Arthur W. Page

Publisher, Public Relations Pioneer, Patriot

BOOKS BY NOEL L. GRIESE

How To Manage Organizational Communication
during Crisis

How To Work
with Angry People and Outraged Publics

Arthur W. Page
Publisher, Public Relations Pioneer, Patriot

ABOUT THE AUTHOR: Noel L. Griese has been a public relations executive in the telecommunications and petroleum industries. He has also been a newspaper editor, a journalism professor at the Universities of Wisconsin and Georgia and a U.S. Army officer. Currently an author and consultant, he resides with his family in Atlanta.

To contact author: email noelgriese@aol.com

To contact publisher: email anvilpub@aol.com
website www.anvilpub.com
phone: 770-938-0289
fax: 770-493-7232

Arthur W. Page

Publisher, Public Relations Pioneer, Patriot

by
Noel L. Griese

ANVIL PUBLISHERS, INC.
Atlanta

Published by
Anvil Publishers, Inc.
3852 Allsborough Drive
Tucker, GA 30084

Copyright © 2001 by Noel L. Griese.

First Edition

Library of Congress Cataloging-in-Publication Data

Griese, Noel L.
    Arthur W. Page : publisher, public relations pioneer,
patriot / by Noel L. Griese. -- 1st ed.
      p. cm.
    Includes bibliographical references and index.
    LCCN: 00-135873
    ISBN 0-9704975-0-4

    1. Page, Arthur W. (Arthur Wilson), 1883-1960
2. Businessmen--United States--Biography 3. Statesmen--
United States--Biography. 4. Corporations--United
States--History. 5. Publishers and publishing--United
States--History. 6. Public relations--United States--
History.   I. Title

HC102.5.P34G75 2001   338'.092
                    QBI00-902079

Printed in the United States of America

June 2001

10 9 8 7 6 5 4 3 2 1

Contents

Illustrations

To
my wife Kathie
ever beautiful, devoted and supportive,
and to Avery, Carolyn, Dawn, Laura,
Mary, Mark, Mitch, Nate,
Nolan and Shannon
around whom
most of my adult life has revolved

Preface

LIKE PEOPLE, corporations struggle to survive and evolve. One mechanism corporations have refined to help them survive is public relations.

Arthur W. Page was one of the nation's foremost contributors to development of the modern concept of public relations. He did that during the period 1927-1946, when he served as the public relations vice president of the American Telephone & Telegraph Co.

Page's philosophy is one of the soundest yet devised for assuring the survival of big business in a democratic society. The breakup of the Bell System, America's largest corporation, into AT&T and the regional Bell operating companies did not occur for more than three decades after he left the AT&T public relations helm.

I first heard of him when I was working in the Public Relations Dept. of Illinois Bell in Chicago. Later, teaching and studying at the University of Wisconsin, I had the opportunity to wade through some 80 boxes of personal papers Page left behind.

That research led me to believe that Page deserves greater stature in the canonical hierarchy of public relations. He was a giant!

Trying to summarize what is important in his life has been a humbling experience. Consider that he lived almost 77 years. In round numbers, that's about 675,000 hours. Exclude the 225,000 or so hours he spent sleeping, and you have 450,000 or so hours left during which he could have been doing things worthy of note by a biographer. The biographer has to distill all this down to a book manuscript that the reader can peruse in about six hours. How do you compress 450,000 hours of activity into a manuscript that can be read in a few hours, retaining all that is relevant and discarding all that is not?

I've done my best to produce an accurate portrait of Arthur Page. The probability is great that in compressing his life into a book I excluded some things that are relevant and included others that are not. I apologize to readers for my inadequacies.

I have much material I was unable to use. The publisher set a page limit—the book length, including front matter, text, notes, bibliography and index—must be no more than 14 signatures of 32 pages each, or a total of 448 pages. Perhaps a future public relations student will contribute to the profession's body of knowledge by developing some of this unused material into another work.

I extend special thanks to those who went out of their way to help me write this life of Arthur Page.

I am grateful to his children—Walter H. Page II, who retired as chief executive officer of Morgan Guaranty Trust (23 Wall Street), John H. Page, who served as president of International Nickel, Arthur W. Page Jr., who rose to a vice presidency at Cities Service, and Mollie Page Hewitt, a Vermont entrepreneur once married to advertising executive Anderson Hewitt. They gave me information on their father, especially about his financial affairs, unavailable from any other source.

Several Bell System officials have also been helpful. I am grateful to:

- *Douglas Williams*, an AT&T public relations executive who gave me documents—including Arthur Page's internal AT&T correspondence-—which helped me a great deal.
- *Paul Lund*, who when serving as AT&T's public relations vice president, gave me access to documents in the AT&T archives that I found helpful.
- *James Ryan*, an AT&T assistant vice president who went out of his way to provide me with facts I needed.

- *John McKay Shaw*, a retired Bell System public relations executive who shared his insights into Page's strengths with me.
- *Prescott Mabon*, another Bell System public relations executive who shared information with me.
- *Ed Block*, a retired AT&T public relations vice president and a founder of the Arthur Page Society, one of Page's greatest admirers.
- *Hale Nelson*, retired public relations vice president of Illinois Bell/Ameritech, one of the first inductees into the Arthur Page Society Hall of Fame, with whom I had the privilege to work early in my career and who encouraged me to publish this manuscript.
- *Jim Tirone*, a Bell System public relations executive who encouraged me during the period I was writing the first draft of this manuscript.

Florence Anderson, onetime secretary of the Carnegie Corporation, performed above and beyond the call of duty in furnishing me with copies of memoranda and other documents about Page's service to that giant philanthropy.

Although I never had the pleasure of meeting him, I am also indebted to Edward Raleigh, whose master's thesis on Page's government service was of great help in my own research.

My niece Victoria Skala Cherne of Minneapolis-St. Paul was an invaluable proofreader and critic.

Above all, I thank my family for their patience while I was working on this manuscript. I took far more time from them than I should have.

Noel L. Griese
Atlanta, Georgia
June 15, 2001

Arthur W. Page in 1928, at age 44, a year after he became public relations vice president at AT&T. Photo property of AT&T Archives. Reprinted with permission of AT&T.

Arthur W. Page is at far left in this assemblage of AT&T executives gathered in New York on March 28, 1928, for the opening of transatlantic telephone service to Paris. AT&T President Walter S. Gifford is seated at center, handset to ear, making the first call to French Minister of Commerce and Industry Maurice Bukanowski. With Bukanowski in Paris was American Gen. John J. Pershing, under whom Page had served as a propaganda officer in World War I. On the table in front of Gifford are the original instruments through which Alexander Graham Bell first transmitted speech in 1876. On the wall behind Mr. Gifford is a map showing the transatlantic route of the phone call. Photo property of AT&T Archives. Reprinted with permission of AT&T.

Arthur W. Page in 1956, at age 73. In 1956, patriots in Hungary unsuccessfully tried to revolt against Soviet domination. Actively involved with the National Committee for Free Europe and its Radio Free Europe affiliate, Page helped handle RFE's public relations response to accusations it had promised American aid for the Hungarian Freedom Fighters.

CHAPTER ONE

The Training of Another American

H E'S GONE NOW, dead since 1960. But his memory lingers on, especially among the nation's public relations executives.

His oil portrait hangs, appropriately for a man who loved books, in the Gordon Reading Room at the Harvard Club of New York. While he was one of the best and the brightest, he avoided the limelight during his life, so newer members glancing at the portrait are likely to ask, "Who was he?"

During his life, he built three separate successful careers. The first was with the publishing house of Doubleday, Page and Co., where he edited the *World's Work* magazine and served as vice president in charge of nonfiction book publishing. Then he worked for 20 years as the public relations vice president of AT&T. During the last 14 years of his life he was a consultant on public relations and other matters to businesses, government, charities and universities.

He is remembered mainly as a public relations counsel. He was one of the most powerful and eloquent public relations practitioners in America from 1927 to 1960, but his aversion to personal publicity made him less well known in his profession than many others.

In 1970, 10 years after his death, when members of the Public Relations Society of America were asked to rank 119 of the nation's most outstanding public relations professionals and educators, he placed only seventh in the field, behind Ivy Ledbetter Lee, John W. Hill, Pendleton Dudley, Carl Byoir, Edward L. Bernays and Earl Newsom.[1]

He shared with those who ranked ahead of him in the poll a reputation for being a sage counsel, but he alone among them was a member of the Eastern establishment. He had far more power and influence than those picked ahead of him.

On the corporate side, he sat on the boards and often executive committees of AT&T, the Chase National (later J.P. Morgan Chase) Bank, Kennecott Copper, Prudential Insurance, Continental Oil, Westinghouse Electric, Southern Bell Telephone, New England Telephone, the Bell Telephone Co. of Canada and Engineers Public Service Co., the last an electric and gas utility holding company.

His influence also stemmed from his membership on boards of trustees of philanthropic and educational organizations such as the prestigious Carnegie Corp. of New York, Metropolitan Museum of Art and Harvard University.

He had many important friends in government. Henry L. Stimson was the statesman to whom he was closest, and who asked most often for his counsel. Stimson's long career included serving as secretary of war for President William Howard Taft, as governor-general of the Philippines for President J. Calvin Coolidge, as secretary of state for President Herbert Hoover and as secretary of war for Presidents Franklin D. Roosevelt and Harry S Truman.

His father, Walter Hines Page, was ambassador to the Court of St. James's (Great Britain) for President T. Woodrow Wilson. The senior Page has been the subject of numerous biographies and historical treatises. Burton Hendrick alone won two Pulitzers for his four-volume *Life and Letters.*

The fourth volume of the Hendrick biography, *Training of an American*, traces the early life of Walter Hines Page from 1885 to the start of his ambassadorship to England in 1913. This chapter traces the training of another American, Arthur Wilson Page, son of Walter Hines Page, from birth in 1883 to graduation from Harvard in 1905. The two most important influences on his life in this period were his father and his education at Harvard. A third influence was the boyhood summers he spent with paternal grandparents in North Carolina.

Birth and childhood of Arthur Page

ARTHUR W. PAGE WAS BORN in Aberdeen, N.C., on Sept. 10, 1883. He was the second child of Walter H. and Willia A. "Allie" Page. The first, Ralph W. Page, was born in Missouri in 1881.[2]

When Arthur was born, his father was struggling to make a success of a newspaper he had started in Raleigh, N.C. The *State Chronicle* was printed in a half-basement under a hardware store.[3]

A circuitous trail had brought Walter Page back to his native North Carolina in 1883. His parents, A.F. "Frank" and Catherine "Kate" Page, had in 1871 sent their young son to Trinity College (now Duke University), one of the few colleges open in the South immediately after the Civil War. Unhappy there, Walter left after a year and completed his undergraduate education at Randolph-Macon College in Ashland, Va.[4]

In the fall of 1876, Walter Page accepted one of the first 20 fellowships offered at the new Johns Hopkins University in Baltimore. For the next two years he studied Greek literature under Professor Basil Gildersleeve, a noted authority.[5] Restless, he left Johns Hopkins in the summer of 1878 to lecture on English literature at the University of North Carolina. Among the undergraduates who attended his lectures was Allie Wilson, a childhood friend who became his wife.[6]

In the fall of 1878, Walter went on to Louisville where he taught English at Male High School and bought a half-interest in a magazine, *The Age*, an imitator of the successful *Nation* in New York. When the magazine failed, he went home to North Carolina.[7]

By mid-1880, he was working as editor of the *St. Joseph* (Mo.) *Gazette*. Late in the year, he married Allie Wilson.[8]

In the summer of 1881, Walter Page left the *Gazette* to become a roving correspondent covering the South for the *New York World, Boston Post* and other newspapers. His letters describing visits with Jefferson Davis on the Mississippi coast and with Joel Chandler Harris (creator of the Uncle

Remus stories) in Atlanta were immediate hits with his editors.[9]

In late 1881, following the birth of his first son, Page went to New York to join the staff of the *New York World*, at that time a polite, respected "journal for gentlemen" controlled by Jay Gould. By May 1883, he had risen to the rank of literary critic and editorial writer. Then Joseph Pulitzer bought the *World* from Gould, and Page resigned.

With his wife and infant son, he returned to North Carolina, where he went to Raleigh to found the *State Chronicle*. His wife Allie stayed with her husband's parents at Aberdeen while awaiting arrival of Arthur, their second child.[10]

As the days passed, Walter Page grew increasingly frustrated with life in the South and his efforts to make the *State Chronicle* a financial success. His personal attitudes were essentially those of the New South movement, of which he was a spokesman along with Henry Woodfin Grady of the *Atlanta Constitution*, Henry Watterson of the *Louisville Courier-Journal* and others.

The Old South was based on an illiterate laboring class, King Cotton and an agrarian Bourbon aristocracy. Advocates of the New South sought to replace it with an order based on industrialization, education of the masses and urbanization. The voices of the New South movement began to be heard in the 1870s, and swelled to stridency in the 1880s. Walter Page became a publicist in the movement at least as early as 1881, when he published an article critical of the old southern order in the *Atlantic Monthly*.[11]

In Raleigh, Page met regularly with a circle of friends with views similar to his own, a group calling itself the Watauga Club after a progressive county in North Carolina.

The *State Chronicle* probably failed not because of Walter Page's iconoclastic views, which were unpopular in many quarters, but for purely economic reasons.[12] Page's newspaper was one of three struggling to survive in Raleigh. The town's depressed economy could not provide enough revenue for all three to succeed. Page tried futilely to breathe life into the *Chronicle* by converting it from a weekly to a daily. When that failed, he went to New York in early 1885 to find employment, turning the paper over to his financial backers.

In New York, he went to work as a writer of leaders (main editorials or articles) for the *Brooklyn Union*. In addition, he freelanced literary and political notes for *The Nation* (at the time the weekly edition of the New York *Evening Post*), *Harper's Weekly* and other publications. He was soon able to bring Allie and the two children north. The family settled in inexpensive rented quarters in Brooklyn.[13]

In February 1887, when Arthur was 3 1/2, his father left the *Union* to join the staff of the New York *Evening Post*, edited at the time by renowned Crimean War correspondent Edwin L. Godkin, who had founded *The Nation* in 1865 and then sold it to Henry Villard of the *Post* in 1881.[14] Godkin became editor of the *Post* in 1883.

A few months later, Walter Page changed employment again, this time to become business manager of *Forum* magazine, a review in its second year of publication. Editor Lorettus S. Metcalf had built the magazine's circulation to around 20,000. Page was hired to relieve him of business duties so he could devote full time to editing the magazine.

In 1891, Metcalf resigned and Walter Page became editor. According to magazine historian Frank Luther Mott, Page was more brilliant as an editor than Metcalf, but less willing to meticulously edit copy.[15]

By 1891, Walter Page had moved his family to New Rochelle, N.Y. Ralph, the oldest child, was 10. Arthur was 8. Frank Copeland Page, born in Brooklyn in 1887, was 4. The fourth and final child of Walter and Allie Page, Katherine Alice, was born in New Rochelle in January 1891.[16]

Under Walter Page's guidance, the *Forum*, which had been losing money, showed a profit in 1893, the year of a great financial panic. Although Walter Page's stock in the Forum Publishing Co. was now of value, the family was far from prosperous. In a Christmas letter to his mother in North Carolina, Walter wrote: "Santa will be pretty low on presents this year. Down in the horrid city, in fact, he'll do mighty well if he manages to get loaves of bread enough to go around. People are starving at a rate I never heard of before—the pitifulest scenes—Oh God, it is awful!"[17]

By 1894, circulation of the *Forum* had climbed to 28,000. The *North American Review*, by comparison, had a circulation of about 18,000.[18] A year later, Walter Page lost a struggle for control of the now successful magazine with its board, headed by Isaac L. Rice and made up of other investors.

Page resigned as editor of the *Forum*, and moved his family to Cambridge, Mass., where he became a literary adviser to Houghton Mifflin's *Atlantic Monthly*, perhaps the foremost intellectual magazine in America.[19] According to Burton Hendrick, Horace E. Scudder was little more than nominal editor of the magazine, with Walter Page in fact exercising editorial control. In 1898, Page was officially named editor. Circulation of the magazine at the time was about 7,000.[20]

At the *Atlantic*, Page went about his editorial duties with his usual bluff, hale spirit. On one occasion, Hendrick recounts, he spanked a young female author of promise in his office because she refused to stop writing stories with themes that were unprintable in the Age of Innocence.[21] According to Josephus Daniels in *Tar Hell Editor*, he once teased William Lloyd Garrison by saying "One of your n——s is waiting outside." "I very much regret that you should insist on spelling 'Negro' with two g's," Garrison rebuked him. [22]

While Walter Page edited the *Atlantic*, sons Ralph and Arthur completed their grammar school education at the prestigious Cambridge Latin School. Walter had already decided they would go to Harvard, or so he said in 1897 in his "Forgotten Man" speech at the State Normal and Industrial School for Women at Greensboro, N.C.[23]

Until Walter Page became editor of the *Atlantic*, the long line of New Englanders who controlled the magazine had been of the opinion that the only justifiable war since the Revolution had been the Civil War. The American war with Spain in 1898 came almost as an insult to the anti-jingo intellectuals of the Boston area. The June 1898 issue of the *Atlantic* must have been an affront to many of them. In a jingoistic salute to American imperialism, Walter Page had placed an unfurled American flag on the cover in imitation of a cover that had appeared on the magazine immediately after the Confederate firing on Fort Sumter.

Boyhood summers in North Carolina

DURING THE PERIOD when Walter Page was moving about the country changing jobs, Arthur spent many of his summers in North Carolina with his grandparents, Frank and Kate Page.

Arthur's grandparents had moved in the 1870s from Cary (near Raleigh) to Aberdeen after Frank Page bought a large tract of pine-forested land in Moore County. With them had come their eight children, five boys and three girls. Arthur's father Walter was the oldest.

With the help of his sons, Frank Page built logging camps, sawmills and a railroad, and the family prospered.[24]

In his *Oral Reminiscences* for Columbia University, Arthur Page stressed that the frequent family moves made when he was a child (from Brooklyn to New Rochelle to Cambridge) led to his inability to identify with northern communities. He came to regard North Carolina, where he was born and spent his summers as a youngster, as his home.[25]

It's important to understanding the mature Arthur Page to realize that he regarded himself as a man both of the North and of the South. As he told Dr. Howard Odum of the University of North Carolina, "It is true that I spent pretty much all my summers, until I went to college, with my grandparents in Aberdeen, and as my parents owned no house in the North at that time and moved several times, I came to look upon Aberdeen as my fixed home in a sense, and always since I have kept an interest in North Carolina... As you know my father and mother are buried there. But not only because I went to college in the North and my parents lived there, but also because I went into publishing, for which the South offered no opportunity, I have lived North—as a matter of fact in and around New York—since 1905...."[26]

Summer life in the sandhill country of North Carolina was simple but ample for young Arthur. There was no refrigeration, so the staple meats were chickens killed when needed and hams from the smokehouse. Packaged foods did not exist, so each morning Arthur's grandmother would measure out foods like sugar and flour from barrels and turn the food over to a cook. As many as 12 to 15 persons gathered for meals: grandmother and grandfather, the visiting grandsons, aunts, uncles and cousins who lived in Aberdeen or nearby.

Travel in the sandhill country was by horse and buggy for the most part, and very slow. The roads were of thick sand which didn't give a horse sound footing. Buggy wheels could sink in the sand.

By standards of the day, Arthur's grandfather Frank was a prosperous small businessman. In addition to owning considerable land, he had a sawmill at Aberdeen to cut pine logs into lumber. He also owned a short railroad that carried the lumber to Asheboro, where the Page rail line connected with the Southern Railway and Seaboard Air Line (later Seaboard Coast Line) Railroad.[27]

Around 1890, Frank Page expanded into banking. When the cashier at the State National Bank in Raleigh, one of the two banks in town, forced closure by absconding with the bank's funds, Frank Page, in partnership with others, formed the Commercial National Bank of Raleigh.

For young Arthur, the sandhills and pine forests provided places for a young boy to roam and explore. He had his older brother Ralph and numerous cousins with whom to play. On summer afternoons when he had nothing better to do, he watched work at the Page sawmill, or rode the daily train from Aberdeen to Biscoe. The train fascinated young Arthur, who in later life would be a director of the Panama Railroad, consultant to the Pennsylvania Railroad and advisor on national transportation policy. He often rode in the cab of the locomotive on the Aberdeen to Biscoe run, feeding cordwood into its firebox. In 1947, he commissioned an artist to paint the train as it had run in the 1890s, with an engine and tender, lumber gondolas and a single passenger car.[28]

The well-known Pinehurst Resort near Aberdeen began when Frank Page in 1895 sold 5,000 acres of logged-off land for $5,000 to Boston soda fountain magnate James Tufts. Local residents thought Page had swindled Tufts, selling him worthless sandhills for $1 an acre. But within a few decades the land on which Tufts built his winter spa was worth more than $1,000 an acre.[29]

The summer of 1897 was tinged with sadness for young Ralph and Arthur, who were again spending a summer with the grandparents. Grandmother Kate was dying. She lingered on, the boys returned to Cambridge, and she died in the fall. From the birth of Walter Hines Page forward, through the birth of seven more children and 16 grandchildren, there hadn't been a single death in the Page family. Walter, perhaps the closest of the children to his mother, dejectedly told his friend Horace Scudder after the death that the boys still talked of their grandmother "as though she were yet alive."[30]

The summer of 1899 was Arthur's last with his grandfather. Frank Page died a few months after Arthur had entered prep school in New Jersey.

In July 1899, while he was in North Carolina, his father changed jobs again, leaving the helm of the *Atlantic* to join the publishing house of the brilliant but erratic S.S. McClure.

McClure had gotten his start running a feature syndicate supplying a number of newspapers. He then founded *McClure's* magazine, the circulation of which zoomed in the period at the end of the 19th century when the first American general interest magazines were approaching circulations of one million and more.

In 1897, McClure had brought Frank N. Doubleday into his firm from *Scribner's* magazine. Doubleday became a vice president of the S.S. McClure Co., and in addition, was given a 51 per cent interest in a new book publishing venture, Doubleday and McClure.

In early 1899, J. Pierpont Morgan, who had invested some $22 million in the Harper and Brothers publishing house, began to look for someone to buy the business which was suffering from nepotistic dry rot. Almost every Harper family male, upon reaching maturity, was given a position in the firm. Morgan invited McClure to buy the House of Harper.

McClure, planning to make the purchase, invited Walter Page to join the enterprise. He was to edit a new magazine dealing with current history and to be editor-in-chief of an encyclopedia McClure hoped to establish.

In October 1899, after Walter Page had joined S.S. McClure, Sam McClure, fearing he had overextended himself financially, canceled his contract with Morgan to purchase Harper. Two weeks later, Frank Doubleday informed McClure that he and Walter Page were leaving. Thus was born the publishing house of Doubleday, Page and Co.[31]

The Lawrenceville years

IN THE FALL OF 1899, with his older brother Ralph a freshman at Harvard, Arthur entered the third form of the Lawrenceville School located near Princeton, N.J.

Lawrenceville was a prep school for boys planning to attend Princeton. About 300 were enrolled. Nominally Presbyterian (the Pages were Methodists), the school required students to take religious instruction, although admission did not depend on denomination. Dr. Simon John McPherson, headmaster, was an ordained Presbyterian minister.[32]

Modeled on the classic English prep school, Lawrenceville was regarded as one of the better schools of its type, in the same class as Groton, St. Paul's, Exeter and the Horace Mann School.

Younger boys were placed in groups of seven to 32, and lived with a housemaster and his family on the school grounds. Older boys in the fourth form (senior year) lived in two separate dormitories, assignment depending on their scholastic performance.[33]

Arthur's nickname at Lawrenceville was "Theus."

His closest friends were Isaac S. "Ike" Kampmann of San Antonio, Texas, later a Harvard graduate, successful lawyer and banker, and Oscar H. McPherson, son of the school's headmaster.[34]

During his senior year at Lawrenceville from 1900 to 1901, young Page was named to the second testimonial (honors) for the first half of the year, and to the first testimonial (high honors) for the second half.[35]

Arthur was active in several extracurricular activities. He was a member of the "Creams," the school's scrub football team, sharing, according to one classmate, the distinction of being one of the two worst ends in the team's history. He was also a member of the school's Philomathean Society, devoted to debate, and won a prize in the school's annual debate contest in 1901.[36]

Being a close friend of the son of the school headmaster did not win the young scholar special privileges. He was suspended for a time after he was caught going from one room of the school to another along a ledge instead of by a less adventurous route.[37]

Although his attainment of honors and high honors in his senior years at Lawrenceville indicates excellent attainment, Arthur did poorly on his Harvard entrance examinations, the beginning of academic problems that plagued him until immediately before graduation in 1905. His son's performance at Harvard may to some extent be attributed to Walter Page having selecting a Princeton prep school for a son going to Harvard.

Soon after Arthur's admission to Harvard, Walter wrote to Dr. McPherson at Lawrenceville to complain that "Arthur barely escaped scholastic disgrace in his Harvard examinations. He is admitted to the college but with the maximum number of conditions that a boy can have and be admitted. He failed in German, Latin and Greek. I regret for Arthur's sake and for the school's that the only Lawrenceville boy that went up this year to our oldest and largest college, though he was a first testimonial boy, entered only with the heaviest possible conditions...."[38]

In later years, Arthur Page severed his ties to Lawrenceville, although he devoted much of his time to other schools. He declined a number of invitations to speak at the school, and refused to contribute to school fund drives when asked.[39] He wrote to Allan V. Heely of Lawrenceville in 1943 to explain:

> Lawrenceville was a good school when I went there—for Princeton. I limped badly getting into Harvard not because I hadn't been taught enough, but I hadn't been taught the right things. I was the only boy in my class who went to Harvard.
>
> It was natural enough that my school ties didn't continue very active, nor have they ever been.
>
> In the meanwhile, I have put four children through Milton, three through Harvard and one through Bennington and I have served on the board of trustees of three colleges.
>
> About all the educational sap in me is already accounted for.
>
> This is an honest account of why you can not count on me to help in promoting scholarship and the school's other objectives.[40]

Arthur spent the summer after graduation from Lawrenceville with the family of his uncle Robert N. Page in Biscoe, N.C. His uncle, who was elected to Congress in 1902, had started a sawmill in Biscoe, and Arthur worked there, building his body, 11 to 12 hours a day, six days a week, for $3.60 per week in pay. His cousin Thad, a member of the family, remembered Arthur during that summer as a bright, serious, hard-working and well-liked member of the Page clan. He was also impressed by Arthur's wearing woolen socks even in the summer. Everyone Thad knew wore cotton socks in summer and winter alike.[41]

The Harvard experience

ARTHUR FOLLOWED his brother Ralph to Harvard in the fall of 1901.

During the first few days, he drifted into contact with a dozen or so young men in his class from the South. At the end of the first week of instruction, the young men from Dixie gathered in the room of one of the students to complain about slights and insults they felt they received from the northern students. Page called the complaints "whining," and went on in four years at Harvard to mix with northern and southern students alike.[42]

Much of his early socializing at Harvard, however, was with the clannish southerners. Although the students from the South made up only a small fragment of the student body at Harvard in the early 1900s, there were perhaps more students from south of the Mason-Dixon line at Harvard in the first years of the 20th century than at any time since the Civil War.

Social clubs were then popular at Harvard, prior students having rejected traditional Greek-letter fraternities. The young men from the South formed their own social outlet, the Southern Club, headquartered in a rented house on Mount Auburn Street. A thriving institution in Arthur's day, the Southern Club wasn't particularly popular with Harvard officials because of a not-unwarranted suspicion that more liquor was being consumed on the premises than propriety justified.[43] The southern students did little to improve their reputations when they campaigned unsuccessfully to have the names of Harvard graduates who died fighting for the Confederacy added to monuments around campus listing the names of Harvard students who died in Union blue.[44]

Early in the 1900s, the South was in another of its periodic efforts to improve education. Typical of the times was Charles B. Aycock, progressive governor of North Carolina from 1901 to 1905. He established a literacy test to remove black voters from electoral rolls while funding new school construction and teacher training for whites.

The Southern Club during young Page's day was the site of a notable undergraduate dinner about education reform. The young men of the Southern Club invited incumbent Gov. Andrew Jackson Montague of Virginia who had campaigned on an educational platform calling for larger appropriations for public schools to speak. Gov. Montague, whose state had restricted black suffrage at its 1902 state constitutional convention, accepted the invitation.

Soon after, Gov. Curtis Guild of Massachusetts called the Southern Club. When Arthur Page answered the phone, Guild said "I understand that Governor Montague is coming to the Southern Club, and Massachusetts and Virginia are the only two commonwealths in the nation." Showing the public relations acumen that would characterize him later in life, young Arthur recalled saying, "Well, Governor, we have just found out that Governor Montague is coming and we were going to ask if you wouldn't come." Guild accepted.

With two governors coming, the Southerners decided they had better invite Harvard President Charles W. Eliot, who also accepted. The boys then had to decide whether to allow liquor at the dinner with so many dignitaries present. After considerable soul-searching, they opted for alcohol.

On the evening of the dinner, Gov. Guild led off with a traditional Blue and Gray speech, allowing that the North and South were friends again. Gov. Montague, one of the great orators of the day, made a moving argument for an educated populace as fundamental to effective democracy.

President Eliot, next on the program, quickly made it clear he wasn't going to have a governor speak about education in his back yard without giving some competition. He told the audience that Harvard would do its duty, allowing blacks who could qualify for entrance to attend, so long as their numbers didn't impede the college.[45]

The danger of a "black tide" at Harvard was far from imminent. There were perhaps five in Arthur Page's class.

While the Southern Club provided a social outlet for Arthur, the classes he took and the extracurricular activities in which he participated gave him the intellectual base for his later careers as magazine editor, book publisher and public relations expert.

He majored in history, also taking a fair number of courses in English literature and composition. His classes in history

are perhaps the most noteworthy because of his later lifelong interest in the subject. In the last 18 years of his life, he
served as a trustee of the American Historical Assn. In those
later years, he also played a key role in arranging publication of an autobiography and biography of Henry L. Stimson,
and in funding the Center for the Study of Liberty in America
history project at Harvard.

Walter Page enjoyed reading history, and Arthur's interest in the subject probably arose in part because of his father. At least one Harvard history professor influenced him
favorably. Recalling the Harvard days in his *Reminiscences*,
he makes no mention of two of his history professors,
Frederick Jackson Turner and Edward Channing. A third, Silas
MacVane, he recalled with distaste. A fourth, Archibald Carey
Coolidge, he remembered fondly.

Page took a course in the development of the American
West from Turner during his junior year. Turner, perhaps
the most distinguished of the historians under whom young
Page studied, was a visiting professor at Harvard at the time.
He had begun to establish his reputation in 1893, when he
read a paper at the American Historical Assn. attacking the
"germ cell" theory of American history which held that
America could best be explained in terms of imported European influences. Turner argued that settlement of the American frontier was a unique influence not imported from Europe that explained much of American history. Although
Turner was well known among historians when Arthur Page
studied under him, he was not a dynamic lecturer, and appears to have made little impression on the young scholar.

Arthur took a two-semester course in European history
from Silas MacVane, Harvard's McLean professor of ancient
and modern history. MacVane seldom introduced new material, and young scholars sometimes purchased for $5 sets
of notes put out by previous students rather than attend his
class. Some of the boys brought collapsible paper checker-
boards to MacVane's lectures to help pass the time.

In his sophomore year, Page took a course in the history
of the United States from 1783 to 1865 from Professor

Channing. Although he makes no mention of Channing in his *Reminiscences*, he devoted much of his later reading to this period in American history.

The teacher Page recalled as having influenced him the most was Archibald Carey Coolidge, independently wealthy, who taught at Harvard for $1 per year.

Page took a course in medieval and modern European history from Coolidge in his freshman year, and an advanced course in 19th century European expansion from him in his senior year. Page was fascinated with Coolidge's mannerisms—a sort of spring-halted walk, and an inability to pronounce "r's," which led him to say "wugged" and "Wenaissance"—but also appears to have been intellectually stimulated by him.

In his *Reminiscences*, Page recalls walking into a class taught by Coolidge with a dozen or so other boys. Coolidge explained that the students, not he, would do the lecturing, reporting on topics he would assign to them.

Arthur's first assignment was to report on the Taiping Rebellion, which occurred in China shortly before the American Civil War. He innocently went to Harvard's library to check out "the book on the Taiping Rebellion." There was no book, he soon learned. Instead, he had to go to 20 or so general histories to learn what they said. The books didn't agree on what had happened or on the significance of the event. For the first time, he recalled, he saw that history wasn't an accurate discipline. Some facts were omitted by authors. Facts that were given were often biased. When you got all done with a collection of facts, you still had to guess about what had happened.[46]

Page also took a number of courses in English at Harvard. Since much of his later life was devoted to applied English—to writing and editing—the courses are worthy of note.

Young Page particularly liked a course in English literature from Dryden through Swift that he took in his junior year from Prof. Charles T. Copeland. A few years after graduating from Harvard, he said in a *World's Work* magazine article that boys went to Copeland's classes voluntarily because they were interested. Copeland wasn't a scholar in the sense of having published a long series of learned works, he said, but he was an inspirer, a teacher rather than a collector of learned facts.[47]

Probably of greater importance to the development of young Page as a writer was his involvement first as a contributor to and then as editor of the *Harvard Advocate.*

Born as a newspaper in 1886, the *Advocate* in the years Page attended Harvard was more a literary magazine.

Arthur's brother Ralph was the first of Walter Page's sons to contribute to the *Advocate.* Arthur soon followed suit.

His first articles were short stories, heavy with dialect in the style of Joel Chandler Harris and Finley Peter Dunne, often with ironic surprise endings of the type popularized by O. Henry, the pen name of William Sidney Porter. In later life, he wrote several appreciations of O. Henry, whose works were published for the most part by Doubleday, Page.

The earliest Arthur Page stories in the *Advocate* are about southern blacks, portrayed in the stereotypes of the time as afraid of thunder, lightning and the dark, and childlike in other ways. His later short stories usually involve Southerners that outsmart "Yankee revenuers" or Union soldiers during the Civil War. The stories are not particularly noteworthy as literature, but they show an early ability in Page to tell anecdotes in dialect, a skill he later put to frequent effective use when speaking before small and large groups.[48]

Page began contributing to the *Advocate* in 1902. By his junior year, 1903-1904, he had become a member of the board of editors, and in his senior year, he became president of the board, or editor-in-chief.

Although it is possible that young Page contributed unsigned editorials to the *Advocate* in his junior year, the first editorials that can definitely be attributed to him appear in his senior year. In that academic year he contributed 34 short editorials, almost the whole of the *Advocate* output.[49]

The editorials deal mainly with Harvard matters—a suggestion that beer be served at the student union, and expressions of support for the football and baseball teams. One editorial, "The Advocate at the Inauguration" notes that President Theodore Roosevelt was a past editor of the *Advocate*, and that the magazine's current "Pegasus"— editor Arthur Page—would have a prominent place at Roosevelt's 1905 inauguration. An editorial earlier in the school year had wished well to the Democratic Club of Harvard, of which Page was a member.[50] Young Page did not let his personal politics stand in the way of attending the installation of a Progressive Republican.

In addition to being active on the *Advocate* and a member of the Democratic Club, Arthur participated in other extracurricular activities. According to Harvard Class Albums for 1904 and 1905, he was a member of:

• *Hasty Pudding,* a social club nominally devoted to patriotic oratory and discussion, composed of 100 men selected annually from the sophomore class.

• *Signet,* a literary and social club composed of undergraduates interested in the arts.

• *"O.K.,"* another literary society, and

• *Amphadon,* a small group consisting of six young men, all seniors, who met fortnightly to discuss whatever topics interested them.[51]

Arthur also went out for the baseball team in his senior year, but had to abandon that enterprise because of faltering grades and afternoon classes that conflicted with the team's practice sessions.[52]

Young Page was not particularly successful as a scholar. In addition to entering Harvard with deficiencies, he was almost expelled in 1902 for failure to attend classes. At the time, Harvard was cracking down on the scions of America's wealthier families, many of whom were being granted degrees despite minimal class attendance. Students were told that if they cut too many classes they could end up in trouble with the dean. One of the stricter rules prohibited the cutting of classes immediately before Christmas vacation.

Arthur went home to New York for Christmas in 1902, but not, according to his later account, before having attended the last lecture in the history course he was taking from Prof.

MacVane. Instead of sitting in his assigned seat, he says he sat near the classroom door. At home, he had dinner on Christmas Eve with his mother, father and sister Kate. His two brothers were away for the holiday. After the cheery dinner, his mother and sister left the room, leaving Arthur alone with his father. Walter Page handed him a letter from Harvard, saying "Arthur, this thing seems to affect you more'n it does me."

"Dear Mr. Page," the letter began. "I regret to inform you that your son Arthur's connection with Harvard College has been severed." It was signed by the dean. Arthur looked at it for a few moments and said, "I don't know what this means."

Walter Page was calm and uncritical. Finally, Arthur said, "I think I'd better go back and find out."

"Yes, I think that would be a good idea," Walter replied.

Arthur returned to Cambridge to see the dean. He was told the monitor taking attendance at MacVane's last class before Christmas had marked him absent. Arthur explained he'd been present, and that several classmates saw him sitting near the door. The dean accepted his word, and he was reinstated—on probation.[53]

As late as the spring of 1905, he was still on probation—or, if he had temporarily removed himself, back on. He wrote to his mother in March to say "I am sorry that I have no good news in regard to my probation or in other words it is still in existance (sic)."[54] His grades in his senior year included a C and B in English, two C's in history, a D in government and a B in a fine arts course in typography and engraving.[55] The B's in English and fine arts apparently saved him. He was taken off probation in April, and graduated in June, without honors or other distinction.[56]

In Arthur's day, a "gentleman's C" was acceptable at Harvard. Grading was harsh, and the class grind who worked only for high grades might be disliked by classmates. Simple graduation from Harvard, even without honors, was an accomplishment. His freshman class had started with 712 members. By his senior year, the class had dwindled to 268.[57] Some of the attrition was due to a program with which

Harvard was experimenting at the time, permitting young men to graduate in three years instead of the normal four by taking courses at an accelerated rate. More of the attrition, however, was due to students dropping out for many reasons, not the least being poor grades.

In later years, Arthur carped a bit about the quality of education at Harvard, contending too many of the professors were boring publishers of erudite scholarship instead of stimulating teachers. He said in a 1910 *World's Work* article, "It is a curious fact that as a rule a teacher gets a position on a college faculty not because he can teach, but by demonstrating that he has been taught. As often as not he wins promotion, not by success in teaching, but by evidence of additional learning."[58]

Despite such occasional jibes, he was a loyal adult alumnus, always ready to serve when Harvard called for help.

In later years, many of the men with whom he associated were Harvard graduates of his era—men like Walter Gifford, Edwin Alderman, Winthrop Aldrich, William Baldwin, Willard Baldwin (a Page Harvard roommate), W.H. "Laird" Bell, Adolf Berle Jr., James B. Conant, Joseph C. Grew, Walter Lippmann and Ellery Sedgwick. Harvard, and particularly the Harvard Democratic Club, provided many of Page's later political contacts, including Robert Johns Bulkley, Clement Haynsworth, Smith Hickenlooper, Charles Evans Hughes, Leverett Saltonstall and Norton Wigglesworth.

Page throughout his adult life was active in public service activities. In his later years, he estimated that he had devoted a third of his active business life to voluntary service.[59] What made him willing to serve government, charities and education?

There is ample evidence that he took on public service assignments because he believed it his responsibility to do so. His willingness to serve in the public interest surely stems at least in part to the influence of Harvard—to what reform President Charles W. Eliot was fond of calling the Harvard "spirit of service." Eliot says of the spirit of Harvard graduates in his *Harvard Memories,* "They differ strongly on political, industrial and religious questions, but they have a common unifying desire to contribute to the public welfare. Here is a Harvard tradition."[60]

Again, he says, "Now, what is the traditional spirit of Harvard University? I should describe it as a spirit of service—not necessarily in what we call public service, but a spirit of service in all the professions, both learned and scientific, including business; a desire, a firm purpose, to be of use to one's fellow men...."[61]

The influence of Walter Hines Page

WHILE HARVARD played an important role in the shaping of young Arthur Page, the influence his father had on him is also profound. Many of his attitudes—on education in the South, on the role blacks should play in America, on the value of corporations to the quality of life in American society—he inherited from his father. Even his political stance, that of a young conservative Democrat in an age when it was more popular in the East to be a Progressive Republican, appears to have been modeled on his father's politics.

Above all, Walter Hines Page made a magazine writer and editor of young Arthur. True, Arthur's first experience as magazine contributor and editor came with the *Harvard Advocate*, but that was mere preparation for the training that would come as Arthur worked on a mass circulation magazine. Already by the summers of 1903 and 1904, during Harvard vacations, young Page was working for his father on the *World's Work*, a major magazine with a circulation building to around 100,000.

The story of the *World's Work* began soon after Frank Doubleday and Walter Page opened their publishing house in New York in early 1900.

The firm's first business was book publishing, with emphasis on novels, then far more profitable than nonfiction. The first authors published by Doubleday, Page were for the most part fiction writers Doubleday had handled at Scribner's

and McClure's. Rudyard Kipling, who nicknamed Frank
Doubleday "Effendi" in a play on his "FND" initials, was the
most popular of the firm's authors. Sam McClure was particularly hurt that the promising young Frank Norris deserted
him for Doubleday, Page. Not so popular, but perhaps the
best writer in the new firm's stable, was Joseph Conrad, who
used ships and the sea as symbolic backdrops against which
to play out dramas in which his characters war with their
alter egos.

In the autumn of 1900, Doubleday, Page began its first
monthly magazine, the *World's Work*, under the editorship
of Walter Page. The first issue was produced in ten hectic
days and nights, and had an initial press run of 35,000 copies.[62]

The first issue set the style for later monthly numbers
through 1926, although minor changes in format were periodically introduced. At first interspersed with the editorials,
but later clumped together in a "portrait gallery," were halftone photos of notable men and women of the world, printed
on slick paper instead of the rough stock used for the rest of
the magazine.

A "March of Events" section was followed by a half-dozen
to a dozen nonfiction feature articles about men at work,
national and international issues, education, art and human
interest topics. The feature articles were printed on an inexpensive grade of paper similar to but of slightly better quality than newsprint, with slick coated paper sandwiched between the text clumps to permit printing of photos to illus-
trate the articles. *World's Work* staffers wrote some of the
signed feature stories. Others were written by freelancers,
usually to Walter Page's specifications.

A "back of the book" section made up of several departments followed the feature articles. Early issues of the magazine contained a "Short Stories of Men at Work" department,
a section entitled "Among the World's Workers," and a department on recently published books, especially those of
Doubleday, Page and Co. Paid advertising was clumped into
a single section.

From the first November 1900 issue forward, the *World's Work* was an apologist for big business. The magazine was, after all, dedicated to covering the ways people earned their livings. This pro-business stance was somewhat unique in a period when muckraking attacks on the trusts were more popular than was conservative defense of industry.

The defense of big business began with the "March of Events" section of the first issue of the magazine, which included two articles pointing out benefits brought by big business often overlooked by the public.[63]

While Walter H. Page had a favorable opinion of big business, he called frequently in his magazine for the trusts to end their policy of secrecy. He wanted big businesses to freely and frankly publicize their affairs so that the public could understand and fairly judge their actions. The first such call for corporate "publicity" appeared in a March 1901 article by Henry G. Chapman entitled "The Progress of Honesty." Publicity, said Chapman, was the remedy for abuses of power. Truth paid in business, he argued. It was better to be open than to be secretive. Publicity would bring better morals to business—and to government.[64]

It seems probable that Arthur Page absorbed his father's philosophy about the need for businesses to be open with the public. He would certainly have read articles and editorials on the subject in the *World's Work*, and have had conversations with his father about it. It is similarly likely that he integrated this philosophy into his mature concept of the public relations function later in life.

The *World's Work* became almost an overnight success, in large part due to the promotional efforts organized by Frank Doubleday, one of the most hardheaded businessmen ever to grace the publishing profession. The mail order department of Doubleday, Page, originally organized to handle subscription book business, was converted to promotion of the magazine, and subscriptions began to pour in at the rate of 300 to 400 per day.[65]

While a few muckraking articles and series appeared in the magazine, Walter Page kept the *World's Work* pretty much aloof from that movement in which many other mass magazines participated.

The targets of muckrake journalism were excessive corporate power, political corruption and things injurious to the middle class. Although many muckraking articles appeared before 1902 (in Benjamin Flowers' *Arena* magazine, for example), the beginning of the movement is usually set at October 1902, when *McClure's* carried "Tweed Days in St. Louis" by Lincoln Steffens and Claude Wetmore, and a notice that the November issue would carry the first installment of Ida Tarbell's "History of the Standard Oil Co."[66]

Like his father, Arthur Page had a distinct distaste for muckraking, preferring articles with "uplift" to those that sought to tear down institutions and reputations. That notwithstanding, the magazine's slant often reflected the biases of the time. In the summer of 1903, when young Arthur spent his first months on the magazine, the *World's Work* was expressing concern over the increased tide of Jewish and non-English European immigration to America (the purity of America's Anglo-Saxon stock had to be protected), the declining birth rate of America's educated, the problems being caused by labor unions (Walter Page and Frank Doubleday didn't like them), railroad frauds, scandals in the U.S. Post Office, concern with lynchings (there were 50 or so nationally in the first half of 1903), irrigation of the West, and of course, the progress of business in America.[67]

In 1902, Progressive economist Henry C. Adams argued that publicity was the solution to the problem of trusts. In 1904, Thomas F. Woodlock's "The Uplift in Business" in the same vein appeared in the *World's Work* while Arthur was spending his second Harvard summer "vacation" on the magazine.

Woodlock, at the time with the *Wall Street Journal,* but later a public relations professional (for a period he employed public relations pioneer William Baldwin), chronicled what he saw as a new, enlightened morality in business—despite what the muckrakers of the day were contending. Woodlock set the beginning of the new morality at 1893 to 1896, the period in which America's railroads were reorganized. The railroads had needed capital from banks, Woodlock contended, and came to realize they were unlikely to get it unless they were honest about their finances. He admitted that the "higher moral standards" he felt had come to prevail originated "from motives of self-interest," but he argued that the "self-interest (had) been enlightened." He believed the public stock of the giant steel trust (U.S. Steel) had been sold rapidly only because of the firm's honesty with the public.[68]

The summers of 1903 and 1904 served to familiarize young Arthur with the *World's Work*. He did no writing for the magazine, devoting his time to menial tasks—collecting photographs for illustrated sections and checking the accuracy of facts in articles others wrote for the magazine. The summers nonetheless were his preparation for working full time on the magazine after he graduated from Harvard.

ENDNOTES

[1] David L. Lewis, "The Outstanding PR Professionals," *Public Relations Journal*, Vol. 26 (October 1970), pp. 78-80 ff.

[2] *The Book of the Children of Allison Francis Page and Catherine Raboteau Page* (Private Printing, 1921), Box 83, Arthur W. Page Papers, Mass Communications History Center, State Historical Society of Wisconsin, Madison. This book hereafter is called *Book of the Children*, and the collection in which it appears the Arthur W. Page Papers.

[3] Josephus Daniels, *Tar Heel Editor* (Chapel Hill, N.C.: University of North Carolina Press, 1939, renewed 1967 by Frank A. Daniels), p. 95. Used by permission of the publisher.

[4] Burton J. Hendrick, *The Training of an American* (Boston and New York: Houghton Mifflin, 1928), pp. 42, 49-50.

[5] *Ibid.*, p. 67.

[6] *Ibid.*, pp. 119-21, 133-34.

[7] *Ibid.*, pp. 123-25.

[8] *Ibid.*, pp. 130-33, and Burton J. Hendrick, *The Life and Letters of Walter H. Page* (Garden City, N.Y.: Doubleday, Page and Co., 1923), Vol. I, p. 37.

[9] Hendrick, *Training of an American, op. cit.*, pp. 134-35, 147-51.

[10] Edwin Emery, *The Press and America* (Englewood Cliffs, N.J.: Prentice-Hall, 1962), p. 376, and Hendrick *Training of an American, op. cit.*, pp. 155-58.

[11] Paul M. Gaston, *The New South Creed: A Study in Southern Mythmaking* (New York: Vintage Books, 1973), pp. 3-61. See also Walter H. Page, "Study of an Old Southern Borough," *Atlantic Monthly*, Vol. 47 (May 1881), pp. 648-58.

[12] Hendrick gives the impression that the *Chronicle* failed because Walter Page attacked the old Southern order in Raleigh. A case can be made that Walter Page was far less an iconoclast than Hendrick makes him out to be.

[13] Hendrick, *Training of an American, op. cit.,* p. 196.

[14] *Ibid.,* p. 197.

[15] Frank Luther Mott, *A History of American Magazines* (Cambridge, Mass.: Harvard University Press, 1957, Vol. IV, pp. 511-16.

[16] *Book of the Children, op. cit.*

[17] Letter from Walter H. Page to Catherine R. Page, cited from Hendrick, *Training of an American, op. cit.,* pp. 223-24.

[18] Mott, *op. cit.,* pp. 511-16.

[19] Hendrick, *Training of an American, op. cit.,* pp. 232-33.

[20] Mott, *op. cit.,* p. 44

[21] Hendrick, *Training of an American, op. cit.,* p. 238.

[22] Daniels, *op. cit.,* p. 257.

[23] Walter Page's "The Forgotten Man" speech can be found in *The School That Built a Town* (New York: Harper and Brothers, 1952), a new edition of a much older book, *The Rebuilding of Old Commonwealths.*

[24] A genealogy of the Page family appears in *Book of the Children*. See also Hendrick, *Training of an American, op. cit.,* pp. 6-17, 218, and *Life and Letters,* Vol. I, pp. 4-5.

[25] Except where specifically footnoted, material on Arthur Page's boyhood summers in North Carolina is from *The Reminiscences of Arthur W. Page* (New York: Oral History Research Office, Columbia University, 1959), pp. 1-4 This document hereafter is referred to as *Reminiscences.*

[26] Letter from Page to Dr. Howard W. Odum of the University of North Carolina, May 20, 1946, Box 13, Arthur W. Page Papers.

[27] Frank Page's railroad, eventually named the Aberdeen and Asheboro, originally ran from Aberdeen to Biscoe, N.C. By 1900 the railroad was extended from Biscoe west to Mount Gilead and north to Asheboro, so that its 90 miles of track formed a "Y." Letter to author from Thaddeus Shaw Page, undated but about May 15, 1973.

[28] Letter to author from Thaddeus Shaw Page, *op. cit.; Reminiscences*; and letters from Page to Ralph Kelly of the Baldwin Locomotive Works, Aug. 5, 1947, to J.N. Reibel of the American Car and Foundry Co., Aug. 12, 1947, and to cousin Robert N. Page Jr., Nov. 28, 1947, Box 16, Arthur W. Page Papers.

[29] *Reminiscences,* pp. 4-5; Daniels, *op. cit.,* pp. 441-42; and letter to author from Thaddeus Shaw Page, *op. cit.*

[30] Hendrick, *Training of an American, op. cit.,* p. 281.

[31] Description of Walter Page's brief employment at the S.S. McClure Co. and of the formation of Doubleday, Page and Co. is essentially from Peter Lyon, *Success Story: The Life and Times of S.S. McClure* (New York: Charles Scribner's Sons, 1963), pp. 146-47 and 160-72, and from Hendrick, *Training of an American, op. cit.,* pp. 345-48.

[32] Pamphlet, "The Lawrenceville School," in *Private Independent Schools, 1971* (Wallingford, Conn.: Bunting and Lyon, 1971), hereafter called "The Lawrenceville School," and letter to author from Edwin C. Bleicher, librarian, Lawrenceville School, May 18, 1973.

[33] Franklin T. Baker, "The Model Preparatory School," *World's Work,* Vol. 6 (September 1903), pp. 3886 and 3889, and photostat of Lawrenceville School pamphlet, "The School," *ca.* 1901.

[34] Letter to Page from Oscar H. McPherson., Nov. 4, 1926, and letter to

Page from Isaac S. Kampmann, Dec. 22, 1930, Boxes 1-2, Arthur W. Page Papers.

[35] *Lawrenceville School Register, 1901*, cited in letter to author from Lawrenceville School Librarian Edwin C. Bleicher, April 30, 1973.

[36] Letter to Page from Newark Attorney Runyon Colie, May 4, 1935, Box 4, Arthur W. Page Papers, and letter to author from Edwin C. Bleicher, April 30, 1973, with accompanying photostats from Lawrenceville School senior class book, *Olla Podrida*, for 1900-1901.

[37] Letter to author from John H. Page, Nov. 11, 1975.

[38] Photostat of letter from Walter H. Page to Dr. S.J. McPherson, Sept. 14, 1901, provided to author by Edwin C. Bleicher.

[39] Page's failure to attend his class reunion is documented by letters from his secretary in reply to letters to him from W.B. Littell, April 30, 1935, from Runyon Colie, May 4, 1935, and from George H. Coughlin, May 7, 1935, Box 4, Arthur W. Page Papers. His refusal to contribute to the school is evidenced by the absence of his name in a list of donors to the school, "Report of the Lawrenceville School," *ca.* 1931, Box 2, and in a letter to Lawrenceville Headmaster Allan V. Heely, Oct. 21, 1943, Box 10. Among the letters in which Page refused to speak at the school are one to Oscar McPherson, Nov. 9, 1926, Box 1, and another to Lawrenceville Headmaster Mather Abbott, Feb. 25, 1932, Box 2.

[40] Letter from Page to Allan V. Heely, *op. cit.*

[41] *Reminiscences*, p. 2, and letter to author from Thaddeus Shaw Page, *op. cit.*

[42] See letter from Page to Owen Wister, Nov. 27, 1931, Box 2, Arthur W. Page Papers.

[43] *Reminiscences*, p. 6.

[44] Letter from Page to Harvard Dean Willard L. Sperry, Dec. 19, 1932, Box 2, Arthur W. Page Papers.

[45] Description of Southern Club dinner is primarily from *Reminiscences*, pp. 7-10.

[46] List of history courses Page took at Harvard is from transcript furnished to author by Harvard Registrar Marion C. Belliveau, May 1, 1973. Page's description of the influence of Professor Coolidge is from *Reminiscences*, pp. 11-12. Description of boys playing checkers in Professor MacVane's course is from Arthur W. Page, "Are the Colleges Doing Their Job?," *World's Work*, Vol. 20 (September 1910), pp. 13431-39.

[47] Based essentially on Arthur W. Page, "Are the Colleges Doing Their Job?", *op. cit.*

[48] Page's fiction contributions to the *Advocate* include: "An Unfinished Sermon," Vol. 73, p. 69, a dialect anecdote about a black preacher who attacks the weaknesses of the flesh only to have to stop preaching because bees are stinging him; "A Half Hour's Freedom," Vol. 73, pp. 88-89, a dialect story about a Negro slave who decides to run away but changes his mind when he grows afraid of the shadows of the night; "Ephraim's Fall," Vol. 74, pp. 37-38, in which a black manservant helps his master cheat at cards until a thunderstorm scares him into falling through a skylight; "The End of Blackwell's Tiger," Vol. 74, pp. 77-79, in which a southern mountaineer outsmarts both a Yankee liquor tax collector and a moonshiner in competition with him; "A War Time Game," Vol. 75, pp. 108-09, a dialect story in which an Irish Union trooper is outsmarted by a Confederate soldier; "On the River Dan," a trick-ending story about captured Confederate soldiers who get their captors to march into the hands of Confederate cavalry; and

"The Strength Test," a short story about a charming but corrupt southern senator who is outsmarted by a newspaper reporter. Story-telling is a southern tradition. The Page stories have the flavor of anecdotes still occasionally told by old men sitting on benches in front of the courthouses of small southern towns.

[49] Letter to author from Mary M. Meehan, assistant, Harvard University Archives, May 24, 1973, with attachments; *Harvard University Register, 1903-04*. p. 66; and *Harvard University Register, 1904-05*, p. 76.

[50] Arthur W. Page, "The Advocate at the Inauguration" and "Campaigning," editorials, *Harvard Advocate*, Vol. 78, pp. 113 and 115 respectively

[51] *Harvard Class Album, 1904*, p. 49; Harvard Class Album, 1905, p. 115; *Harvard University Register, 1904-05*, Vol. 31, p. 134, *The First Catalogue of the Hasty Pudding Institute of 1770* (Cambridge, Mass.: Harvard University Press, 1936), p. 174; Nathan C. Shiverick, "A Short History of the Signet Society," *The Signet: A Centennial Catalogue, 1870-1970* (Cambridge, Mass.: The Signet Society), pp. 2-3; and *Catalogue of the Officers and Members of the O.K. in Harvard College* (Cambridge, Mass.: Harvard University, 1885), pp. i-iii. Copies of pertinent portions of these documents were provided by Mary Meehan of the Harvard University Archives, who knows about such things.

[52] Letter from Arthur W. Page to his mother, March 5, 1905, File 811, Walter Hines Page Papers, Houghton Library, Harvard.

[53] *Reminiscences*, pp. 12-13.

[54] Letter from Arthur Page to his mother, March 5, 1905, *op. cit.*

[55] Harvard grade sheet for Arthur Page's senior year, File 811, Walter Hines Page Papers.

[56] Letter to Page from B.S. Hurlbutt, April 4, 1905, File 811, Walter Hines Page Papers.

[57] Arthur W. Page, "Some Profitable Statistics," *Harvard Advocate*, Vol. 78 (Oct. 21, 1904), pp. 15-16.

[58] Arthur W. Page, "Are the Colleges Doing Their Job?", *op. cit.*

[59] Edward C. Raleigh, *In the Public Interest: The Government Service of Arthur Wilson Page*, unpublished master's thesis (Madison: University of Wisconsin, 1965), p. 92.

[60] Reprinted by permission of the publishers from Charles W. Eliot, *Harvard Memories* (Cambridge, Mass.: Harvard University Press, Copyright © 1923 by the President and Fellows of Harvard College), p. 8.

[61] *Ibid.*, p. 36.

[62] Walter H. Page, "On a Tenth Birthday," *World's Work*, Vol. 21 (January 1911), pp. 13903-17.

[63] "Froth and Truth about Trusts," and "The Trusts and Wages," *World's Work*, Vol. 1 (November 1900), pp. 18-19.

[64] Henry G. Chapman, "The Progress of Honesty," *World's Work*, Vol. 1 (March 1901), pp. 509-14.

[65] "The Autobiography of a Magazine," *World's Work* Advertiser, *World's Work*, Vol. 1 (November 1900 to April 1901).

[66] See Cornelius C. Regier, *The Era of the Muckrakers* (Chapel Hill: University of North Carolina Press, 1932) especially Chs. One and Five.

[67] See *World's Work*, Vol. 6 (July and August 1903).

[68] Thomas F. Woodlock, "The Uplift in Business," *World's Work*, Vol. 8 (July 1904), pp. 4955-58.

CHAPTER TWO

Magazine Reporter to *World's Work* Editor, 1905-1915

W ALTER PAGE wanted one of his sons to join him at Doubleday, Page. Ralph, the oldest, decided to become a lawyer, removing himself from competition. Frank, the youngest, had to complete his undergraduate education at Harvard. That left Arthur.

Although he wanted to be an architect, Arthur obeyed his father's wish that he join the *World's Work* staff after graduation in 1905.[1] In his *Reminiscences*, he says he did so because of gratitude for the gracious way his father had handled his near expulsion from Harvard.[2]

When Arthur told his father he would join the *World's Work*, Walter Page asked him how soon he could start. Arthur replied "at any time," expecting his father to tell him to take a summer vacation and report in the autumn. But Walter Page told him to come immediately after graduation. He reported in early July 1905.[3]

The officers of the publishing house at the time were:

President, Frank N. Doubleday;

Vice Presidents, Walter H. Page and Herbert S. Houston;

Secretary, Henry W. Lanier, son of southern poet Sidney Lanier; and

Treasurer, Samuel A. Everitt, a Scribner's staffer who had followed Frank Doubleday first to *McClure's* and then to Doubleday, Page.[4]

Although the *World's Work* was at first printed by out-side firms, in 1904 Doubleday, Page began printing the magazine on its own presses in its building on E. 16th St. in New York.[5] Then as now, most publishing houses had their printing done by printing firms. Doubleday, Page cut costs by printing its own books and magazines. This, coupled with paying of wages that were below those of most other New York houses, contributed to the firm's prosperity.

In addition to Walter and Arthur Page, the *World's Work* staff in this early period included Michael G. Cuniff, French Strother and Isaac "Ike" Marcosson. The magazine also had occasional staffers, largely because Walter Page was willing to give a chance to almost any aspiring writer who walked in off the street.

Cuniff at 26 had left his post as an English instructor at Harvard to become literary editor of the *World's Work*. He wrote mainly on unionism before being named managing editor of the magazine in 1903. That same year he spearheaded the *World's Work's* first mild plunge into muckraking with an exposé about corruption in the U.S. Post Office.[6] He left the magazine in 1907 to pursue a career in Arizona mining and politics.

Strother was Arthur's closest friend on the staff in this period. Son of a southern lawyer, he worked as a reporter for Walter Page from 1901 to 1907, and again from 1911 to 1913. From Fresno, Calif., and about Arthur's age, Strother published his first *World's Work* article in March 1905.[7]

The egocentric Marcosson was, in his brief tenure at the magazine, one of the office joys. When he left, he laughingly contended it was because Walter Page was a great man, and the magazine didn't need another.[8]

Walter Page was the undisputed chief of the magazine. He wrote perhaps three-fourths of the editorials for each issue, sometimes hiding in a nearby hotel to work without being disturbed when deadlines were near. He also decided the topics for feature articles. Once a topic for an article was selected, the article was either assigned to a staffer to write, or an outside "expert" was commissioned to do the story.[9]

Arthur's training as a reporter didn't end when he left the office for the evening. Until he married in 1912, he lived at home with his father and mother. Evenings, he and his father spent much of their time discussing magazine affairs. Many nights they worked together preparing the next issue. Even casual conversations at home were devoted to discussing topics for *World's Work* editorials.[10]

One of Arthur's first assignments was to collect photos for an article by Sereno Pratt listing the 76 most powerful industrialists and financiers in America, the men Pratt, associate editor of the *Wall Street Journal*, called the "business senate" of the United States.[11]

"This was my first acquaintance with the great," Page recalled years later. He fixed most of the names in his mind, and noted that by 1935 almost all of them had faded into oblivion. Late in life, he said he learned a valuable lesson from the assignment—that as long as American government guaranteed opportunity for people on the way up, power could not be stratified here as it had been in Europe.[12] His view is notable not so much for its accuracy—critics will contend that power has indeed been stratified in America, but in a different way than in Europe—as because it became an integral part of his attitudes.[13]

Staff writer for the World's Work

ARTHUR PAGE'S APPRENTICESHIP on the *World's Work* lasted from 1905 to early 1913, when he replaced his father as editor of the magazine.

During the period, Arthur published a total of 21 feature articles under his own byline. In addition, he helped to solicit manuscripts for publication as part of Doubleday, Page's nonfiction book line and probably wrote some of the *World's Work* editorials, which were unsigned.

The first article carrying young Page's byline appeared in the January 1906 issue of the *World's Work*. An illustrated feature entitled "The Cotton Growers," the story optimistically noted that the price of cotton had risen to 10 cents per pound, a rate likely to restore prosperity to the 11 million or so Americans in the South engaged in growing and marketing cotton.[14] Walter Page particularly liked stories about progress that evidenced emergence of the "New South."

A few months later, the *World's Work* had another brief fling at muckraking. The April 1906 issue was devoted to the life insurance industry in America. Much of the material in the issue dealt with scandals in the business.[15] It was a timely topic. In 1905, New York Attorney Charles Evans Hughes exposed chicanery in big insurance companies, touching off other investigations and a reform movement. That catapulted Republican Hughes to an unsuccessful run in 1916 for the presidency.

The same issue carried a short article about Socialism by Upton Sinclair, whose sixth novel, *The Jungle*, a sensational exposure of unsanitary conditions in meat-packing, had just been published by Doubleday, Page. Sinclair said of the novel, which was originally commissioned by a Socialist weekly, "I aimed at the public's heart, and hit it in the stomach." The issue included a promise that the *World's Work* would shortly publish further information about the threat to public health posed by the meat-packers.[16]

The May 1906 issue of the *World's Work* carried three articles on meat-packing as promised. Despite a pious disclaimer that the stories were not "literature of exposure," but rather, a plea for federal regulation of meat-packing, they were muckraking at its best.

Perhaps the most explosive article in the series was "A Picture of Meat Inspection" by W.K. Jaques, a former head of meat inspection at the Chicago stockyards. Jaques confirmed the unhealthy practices that Sinclair had treated as naturalistic fiction in *The Jungle*.[17]

The *World's Work* got the federal regulation of meat-packing it advocated. After reading *The Jungle*, Teddy Roosevelt ordered his secretary of agriculture to conduct an investigation. On hearing that the *World's Work* was going to back up the book with further articles, he appointed a commission to conduct a more thorough inquiry. New pure food laws were the eventual outcome.[18]

Walter Page believed, and Arthur Page inherited his view, that if corporations openly publicized their affairs, abandoning secrecy, muckraking literature attacking big corporations would go away.

The July 1906 issue of the *World's Work* carried an editorial, "The 'Publicity Men' of Corporations," which praised the trend in big business to hire publicity agents as a step toward abandonment of secrecy.[19] A draft of this editorial is in the early Arthur Page Papers, suggesting he probably wrote it. If so, young Page early in life was favorably predisposed to the public relations vocation to which he devoted most of the last 34 years of his life.[20]

The editorial endorsed hiring these "publicity men" from the ranks of working journalists for two reasons. First, the editorial held, publicity men with newspaper or magazine backgrounds would be more accurate sources of news than corporation men who knew nothing about writing news. (In later life, heading AT&T public relations, Arthur Page held the reverse, that Bell System public relations ranks could best be staffed from within, by men who knew about the business rather than about writing news.) The second advantage was that publicity men, by making information readily available, would hasten the day when corporations and consumers could get along amicably and government investigators would fade away. The editorial warned that news prepared by publicists would be distrusted by the public "as an attorney's givings-forth are received." The magazine concluded that truth could be as elusive as ever "in spite of the multiplicity of her salaried ministers."

Arthur Page's second *World's Work* article, "Communication by Wire and 'Wireless,'" about AT&T just before Theodore N. Vail became president, appeared in the January 1907 issue. A summary of what was happening in the communications industry, the article flattered AT&T, which by late 1906 controlled a little more than half the telephone business in America. The *World's Work* liked big business.

Arthur Page, in turn, liked AT&T, for which he would later work. The article noted that by late 1906 AT&T handled 75 times as many messages annually as America's two telegraph companies, Western Union and Postal Telegraph. Young Page was impressed by AT&T's technology and the firm's regular eight per cent stock dividend. He argued that the telephone was a natural monopoly (a position advocated by Vail, at the time a director of AT&T). He noted that customers were the losers when two competitive telephone companies served the same town. In such a case, a subscriber, under the practices of the day, had to take service from both companies in order to talk to all the telephones in a town.[21]

The remaining bylined articles Arthur wrote from 1905 to 1913 cover conservation of natural resources, developments in agriculture, education in America and technological innovations. The articles are on balance pro-business, although he criticized the lack of conservation practices in a few industries.

Working day by day with his father, Arthur developed a closer relationship with him than had either of his brothers. Walter Page's attitudes, writing style, ability to pick out central issues in complex matters and other traits became his. One thing he didn't inherit was his father's informality. Throughout life, he was less exuberant, more reserved and formal when dealing with others. Both men, perhaps influenced by a southern tradition that valued good manners, were unfailingly kind and courteous to others except when they felt themselves wronged or their honor questioned.

Arthur Page's inheritance of his father's writing style is especially worth noting. Walter Page believed in simplicity and clarity in writing. He would not permit writers—particularly his son—to use two-syllable words when one-syllable words would do. He abhorred use of foreign words and phrases. According to French Strother, Walter Page was determined to make his magazine understandable to readers. A staff joke held that the *World's Work* was edited "for the comprehension of the Kansas farmer's hired man's 14-year-old daughter."[22]

In later life, those who worked with Arthur Page said he had an uncanny knack for sitting in meetings listening to controversy until an impasse was reached. Then he would sum up the critical issues in a few words and lead the others to a decision. This ability too Arthur appears to have inherited from his father. Arthur Goodrich, who had known Walter Page well, told Burton Hendrick in 1925 that Walter Page "had an extraordinary way of seeing straight through to the essential thing in any question which came up. I can remember dozens of times during conferences when he would sit silent, with the smoke from his inevitable cigar drifting in a leisurely haze about his head . . . Then he would suddenly, in a few words, dispose of the whole problem which had been agitating us, by cutting cleanly through the surface to its heart. He thought simply and clearly, just as he wrote..."[23] Place a pipe in Arthur Page's mouth instead of a cigar, and he and his father are one.

Meeting with the power elite

DURING HIS APPRENTICESHIP YEARS on the *World's Work*, Arthur Page began to come into regular contact with men of prestige and power.

In the summer of 1907, he accompanied Secretary of the Interior James Garfield on a trip through the West to inspect the work of the U.S. Reclamation Service, which was building irrigation networks to open arid federal lands to settlers. Young Page wrote several articles about development of national resources after the trip.[24]

At about the same time, he traveled with Gifford Pinchot on an inspection tour. The trip with Theodore Roosevelt's irascible, conservation-minded chief of the Bureau of Forestry stimulated Arthur to write a series of articles about the need for better conservation policies in America.[25] Pinchot and Roosevelt at the time were conducting a major public relations campaign on behalf of forestry, and young Page became a publicist in the movement. Among the firms he criticized in his articles was the Weyerhaeuser Co., owner of millions of acres of timber, a firm that many years later would retain him as a public relations consultant.

In 1908, the *World's Work* began publishing the reminiscences of John D. Rockefeller, a coup magazine historian Theodore Peterson calls the *World's Work*'s "first great scoop."[26]

Rockefeller's Standard Oil Co. had come under attack at the turn of the century from a variety of sources for secrecy and unethical practices. Perhaps the most damaging attack came in Ida Tarbell's "History of the Standard Oil Company" serialization that began in *McClure's* in 1902.

In 1905, Rockefeller's philanthropic adviser, Rev. Frederick T. Gates, urged him to become less secretive. A short time later, Standard Oil hired newsman Joseph I.C. Clarke to handle publicity, and he began working to make the corporation more open.[27] Standard Oil executives for a time caught the spirit. In late 1907, Standard operating head John D. Archbold (or more likely someone writing for him) published "The Standard Oil Company: Some Facts and Figures" in the *Saturday Evening Post*. The article, containing information which had previously been kept confidential, grudgingly admitted secrecy was a bad policy for corporations.[28]

In August and September of the following year, the *World's Work* paved the way for publication of the first installment of Rockefeller's memoirs with three teaser articles, two about the oil magnate by C.M. Keys, and a third by Frank Doubleday about encounters he had had with Rockefeller.[29]

The Rockefeller series proper, "Some Random Reminiscences of Men and Events," published in seven installments, began in October 1908. In the series, Rockefeller defended big business as efficient, denying charges of corruption at Standard leveled by Ida Tarbell and others.[30]

In addition to publishing the Rockefeller reminiscences, the *World's Work* in this period editorially defended Standard Oil against judicial attack by Judge Kennesaw Mountain Landis (who later broke up the Standard Oil combine) and from press attack by the Hearst papers, which at the time were exposing payoffs Archbold had made to Sen. Joseph B. Foraker in return for favors to Standard Oil.[31]

Publication of Rockefeller's memoirs in the *World's Work* led to gossip that Rockefeller was a financial "angel" for Doubleday, Page. The rumors were further fueled when Doubleday, Page in 1908 bought the book-publishing business of S.S. McClure and Co. Standard Oil in this period was known to subsidize magazines and newspapers in return for favorable coverage. Some people in publishing circles believed Rockefeller provided the capital for the acquisition.

Walter Page vehemently denied any financial connection between Rockefeller and Doubleday, Page, other than that the *World's Work* had paid Rockefeller for the right to publish his memoirs. Doubleday, Page was well managed financially, and the acquisition of the McClure book-publishing venture was probably nothing more than another astute business deal by Frank Doubleday, who bought a property valued at $225,000 for $118,750.[32]

In mid-1910, Arthur Page added Wilbur and Orville Wright to the expanding list of influential people he knew. Arthur first saw the Wrights in New York, seven years after their historic flight at Kitty Hawk, when they came to fly an airplane around the Statue of Liberty. Soon after that flight, Arthur went to Dayton, Ohio, to interview the normally taciturn brothers. They received him politely. He published an article about them, "How the Wrights Discovered Flight," in the August issue of the *World's Work*.[33] He kept in touch with them during the ensuing years.[34]

Country Life, one of the magazines published by Doubleday, had for years been advocating that people move from the congested, unhealthy cities to the country. In the fall of 1910, the firm followed its own advice, moving from its overcrowded plant in New York City to a new plant with 150,000 square feet of floor space in Garden City, a small town on Long Island. Modern machinery was installed in the new plant, and employment and production shot upwards. The 40-acre site in Garden City provided plenty of room for expansion.[35]

Walter Page moved his family from a duplex in New York City to a more spacious home in Garden City. The home, a mansard-roofed, green-shuttered wooden house painted white, was one of a dozen duplicates that stood in a row and were collectively nicknamed "the 12 Apostles."[36]

Arthur at about this time traveled with American correspondents to Mexico City to attend ceremonies marking the 100th anniversary of Mexican independence and the 80th birthday of dictator Porfirio Díaz, whom Teddy Roosevelt once praised as the "greatest statesman now living."

On the long train ride to Mexico through the hot, dusty plains of Texas, Arthur got his first experience with tequila, and with a voluble student of Roman history, Col. Bill Stirrit of the *Dallas News*. Self-educated, Stirrit had read the Bone classics "from kiver to kiver," and amused the correspondents by drawing parallels between Roman and American political figures.

At the celebration in Mexico City, Page met the walrus-moustached Díaz, who had brutally ruled Mexico through eight terms from 1876 forward. Although a believer in democracy, Arthur nonetheless formed an admiration for the Mexican strongman who had made his country safe for American investment—which in turn led steel magnate Andrew Carnegie to regard him as "The Moses and Joshua of Mexico."

Dictator Díaz a few months later in 1911 provided young Page with another lesson in the transitory nature of power. Francisco Madero, aided by Francisco "Pancho" Villa and Emiliano Zapata, overthrew Díaz and drove him from the country. The revolt touched off a spate of coups and countercoups in Mexico. Gen. Victoriano Huerta replaced Madero (who had been assassinated) and in turn was supplanted by Gen. Venustiano Carranza. Each successive event was reported by the *World's Work* with mounting disapproval.[37]

Another article in the *World's Work* worth noting can be traced to a court decision in the late 19th century that conferred the status of a person on corporations. While the courts might make a corporation into a person, a common argument of the time charged, they could not give the corporation a soul. As corporations and trusts grew in scale and impersonality, so grew the charges that big business was profit-motivated and soulless. Many executives took such charges seriously, and sought to refute the charge by publicizing various altruistic and charitable behaviors.

A March 1912 article in the *World's Work* was characteristic of the "soul" movement and also presaged the modern concept of public relations. "The Soul of a Corporation," bylined by President William Gibbs McAdoo of the Hudson and Manhattan Railroad, outlined how the railroad had arrived at its enlightened self-interest. Good service was the necessary foundation for good relations with the public, McAdoo allowed.

The article began with the Hudson and Manhattan creed, what today would be called a mission or vision statement:

> We believe in "the public be pleased" policy; we believe that the railroad is best which serves the public best; that decent treatment of the public evokes decent treatment from the public; that recognition by the corporation of the just rights of the people results in recognition by the public of the just rights of the corporation. A square deal for the people and a square deal for the corporation![38]

In later life, Arthur Page held that good public relations begins with sound policies in the public interest, and that if policies were not sound, no amount of publicity whitewash would help. Other later tenets of Arthur Page's public relations creed foreshadowed in the McAdoo article include:

1. Employee courtesy is an important element in good customer relations.
2. The public is basically reasonable. It becomes unreasonable when uninformed.
3. Good service in the public interest must precede any calls for public support.

4.   Actions speak louder than words.

5.   The public must be taken into the company's confidence when changes in policies and procedures are introduced if good public relations are to be maintained.

6. Even when the corporation has the legal right to do something, it is better to do it with public approval than without.

7. Complaints from the public must be answered promptly with information in defense of the company. Complaints must not be ignored.

8. Customer good will is particularly valuable when a regulated industry goes before a government agency to ask for rate or fare increases.[39]

Husband and son of an ambassador

FROM 1905 to the early summer of 1912, Arthur Page was an apprentice to his father. Then two things occurred that assured his independence.

He married Mollie W. Hall of Milton, Mass., on June 1, 1912. Almost 30 years old, the groom was 5 feet 11, weighed about 170 pounds, brown-eyed, not particularly handsome (rather plain, in fact), and like his father, prone to be somewhat careless in dress. Two years his junior, Mollie was attractive (even Bruce Barton, who had a keen eye for women, said so) and vibrant. Like Arthur, she had waited longer than most young people to marry. The two swore their vows of fidelity in St. Peter's Church in Milton.

Arthur and his bride moved to separate quarters from the Walter Page home in Garden City. Now the meetings with his father occurred on the job, and only occasionally during evenings or on weekends. The first child of Arthur and Mollie Page, a daughter, Mollie Jr., was born in New York City on March 17, 1913. Arthur's independence from his father was by this time almost complete.

The second thing assuring Arthur's independence, although public announcement had not yet been made, was that Walter Page had agreed to be appointed U.S. ambassador to the Court of St. James's (Great Britain) by President Woodrow Wilson. Arthur was to replace his father as editor of the *World's Work*.

The connection between Walter Page and (Thomas) Woodrow Wilson began before Arthur was born. Walter Page met Wilson in Atlanta while covering meetings of the Tariff Commission of 1882 for the New York *World*. An aspiring young lawyer whose practice would be short and unsuccessful, Wilson asked Page to appear as a witness at the hearings. A casual friendship began.

In the early 1900s, the *World's Work* applauded Wilson's appointment as president of Princeton, and his successful bid in 1910 for the governorship of New Jersey.[40] Beginning in late 1910, Walter Page helped to pump him up to presidential stature, contending in his magazine that Wilson was one of the three strongest candidates for the 1912 Democratic nomination, "the best example in present life of the old-fashioned Democrat,"[41] code-words for "southern Democrat." Wilson represented Page's best hope of seeing a southern president in the White House. He published more articles booming Wilson,[42] and eventually assigned Frank Parker Stockbridge, a staffer on the magazine, to oversee publicity for Wilson.[43] His support of Wilson was not deterred by other executives of the publishing house who opposed Wilson.[44]

Wilson was nominated on the 46th ballot of the Democratic Convention, and then elected in a landslide plurality when Republican William Howard Taft and Progressive Bull Mooser Teddy Roosevelt split the majority vote.

In January 1913, the *World's Work* began publishing in seven installments the text of Woodrow Wilson's *The New Freedom*, a publishing coup that left the impression the magazine was the official voice of the newly elected president. Later published in book form by Doubleday, Page, *The New Freedom* was the work of *World's Work* staffer William Bayard Hale, who pieced the manuscript together chiefly from Wilson's campaign speeches. Hale earlier, at the bidding of

Walter Page, had written Wilson's campaign biography.[45] During the months The *New Freedom* articles ran, newsstand sales of the magazine went up 40 per cent and paid subscriptions increased by 10,000.[46]

Wilson considered Walter Page for his cabinet, but Col. Edward M. House, his closest adviser, objected to Page being named secretary of agriculture or interior, the posts Wilson had in mind. Wilson finally offered Page the less attractive ambassadorship, and then only after Richard Olney and Charles W. Eliot had both turned it down.

Walter Page, worried about money, hesitated to accept the job. The British ambassadorship usually went to wealthy men. The State Dept. salary, $17,500 per year in 1913, did not come close to covering expenses an ambassador in London incurred. He accepted only after Frank Doubleday, in a gesture motivated by patriotism and realization the appointment would enhance the publishing house prestige, agreed to continue his Doubleday salary while he was in England.[47]

The appointment was announced on March 31, 1913.[48] The new ambassador sailed for England in May, taking with him his son Frank. His wife and daughter would follow shortly. Arthur stayed behind to edit the *World's Work* and look after his father's interests at the publishing house.

Walter Page's concern about being able to afford the ambassadorship turned out to be justified. In his first year, he had to dip into personal savings for $30,000. Alarmed, he wrote to President Wilson saying he could not continue in the post without more money. Wilson arranged for a contribution of $25,000 per year from Cleveland Dodge. The money went from Dodge to Col. House to Arthur, who sent it on to his father. According to an entry Col. House made in his diary, Walter Page never knew the source of the subsidy.[49]

Metamorphosis from writer to magazine editor

THE JUNE 1913 ISSUE of the *World's Work* was the first to carry the name of Arthur Page as editor.

Aside from leaving a thick sheaf of editorials behind for Arthur to use until he had time to begin writing his own, Walter Page withdrew from active management of the magazine, leaving Arthur to make the decisions.

There was no real need for Walter Page to send detailed instructions on management across the Atlantic to his son. The magazine went on as though Walter Page were still editing it. The son he chose to succeed him as editor was probably the single man closest in thought and opinion to him. Arthur was cast in his father's image.

Many of the editorials Arthur wrote for the *World's Work* while his father was ambassador sound like excerpts from letters Walter Page was writing to friends and government officials. Father continued to communicate with son at the publishing house, and Walter wrote to Arthur many of the same things he was saying in letters to others.

Walter Page read his son's editorials in the *World's Work*, and reacted to them. More importantly, Arthur each week or so sent his father a thick 15- to 20-page letter. This weekly sheaf consisted of Arthur's analysis of American public reaction to news events and a summary of the state of public opinion in the nation.[50] Raleigh refers to Arthur's regular written briefings for his father as "the Page News and Special Events Service."[51] To some extent Arthur probably helped shape his father's impressions of opinion in America, a possibility that becomes especially important in view of the split that developed between Walter Page and President Wilson in the early years of World War I. Thus the magazine's editorial stance continued as though there had been no change in editors. Walter Page moved his physical presence from Garden City to London, but his spirit lived on in his son.

That is not to say that Arthur Page made no changes in the magazine. Editorials often covered matters Walter Page had not treated during his years as editor. Arthur subtly changed feature article content of the magazine to provide more coverage of political affairs, and made other changes.

Once he became editor, Arthur shifted his own writing output from feature articles to editorials. He contributed 21 feature articles from 1905 to early 1913, only nine from 1913 through 1926. From 1913 to 1916, his most important writing was of *World's Work* editorials, although he wrote far from all of them.

Perhaps the most notable of Arthur's feature articles during his early editorship years are a character sketch of Secretary of War Lindley M. Garrison, and a series of four articles about 0. Henry, the latter written not for the *World's Work*, but for *Bookman*.[52]

In mid-1913, Arthur hired Burton Hendrick from *McClure's* to serve as associate editor of the *World's Work*. Hendrick became one of the magazine's best writers. Three of his *World's Work* feature article series, when published as books, won Pulitzer Prizes. His first article for the *World's Work*, a sketch of Secretary of the Interior Franklin K. Lane, part of the magazine's "Who Governs" series initiated by Arthur Page, appeared in the August 1913 issue.[53] Hendrick, interviewed by Allan Nevins and Dean Albertson for the Columbia University Oral History Project in 1949, said he left *McClure's* because it was about to fold, and more importantly, he contended, because "... Arthur Page was not a very good writer and he was supposed to do the editorials which were then very important... I wrote the editorials after three or four years—all of them. That was my main job."[54]

In November 1913, Arthur contributed another bylined article for the "Who Governs" series, this one on Secretary of Agriculture David F. Houston, a friend of his father.[55] Born in North Carolina and raised in South Carolina, Houston played a round of golf with Arthur to permit a long interview, and the two, if not already friends, became so. A decade and a half later, Arthur replaced Houston as president of the Bell Telephone Securities Co., an AT&T subsidiary.

Covering the start of the World War

THE CIRCULATION OF THE *WORLD'S WORK* fell a bit in the first year of Arthur Page's editorship. Then World War I erupted in Europe. By shifting much of the magazine content to coverage of the conflict, Arthur was able to increase circulation.

When Germany invaded Belgium on Aug. 3, 1914, the September edition of the *World's Work* was already on press. Arthur ordered the presses stopped. The staff of the magazine, with the help of a few freelancers, put together in a single week a 136-page War Manual crammed with facts. Nearly 300,000 copies of the special issue were sold on newsstands, and attention in subsequent issues to events in Europe boosted circulation to around 140,000 copies per month, the largest in any five-year period of the magazine's history.[56]

In the first months after outbreak of the war, the *World's Work* devoted most of its editorials and features to covering the hostilities. In another stroke of ingenious editorial opportunism, Page inserted a last-minute supplement on the war in the October 1914 issue. It included an outstanding feature by Arno Dosch-Fleurot, one of the two American journalists who witnessed the fall of Louvain in Belgium to German troops invading France through the neutral nation.[57] A priceless medieval library and other gothic monuments were laid waste by the green German troops. The November 1914 and January 1915 *World's Work* issues were wholly devoted to war coverage.

The December 1914 number took a brief respite from the war for Arthur Page to introduce another innovation, a special issue devoted to foreign trade, especially American trade with Latin America. A few months later Page announced the *World's Work* would begin publishing a special quarterly edition in Spanish for circulation south of the border.[58]

Arthur sought to recruit former President Teddy Roosevelt to contribute to the Spanish edition. He was unsuccessful, as he had been in his efforts to get Roosevelt to attend the annual dinners for former editors of the *Harvard Advocate* in New York in 1912 and 1913, but his efforts led to an eventual friendship with the combative former president.[59]

During the first months of the Wilson presidency, when Woodrow Wilson, Walter and Arthur Page were in agreement on issues such as the Panama Canal tolls controversy and unrest in Mexico, the *World's Work* had a honeymoon with the administration. Soon after the outbreak of the war in Europe, however, Walter Page, under the sway of British statesmen who went out of their way to influence the American ambassador, took the side of the English against the Central Powers and Wilson's policy of neutrality.

Beginning in February 1915, the *World's Work* became mildly critical of the administration. There was no sharp split. The magazine began gently, avoiding direct attack of the neutrality policy, but calling for military preparedness in a steadily increasing stream of editorials and articles.

As the war dragged on, Walter Page became ever more strident in his letters to Wilson, cabinet officials, presidential advisers and friends. He called for an end to neutrality and active American aid to the Entente Allies. The *World's Work* simultaneously became more strident, voicing the same views Walter Page was sending privately to Washington.

Walter Page may never have enjoyed the confidence of Wilson. If he did, he soon lost it because of his support of Great Britain in the war. Wilson thought with good reason that his ambassador was the victim of British propaganda. The break began at least as early as September 1914, by which time Walter Page began making clear his views in messages to the president and Col. House.[60] By November 1914, Walter Page had told son Arthur he favored the Allies.[61]

The *World's Work* in 1915 began campaigning for a federal budget system. Henry L. Stimson, educated at Yale and Harvard, had proposed such a federal budget two years earlier when he was secretary of war in the cabinet of President William H. Taft. The *World's Work* had noted Stimson's unsuccessful run for the governorship of New York in 1910 and the Taft appointment in 1911. A 1915 editorial about Stimson's work for a federal budget appeared as Arthur Page and Stimson were becoming close friends.[62]

The friendship began soon after Arthur Page bought a country estate. The estate, County Line—which Page was more apt to describe as "a run-down farm"—was about eight miles from Garden City near Cold Spring Harbor, Oyster Bay and

Huntington on the tony north shore of Long Island. Stimson's Highhold estate was located nearby.

A few weeks after Arthur, Mollie Sr., and baby Mollie moved to County Line, Stimson—not yet Col. Stimson (that would come after he served as a colonel of artillery with the AEF in World War I)—rode up on one of his horses and introduced himself to Arthur. The handshake became the start of a lifelong friendship between the Arthur Page family and the childless Henry and Mabel Stimson.

For many years after, when the Stimsons were at Highhold, perhaps three Sunday evenings out of four, Arthur and Mollie would have dinner at Highhold with the Stimsons. While Mollie and Mabel chatted about household affairs, Arthur and Henry discussed politics, economics and world affairs. Other frequent diners at Highhold, and at Woodley, Stimson's northwest Washington estate, especially after 1940, included Harvey and Kate Bundy and John and Ellen McCloy.

Stimson became for Arthur the sounding board and adviser that his father had been. Years later, Arthur Page observed of the relationship: "Father having started this (discussions about current events), I carried it on with Colonel Stimson, and while they were completely different in their approach to things—they were not so far different in their opinions. Although the Colonel was as inherited a Republican as we were inherited Democrats, actually I could never see any real difference on any important subject. They might vary on minor matters, but as far as general conception of life and what went on in the United States and what ought to go on, there was almost no difference."[63]

Walter Hines Page II, the second child of Arthur and Mollie Page, was born at County Line on July 7, 1915.

On Aug. 4, Arthur's sister Katherine married Bostonian Charles Greeley Loring in the Chapel Royal of St. James's Palace in London. Among the children, Ralph in 1911 had married Leila H. Tuckerman of Brookline, Mass., abandoning a law career in favor of settling in North Carolina to pursue the life of a gentleman farmer. He returned briefly in 1915 to attend, along with 1,200 other carefully selected young men of substantial wealth, the four-week businessman's military training camp at Plattsburg, N.Y. There the upper-class elite were converted to patriots. Frank Page, youngest son of the ambassador, married Katherine Sefton of Auburn, N.Y., in June 1916. After his marriage, Frank settled in Garden City to work with Arthur on the staff of the *World's Work* and other Doubleday magazines.[64]

From the 1915 sinking of the *Lusitania* by a German submarine on, the *World's Work* grew ever more critical of the Central Powers and American neutrality. It lashed out against the $100 million German propaganda effort in America, conveniently failing to notice British propaganda—equally as extensive if not as costly, although far more skillfully managed. Editorials alleged that German propaganda found particular success in New York because of German-American control of the city's major newspapers through Ochs of the *New York Times*, Villard of the *Evening Post*, Reich at the *Sun* and *Evening Sun*, and the younger Pulitzer at the *World*. Arthur's most barbed editorials were directed at American propagandist in German employ George Sylvester Vierick and his pro-German *The Fatherland* publication. Page disliked Vierick at least as much as Socialist Upton Sinclair.[65]

In July, the magazine applauded the resignation of pacifist Secretary of State William Jennings Bryan, interpreting it as a turnaround in Wilsonian policy,[66] which it certainly was not. Bryan, who knew next to nothing of foreign affairs, was named to head State in return for having gotten Wilson nominated in 1912. As a pacifist who treated the warring factions in Europe equally, he had been useful to Wilson.

Bryan's successor, Robert M. "Bert" Lansing, was like Walter Page an anglophile who worked to advance the Entente cause. He was married to one the daughters of John Foster, who was secretary of state for Benjamin Harrison. Uncle to Allen and John Foster Dulles, who would serve in years ahead as head of the Central Intelligence Agency and secretary of state in the Eisenhower administration, Lansing was a close friend of the two principal British intelligence agents in America during the war, Sir Courtney Bennett and the Australian Captain Sir Guy Gaunt. Gaunt gave American officials their first evidence of German intrigue on neutral U.S. soil. While outwardly maintaining a strict stance of neutrality, Lansing worked behind the scenes in the Wilson administration to undermine the Central Powers.[67]

As for Wilson and his policy of neutrality, it would be simplistic to say he was simply a peace-loving, idealistic academic trying to remain aloof from the intrigues of a decadent Europe. He wanted to be a president devoted to domestic affairs, but hoped also to be the mediator who would bring peace to Europe. He was no stranger to foreign intrigue. During his presidency, American troops occupied Veracruz in 1914, Haiti in 1915, the Dominican Republic in 1916 and part of Mexico in 1917. He sent Gen. John Pershing with 10,000 soldiers deep into Mexico in pursuit of Pancho Villa in 1916. At the time Walter and Arthur Page were calling for him to intervene in World War I, Wilson perhaps wisely meant to keep the country out of the ghastly trench war in Europe. He was horrified by the hundreds of thousands of soldiers being killed in battles that had little or no importance.

As the twin pressures of American economic involvement with the Allies and German submarine warfare sucked Wilson inexorably toward war, he continued to resist even when Teddy Roosevelt called him a coward and traitor. More of that and what pushed him into the war in the next chapter. At the beginning of 1916, Arthur Page became a vice president of Doubleday, Page, and his duties were considerably enlarged. That too is discussed in the next chapter.

ENDNOTES

[1] Page discusses his desire to become an architect and the circumstances that led him instead to the *World's Work* in *Reminiscences*, p. 12.

[2] *Ibid.*

[3] *Ibid.*, p. 15.

[4] Contents page, *World's Work*, Vol. 14 (August 1907). See also "The Doubleday and McClure Co.," *New York Times*, Dec. 19, 1899, p. 16.

[5] "Publisher's Housewarming," *New York Times*, Nov. 18, 1904, p. 7, and *The Country Life Press* (Garden City, N.Y.: Doubleday, Page and Co., 1919), p. 9.

[6] M.G. Cuniff, "The Post-Office and the People," *World's Work*, Vol. 7 (December 1903), pp. 4074-85. The same issue of the magazine contains another exposé, Adele Marie Shaw's criticism of public schools, "The True Character of New York Public Schools," pp. 4204-21.

[7] "Notes from Mr. Strother," May 3, 1926, Burton J. Hendrick Papers, in private hands in Plano, Ill. Hendrick interviewed Strother as part of his work on the fourth volume of his biography of Walter H. Page.

[8] Miss J.N. McIlwraith, "A Few Unimportant Jottings about Mr. W.H. Page," Jan. 27, 1925, Burton J. Hendrick Papers, Plano, Ill.

[9] Based essentially on *Reminiscences*, pp. 18-19. See also Mott., *op. cit.*, p. 778.

[10] *Reminiscences*, p. 17.

[11] Sereno S. Pratt, "Our Financial Oligarchy," *World's Work*, Vol. 10 (October 1905), pp. 6704-14.

[12] *Reminiscences*, pp. 20-21.

[13] Views that wealth and power in America is stratified are presented in Ferdinand Lundberg's *The Rich and the Super-Rich*, and in the scholarly publications of University of Wisconsin economist Robert Lampman and Harvard economic historian Gabriel Kolko.

[14] Arthur W. Page, "The Cotton Growers," *World's Work*, Vol. 11 (January 1906), pp. 7049-59.

[15] *World's Work*, Vol. 11 (April 1906).

[16] Upton Sinclair, "The Socialist Party," *ibid.*, pp. 7431-32, and "The Talk of the Office" column, World's Work Advertiser, *ibid.*

[17] See W.K. Jaques, "A Picture of Meat Inspection," and related articles, *World's Work*, Vol. 11 (May 1906), pp. 7491-505, and Mott, *op. cit.*, p. 778.

[18] Lyon, *op. cit.*, p. 245.

[19] "The 'Publicity Men' of Corporations," *World's Work*, Vol. 12 (July 1906), p. 7703

[20] A typewritten draft of the editorial is attached to a letter to Page from D.S. Freeman of the Richmond (Va.) *News Leader*, Box 1, Arthur W. Page Papers. Apparently Freeman, whose letter is undated, was returning the typewritten copy of the editorial to Arthur Page, who had sent the draft to him. There is no hard evidence that Arthur Page wrote the editorial.

[21] Arthur W. Page, "Communications by Wire and 'Wireless,'" *World's Work*, Vol. 13 (January 1907), pp. 8408-22.

[22] Hendrick discusses Walter Page's editing style in *Training of an American* and to a lesser extent in *The Life and Letters*. French Strother's comment about the reading level at which the *World's Work* was aimed is from Hendrick, "Notes from Mr. Strother," *op. cit.*

[23] Memo from Arthur Goodrich to Burton J. Hendrick, Jan. 24, 1925.

[24] See Arthur W. Page, "The Real Conquest of the West," *World's Work*, Vol. 15 (December 1907), p. 9691 ff., and "Running a River through a Mountain," *ibid.*, Vol. 14 (September 1907), pp. 9322-30.

[25] *Reminiscences*, p. 28; and Arthur W. Page, "The Fight for a Land Conscience," *World's Work*, Vol. 15 (November 1907), pp. 9588-93, "The Statesmanship of Forestry," *ibid.* (January 1908), pp. 9734-57, "The Rediscovery of Our Greatest Wealth," *ibid.*, Vol. 16 (May 1908), pp. 10223-28, and "A Fight for Conservation," *ibid.*, Vol. 21 (November-December 1910), pp. 13607-11 and 13748-60.

[26] Theodore Peterson, *Magazines in the Twentieth Century* (Urbana, Ill.: University of Illinois Press, 1956), pp. 140-41. Author incorrectly sets publication at 1907; the series appeared in 1908-1909.

[27] Scott M. Cutlip and Allen H. Center, *Effective Public Relations* (Englewood Cliffs, N.J.: Prentice-Hall, 1971), p. 79.

[28] John D. Archbold, "The Standard Oil Co.: Some Facts and Figures," *Saturday Evening Post*, Vol. 80 (Dec. 7, 1907), pp. 3-5, 32.

[29] C.M. Keys, "The Large Corporations," *World's Work*, Vol. 16 (August and September 1908), pp. 10571-90 and 10683-702, and Frank N. Doubleday, "Some Impressions of John D. Rockefeller," *ibid.* (September 1908), pp. 10703-15.

[30] John D. Rockefeller, "Some Reminiscences of Men and Events," *World's Work*, Vol. 16 (October 1908), pp. 10755-68, and Vol. 17 (November-December 1908, and January-April 1909), pp. 10878-94, 10992-11004, 11101-10, 11218-28, 11341-55 and 11470-78.

[31] "The Great Standard Oil Fine," *World's Work*, Vol. 16 (September 1908), pp. 10633-34, and second editorial critical of Hearst attack on Standard Oil, *ibid.*, Vol. 17 (November 1908), pp. 10851-53.

[32] Lyon, *op. cit.*, p. 322.

[33] Arthur W. Page, "How the Wrights Discovered Flight," *World's Work*, Vol. 20 (August 1910), pp. 13303-18.

[34] *Reminiscences*, p. 24.

[35] *The Country Life Press, op. cit.*, pp. 7-20.

[36] *McIlwraith Reminiscences, op. cit.*

[37] *Reminiscences*, pp. 25-28, and "Is Mexico Ready Now To Dig Up a Dictator and Repatriate Him?," *Wall Street Journal*, Dec. 14, 2000, p. 1

[38] William Gibbs McAdoo, "The Soul of a Corporation," *World's Work*, Vol. 23 (March 1912), pp. 579-92 at p. 580.

[39] *Ibid.*

[40] See photo of Wilson when he was appointed Princeton president, *World's Work*, Vol. 4 (October 1902), p. 2585, and frontispiece and editorial, "Presidential Weather and Timber," *ibid.*, Vol. 21 (November 1910), p. 13574.

[41] "Presidential Weather and Timber," *op. cit.*

[42] See, for example, William Bayard Hale, "Woodrow Wilson: Possible President," *World's Work*, Vol. 22 (May 1911), pp. 14399-53, and Frank Parker Stockbridge, "With Governor Wilson in the West," *ibid.* (August 1911), pp. 14713-16.

[43] *Reminiscences*, p. 34.

[44] Walter H. Page, "What the *World's Work* Is Trying To Do," *World's Work*, Vol. 25 (January 1913), pp. 265-68.

[45] William E. Leuchtenburg, "A Note about This Edition," *Woodrow Wilson: The New Freedom* (Englewood Cliffs, N.J.: Prentice-Hall, 1961), p. ix. Barbara Tuchman in her mistressful *The Zimmermann Telegram* says William Bayard Hale was a paid German agent during World War I.

[46] "Talk of the Office," World's Work Advertiser, *World's Work*, Vol. 25 (April 1913).

[47] Ross Gregory, *Walter Hines Page, Ambassador to the Court of St. James's* (Lexington, Ky.: University Press of Kentucky, 1970), pp. 22-24, 31, and Hendrick., *Life and Letters, op. cit.*, Vol. 1, pp. 130-31.

[48] "W.H. Page Chosen Envoy to England," *New York Times*, April 1, 1913, p. 7.

[49] Explained in *Diary* of Edward M. House, Sept. 5, 1914, Yale University Library, and letter from Walter H. Page to Woodrow Wilson, Nov. 5, 1914, Walter H. Page Papers, both items cited here from Gregory, *op. cit.*, p. 31.

[50] Arthur Page's weekly letters briefing his father in London are in

possession of Arthur's sons. Raleigh, *op. cit.*, discusses the letters at p. 12. They are also mentioned in George E. Moranda, "Arthur Wilson Page: His Formative Years," term paper, University of Wisconsin, May 1963, p. 11.

[51] Raleigh, *op. cit.*, p. 92.

[52] Arthur W. Page, "Who Governs the United States—Secretary of War Lindley M. Garrison," *World's Work*, Vol. 26 (July 1913), pp. 292-301, and "Little Pictures of O. Henry," *Bookman*, Vol. 37 (June-August 1913), pp. 381-87, 498-508 and 607-16, and Vol. 38 (October 1913), pp. 169-77.

[53] "From the Editor's Desk," World's Work Advertiser, *World's Work*, Vol. 26 (August 1913); Burton J. Hendrick, "The American 'Home Secretary,'" *ibid.*, pp. 396-405; and Burton J. Hendrick, *Oral History Project: The Reminiscences of Burton J. Hendrick* (New York: Oral History Research Office, Columbia University, 1972), especially p. 25. The last document hereafter is referred to as *Hendrick's Reminiscences*. Hendrick makes a number of interesting statements and allegations in the document. He contends, for example, that it wasn't true that Frank N. Doubleday was the financial genius and Walter H. Page the literary genius of the publishing house; that it was Frank N. Doubleday who obtained the Rockefeller memoirs for the *World's Work*; and that Walter H. Page as a publisher was not as successful as many people believed (pp. 55-59).

[54] *Hendrick's Reminiscences*, pp. 25-26.

[55] Arthur W. Page, "Houston of Agriculture," *World's Work*, Vol. 27 (December 1931), pp. 149-59.

[56] "Talk of the Office," World's Work Advertiser, *World's Work*, Vol. 28 (September 1914), and Mott, *op. cit.*, p. 783.

[57] Arno Dosch-Fleurot, "Louvain the Lost," *World's Work*, Vol. 28 (October 1914), pp. A-H.

[58] "A Spanish Edition of the *World's Work*," *ibid.*, Vol. 29 (February 1915), p. 374.

[59] See especially letters from Page to Theodore Roosevelt, April 28, 1913, and June 15, 1915, and letter from Roosevelt to Page, June 17, 1915, Box 1, Arthur W. Page Papers.

[60] See telegram from Walter H. Page to Woodrow Wilson, Sept. 11, 1914, in Hendrick, *Life and Letters*, *op. cit.*, Vol. 1, pp. 325-26, and letter from Walter H. Page to Edward M. House, *ibid.*, pp. 327-35.

[61] Letters from Walter H. Page to Arthur W. Page, one undated but probably Sept. 1914, the other Nov. 6, 1914, *ibid.*, pp. 335-38 and 343-47.

[62] "The Federal Budget System," editorial, *World's Work*, Vol. 30 (May, 1915), pp. 13-14, and *Reminiscences*, p. 56.

[63] *Reminiscences*, pp. 55-56.

[64] "Miss K.A. Page To Wed.," *New York Times*, March 13, 1915; "To Wed in Chapel Royal," *ibid.*, July 3, 1915, p. 7; "Miss Page Weds in Chapel Royal," *ibid.*, Aug. 5, 1915, p. 11; "Frank C. Page Takes Miss Katherine Sefton as Bride," *ibid.*, June 4, 1916, p. 21; Ralph W. Page, "From a Law Office to a Cotton Farm," *World's Work*, Vol. 23 (November 1911), pp. 114-17; and letter to author from Arthur W. Page Jr., Oct. 23, 1975.

[65] See especially "Pan-Germanism in the United States," editorial, *World's Work*, Vol. 30 (June 1915), pp. 135L-135P.

[66] "The Editor" and "Mr. Bryan's Retirement and Its Significance," editorials, *ibid.* (July 1915), pp. 269-72.

[67] Leonard Mosley, *Dulles: A Biography of Eleanor, Allen, and John Foster Dulles and Their Family Network* (New York: The Dial Press/James Wade, 1978), p. 37

CHAPTER THREE

The Doubleday, Page Vice President, 1916-1926

Effective with the January 1916 issue of the *World's Work*, Arthur Page became a vice president of Doubleday, Page and Co. He continued as editor of the *World's Work*, but his duties at the publishing house were considerably expanded.

While a vice president he took one leave of absence from the firm to serve with the intelligence staff of the American Expeditionary Force, the American army that fought in Europe.

Managing Doubleday magazines and nonfiction books

As a vice president, Page assumed two important new duties. While continuing as *World's Work* editor, he became the "serious" or nonfiction book editor, and was placed in charge of all Doubleday magazines. The firm published a half-dozen magazines at the time, including *Country Life* and the South American and British editions of the *World's Work*.

To give him time for the new duties, Burton Hendrick began writing most of the *World's Work* editorials.

In the reorganization, Frank Doubleday, majority stockholder, continued as president, Herbert S. Houston remained a vice president and Arthur Page assumed the vice presidency formerly held by his father. Samuel Everitt continued as treasurer. Russell Doubleday, Frank's brother who had replaced Henry Lanier as secretary, continued in that post.

In 1916, nonfiction books accounted for only 20 percent of Doubleday's book sales. However, nonfiction's popularity increased dramatically from 1916 to 1926. One stimulus was the war in Europe, which triggered a demand in America for information on military topics that was met with a flood of titles. Over the long term, increased education fueled demand. As more citizens got high school and even college educations, they became a ready market for nonfiction.

After the *World's Work*, histories, biographies, autobiographies and "how-to-do-it" books were Page's chief interest at Doubleday. He occasionally got involved in the fiction end of the business, but didn't like the naturalism movement of the period. "...I didn't care much for fiction," he said, "and I cared less so as it went along, because we got into the so-called realist era in which it got to be a great book if it described in intimate detail the worst hour of the worst day in the worst town in the country. The less of that I read, the better I liked it."[1]

He also liked his American history on the idealistic side. His temperament suited him for a later career in public relations where, denials to the contrary, the ability to create myth and romantically portray institutions is important to the job.

His new responsibility as nonfiction book editor put him even more in touch with influentials whose biographies and autobiographies Doubleday sought. His main duty in 1916-1926, though, continued to be editing the *World's Work*. Burton Hendrick relieved him of the chore of writing editorials, but he still had to decide what stance the magazine would take on issues. Up to American entry into the war in Europe, the editorials continued to call for military preparedness, an end to neutrality and active aid to the Allies.

After Woodrow Wilson forced Secretary of State William Jennings Bryan to resign, the *World's Work's* main target in the administration became Secretary of the Navy Josephus Daniels. A North Carolinian, Daniels became a friend of Walter Page in the 1880s, helping him with occasional editing chores at the *State Chronicle*. After Page returned to the North, Daniels visited him now and then in Brooklyn and New Rochelle. Still the men had differences. The two quarrelled in their respective media over such issues as academic freedom. When Daniels demanded the resignation of a white North Carolina professor who praised black educator Booker T. Washington, Page rose in defense of the educator.[2]

The *World's Work* charged that Daniels, a pacifist, failed to get the Navy ready for war, and when war came, failed to use it aggressively against the enemy in European waters.[3] The tiff was not serious. Years later, when Daniels was U.S. ambassador to Mexico, Arthur visited him at the embassy in Mexico City, where Daniels received him cordially.

In July 1916, Secretary of State Robert Lansing ordered Ambassador Page home for a month. The home leave was ostensibly to permit Page to attend a round of conferences in Washington and to give him a chance to revisit the country from which he had been absent for three years.[4] In reality it was staged so President Wilson could give his British ambassador an object lesson in the meaning of neutrality.

The visit proved doubly sad for Walter Page. The ambassador and his wife arrived in New York on the evening of Aug. 11. They planned to spend a few days with sons Arthur and Frank in Garden City, then go on to Washington. But upon landing, they were told Frank Page's bride of two months, Katherine Sefton Page, had been stricken by poliomyelitis. The ambassador and his wife, Arthur and his wife, and daughter Katherine (Page) Loring established a vigil at the Garden City Hotel, calling Frank regularly to check on his wife's condition. She died the next day.[5] The ambassador postponed his trip to Washington to attend the funeral at Auburn, N.Y.[6]

Walter Page then received a chilly reception in Washington. President Wilson, Secretary Lansing and other officials refused to discuss the subject of the war with him.[7] Only after Page repeatedly insisted did Wilson finally sit down with him for a morning of serious discussion that failed to change the mind of either. Bainbridge Colby, who succeeded

Lansing as Wilson's secretary of state, summed up the president's attitudes toward Walter Page in a 1925 *New York Times* interview. "I had occasion during one of the darkest hours of the war, to visit England on an official mission," he said, "and when I took my leave of the President at the White House he said to me: 'Now be an American. Our men only last about six months in England and then they become anglicized.' The President was referring to that subtle and encompassing and penetrating charm which is English. Page fell a victim to it... His sincerity is beyond question and his popular success in England was unmistakable, but he had ceased to be a serviceable spokesman of the President or a dependable Ambassador of the United States."[8]

The ambassador and his wife returned to England in September.[9] The *World's Work* thereafter praised Wilson for signing a bill authorizing a five-year naval building program, but urged for an end to neutrality and for America to actively intervene on the side of "democracy" in the war against autocracy.[10] The magazine finally in its November number gave its grudging endorsement to Wilson.[11]

Much of Arthur Page's correspondence at this time is with Theodore Roosevelt, whom he now and then visited at the ex-president's Oyster Bay home near his own County Line. He discussed politics with Roosevelt, and tried unsuccessfully to get him to write for Doubleday, Page.[12]

In November 1916, Wilson was reelected. Walter Page offered to resign, but Wilson refused the offer. In February 1917, behind Page's back, Wilson offered the job to Cleveland Dodge, who delined it.

Arthur Page spent November-December 1916 in Europe, interviewing officials of the Entente governments. Much of the fighting in 1916 centered on Verdun, where Henri Philippe Pétain was placed in charge of the French Second Army's operations in the spring following a German offensive. Page was a war correspondent in the frontline area at the time of the French recapture of Forts Douaumont and Vaux and other successes at Verdun. Overlooking the battlefield where some 500,000 Allied and German soldiers were sacrificed, he interviewed French Gen. Robert Nivelle, who succeeded Joseph J. Joffre as commander in chief of the French army. Nivelle became an overnight hero when he led the successful counterattacks at Verdun. Within months, he would be discredited and replaced by Pétain after leading a disastrous offensive in April 1917 that resulted in a mutiny eventually affecting 68 of 112 French divisions.

From Verdun, Page went to Paris, then back to London where he had a long meeting with British Prime Minister and War Secretary Lloyd George. After that he returned home.[13]

American public indignation against Germany, fueled by print media coverage, grew in the early months of 1917. Sabotage had been suspected when a munitions dump on Black Tom Island in the New York Harbor blew up in July 1916. John J. McCloy would not prove that German agents were responsible for that until 1939. Other hostile acts by Germany were regularly fed by British Intelligence to the *Providence Journal* and simultaneously published in the *New York Times*.

Of far greater import, Germany resumed unrestricted submarine warfare on Feb. 1. On Feb. 3, President Wilson announced an end to American diplomatic relations with Germany. The *U.S.S. Housatonic* was sunk by a German submarine the same day. Four more U.S. flag vessels were torpedoed in March.

Walter Page played a role in fueling war fever. In mid-January, German Secretary for Foreign Affairs Arthur Zimmermann sent an explosive telegram to his minister to Mexico. The British Navy's Room 40 intercepted it in three different ways and decoded it. The message ordered the ambassador to persuade Mexico, if America went to war over the submarine issue, to declare war on the United States and enlist the support of Japan in the cause. Germany in return would provide generous financial aid and diplomatically support Mexican recovery of Texas, New Mexico and Arizona. The decoded Zimmermann telegram was given to Ambassador Page in London in late February. The ambassador sent it on to the State Dept. President Wilson released the paraphrased text to the Associated Press late on Feb. 28. Public outrage to the news was widespread, especially in the Midwest and West where neutralist sentiment was strongest.[14]

These were the final events that pushed Wilson, who had wanted to be a domestic-issues president, and who only a few months before in his bid for reelection had campaigned on keeping America out of the war, into joining the war on the side of Britain and France.

The March 1917 issue of the *World's Work* was another War Manual, this one devoted to America's military and industrial preparedness for the intervention in the war that Arthur Page saw as imminent.

On April 2, President Wilson asked a special joint session of Congress that he had convened for a declaration of war against Germany (but not Austria-Hungary, which came in December). The Senate approved on April 4, and the House on April 6. The declaration of war contained many of the same arguments Walter Page had been making in his barrage of ignored letters and messages to the president and other government leaders.

Immediately after the declaration of war, the *World's Work* found new figures to praise and criticize. Among those criticized was Progressive journalist George Creel, head of the Committee on Public Information (CPI), America's massive propaganda office formed to coordinate and censor war information. The magazine was critical of Creel for his censorship policies and alleged lack of credentials. It was especially critical of a CPI pamphlet put out to justify Wilson's neutrality up to U.S. entry into the war. Among those praised were the impetuous Adm. William S. Sims, commander of American naval operations in European waters, and Hugh Gibson, who had been first secretary of the American Legation in Brussels until driven to France by the Central Powers. Gibson's "A Journal from Our Legation in Belgium" was a successful *World's Work* serial in 1917.[15]

Caught up in the war hysteria, the *World 's Work* lashed out at real and imagined enemies of America. The magazine in prior years had published occasional barbs aimed at "hyphenate" Americans—German-Americans, Polish-Americans, and so on. it became more aggressive in the World War I years in its criticisms of immigrant minority groups outside the white Anglo-Saxon Protestant "old stock." It was particularly critical of hyphenate Americans who had voted Socialist tickets in New York, Chicago and Milwaukee.[16]

Propagandist for the Allies

IN THE SUMMER of 1918, Walter Page became seriously ill. Arthur sailed for England to accompany his father on a voyage back home. Instead of returning to America with his father, however, he stayed in Europe, going from England to France to serve with the American Expeditionary Force (AEF).

Walter Page embodied the Greek tragic hero, a man blind to an internal flaw that leads to his downfall. He gave his health to getting America involved in the war, but failed to realize his efforts were totally ignored by President Wilson.

After both Wilson and Walter Page were dead, Burton Hendrick obtained the more sensitive letters Page had sent to Wilson before America entered the war. Many of the letters over which Walter Page had labored himself to death were unopened. Hendrick concluded that Wilson refused to open them knowing they would be pro-British.[17]

In October 1917, Walter Page in London had written Frank Doubleday that he was ill.[18] He nonetheless stubbornly stayed at his post as his health deteriorated. In March 1918, extreme fatigue forced him to take a vacation. Even after that, he returned to his job, ignoring the advice of doctors who told him to resign and return home if he wanted to live.

In July, Arthur's brother Maj. Frank Page, who had left the *World's Work* to command an air base in France, visited his father in England. Alarmed, he called for Arthur to come to London. When Arthur arrived, he and Frank coaxed their father to resign. He finally complied on Aug. 1.

When news of the resignation was made public, Prime Minister (David) Lloyd George, the King and other British officials did what they could to let Walter Page know his service as ambassador had been appreciated.

Because Walter Page was not well enough to make the Atlantic crossing immediately, Arthur took him to Banff, Scotland, for a rest. There father and son held their last editorial conferences, deciding among other things that young Briton Winston Churchill had the makings of greatness.[19] Walter Page, accompanied by son Frank, sailed for America in October. Arthur, who had intended to return home with his father, instead went to France to serve with American forces.

Delirious during much of the trip home, Walter Page was hospitalized in New York. He rallied briefly in the hospital. In November, he was sufficiently strong to hold a pen. His first letter was a final report to his commander-in-chief, President Wilson. Then his health failed again. Doctors granted his last wish, permitting him in early December to return to North Carolina where he died on Dec. 21.[20]

Perhaps as early as August, and definitely by September 1918, Arthur Page in England had decided to join American armed forces in France, leaving the World's Work to the care of staffers Burton Hendrick and French Strother.[21]

While with his father in England, Arthur met a number of American military officers, one or another of whom suggested that his editing experience suited him to preparing propaganda for the AEF. Hugh Gibson, a friend of the Pages and author of a 1917 serial in the World's Work, suggested to Gen. Dennis E. Nolan, head of AEF Intelligence (G-2), that he contact Arthur about serving in the G-2 propaganda section. Gibson, working for the Creel Committee in Paris, was in close touch with Allied propaganda officers.[22]

In the autumn of 1918, Arthur moved to Paris to begin working in Unit G-2-D, the Psychological Subsection of AEF Intelligence responsible for propaganda production. In Paris, he shared an apartment with Hugh Gibson, Eugene Stetson and a North Carolinian named Blunt who was the Creel Committee's chief censor in France.

Page was in France when the two major battles involving the late-arriving AEF were fought. At the St.-Mihiel salient in mid-September, the AEF won a great victory and took 15,000 German prisoners. Less than two weeks later, in the Meuse-Argonne, "Black Jack" Pershing spread himself too thin. Because of chaotic lines of communication and supply, the offensive in the Argonne Forest dragged on for more than six weeks, with the AEF suffering 117,000 casualties to 100,000 for German forces.

Unit G-2-D was commanded by Capt. Heber Blankenhorn, who had his headquarters with AEF commander Pershing at Chaumont. The Paris section of Blankenhorn's unit included Page and Capt. Walter Lippmann, the latter a young American intellectual and journalist destined to become one of America's most influential newspaper columnists. A 1910 Harvard graduate who published *Drift and Mastery* in 1914, Lippmann with Arthur Bullard in 1917 had persuaded President Wilson to create what became the Committee on Public Information. Lippmann was named to head CPI's propaganda wing. Another member of the small G-2-D unit, Lt. Charles Merz, based in England, in later life became a distinguished editor of the *New York Times.*

The unit's operations were already under way when Page began work, the first leaflet having been produced on Aug. 28 by Blankenhorn, Lippmann and a helper.

Page was assigned to helping Lippmann and another officer write and print the propaganda in Paris. Blankenhorn and a small contingent at Chaumont handled distribution by aircraft, artillery shell, balloon and other means. As the war progressed, Lippmann became responsible for writing the propaganda, and Page for getting it printed and delivered to Chaumont and elsewhere.[23]

The first messages emphasized that prisoners would be treated humanely and fed well. From American capture of the St.-Mihiel salient in September on, much of the material stressed amounts of territory, enemy weapons and prisoners captured. Near the end of the war, statements from speeches by Woodrow Wilson were popular topics.

The propaganda flow increased dramatically in September-October, peaking just before hostilities ended. On Nov.

10, Capt. Blankenhorn wired Page to stop further shipments of leaflets to the front lines.[24] The armistice went into effect at 11 a.m. the next day.

Between Sept. 6 and the armistice, Page shipped 4.8 million leaflets to Chaumont, Bar-le-Duc and Toul. He sent nearly a million pamphlets forward in the last full week of the war, an indication the American propaganda effort was just swinging into high gear as the conflict ended.[25]

After the war, Capt. Blankenhorn wrote that the propaganda had been extremely effective.[26] He argued that two out of every three German and Austro-Hungarian soldiers who surrendered just before the armistice were carrying American propaganda leaflets.[27] Further, the Germans obviously feared the *verdammte Flugblaetter*, threatening severe punishment to troops caught with it. Allied fliers downed in normal aerial combat were imprisoned by the Germans, but ordered executed if caught carrying propaganda.[28]

Arthur Page took a skeptical view of propaganda, noting that soldiers who surrendered were ready to do so because they were beat—the propaganda merely provided a convenient stimulus to action.[29] Such was the case at St.-Mihiel, where Col. "Wild Bill" Donovan's Rainbow Division took more than 13,000 demoralized German prisoners in 48 hours, some 300 of them surrendering from a bunker to a lone AEF sergeant armed with an empty pistol. In their 110 days of fighting, American forces took a total of 43,000 prisoners.

Page became doubtful about Allied propaganda after asking British and French officers how successful their leaflets were when the other side was winning. He was told that when the other side was winning, there was no time to prepare and distribute propaganda.[30] This early skepticism, which became an integral part of Page's public relations philosophy, kept him from making the mistake of many public relations pioneers who assumed propaganda to be all-powerful. Nor did he come to believe, as did many propagandists, that appeals to emotion were more effective in persuasion than appeals to reason.

In the big picture, the German army had launched its last

offensive of the war on the Western Front in March 1918. By the end of May, the army stalled still 37 miles from Paris. The Allies, refreshed by American troops, launched their counteroffensive in August. The demoralized German army literally went on a soldiers' strike. Seeing that the war was lost, the General Staff restructured the government and negotiated an armistice through Woodrow Wilson. It went into effect to wild jubilation at the 11th hour of the 11th day of the 11th month of 1918—at 11 a.m. on Nov. 11.

In all, more than 70 million men had been called to arms. Perhaps nine million died. American deaths came to 113,000, almost as many from the Spanish flu as from combat. The war, an economic disaster for Europe, shifted the center of capitalism from there to the United States.

Page was one of many Harvard men who served, half of them as officers. He ended his participation in the war as he had begun it, out of uniform. A recommendation that he be commissioned a captain had been forwarded to the War Dept. He had purchased Army uniforms in anticipation of the commission. Either it did not arrive by the armistice, when the War Dept. halted new commissions, or it came and he declined it to speed his return home.[31]

He had been a private in the New York National Guard from 1906 to 1910. At some time after 1918, he accepted a commission as a major in the Army Reserves.

Soon after the armistice, Page left France for England, and from there sailed home. He arrived in mid-January 1919, a month after his father's death.[32] After a brief interlude with his family, he returned to Doubleday, Page. His name reappears as editor of the *World's Work* in the April 1919 issue.

Back at the helm of the World's Work

WHEN ARTHUR RETURNED FROM THE WAR, his wife Mollie and the children—there were three now, Arthur Wilson Jr. having entered the world in New York in January 1917—were living at Pinehurst, N.C., where Walter Page died.

For three months, until Mollie and the children rejoined him, he lived at the University Club in New York City. There in his spare time he wrote a series of articles that became his first book. There he also read the extant letters of George Washington, remembered among other things for his advice that America avoid "entangling alliances."

Years later, Page used what he'd read in the Washington letters to try to persuade Walter Lippmann and Allen Dulles that America's first president had favored rather than opposed treaties with foreign nations.[33]

Page's interest in foreign treaties was related to his developing philosophy of internationalism, the antecedents of which can be found in his father's pleas for American intervention in World War I, in the editorials he wrote for the *World's Work* or directed Burton Hendrick to write and in his introduction of foreign editions of the magazine. In his developing philosophy, he was far more pragmatic than Woodrow Wilson, who could not take the race of man as it exists with all its imperfections, and who believed that if ideal peace-keeping terms could be struck at Versailles, people would become idealistic and a new millennium would dawn.

The February 1919 issue of the *World's Work* endorsed American participation in the League of Nations. As time went by, however, Page developed reservations about the League, the beginning of his skepticism about American participation in international peacekeeping organizations. In 1920, he expressed his reservations to Ray Stannard Baker, who handled President Wilson's public relations at Versailles and after. Embittered by the way Wilson treated his father, Arthur said of Wilson "...He appointed himself the spokesman of idealism and he failed and in his failure made idealism ridiculous and left us prey to materialistic reaction."[34] That notwithstanding, the problem with Wilson had been that he was so confident of the purity of his motives that he did what he thought right rather than what was practical.

The April 1919 issue of the *World's Work* carried the first installment of a series of articles by Arthur Page entitled "The Truth about Our 110 Days' Fighting."[35] A defense of the

American Expeditionary Force's performance in Europe, the articles were well received by critics, largely because of the excellent maps that accompanied them.[36] The articles, with some unit histories added, became Page's first book, *Our 110 Days' Fighting.* Doubleday, Page published it in 1920.[37]

In the same period, the *World's Work* published in serial form a biography of AEF commander Gen. John Pershing and a history of American naval operations in European waters by Adm. William S. Sims.

The Sims series, "Victory at Sea," written in collaboration with Burton Hendrick, is the more noteworthy.[38] The articles collected in book form earned a Pulitzer for Sims and Hendrick. The articles, overgenerous in their appraisal of Sims' naval genius, were still running in 1920 when a public controversy involving Sims erupted. He had sent a memorandum to pacifist Secretary of the Navy Daniels highly critical of the way the Navy had been handled during the war. Daniels made Sims' criticisms public, charging the outspoken admiral with insubordination. The resulting furor in the American press provided considerable publicity for the Sims series in the *World's Work*. The magazine, as might be expected, sided with the admiral against Daniels.[39]

A wave of anticommunist and anti-socialist sentiment— the "Red hysteria" or "Red scare"—swept America in 1919-1920. Sparked by overreaction to anarchist bombings and suspicion of leftist leanings among immigrants, it led to mass deportation of radicals and to J. Edgar Hoover being named to head a new antisubversive unit in the Justice Dept.

The *World's Work* helped fan the flames with several articles critical of the International Workers of the World (IWW) labor union and "parlor pinks." The magazine became disgusted following the arrest of five socialists in New York who had been legally elected to public office.[40] After that, the magazine's participation in the red-baiting dwindled and died.

In the 1920 political conventions, the *World's Work* backed Woodrow Wilson protégé William Gibbs McAdoo for the Democratic nomination, and Gen. Leonard Wood for the Republican nominee. The nominations went to James Cox and Warren G. Harding, neither of whom the *World's Work* admired.[41] Page contributed a personal article, "The Meaning of What Happened at Chicago," critical of the Republicans for nominating what the magazine termed "a party hack" instead of Gen. Wood.[42] The *World's Work* and Arthur Page personally went on to endorse Republican Harding over Democrat Cox.[43] The Harding endorsement may be the beginning of Page's political metamorphosis from Democrat to Republican, a transition he later contended did not occur until Franklin Roosevelt decided to run for more than two terms as president. He moved back into the Democratic camp in 1924, but from 1928 forward, he was a Republican.

In March 1920, John Hall Page, the fourth and final child of Arthur and Mollie, was born in New York. Mollie Jr. was then 7, Walter Hines II was not quite 5 and Arthur Jr. was 3.

Doubleday, Page prospered in the Roaring Twenties boom. Early in the decade, it bought a controlling interest in William Heinemann Ltd., which published the British edition of the *World's Work*, and concluded an agreement with the Oxford University Press to handle all its children's books in America.[44]

Immediately after Arthur became editor of the *World's Work*, he launched the magazine's innovative "Who Governs America" series of short biographical sketches of government leaders. The sketches led naturally to the magazine publishing longer sets of monthly articles on or by leaders, and eventually, to issuing the longer sets of articles in book form. Among the earliest of the serials published as books were Hugh Gibson's *Diary*, the Pershing and Sims series, the memoirs of Henry Morgenthau and Page's own series on American fighting performance in Europe.

In 1921, the magazine began publishing two notable new series. The first was based on the diary of T.E. (Thomas Edward) Lawrence, the legendary "Lawrence of Arabia." The other was based on the edited letters of Walter Hines Page.[45] Burton Hendrick's serial publication of Walter Page's letters is far and away the more important to American history.

While ambassador to Great Britain, Walter Page had written many persuasive letters to friends, to President Wilson and to administration officials. Hendrick and Arthur Page were unable to get most of the letters he wrote to President Wilson, but they did get some of those letters, and many more that the ambassador had written to friends and other political figures.

The letters dealt with many topics, often patriotic, but especially with the need for America to defend the ideals of democracy (the Entente Powers or Allies) against autocracy (the Central Powers). Hendrick edited them, writing a historical narrative to provide continuity. Arthur and his mother read the proofs of each installment before publication, now and then demanding that material be deleted or interpreted differently.[46]

What emerged from the series was a highly flattering portrayal of Walter Page and a derogatory portrait of Wilson. Over the 14 months that the articles ran in the *World's Work*, press and public comment on the articles was highly complimentary. Many Americans became familiar with Walter Page through the magazine articles. In death, the ambassador assumed a greater luster than he had in life. He acquired a posthumous reputation for having been one of America's greatest letter-writers. Published in book form as volumes I and II of *The Life and Letters of Walter H. Page*, the series won Hendrick his second Pulitzer Prize.

A major *World's Work* editorial theme in the early 1920s was opposition to interest groups seeking favors in Washington. Walter Page had criticized the "Mummies," his pejorative term for the southern old guard that resisted the dawn of the New South. The *World's Work* under his son ridiculed the "Mystics" who thought the federal government's resources to be limitless.[47] The Farm Mystics, Labor Mystics, Railroad Mystics and others—what would be called "special interests" today— all came in for their share of the magazine's barbs. Typical editorials lashed out at bills that would have provided farm subsidies, a bonus for World War I veterans, protective tariffs and subsidies for the shipping industry.

Other editorials called for a federal budget (which became reality during the Harding administration), for naval
disarmament, for denial of independence to the Philippines
and Puerto Rico, and for American economic aid to Europe.
The last is worth noting in light of Page's work after World
War II for the Stimson Committee for the Marshall Plan.

In 1921, Frank Doubleday appointed his son Nelson to a
new vice presidency in the publishing house. Later the same
year, Arthur became the firm's senior vice president when
Herbert Houston left to start his own magazine.[48]

Beginning in June 1922, the *World's Work* participated in
one of the periodic waves of xenophobia that sweep America.
The initial editorial, "Keep Up the Bars against Immigration,"
marked a revisiting of the old theme of the "hyphenates," or
immigrant minorities, in America.[49] The new editorials argued that non-English-speaking immigrants did not integrate
in American society and did not abide by American ideals—
the latter a reference to the leanings of some Central European immigrants toward socialism and labor syndicalism.

The *World's Work* was reflecting popular American sentiment. In the early 1920s, the post-World War I Red hysteria
had given way to a wave of anti-alienism and demands for
restrictions on immigration. The pseudo-science of eugenics
encouraged "scientific racism," which further fanned the fires
of ethnic bigotry. One manifestation of popular sentiment
was the rise of the revitalized Ku Klux Klan with its "pure
Americanism" gibberish.

In its August 1922 issue, the magazine called for Harvard
to restrict enrollment of Jews who had emigrated from Eastern Europe. The *World's Work* argued that Harvard would
lose its "national character" if it admitted too many Jews
with Russian and Polish backgrounds.[50] The magazine was
particularly critical of demands being made by some ethnic
minorities that American history texts used by school children be rewritten to more accurately portray the role of
non-English settlers in the nation's history.[51]

Perhaps the most ridiculous series to appear in the *World's
Work* was published in this period. By Gino Speranza, the

articles attacked minority populations for failing to integrate into Anglo-Saxon mainstream America, for refusing to admit the superiority of the English "old stock" and for failing to recognize the inherent superiority of England in America.[52]

Two factors led the magazine to temper its criticism of "hyphenate" Americans: passage of alien restriction laws that in 1924 swung shut the doors of easy immigration from non-Anglo-Saxon countries, and a series of articles by Robert L. Duffus exposing how Atlanta publicity agent Edgar Young Clarke had rebuilt the Ku Klux Klan into a national force using hatred as a motivator.[53]

In fairness, the *World's Work*, while critical of ethnic minorities, also criticized injustices done them. It continued to attack lynchings (which escalated sharply in the summer of 1919 after a bloody race riot in Chicago), to crusade against the Klan and to argue on behalf of American Indians against land speculators seeking to deprive them of tribal lands.

In November 1922, Page made a major format revision in the *World's Work*, experimenting with run-of-press coated paper to permit use of photo illustration on any page. Until this time, halftones had been used only in illustrated sections of the magazine sandwiched between text-only sections. (During the paper shortages of World War I, the magazine had used a low-grade slick stock throughout, but had not taken advantage of the illustration potential.) Of the 112 pages in the November 1922 issue, 68 carried photos, well over twice the number of illustrated pages in prior issues.

The next month's issue carried the first installment of Burton Hendrick's "The Jews in America," the avowed purpose of which was to examine the rising tide of anti-Semitism in England and America as evidenced by immigration restrictions and college quotas.[54]

Arthur Page was by this time a part of New York's "high society," although he disdained the more frivolous activities and snobbishness of some members of the *Social Register*. His position as officer, owner and editor at a major New York publishing house was sufficient to qualify him for the *Social Register*. His standing in society came also from being the son of one of America's best-known ambassadors to Great Britain. Various honors conferred posthumously on the ambassador demanded Arthur's participation in publicized ceremonies. These increased his prestige.

In the summer of 1923, Page sailed to England with wife Mollie, his mother, his sister Katherine and three of Walter Page's grandchildren to attend a fête at Westminster Abbey unveiling a marble tablet in his father's memory. Among the dignitaries present were Viscount Grey of Fallodon, Prime Minister Stanley Baldwin, six members of Baldwin's cabinet, American Secretary of the Treasury Andrew Mellon and the entire staff of the American Embassy in London.[55]

Bearing the Presidential standard of Carter Glass

WHILE ARTHUR WAS IN England for the Westminster ceremonies, the July 1923 issue of the *World's Work* carried the first article promoting the presidential candidacy of the irascible Sen. Carter Glass of Virginia.[56] Page's promotion of Glass, a major architect of the Federal Reserve banking system who replaced William Gibbs McAdoo as secretary of the treasury in the Wilson administration, in many ways resembles his father's boosting of Woodrow Wilson.

By March 1924, Page had been selected a delegate from New York to the Democratic nominating convention. In a letter to his uncle Robert Page, a former U.S. congressman and member of the North Carolina delegation, he perceptively said he thought the strongest Democratic contenders, William Gibbs McAdoo and Al Smith, had already all but been eliminated, and that the nomination would probably go to a "dark horse," either John W. Davis or Carter Glass.[57]

As the convention drew near, John Stewart Bryan, publisher of the Richmond (Va.) *News Leader*, encouraged Page to work for the candidacy of Glass. He asked for permission to reprint a May 1924 *World's Work* article about Glass,[58] a request Page refused because he had already turned down a similar request from President (J.) Calvin Coolidge.[59]

Page contacted Sen. Glass to ask if he welcomed support. Glass said he'd not be embarrassed by a campaign, but couldn't actively participate because he was committed to McAdoo. Page then wrote Bryan, urging him to form a committee to boom Glass. Henry Morgenthau agreed to raise funds.[60] A Mark Sullivan article in the June *World's Work* held that the leading Democratic contenders were Glass, Davis and Sen. Samuel Ralston of Indiana. Sullivan noted that McAdoo's candidacy had been seriously hurt by revelation he'd been a lawyer for Eugene L. Doheny, implicated in the Harding administration Teapot Dome oil lease scandals.[61]

Glass's convention headquarters was established in New York in June, with Sen. Claude Swanson of Virginia in charge of the effort and Bryan responsible for publicity.[62]

The Democratic Convention opened in New York on June 24 with Arthur Page among the delegates from New York. Glass was placed in nomination on June 27. Gov. Lee Trinkle of Virginia said of Glass in his nominating speech, "No man can point the finger of scorn at him except with pride."[63]

Before balloting began, a bitter floor fight broke out over a platform plank condemning the Ku Klux Klan. Al Smith's forces favored a plank strongly condemning the Klan. McAdoo's forces wanted a weaker version. The McAdoo forces won by a few votes. The close vote on the Klan deadlocked the two sides. After interminable ballots in which neither Smith nor McAdoo could muster a majority, McAdoo released his delegates.[64]

Page was correct in predicting that the nomination would go to a dark horse. On the 103rd ballot, delegates nominated John W. Davis, who in 1918 had succeeded Walter Page as ambassador to England.

Glass never did better than 78 votes on any single ballot.[65] Despite Glass's loss, John Stewart Bryan was elated. On July 9, he wired Page: "THANK YOU COMPANION IN ARMS WE WON A REAL VICTORY IN SELECTION OF DAVIS AND BIGGER VICTORY LIES AHEAD LEFT TOBACCO WITH F V MARTIN MANAGER WALDORF FOR YOU SCOTTS AND MCADAMS SALUTE YOU DIDN'T WE COME NEAR WINNING"[66]

Glass never had a chance of nomination. Party chieftains distrusted Sen. Swanson, his campaign manager.[67] Of greater consequence, most party insiders disliked the temperamental Glass, of whom an opponent once said, "Elevating him to the U.S. Senate was worse than Caligula naming his horse a Roman consul because Caligula had the good sense to appoint both ends of the horse."

Democratic nominee John Davis was a Page family friend and a trustee of the committee raising funds for the proposed Walter Hines Page School of International Relations at Johns Hopkins. The *World's Work* endorsed Davis for the presidency. Arthur Page personally spoke out for him in a *New York Times* interview.[68]

Publishing the story of the Zimmermann telegram

WITH *WORLD'S WORK* CIRCULATION again declining in the 1920s, Page tried to halt subscriber erosion. His experiment with run-of-the-magazine illustration has already been noted. In late 1923, he briefly tried four-color illustrations.[69] In early 1924, he restructured the staff of the magazine. Ralph Graves became managing editor. French Strother became an associate editor, equal in rank to Burton Hendrick.

At the time of the restructuring, Hendrick was working on a new series of Walter Page letters for serialization in the *World's Work*. The death of Wilson had freed some 80 of the 100 or so letters Walter Page had written to him during the London years. The new series began to appear in June 1925.[70] Published in book form, the articles became the third volume of Hendrick's *Life and Letters of Walter H. Page*.

The most noteworthy installment appeared in November 1925. The article detailed the role of Walter Page in transmitting the Zimmermann telegram to President Wilson in 1917. The story, unknown to the American and British publics, touched off a flurry of press comment in the United States and in England.[71]

Hendrick and Arthur Page had intended to publish details

of the Zimmermann affair in the first two volumes of the Walter Page biography. That could have posed diplomatic problems. Secretary of State Charles Evans Hughes asked them to suppress the information. No such prohibition applied when the bulk of the Walter Page letters to Wilson were cleared for publication in 1925.

The message that had inflamed American public opinion in 1917 was sent in code in mid-January by German Foreign Secretary Arthur Zimmermann to Heinrich von Eckhardt, the German minister in Mexico City. Germany would resume unrestricted submarine warfare on Feb. 1, it said. If America retaliated by declaring war, Eckhardt was to persuade Mexican President Carranza to declare war on the United States. In return, Germany would provide generous financial aid and support Mexico's territorial ambitions for recovery of Texas, Arizona and New Mexico when peace was made.

The cable was intercepted and decoded by British naval intelligence. Adm. Sir William Reginald Hall decided to withhold it from the United States until an opportune moment.

At 4 p.m. on Jan. 31, too late for protest, Germany informed the United States it was resuming submarine warfare the next day. A few days later, Wilson surprised the German statesmen. He told Congress he had broken off diplomatic relations with Germany, and warned that if American ships were sunk, he would take further steps—which was *perhaps* a war warning in Wilsonese.

In London on Feb. 23, Adm. Hall, nicknamed "Blinker" because of an eyelid twitch, gave Ambassador Page the text of the Zimmermann telegram. Page is said to have remarked on reading it, "Why not Illinois and New York while they were about it?" He dispatched the message to Acting Secretary of State Frank L. Polk (Bert Lansing was on holiday), who had it in hand the next day. Wilson, after reading it, worked himself up from indignant to angry.

To add insult, one of the three copies was sent through American diplomatic channels. President Wilson had intermittently, over objections of Lansing, given the Germans permission to use American communication channels to send peace feelers. Under an offer still in effect, Zimmermann sent his note from Berlin to the State Dept. in Washington, where it was handed undeciphered to the German ambassador who forwarded it to Mexico City. Polk provided a copy to Lansing when he returned from vacation. The State Dept. was able to compare cipher groups it had logged to the British copy, verifying authenticity. If that wasn't enough, Zimmermann clumsily admitted the message was not a hoax.

Paraphrased text of the Zimmermann telegram was released to the Associated Press in Washington on the evening of Feb. 28. Public outrage ensued. The telegram, along with the sinking of several American-flag ships by German torpedoes, led to the American declaration of war against Germany on April 6, 1917.[72]

Businessman Page broadens his horizons

IN HIS FINAL SIX YEARS at Doubleday, Arthur began to broaden his horizons. He accepted positions in charities and education, and became a director of two corporations.

One of his earliest philanthropic involvements was with the Roosevelt Memorial Assn., which worked in the 1920s to develop Africa Hall, a wing of the American Museum of Natural History in New York, and other memorials to deceased ex-President Teddy Roosevelt. Page was named to the organization's executive committee in October 1921.[73] Among the other members were Henry Stimson, novelist Upton Sinclair and Africologist Carl Akeley, the museum officer responsible for the Roosevelt (later Akeley) wing. Akeley gained renown for revolutionizing American taxidermy and for his realistic bronze statues of African animals.

Although Doubleday had published Upton Sinclair's novel *The Jungle*, Arthur intensely disliked him, and sparks flew. He objected to serving on the Roosevelt executive committee with Sinclair, and prepared a blistering letter to the Socialist novelist which Stimson dissuaded him from sending.[74]

In January 1922, Page became a member of the central

committee of New York's old and prestigious Charity Organization Society, formed by Josephine Shaw Lowell in 1882 to coordinate the work of churches and other charities in New York City. The Society functioned in the 1920s much as later Community Chests and United Ways. In 1924, Page was elevated to a vice presidency of COS, and became a member of its executive committee. In 1926, he became chairman of the Society's Extension (Membership) Committee.[75]

Another of the organizations in which he became active was the Long Island Biological Assn. (LIBA), which operated a research laboratory at Cold Spring Harbor near Page's County Line estate. The laboratory, created in 1890, was one of the oldest research institutions in America. It became best known as the site for annual summer seminars in genetics and bacteriophages that were among the most prestigious in the scientific world. In 1924, Mortimer Schiff, William Vanderbilt and other Page neighbors incorporated LIBA to operate the laboratory. Later in 1924, Page was elected a director.[76] He remained active for many years. [77]

At the time he was elected a director of LIBA, the Cold Spring Harbor Laboratory shared its site with the Genetics Station of the Carnegie Institution of Washington. He became familiar with the work of both, which may explain some of the pseudo-scientific articles about eugenics that appeared in the *World's Work* in the mid-1920s.[78]

Eugenics was a popular topic at the time, and a lot of foolishness was published on the subject. Perhaps the most absurd statement on it in the *World's Work* appeared before Page was named a director of LIBA. An editorial in the February 1924 issue, apparently serious and probably written by Burton Hendrick, contended that Japanese immigrants in California were genetically best suited to work as farm laborers because their short stature put them closer to the ground where vegetables grew.[79]

In October 1925, Page was elected a director of the British Apprentice Club.[80] Two of his friends—Katherine Mayo, a prolific authoress of contemporary history books, and Moyca Newell—founded the charity shortly after World War I. It provided care and recreation for young apprentices in the British merchant marine visiting the United States.

Page was a member in the 1920s of the North Carolina Society, a social club for natives of North Carolina living in the New York City area. His father had been active in the same group.

He also served as a director of the American Federation of the Arts.[81]

Early service to education

ARTHUR PAGE, LIKE his father, had an enduring faith in the importance of education, and devoted much of his *pro bono* work to serving educational institutions.

His first significant involvement in education was with Teachers College of Columbia University. In February 1923, he was named a member of the college's Finance Committee.[82] At the time, Teachers College, under the deanship of James Earl Russell, was one of the most influential training grounds for teachers in America.

In 1924, Page became a member of Harvard's Committee to Visit the Bussey Institute, the start of more than 35 years of dedicated service to his *alma mater.*[83]

In late 1924, he was elected a director of the St. Bernard's Fund, created to raise money for the private academy in New York attended by his three sons. In 1925, he became president of the Fund, and immediately thereafter, of the St. Bernard's School Building Co., an affiliated fund-raising arm.[84] Other trustees and officers of St. Bernard's included Frank Altschul, who would later play a role with Page in forming Radio Free Europe, and Page friends George Franklin of Cotton and Franklin and William Nichols.[85] Others with whom Page worked and socialized, such as Elihu Root Jr., had children in the school.

In late 1925-early 1926, Page was involved in raising funds for the Rabun Gap-Nacoochee School in the mountains of North Georgia. That institution became well known in the latter 20th century as the source for the bestselling *Foxfire* books about pioneer skills in the Georgia mountains.

Harvard alumnus Andrew J. Richie founded the experimental Rabun Gap School to provide an education for mountain children unserved by a public school system. In late 1925, Richie asked Page to help raise money by becoming a member of the school's New York Committee. Other members of the New York Committee included public relations pioneer Ivy Lee (a sometimes contributor to the *World's Work* and counsel to the Rockefeller family) and financier Henry James, with whom Page worked closely in later years to raise money for Harvard.

In February 1926, shortly after Page became involved, fire destroyed the school's main building. Page publicized the institution's plight in the *World's Work*. He also went to Dr. Wallace Buttrick, an old Page family friend and chairman of the General Education Board, to ask for a $25,000 grant to restore the building. Then the Nacoochee Institute, located about 40 miles from the Rabun Gap School and with a similar experimental program, also burned down. The two schools combined efforts to build a single plant. John D. Rockefeller Sr., financial power behind the General Education Board, agreed to contribute $1 for each $2 the schools raised from other sources. The consolidated Rabun Gap-Nacoochee School was then built in Rabun County, Ga.[86]

Perhaps the most important education work in which Page was involved in these last years at Doubleday was aimed at funding a proposed Walter Hines Page School of International Relations at Johns Hopkins University, where the senior Page had done his graduate work.

A group of distinguished Americans met in New York in April 1924 to discuss formation of the new institution. Franklin D. Roosevelt was named to chair a committee of exploration. Members of his committee included a number of Page family friends—John W. Davis, Edward Bok, Adm. William Sims and Dr. Albert Shaw of the *Review of Reviews*.

In May, Roosevelt announced plans for a $1.86 million campaign for the proposed school.[87] His exploratory committee became the executive committee for a board of trustees formed to fund the Page School. Trustees included Henry Stimson, Sen. Carter Glass, Mrs. Herbert Hoover, Henry Morgenthau, Harry Chandler of the *Los Angeles Times* and Wilson adviser Col. Edward House.[88] The $1 million drive for the Page School opened in June 1924.[89] Arthur served as the family contact with the fund-raising committee.

Although the Page School was scheduled to open in the fall of 1927, by early 1926 only $276,000 of the $1 million goal had been raised.[90] Arthur became actively involved in fund-raising, writing, for example, to Howard Coffin of the Hudson Motor Car Co. to ask him to take responsibility for raising the Detroit quota.[91]

Director of Engineers Public Service and Vitaglass

ARTHUR WAS ELECTED in 1925 to his first corporate directorship. It was with Engineers Public Service Co., an electric and natural gas utility holding company.[92]

In 1926, he was elected a director of the Vitaglass (also spelled Vita-Glass and Vita Glass) Corp. The company made window glass that permitted some ultraviolet light to pass through. Most window glass then and now filtered out such light. Vitaglass advertised that its ultraviolet-transmitting glass was healthful, preventing rickets and permitting indoor tanning.

Bruce Barton, a principal in the Barton, Durstine and Osborn (later Batten, Barton, Durstine and Osborn) advertising agency, was among the early promoters of Vitaglass. Author of a book on evangelical salesmanship contending Jesus was the greatest salesman of all time, Barton was a good friend of Page. He and his wife regularly played bridge with Arthur and Mollie during the New York social season.

Barton wrote a personal testimonial for Page to use in promoting Vitaglass, about how his own health had been rejuvenated after he spent a few days soaking up sun at a health spa while stretched out under a pane of the glass.[93]

Vitaglass claims were at best spurious. Page had the good sense to resign his directorship in 1927, well before debunking that began in 1929 when Dr. Janet Clark of Johns Hopkin revealed that a child spending two minutes outdoors at noon got as much ultraviolet radiation as one sitting for 20 hours 16 feet from a window glazed with the glass. The U.S. Bureau of Standards further noted that many of the special glasses didn't transmit as much ultraviolet light as claimed.[94]

After the debunking, Vitaglass gradually faded into oblivion, disappearing around 1940.[95]

The break with F.N. Doubleday

IN LATE 1926, ARTHUR PAGE resigned his Doubleday vice presidency and sold his common stock in the firm to Frank Doubleday. He did so feeling clashes with the Doubledays, especially "Effendi," had grown unbearable.

Some of the friction between the Pages and Doubledays was over materialism versus idealism. However, Doubleday's critics perhaps overemphasize that. True, Frank Doubleday was an astute businessman who detested being bettered in a deal. He was to a large extent motivated by commercialism. Publisher George Doran, after serving in a publishing partnership with Doubleday, waspishly described him as "a book-lover—with a complete fidelity to one red russia leather-bound book, the book of the law and the profits... It contained his matins, his vespers, and his collects. Long since I had learned that in the Doubleday economics of publishing the auditor-in-chief and not the editor-in-chief was the final arbiter of the publishing policy."[96]

While Walter and Arthur Page were not opposed to making money, they were more motivated by idealism than Doubleday. As Arthur put it, "I would say from the commercial point of view, both my father and I were more concerned with the success of certain ideas than we were with the maximum of sales, although we understood perfectly that no idea got circulation in a magazine that didn't sell...."[97]

In Doubleday's defense, Burton Hendrick says in his *Reminiscences* that he had found him amiable, less devoted to commercialism than accused and more of a publishing genius than was generally believed.[98]

Two factors influenced Arthur Page to leave the publishing house—a growing irritability in Frank Doubleday, and what Page regarded as his interference in the magazine side of the business, which the Pages regarded as their private domain at the publishing firm.

In Arthur's final days at the publishing house, Frank Doubleday is said to have suffered from a nervous disorder that made him more than normally irascible. Because motion alleviated the symptoms, he conducted much of his business from the back seat of his chauffeured Packard as it cruised around Long Island.

Perhaps because the illness made him short-tempered, Doubleday began to point out to Arthur that the name "Page" was worth less and less as the memory of Walter Page faded.[99]

The matter that crystallized Arthur's decision to leave was Frank Doubleday's order, supported by his son Nelson, that Arthur keep the *World's Work* a magazine with the capability of run of press photographic illustration.

Page had experimented with using photo illustrations throughout the magazine in 1922. In 1926, however, he began a reformatting aimed at reducing pages illustrated by photos to a minimum. The reduction in photos began with the January 1926 issue. By July, the magazine carried only a single sandwich of 16 illustrated pages, a format that persisted with only slight variation through the December number, the last edited by Page.

Because of his differences with the Doubledays, particularly over the format of the *World's Work*, Arthur had already decided to resign from the firm when Walter Gifford offered him the new AT&T public relations vice presidency.[100]

The *New York Times* on Nov. 24, 1926, announced that Page planned to leave Doubleday for AT&T.[101] A few days after the announcement, Frank Doubleday wrote to Arthur to offer him $250 per share for the common stock he held in the publishing house. Page did some quick calculating on the back of Doubleday's letter, multiplying 2,786 by 250, an indication that Doubleday was offering him $696,500 for the stock.[102]

Another letter from Doubleday to Page a few days later makes it clear Arthur wanted more for his stock than Doubleday was offering. He was probably justified. Doubleday, Page in late 1926 was a highly profitable, multi-million dollar enterprise. And Frank Doubleday, by his own admission, felt cheated in a business deal unless he got the better of the other party.[103]

Doubleday refused to meet Page's asking price. He told Page to either keep his stock or sell it for what he could. It was unlikely that Page could have found another buyer when Doubleday controlled the majority of stock in the business. Arthur apparently sold his common stock to Doubleday on Doubleday's terms, retaining only some preferred stock.[104]

The January 1927 issue of the *World's Work* was the first published after Page left. Edited under the personal supervision of Frank Doubleday, it was heavily illustrated, with slick coated stock throughout. In all, 76 of the 114 pages carried halftone photos, more than even Arthur had used when experimenting with heavy illustration from 1922 through 1925. Other changes were instituted after Page left. Circulation of the magazine, which had dipped to 100,000 in 1923, began to rise, reaching a high-water mark of about 150,000 after the magazine page size was increased to quarto format.[105]

Then the Great Depression began in 1929. Advertising revenue declined until publication became unprofitable. The last issue of the *World's Work* was published in the early 1930s. The remaining assets of the magazine were sold to the *Review of Reviews*, which merged into the *Literary Digest*, which in turn was taken over by Henry Luce's *Time* in 1938. It is perhaps fitting that the final resting place of the *World's Work* was *Time*, the modern magazine which in many ways it had foreshadowed.[106]

Page was angered at the price Doubleday had paid him for his stock in the publishing house. He felt Doubleday had cheated the Page family several times. His first act of retaliation was to demand that the Page name be removed from the firm's title. He argued to Samuel Everitt, still a Doubleday, Page officer, that it was embarrassing to the Page family to have its name used when no member of the family was still connected with the publishing house. If Everitt couldn't get Doubleday to delete the Page name voluntarily, Arthur threatened to do his best to give the public the knowledge that the Pages had severed their connections with the firm by whatever means he could devise.[107]

Perhaps for financial or nostalgic reasons, perhaps because he wanted to irritate Arthur, Frank Doubleday insisted on retaining the Page name. He argued that when Arthur sold his stock, he had sold his interest in the "good will" or trademark value of the name Doubleday, Page and Co.[108]

Arthur responded angrily that, "As for that (the 'good will'), — when you bought some of father's stock in 1912 at your insistance (sic), you paid no good will; when you bought mother's stock at your insistance (sic), you paid no good will, for your contract provided for none; when you bought my stock, you paid for some, for the contract was abrogated then, but you were unwilling then to arbitrate a fair price."[109]

There the impasse might have stood had not George H. Doran of the Doran publishing house decided to enter partnership with Doubleday. Doran insisted that unless the firm name was changed to Doubleday, Doran and Co., he would not approve the merger. Doubleday conceded to Doran and the Page name was deleted.[110]

When the Doubleday, Doran partnership ended, the firm name was changed to Doubleday and Co., its name at the beginning of the 21st century, although the publishing house was by then owned by a German media conglomerate.

In the fall of 1927, Page moved publication of the fourth volume of his father's biography, *Training of an American*, from Doubleday to Houghton Mifflin. He also moved publication of a planned inexpensive edition of the first three volumes of the biography and letters to the new publisher.[111] Burton Hendrick objected unsuccessfully to movement of the fourth volume from Doubleday, contending the move might hurt sales.

As it turned out, the fourth volume won Hendrick his third Pulitzer Prize. However, sales were only 10,000 to 15,000 copies, compared to sales of about 150,000 copies of the first three volumes.[112]

Arthur turned his back on Doubleday thereafter, as he had severed his ties to the Lawrenceville School. However, he was willing in later years to help colleagues who had worked with him, particularly if they had left Doubleday.

ENDNOTES

[1] *Reminiscences*, p. 77.

[2] See especially "A Notable Victory for Academic Freedom," editorial, *World's Work*, Vol. 7 (January 1904), pp. 4284-87, and Josephus Daniels, *Editor in Politics* (Chapel Hill, N.C.: University of North Carolina Press, 1941), pp. 428-35.

[3] Lead March of Events editorial, *World's Work*, Vol. 32 (May 1916), p. 3; Burton J. Hendrick, "The Case of Josephus Daniels," *ibid.* (July 1916), pp. 281-96; "Destroyers to the Rescue," editorial, *ibid.*, Vol. 34 (October 1917), pp. 589-91; William Sowden Sims and Burton J. Hendrick, "The Victory at Sea," *ibid.*, Vols. 38-40 (September 1919-July 1920); and "Admiral Sims and Mr. Daniels" and "The Gist of Sims' Criticisms," editorials, *ibid.*, Vols. 39 and 40 (March and May 1920), pp. 425-28 and 122-23. In 1921, the *World's Work* reversed its direction of attack on Daniels, contending he should be disarming the Navy instead of building it up.

[4] "Page To Visit America," *New York Times*, July 22, 1916, p. 9.

[5] "Walter H. Page Returns," *ibid.*, Aug. 12, 1916, p. 16; "Paralysis Kills Mrs. Frank Page," *ibid.*, Aug. 13, 1916, p. 1; and "Ambassador Page," editorial, *ibid.*, Aug. 14, 1916, p. 8.

[6] "Mrs. Page Buried," *ibid.*, Aug. 16, 1916, p. 16.

[7] See Burton J. Hendrick, "Washington in the Summer of 1916," *World's Work*, Vol. 44 (June 1922), pp. 150-68, and Gregory, *op. cit.*

[8] "Colby Estimates Page as Ambassador," *New York Times*, Dec. 6, 1925, sec. 2, p. 11. Copyright © 1925 by the New York Times Co. Reprinted by permission.

[9] "Honor Ambassador Page at Dinner," *ibid.*, Sept. 19, 1916, p. 9.

[10] "The President—Why He Should and Should Not Be Reelected," editorial, *World's Work*, Vol. 32 (August 1916), pp. 367-69; lead March of Events editorial and "An American Navy at Last," editorial, *ibid.* (October 1916), pp. 591, 608-09.

[11] Lead March of Events editorial, *ibid.*, Vol. 33 (November 1916), p. 3.

[12] See especially letters from Page to Theodore Roosevelt, Oct. 15, Nov. 3 and Dec. 7, 1915, and Aug. 24 and Sept. 15, 1916, and Roosevelt's replies, Box 1, Arthur W. Page Papers. Page comments on his visits with Roosevelt in his *Reminiscences*.

[13] Arthur W. Page, "Why the Allies Expect To Win," *World's Work*, Vol.

33 (February 1917), pp. 356-62, and *Reminiscences*, pp. 39-40.

[14] Telegram from Arthur Zimmermann to Count Bernstorff, Jan. 16, 1917, quoted in telegram from Walter H. Page to Secretary of State Robert M. Lansing, Feb. 24, 1917, as quoted in Hendrick, *Life and Letters, op. cit.*, Vol. 3, pp. 332-33.

[15] "Public Confidence and the Censor," editorial, *World's Work*, Vol. 34 (July 1917), pp. 243-44; "Information, Not Argument," editorial, *ibid.* (August 1917), pp. 359-60; Robert F. Wilson, "Sims, of the Successful Indiscretions," *ibid.* (July 1917), pp. 333-40; and Hugh S. Gibson, "A Journal from Our Legation in Belgium," *ibid.*, Vols. 34-35 (August-December 1917).

[16] "Those Who Voted against the Republic," editorial, *ibid.*, Vol. 36 (May 1918), pp. 13-14.

[17] *Hendrick's Reminiscences*, p. 34.

[18] Letter from Walter H. Page to F.N. Doubleday, quoted from Hendrick, *Life and Letters, op. cit.*, Vol. 2, p. 324.

[19] *Reminiscences*, p. 52.

[20] Discussion of Walter Page's last days in England and his death in the United States is based on: *Reminiscences*, pp. 43, 52; Gregory, *op. cit.*, pp. 203-07; "Ambassador Page Taken to St. Luke's," *New York Times*, Oct. 13, 1918, p. 22; Raleigh, *op. cit.*, p. 65; Hendrick, *Life and Letters, op. cit.*, Vol. 2, pp. 369, 371-72; and "Walter Hines Page Dies at Pinehurst," *New York Times*, Dec. 23, 1918, p. 11.

[21] Letters from Arthur Page to Burton J. Hendrick, one undated but probably August 1918, the other Sept. 14, 1918, Burton J. Hendrick Papers.

[22] *Reminiscences*, p. 44.

[23] Heber Blankenhorn, "The War of Morale: How America 'Shelled' the German Lines with Paper," *Harper's*, Vol. 139 (September 1919), pp. 514-15, and Blankenhorn, *Adventures in Propaganda* (Boston and New York: Houghton Mifflin, 1919), pp. 47-49. See also *Reminiscences*, pp. 44-47; and Historical Division, Department of the Army, Reports of Commander-In-Chief, A.E.F., Staff Sections (Part II) (Washington, D.C.: 1948), p. 122, and Raleigh, *op. cit.*, pp. 70-71.

[24] "Drop News from Sky on All Fronts," *New York Times*, Nov. 1, 1918, p. 4, and "Germans Impressed by Our Propaganda," *ibid.*, Nov. 9, 1918, p. 5.

[25] Telegram from Heber Blankenhorn to Page, Nov. 10, 1918, Box 65, Arthur W. Page Papers.

[26] Blankenhorn, "War of Morale," *op. cit.*, p. 523, and two memoranda, one undated and unheaded, Box 3, Arthur W. Page Papers, the other undated and headed "C O P Y," prepared by Page, and in hands of author.

[27] Blankenhorn, "War of Morale" and *Adventures in Propaganda, op. cit.*

[28] Mrs. Heber Blankenhorn, in introduction to *Adventures in Propaganda, op. cit.*, and Page's "C O P Y" memorandum cited in fn. 26 above.

[29] *Reminiscences*, p. 45

[30] Arthur W. Page, "What Publicity and Advertising Can Do To Help Operation," speech at AT&T General Operating Conference, May 1927.

[31] *Reminiscences*, pp. 45-46, and letter to Page from Brig. Gen. D.E. Nolan, Chief of AEF G-2, Dec. 26, 1918, Box 68, Arthur W. Page Papers.

[32] *Reminiscences*, p. 47.

[33] Regarding Page's attempts to persuade Lippmann and Dulles, see especially his letter to Walter Lippmann, May 21, 1943, Box 91 Arthur W. Page Papers.

[34] Letter from Page to Ray Stannard Baker, Aug. 6, 1920, Box 1, Arthur W. Page Papers.

[35] Arthur W. Page, "The Truth about Our 110 Days' Fighting," *World's Work*, Vol. 37 (April 1919), p. 662 ff., and Vol. 38 (May-June 1919), pp. 69-85 and 159-83.

[36] See, for example, letter to Page from Douglas S.F. Freeman of *Richmond (Va.) News Leader*, and accompanying clipping, "In Today's Magazine," March 26, 1919, Box 1, Arthur W. Page Papers.

[37] Arthur W. Page, *Our 110 Days' Fighting* (Garden City, N.Y.: Doubleday, Page, 1920).

[38] The first installment of "The Victory at Sea" appeared in the September 1919 issue of the *World's Work*. Successive installments appeared through July 1920.

[39] See especially "Admiral Sims and Mr. Daniels," editorial, *World's Work*, Vol. 39 (March 1920), pp. 425-28. Other material about the controversy appears in the magazine through 1924.

[40] See especially Charles Holman, "How Siberia Got Rid of Bolshevism," *ibid.*, Vol. 38 (June 1919), pp. 135-47; John Spargo, "Bolshevism, A Caricature of Marx's Theories," "The Psychology of the Parlor Bolsheviki," and "Why the I.W.W. Flourishes," *ibid.*, Vol. 39 (November 1919-January 1920), pp. 28-36, 127-31 and 243-47; Ole Hanson, "On the Trail of the Reds," "Fighting the Reds in Their Home Town," and "Smashing the Soviet in Seattle," *ibid.* (December 1919-March 1920), pp. 123-26, 302-07, 401-08 and 484-87; Samuel Crowther, "On the Trail of the Reds" and "Radical Propaganda—How It Works," *ibid.* (February-April 1920), pp. 341-45, 477-83, and 618-24; and lead March of Events editorial, *ibid.* (March 1920), p. 419.

[41] "Mr. McAdoo, Mr. Palmer, and Others," and "Wood and the 'Leading' Republican Candidates," editorials, and lead March of Events editorial, *ibid.*, Vol. 40 (May and August 1920), pp. 10-11, 12-13 and 315.

[42] Arthur W. Page, "The Meaning of What Happened at Chicago," *ibid.* (August 1920), pp. 361-77

[43] See especially "Governor Cox's Pro-Germanism," *ibid.* (September 1920), pp. 427-28; "This Is To Be No Pink Tea Campaign," *ibid.*, Vol. 41 (November 1920), p. 10; and letter from Page to Henry L. Stimson, Aug. 20, 1920, Box 1, Arthur W. Page Papers.

[44] "Talk of the Office," World's Work Advertiser, *World's Work*, Vol. 41 (January 1921).

[45] Col. Thomas E. Lawrence, "Arabian Nights and Days," *ibid.*, Vol. 42 (July-October 1921), pp. 277-88, 381-86, 516-20 and 617-21, and Burton J. Hendrick, ed., series of articles beginning with "America and England: The London Letters of Walter H. Page," *ibid.* (August 1921), pp. 246-60. Regular monthly articles in the Hendrick series continued through the October 1922 issue

[46] See letter from Page to Burton J. Hendrick, Aug. 25, 1921, and letter from Alice W. Page (Walter Page's widow) to Hendrick, Sept. 3, 1921, in Burton J. Hendrick Papers.

[47] See especially "The Mystics Descend upon Washington," editorial, *World's Work*, Vol. 43 (March 1922), p. 457.

[48] See title page, *World's Work*, Vol. 44 (May 1922), and "A Magazine of International Affairs," *ibid.*, pp. 13-14.

[49] "Keep Up the Bars against Immigration," *ibid.* (June 1922), pp. 127-28.

[50] "The Jews and the Colleges," editorial, *ibid.* (August 1922), pp. 351-52.

[51] See especially "England Is 'The Mother Country' in New York Public

Schools," *ibid.* (September 1922), pp. 458-60.

[52] See Gino Speranza "Playing Horse With American History," *ibid.*, Vol. 45 (April 1923), pp. 602-10, and "The Immigration Peril," *ibid.*, Vols. 47-48 (November 1923-May 1924).

[53] See Mark Sullivan, "Congress and the Alien Restriction Law," *ibid.*, Vol. 47 (February 1924), pp. 436-42, and Robert L. Duffus, "Salesmen of Hate: The Ku Klux Klan," *ibid.*, Vol. 46 (May-September 1923), pp. 31-38, 174-83, 275-84, 363-72 and 527-36.

[54] Burton J. Hendrick, "The Jews in America: How They Came to This Country," *World's Work*, Vol. 45 (December 1922), pp. 144-61.

[55] "Walter Hines Page Honored in Abbey," *New York Times*, July 4, 1923, p. 12.

[56] Mark Sullivan, "The Democratic Dark Horse Pasture," *World's Work*, Vol. 46 (July 1923), pp. 285-92.

[57] Letter from Arthur W. Page to Robert N. Page, March 27, 1924, Box 1, Arthur W. Page Papers.

[58] Letter to Page from John Stewart Bryan, May 6, 1924, Box 1, Arthur W. Page Papers. The article Bryan wanted to reprint was Mark Sullivan's "Carter Glass—Sound Democrat," *World's Work*, Vol. 48 (May 1924), pp. 78-82

[59] Letter from Page to John Stewart Bryan, pencilled at bottom of letter from Bryan to Page, May 6, 1924, *op. cit.*

[60] Letter from Page to John Stewart Bryan, June 6, 1924, Box 1, Arthur W. Page Papers.

[61] Mark Sullivan, "Who Will Lead the Democrats," *World's Work*, Vol. 48 (June 1924), pp. 146-53.

[62] "Boom Crop Grows; Two More Arrive," *New York Times*, June 20, 1924, p. 22, and "Booms from West Plead for Farmers," *ibid.*, June 23, 1924, pp. 1, 6. See also "Dark Horse Jockeys Put Hopes Higher," *ibid.*, June 26, 1924, p. 3.

[63] Elmer Davis, "Last Nominees in Field," *ibid.*, June 28, 1924, pp. 1, 3.

[64] "Anti-Klan Men Lost by 430 Vote Margin," *ibid.*, June 30, 1924, p. 1.

[65] Davis's nomination was a compromise between managers of the Smith and McAdoo forces. For details on the nomination and how J.D. Ferguson of the *Milwaukee Journal* scooped the country on the Davis choice, see Elmer Davis, "Davis Is Put Over in Wild Stampede," *ibid.*, July 10, 1924, pp. 1, 4, and Will C. Conrad, Kathleen Wilson and Dale Wilson, *The Milwaukee Journal: The First Eighty Years* (Madison, Wis.: University of Wisconsin Press, 1964), p. 112

[66] Telegram from John Stewart Bryan to Page, July 9, 1924, Box 1, Arthur W. Page Papers.

[67] James Kerney told Arthur Page the details of the Davis nomination in the fall of 1924. See letter from Page to John Stewart Bryan, Oct. 3, 1921, Box 1, Arthur W. Page Papers.

[68] See lead March of Events editorials, *World's Work*, Vol. 49 (October-November 1924), pp. 345 and 3, and William H. Crawford, "Issue of Bryanism Is Derided by Page," *New York Times*, Oct. 28, 1924, p. 5.

[69] See *World's Work*, Vol. 46 (October 1923), front cover and pp. 587-90, 595-98.

[70] Burton J. Hendrick, ed., "New Page Letters," *ibid.*, Vol. 50 (June 1925), pp. 139-40. See also "A New Series of Letters from Walter Hines Page to President Wilson," *ibid.* (May 1925), pp. 25-26.

[71] Burton J. Hendrick, ed., "The Zimmermann Telegram to Mexico, and

How It Was Intercepted," *ibid.*, Vol. 51 (November 1925), pp. 2336. See also "World's Workshop," *ibid.* (December 1925), p. 223 ff.

[72] Information on Page and Hendrick publishing details of the Zimmermann Telegram is from *Hendrick's Reminiscences*, pp. 37-39, and letter from Page to Burton J. Hendrick, Aug. 2 , 1921, *op. cit.* Background on the telegram is from Barbara W. Tuchman, *The Zimmermann Telegram* (New York: Macmillan, 1958, 1966), pp. 107-200; J.M. Winter, *The Experience of World War I* (New York: Oxford University Press, 1989), p. 59; Alvin M. Josephy, Jr., ed., *The American Heritage History of World War I* (New York: American Heritage Publishing/Simon & Schuster, 1964), pp. 203-4; and Martin Gilbert, *The First World War: A Complete History* (New York: Henry Holt, 1994), pp. 308, 312.

[73] Memorandum from Page to AT&T executive R.H. Strahan, Dec. 9, 1935, in possession of author.

[74] Letters from Page to Henry L. Stimson, Feb. 11 and 14, 1924, Box 1, Arthur W. Page Papers.

[75] Memorandum from Page to R.H. Strahan, Dec. 9, 1935, *op. cit.*, hereafter referred to as the Strahan memorandum, and personal biography of Arthur W. Page, Jan. 4, 1947, furnished to author by American Telephone & Telegraph Co., and hereafter referred to as 1947 Page résumé.

[76] Strahan memorandum, and certificate of incorporation of Long Island Biological Assn., Feb. 13, 1924, Box 68, Arthur W. Page Papers.

[77] Letter to author from Walter H. Page II, Sept. 9, 1975, and Cold Spring Harbor Laboratory, *Annual Report* (1974).

[78] In the mid-1920s, the *World's Work* ran several articles about the influence of genetics on criminal behavior, mental retardation and similar socially undesirable traits. The articles are for the most part heavy with fear appeals. See especially French Strother, "Crime and Eugenics," Part 1, *World's Work*, Vol. 49 (December 1924), pp. 168-74, and Albert E. Wiggam, "The Rising Tide of Degeneracy," *ibid.*, Vol. 53 (November 1926), pp. 25-33.

[79] "California's Japanese Problem Solved," editorial, *ibid.*, Vol. 47 (February 1924), pp. 355-57.

[80] Strahan memorandum.

[81] Listing for Arthur Page in *Who's Who in New York* (1924), and "A.W. Page Quits Publishers," *New York Times*, Nov. 24, 1926, p. 16.

[82] Strahan memorandum.

[83] 1947 Page résumé.

[84] Strahan memorandum.

[85] Letter to Page from St. Bernard's School Headmaster F.H. Tabor, May 16, 1924; Page's reply, May 19, 1924; St. Bernard's Fund circular letter, March 9, 1925; and letter from Page to George S. Franklin, March 25, 1924; Box 1, Arthur W. Page Papers.

[86] Discussion of Page's role in the Rabun Gap-Nacoochee School project is based on: "The Rabun Gap-Nacoochee School," background sheet attached to letter to Page from Andrew J. Richie, Nov. 30, 1926; letter from Page to New York Committee for the Rabun Gap School Chairman James F. Curtis, March 11, 1926; Dan Magill, "Fire Temporarily Suspends Operation of One of Most Unique Schools in Georgia," clipping from *World's Work*; letter from Richie to Henry James, July 27, 1926; and letter from Richie to Page, with attached letter from Thomas B. Appleget to Richie outlining John D. Rockefeller proposal, Jan. 24, 1927; all in Box 1, Arthur W. Page Papers.

[87] "Names Committee on Page Memorial," *New York Times*, May 5, 1924, p. 6, and "Fund for Page Memorial," *ibid.* May 26, 1924, p. 19.

[88] "Page School Trustees," *ibid.*, May 29, 1924, p. 20.

[89] "Drive Begins Here for Page Memorial," *ibid.*, June 2, 1924, p. 8.

[90] Letter to Arthur Page from Walter Hines Page School of International Relations Committee Executive Director Herbert L. Gutterson, Jan. 19, 1926, Box 1, Arthur W. Page Papers.

[91] Letter from Arthur Page to Howard Coffin, Jan. 4, 1926, Box 1, Arthur W. Page Papers.

[92] Letter to Arthur Page from Charles Augustus Stone, Sept. 24, 1925, Box 1, Arthur W. Page Papers, and Strahan memorandum.

[93] Letter to Page from Bruce Barton, May 9, 1927, Box 1, Arthur W. Page Papers.

[94] See especially Albert Ingalls, "Ultraviolet Transmitting Glass—Has It Made Good?", *Scientific American*, Vol. 140 (April 1929), pp. 338-43; report of D.W. Coblentz, U.S. Bureau of Standards, summary in "Ultra-Violet Windows," *Science*, Vol. 70, special supplement, pp. x-xii; and 1947 Page biography.

[95] "Vitaglass Adds to Capital," *New York Times*, July 28, 1927, p. 29; "Vitaglass To Increase Capital," *ibid.*, June 24, 1928, sec. 2, p. 9; and "Vitaglass Offers $425,000 Preferred," *ibid.*, July 1, 1928, sec. 2, p. 15.

[96] George H. Doran, *Chronicles of Barabbas 1884-1934* (New York: Harcourt, Brace, 1935), p. 46.

[97] *Reminiscences*, pp. 69-70.

[98] *Hendrick's Reminiscences*, pp. 55-59.

[99] Doran, *op. cit.*, pp. 46-47, and letter from Page to F.N. Doubleday, May 2, 1927, Box 1, Arthur W. Page Papers.

[100] *Reminiscences*, pp. 70-72, and letter to author from Arthur W. Page Jr., Aug. 19, 1975.

[101] "A.W. Page Quits Publishers," *op. cit.*

[102] Letter to Page from F.N. Doubleday, Nov. 30, 1926, Box 1, Arthur W. Page Papers

[103] Letter from Page to F.N. Doubleday, Dec. 6, 1926, Box 1, Arthur W. Page Papers, and Lyon, *op. cit.*, p. 322.

[104] Letter from Page to F.N. Doubleday; May 2, 1927; letters from Page to S.A. Everitt, Dec. 6 and 14, 1926; and letters from Everitt to Page, Dec. 5 and 8, 1926; Box 1, Arthur W. Page Papers. Everitt unsuccessfully tried to buy Page's preferred stock.

[105] Mott, *op. cit.*, pp. 786-88.

[106] *Ibid.*, pp. 579, 663-64, 788.

[107] Letter from Page to S.A. Everitt, March 19, 1927, Box 1, Arthur W. Page Papers.

[108]

[109] Letter from Page to F.N. Doubleday, May 2, 1927, Box 1, Arthur W. Page Papers.

[110] Doran, *op. cit.*, pp. 41-45.

[111] See letters from Page to S.A. Everitt, Sept. 16, 1927, and Nov. 17, 1928, and letter to Page from Everitt, Oct. 25, 1928, Box 1, Arthur W. Page Papers.

[112] *Hendrick's Reminiscences*, p. 40.

CHAPTER FOUR

The New AT&T Vice President, 1927-1929

Arthur Page reported for work at American Telephone & Telegraph Co. headquarters at 195 Broadway in New York on Jan. 3, 1927. He was probably the first real public relations vice president at a major American corporation, although some "luncheon vice presidents" at smaller firms may have held the title before him.[1]

When Arthur Page started at AT&T, the company was the largest business in America, with more than 300,000 employees and assets in excess of $3 billion.[2]

It's accepted in the literature of public relations and at many Fortune 500 corporations that the head of public relations to be effective needs access to the chief executive officer and top policy councils. AT&T, the nation's biggest corporation in 1927, was the first major American company to give public relations the stature of reporting directly to the company president. The Page appointment in 1927 set an important precedent.

The AT&T department Page was hired to head was the Information Dept. It was also sometimes called the Publicity Dept., and occasionally Page referred to it as the Public Relations Dept. AT&T did not officially name it the Public Relations Dept. until 1971.

By hiring Page at the rank of vice president, AT&T President Walter Gifford signaled to the companies owned or controlled by AT&T that the parent company was placing an even greater emphasis on public relations. An example was being set for the associated Bell System companies to follow.

The role of Walter Gifford in bringing Page to AT&T

WALTER GIFFORD WAS in the main responsible for bringing Arthur Page to AT&T. Page family friend David Houston, an AT&T officer and director, may have influenced Gifford's decision.

Gifford and Page had started in the same Harvard class in 1901. Gifford completed his education in three years, graduating a year ahead of Page.

After graduating in 1904, Gifford applied for a job at Western Electric, the manufacturing and supply unit of the Bell System. He is said to have mistakenly thought that he was writing to Westinghouse Electric. Whether or not that's true, he was hired as a clerk at Western. He soon caught the eye of AT&T President Theodore Vail, who rapidly elevated him to the post of chief statistician.[3] Gifford was named to the post at the start of what would come to be called "the first measured century" in American history.

In 1916, Gifford took a leave of absence from AT&T to serve as the supervising director of the Wilson administration's Committee on Industrial Preparedness of the Naval Consulting Board, and then as director of the Council of National Defense with responsibility for mobilizing American industry for war. His work for Wilson vaulted him into national prominence. The *World's Work* commented favorably on his performance.

In 1925, at age 40, he was named president of AT&T.

The June 1926 issue of the *World's Work* carried a flattering article about Gifford by French Strother, and an article by Gifford himself, "The Changing Character of Big Business."[4] In his article, Gifford contended that the old "robber barons" of industry were being replaced by a new class of business statesmen who "realize more accurately what the limits of their powers are, and have a much keener sense of their responsibilities to the public." The task of the new industrial statesmen, he said, was not to carve out a place for a new corporation, but to carry on the work of highly organized undertakings that would be around long after they were dead. "Corporations," Gifford said, "owe their success and even their existence to the good-will of the public; and where their views seem to clash, the corporation must either persuade the public to its view, or alter its own."[5]

Here was a corporate philosophy to provide fertile ground for public relations to flourish. Gifford was among the new breed of corporate oligarchs and professional managers more interested in the long-term survival of their enterprises than in carving out new empires. A small group of industrial leaders concerned about public opinion, Theodore Vail among them, began to emerge in the 1890s. Gifford and industrial leaders with similar viewpoints continued to evolve in the 1920s. They saw the need to run America's great corporations with at least a semblance of social responsibility because the cutthroat tactics of the old breed of managers had invited Progressive public attack. Public dissatisfaction with business had in turn led to restrictive new laws and stronger government regulation. Motivated sometimes by honest-to-goodness altruism, sometimes by enlightened self-interest, the new corporate oligarchs sheathed the iron fist in a velvet glove.

Like Gifford, Arthur Page believed business had to perform in a socially acceptable manner to survive. A month before the Gifford article appeared, a *World's Work* editorial set forth the criteria the public might use to judge whether or not a business was performing in the public interest. "From the broad point of view of public policy, the first criterion by which to judge great companies is their service to the public," the editorial pontificated. "The second is, do they provide proper returns to those who take responsibility for serving the public—the civil service of these companies. The third criterion is, do these companies play fair with the people who lend them money."[6]

That brief paragraph summarizes the three great publics corporate public relations practitioners must balance and placate—the customer public, the employee public and the owner public, the last including stockholders, bondholders and banks. When a corporation was fairly serving all three, the *World's Work* contended (neglecting the government public), it was performing in a socially responsible manner.

The same year the Gifford article and related editorial appeared in the *World's Work*, Gifford was looking for someone to replace James Ellsworth, who had headed AT&T's publicity and advertising operations since 1908. Ellsworth was due to retire in a few years. He and Gifford were from different worlds. Ellsworth, onetime newspaperman, patent medicine promoter, press agent, sometimes Machiavellian corporate publicity and advertising man, had many of the rough edges of a man who'd spent years on the western frontier. Gifford was polished, sophisticated and urbane, a Harvard graduate, former high-ranking government official and chief executive of the nation's biggest business—a prince of power. He needed a sophisticated public relations counsel, not a press agent.

In the fall of 1926, Gifford called Arthur Page at the publishing house and asked him to come to his office. He wanted Page's ideas about a book the telephone company sought to publish. The request was not unusual. Prior to 1926, AT&T had subsidized publication of at least two books, Herbert N. Casson's *The History of the Telephone* (1910) and James Mavor's *Government Telephones* (1916).[7]

Early in 1926, AT&T had trouble finding a publisher for a third subsidized book, Arthur Pound's *The Telephone Idea*. Both MacMillan and Payson and Clarke had turned down the manuscript because of its obvious propaganda content. AT&T finally had to arrange publication at a vanity press publisher. Distribution of the book began in December.[8]

Shortly before Gifford called him, Page had discussed with Nelson Doubleday his growing dissatisfaction. Immediately before the meeting in Gifford's office—perhaps even the night before—he told his wife, who agreed with his decision, that he was going to leave the publishing house the first time a good opportunity presented itself.[9]

The manuscript Gifford discussed with Page was probably Dr. Thomas Watson's *Exploring Life*. Whatever the book, Page said he didn't think publication would either much help or hurt AT&T. He told Gifford publication might feed the vanity of some AT&T executives, but that the book would likely have little impact on public opinion.

By Page's account, as he started to leave, Gifford motioned for him to stay. He asked if Page was wedded to the publishing business. He pointed out that for years the *World's Work* had been telling business how to run its affairs. Now he offered Page a chance to put the magazine's theories about socially responsible performance to the test at AT&T. Page accepted Gifford's offer of employment, but only after getting assurances he would be more than a publicity man and would have a voice in making policy and encouraging good performance as a general policy of the Bell System.[10] As he put it later, "....(I)f I was convinced that the Bell System meant to sincerely study the public's needs and serve them, I thought the job offered me would be as interesting as any in the country. If, on the other hand, the intention was not bona fide, I didn't want the job. I was interested in participating in a sincere show, but neither interested nor able to camouflage an insincere one."[11]

In addition to becoming a vice president of AT&T in 1927, Page later in the year was named president of the Bell Telephone Securities Co., an AT&T subsidiary formed to promote broader ownership of company stock. The subsidiary distributed information to potential stockholders and supervised, with AT&T's Legal, Treasury and other departments, the program under which anyone could buy AT&T stock at local Bell System offices around the country.

Soon after the Bell Telephone Securities Co. was incorporated in 1921, Page family friend David Houston was named president. Arthur Page replaced him late in 1927, although Houston retained his post as a vice president of AT&T for a time, and continued as a director of the firm through 1940.[12]

Houston, Woodrow Wilson's first secretary of agriculture and last secretary of the treasury, had been a friend of Walter Page. He extended that friendship to Arthur at least as early as 1913. In ensuing years, Houston wrote occasional articles for the *World's Work*. In 1926, at about the same time Page was offered the AT&T job, the final installments of an eight-part autobiographical series by Houston, "Eight Years with Wilson 1913-1921," were appearing in the magazine.[13] Houston may well have played a role in Page's hiring. As a vice president and director of AT&T, he was certainly in a position to make suggestions to Walter Gifford.[14]

Public relations at AT&T before Arthur Page

WHEN ARTHUR PAGE began working at AT&T, the public relations function was already well established, although thinly staffed. Responsibilities of the Information Dept. included preparation of advertising and publicity and counseling of management.

To understand what Page accomplished as head of public relations, it's necessary to understand how the public relations function evolved at AT&T before he came.

The Bell Patent Assn., a forerunner of AT&T, produced its first crude advertising flyer in 1877, just months after Alexander Graham Bell successfully demonstrated his talking machine at the 1876 Philadelphia Centennial Exposition.[15]

AT&T's emphasis on providing good telephone service as the essential foundation of a good public relations program dates at least to Theodore N. Vail's first term of service with American Bell from 1878 to 1887. A human dynamo, Vail, son of an Ohio Quaker farmer and ironworker, was hired away from the U.S. Postal Service to head the long distance subsidiary of American Bell. He had an acute awareness of the importance of customer good will to business success.

Vail's public relations sensitivity is shown by an 1883 letter he wrote as general manager of the American Bell Telephone Co. to the heads of American Bell licensee companies.

In the letter, Vail asked if service being furnished was acceptable to customers, if lower rates should be introduced and if there had been any disputes between the licensees and customers.[16] In short, he wanted to know that good customer relations were being maintained, particularly through the furnishing of satisfactory service at acceptable rates.

Vail's interest in providing good service led him to clash with American Bell President William H. Forbes. Vail wanted to plow more earnings back into the business, while Forbes wanted to take more profits out to pay as dividends to stockholders. When the Boston financiers who controlled American Bell had to replace Forbes in 1887, they passed over Vail, opting for Howard Stockton, another Boston Brahmin cut from much the same cloth as Forbes. Vail resigned in disgust and went to South America where he made a fortune developing city utility systems.[17]

Two years later, John Hudson succeeded Stockton as president of American Bell. During his presidency, which lasted to 1901, public relations problems multiplied. Perhaps to cope with public criticism already mounting when Hudson became president, but more likely because press agents could help a firm cope with growing public demands for an end to corporate secrecy, American Bell around 1890 organized its first press or "literary" bureau in Boston.[18] Despite the output of the literary bureau, animosity to American Bell grew.

The public was eager for competition in the telephone business when Alexander Graham Bell's patents expired in 1893 and 1894. While its monopoly was protected, American Bell built up an employee force of 10,000 serving 240,000 phones. Six years after the patents expired, 6,000 independent companies were struggling with the Bell System for control of the industry. In the brawling, rough-and-tumble competition, customers were sometimes the winners but more often the losers. Independent companies offered telephone service for as little as $40 per year, compared to the $125 to $150 Bell licensees were charging. However, the independents couldn't provide adequate service at low rates and still pay the high dividends they promised investors. A customer desiring to reach all subscribers in an exchange served by two competing companies had to buy service from both.[19]

The public disliked the early Bell System's ruthless suppression of competition. American Bell made no friends when, upon destroying a competitor, the Bell licensee would publicly burn telephones of the rival in the street as a warning to local citizens. The Populist Party and other groups began to advocate government ownership of telephone and telegraph services.[20]

The foreshadowings of later elaborate Bell System employee information programs date to this period. In the early 1890s, the Western Electric Co., which American Bell acquired in 1881 and made its manufacturing arm, began publishing an employee newspaper called the *Western Electrician*.[21]

As the 1890s drew to a close, American Bell, incorporated in Massachusetts with headquarters in Boston, needed more capital than it was allowed to raise by its state charter. American Telephone & Telegraph, a subsidiary of American Bell incorporated in New York, had no such limits. American Bell was merged into AT&T to permit greater capitalization of the Bell System, the process completed in March 1900.[22]

In 1901, the Boston financiers who still controlled AT&T needed a new president to replace Hudson. According to one story, they first went to Theodore Vail who had retired to a farm in Vermont. He is said to have refused the presidency denied him in 1887.

With Vail unavailable, the Bostonians named Frederick P. Fish, a patent lawyer with General Electric (originally the Edison Electric Co.), to replace Hudson. Far more sensitive to public opinion than Hudson, Fish began immediately to worry about widespread animosity to AT&T.

In 1902, Vail became a director of AT&T. He was ostensibly elected to vote the shares of Clarence Mackay, head of the Postal Telegraph Co.[23] Vail's election coincided with election of two other directors representing New York financial interests vying for control of AT&T. The four groups struggling with the Bostonians were the Rockefeller-Stillman-Gould combine, the Widener-Elkins utility magnates, Mackay's Postal

Telegraph group and the J.P. Morgan-First National Bank-Old Colony Trust interests. While Vail may have gone on the board to vote Mackay's stock, it's clear his loyalties were to the House of Morgan.[24]

Fish's presidency and Vail's directorship mark the start of a new emphasis on public relations at AT&T. Fish shifted company policy from destruction of competitors to bringing independent telephone companies peacefully into the Bell System fold. According to Alan Raucher, Fish hoped that by continuous wooing of the public through efficiency, courtesy and rapid response to complaints, much of the criticism of AT&T would dissipate. Fish's 1903 *Annual Report* reveals his emphasis on AT&T's intent to provide satisfactory, courteous service.[25]

In 1903, Fish hired the Publicity Bureau of Boston, probably America's first public relations agency, to represent AT&T in the court of public opinion. James D. Ellsworth, a Publicity Bureau employee and later partner, was assigned to handling the AT&T account.[26] In his memoirs, Ellsworth recalls that soon after starting work, he learned AT&T already had an extensive nationwide newspaper monitoring operation. Stories published throughout Bell System territory were clipped and sent to national headquarters. During 1903 to 1907, when he handled the AT&T account, he saw the clippings change from 90 per cent unfavorable to the Bell System to more than 80 per cent favorable.[27] The dramatic reversal was likely due less to material put out by the Publicity Bureau than to Fish's policy of providing better and more courteous service.

In 1906-1907, the New York-based Morgan interests won control of AT&T. In April 1907, two Boston directors resigned from AT&T's executive committee and were replaced by Morgan men. A few weeks later, Fish resigned as president and was succeeded by Theodore Vail. The AT&T presidency denied Vail by the Bostonians in 1887 was now his from the Morgan combine that destroyed the Boston interests.[28]

During his presidency of AT&T from 1907 to 1919, Vail forged much of the policy that guided the Bell System for decades. He devoted considerable attention to public relations and the search for a corporate soul for the Bell System.

Vail was convinced that public sympathy had to be cultivated. In 1911 he wrote, "In all times, in all lands, public opinion has had control at the last word... It is based on information and belief. If it is wrong it is wrong because of wrong information, and consequent erroneous belief. It is not only the right but the obligation of all individuals, or aggregation of individuals, who come before the public, to see that the public has full and correct information."[29]

Vail used the term "public relations" to describe the building of good will. His 1907 *Annual Report* was entitled "Public Relations," and he used the words in other annual reports and sections of them.[30]

At the start of his presidency, independent telephone companies served almost as many telephones as the Bell System. By the end of his presidency in 1919, AT&T controlled the lion's share of the telecommunications business in the nation. That posed the problem of monopoly and antitrust laws. One of the major themes Vail stressed was the need for the telephone business to be treated by government as a natural monopoly as were the railroads.

Vail relied heavily on publicity to inform the public of AT&T affairs. He made himself readily available to newsmen for interviews. Pendleton Dudley of the *Wall Street Journal* was among the newsmen with whom he was friendly. When Dudley opened his own public relations agency, Vail retained him as a consultant to AT&T, a relationship that lasted to Dudley's death in the 1960s.[31]

Although Vail was a tough-minded, sometimes ruthless manager, he had an essentially idealistic view regarding the need for big corporations to avoid secrecy and openly communicate. Early in his AT&T presidency, he said:

> The only policy to govern the publicity (of AT&T) is that whatever is said or told should be absolutely correct, and that no material fact, even if unfavorable but bearing on the subject, should be held back. When

we see misstatements, make it certain that those making them have correct facts. This will not only tend to stop the making of them, but will lessen the influence of them by decreasing the number of misinformed, and any excuse for misstatements. Attempted concealment of material fact cannot but be harmful in the end.[32]

In 1907, he hired James Ellsworth to head AT&T's advertising and publicity.[33] Ellsworth had left the Publicity Bureau, which Vail fired when it tried to take credit for having written some stories produced by Col. George Harvey. Because the Publicity Bureau had been dishonest, and Ellsworth had been a partner in the firm, Vail was at first reluctant to put him on the AT&T payroll. However, he acceded to colleagues who liked Ellsworth.[34]

In 1908, Vail launched a pioneering institutional advertising campaign in national magazines. The ads were prepared by the N.W. Ayer and Son advertising agency, the nation's oldest and largest. According to George Griswold Jr. of AT&T, it was S.A. Conover of Ayer who convinced Vail to begin the program.[35] The ads sought to protect AT&T from the threats of government ownership and hostile regulation by improving the public's unfavorable perception of the company. They argued that a telephone monopoly providing "one system" and "universal service" was beneficial. The first of the ads explaining AT&T and its policies appeared in the summer of 1908. They were the start of what would become the most persistent institutional advertising campaign in America. The ads gave Vail a new and potent channel for telling the public about the nature of AT&T's corporate soul,

Ellsworth was assigned to cajole associated Bell System companies into preparing similar ads for newspapers published in their territory, and to writing related publicity.[36]

AT&T's corporate identity program began soon after the first of the institutional magazine ads appeared in June 1908. The original prototype of the Bell Seal—a blue bell inside a circle—was designed in 1889 by Angus Hubbard of AT&T,

but was not widely used.[37] Soon after the institutional ads began to appear, Vail made a trip to Denver. At a party there, he was introduced as the president of AT&T, and someone— or perhaps several people—didn't know what AT&T was. Vail returned to New York and ordered that all future national ads prominently display the Bell Seal and the American Telephone & Telegraph Co. name. It soon became one of the most recognized corporate symbols in America.

In 1910, Ellsworth was moved from the old American Bell headquarters in Boston to a permanent base at AT&T headquarters in New York. His responsibilities were expanded to writing illustrated lectures for Bell System employees to give to local audiences—the beginning of AT&T's speakers bureau programs. The illustrated magic-lantern lectures led to production of AT&T's first company-sponsored film, a silent movie entitled "Spinners of Speech." The film, released on the commercial Pathé circuit, showed how telephones were made, how they worked and how they could be especially useful in emergencies.[38]

Institutional ads glamorizing AT&T employees began in Vail's tenure, with a 1914 "Spirit of Service" ad about telephone linemen and a 1915 "Weavers of Speech" ad idealizing female switchboard operators who had replaced unruly and often rude boys.

AT&T's use of pseudo-events—publicity stunts staged to attract mass media coverage—dates to the late 1870s, when Alexander G. Bell held meetings highlighted by live telephone calls to publicize his invention. Ellsworth refined the publicity stunt, particularly the "first call ceremony." In 1915, he orchestrated a first call ceremony opening the nation's first transcontinental long distance line stretching from New York to San Francisco. Participants included Bell in New York, Thomas Watson in San Francisco, U.S. President Woodrow Wilson in Washington and AT&T President Vail at the Millionaire's Club on Jekyll Island, Ga. Along the line, hundreds of Bell System employees were poised in wagons, on horseback and on snowshoes to make immediate repairs if needed. To assure the best possible publicity, Ellsworth hired extra writers to prepare answers to any questions that might arise from news reporters covering the event.[39]

From Aug. 1, 1918, through July 31, 1919, AT&T was nationalized for the war emergency. The company was placed under control of Postmaster General Albert Burleson and an Operating Board later called the U.S. Telegraph and Telephone Administration. Burleson, who had first proposed government ownership of AT&T in November 1913, now had it, but it lasted only briefly. Ellsworth, told he would not be needed, sat out government control, returning to his old job when AT&T returned to private hands.[40]

Despite allegations that the Bell System was mismanaged by the federal government, AT&T fared well during nationalization. Generous rate increases were granted, and Bell System companies were given permission for the first time to charge for installation of telephones.[41]

In 1919, Harry Bates Thayer succeeded Vail as president of AT&T. He moved immediately to protect rate increases won during nationalization and to map strategy for obtaining more rate relief. In early 1920, he named Eugene Wilson, general counsel to a group of Bell companies, to an AT&T vice presidency responsible for coordinating the national rate increase campaign. Much of Wilson's work was of a public relations nature. He made sure the associated companies used intensive advertising and publicity before asking local public service commissions for rate hikes. He furnished elaborate instructions on how to prepare the general public for higher rates. He gave the operating companies sample ads for local adaptation, news releases, employee information items, instructions for canvassing local opinion leaders to inform them and get their approvals, speeches, window posters and even sample resolutions for local chambers of commerce to adopt. As Wilson put it, "if public sentiment is with us, I think the Commission will more readily grant our request for temporary relief."[42]

Wilson melded the Bell System into an unstoppable juggernaut to lobby for higher rates. More than any other, he deserves credit for introducing the public relations campaign to AT&T. By 1925, publicists throughout the Bell System recognized that "rate cases are always held before two juries—one is the jury of public opinion, the other the jury consisting of the constituted authorities hearing the case."[43]

Edward K. Hall was another of the AT&T vice presidents with public relations responsibilities separate from those of Ellsworth. Vail assigned him the mission of building public esteem for the Bell System. President Thayer extended that mission, asking Hall to encourage employee courtesy. Hall understood that if customer contacts with employees were pleasant, there would be little opposition to requests for rate increases. At the 1921 AT&T Commercial Conference, Hall urged establishment of local public relations committees so that employees could discuss with management how best to "mould this public opinion in the right direction."[44]

In his six years as president of AT&T from 1919 to 1925, Thayer attained many of the goals toward which Vail had worked. Bell System growth continued to outstrip that of independent companies. He carved out almost as big a chunk of the total telecommunications business as Vail had captured in 12 years. The Graham Act of 1920 made the telephone business a legal monopoly and exempted AT&T from prosecution under anti-trust laws. Further, Thayer carried out Vail's desire that smaller telephone companies owned by the Bell System be consolidated into larger units. Indiana Bell was thus created in February 1920. Illinois Bell was born in December 1920 by merger of the Chicago Telephone Co. and Central Union of Illinois. Northwestern Bell was created on Jan. 1, 1921, through consolidation of the Nebraska Telephone Co. and Northwestern Telephone Exchange. Other consolidations followed. The larger operating units had sufficient resources to support specialized staffs, including public relations departments.

Thayer made a major contribution to Bell System public relations in 1921 when he presented a paper at the annual Bell System Presidents Conference entitled "Mobilization of the Forces for Better Public Relations." In the paper, Thayer urged the operating company presidents to encourage employee memberships, at Bell System expense if necessary, in local chambers of commerce, labor and farm organizations, Rotary clubs and similar civic organizations, neighborhood and community improvement societies, church clubs and consumer leagues. "Employees should be encouraged to join organizations which will enable them to be better citizens and of more value to the company," he said.[45] Thus the Bell System locked itself into communities it served through a web of employee memberships. The memberships enhanced public and community relations, but in addition, they provided an early warning system should one or another group become dissatisfied with telephone company service or rates.

In the 1950s, Arthur Page was asked what year AT&T's Information Dept. was organized. He replied that 1922 was the most logical date. In that year, James D. Ellsworth was formally named publicity manager of AT&T. His department was given responsibility for all AT&T advertising and publicity, and more importantly, given the mission of advising management on public relations problems. Publicity and advertising men (women did not become prominent in other than secretarial positions until the 1950s-1960s) existed in the associated companies. Ellsworth's department had responsibility for guiding them. Further, Ellsworth was given authority in 1922 to hold an annual Publicity Conference for AT&T and associated company publicity staffers, a strong indication of departmental status.[46] However, Ellsworth lacked the rank of the heads of other AT&T departments. Further, his "department," if it could be called such, consisted only of himself, an assistant and a secretary.

Two years later, in 1924, with advertising and publicity staffs in the associated Bell System companies expanding, Ellsworth was promoted to assistant vice president.[47] Public relations was edging closer to the top policy-making councils at AT&T. A Motion Picture Bureau was established in Ellsworth's department at about this time. In a matter of two years, the estimated annual audience for AT&T films shot from about two million to more than 20 million per year.[48]

On Jan. 20, 1925, Walter S. Gifford succeeded Thayer as

president of AT&T. When he donned the purple mantle of AT&T control, the company held 51 per cent or more (usually more) of the stock of 20 operating telephone companies such as New York Telephone, Illinois Bell and Southern Bell. It owned almost all the stock of the Western Electric Co., one of the largest manufacturing firms in America. Jointly with Western Electric, it owned the new Bell Telephone Laboratories, formed in 1924 and destined to become the largest industrial research organization in the world. In addition, AT&T and its subsidiaries had miscellaneous holdings, most in the telecommunications business but some not.

To keep the Bell System intact, Gifford needed public approval. Jim Ellsworth was not the sophisticated public relations leader to keep the public docile. Enter Arthur Page.

The new vice president takes charge

WITH THE APPOINTMENT of Page as a vice president, public relations reached the top policy councils at AT&T.

Alan Raucher contends that "the transfer of authority from James D. Ellsworth to Arthur Page (brought) no significant alteration in policy."[49] However, the appointment of Page at the vice presidential level in a rank-conscious corporation was a significant change in AT&T public relations.

Page himself made subtle but important changes in AT&T public relations policy. He began almost immediately to stress that listening to the various publics was as important as sending messages to them. He led associated company public relations from press agentry to action in the public interest as the necessary keystone to building good will.

The *New York Times* in 1927 interpreted the Page appointment as a sign of the likelihood of an increased flow of publicity from AT&T.[50] That was wrong. Page was hired not to be a generator of news releases, but to be a generator of policy. He came to AT&T with an idealism tempered by pragmatism—an amalgam similar to the realistic idealism (or "enlightened self-interest") of Walter Gifford.

In addition to having higher corporate rank than Ellsworth, Page differed from him in other important ways. He was more eloquent than Ellsworth, better able to express himself. Where Ellsworth lacked the complete faith of Theodore Vail and Harry Thayer, Page had the full confidence of Walter Gifford. Ellsworth lacked the social status and familiarity with men of prestige that Page possessed. Ellsworth had attended a little-known college on the western frontier and never graduated; Page had a degree (albeit narrowly) from perhaps the most prestigious university in America. Ellsworth came to AT&T as a former newspaper reporter, patent medicine promoter and press agent; Page came as the editor of an influential national magazine, a publisher of thought-provoking books, independently well-to-do, the son of a widely respected former ambassador to Great Britain.

These factors combined to make it possible for Page to accomplish things Ellsworth could not. He came to AT&T commanding the respect and admiration of his new colleagues. AT&T executives were ready to listen to him, believe him and follow his advice.

When Page began work, Assistant Vice President Ellsworth had already been eased out of the Information Dept. He had been moved to Walter Gifford's office as assistant to the president, a title he retained until he retired in 1930.

From the start of his vice presidency, Page stressed (through constant "preaching and teaching," as he was fond of calling it) that public relations was not the sole job of the Information Dept., but rather, was the responsibility of every employee of the Bell System, high and low alike. In his first few months, he set about making public relations consciousness part of the warp and woof of AT&T and its associated companies.

As early as April 1927, Page made it clear to Bell System publicity and advertising forces that he expected public relations to act as the corporate conscience of the Bell System. Since the Information Dept. was not pressed by day-to-day business concerns of the other departments, he said at the 1927 AT&T Publicity Conference, it was "freer, if it had the brains and perspective and intention, to be the custodian of the ideals of the Company."[51]

While Page waxed idealistic about public relations at the 1927 Publicity Conference, an executive of Ohio Bell presented a view from the front lines. He noted that Ohio Bell's relations with newspapers had improved dramatically since 1923 due to careful nurturing of publishers, editors and news reporters. Many of the Ohio papers, he said, were using stories about rate hearings exactly as they had been written and released by Ohio Bell. The Columbus papers had stopped sending reporters to cover rate hearings, and instead were relying on accounts furnished by Ohio Bell. Further, the papers were giving Ohio Bell more space, printing fewer unfavorable stories and editorials, and even making unsolicited offers to "cooperate" with the company.[52]

According to many public relations texts, the first task of public relations in an institution is to sell the function internally. Unless everyone in the institution believes in public relations, the few people assigned to building good will won't be able to accomplish their mission. Although Page came to AT&T already possessing high credibility, he devoted much of his time to "preaching and teaching" aimed at convincing AT&T employees of the value of public relations.

He appeared before conferences of AT&T's Traffic, Commercial, and Engineering Depts., and at other meetings, to talk about the importance of public relations to overall Bell System success.

In a 1927 speech at the AT&T General Operating Conference, Page showed his thinking to be considerably advanced. Some of his statements that are now accepted as axioms by public relations practitioners include:

• Publicity's first and greatest limitation is that it cannot change the facts. "It can act as a loud speaker to broadcast the good service that you people provide, but its effectiveness has a very fading quality if there is any bad service."

• One must learn by trial and error, evaluating each

public relations effort... making what is learned in each project available to all, so that mistakes can gradually be eliminated.

• Messages must be simple and repeated often if they are to penetrate the public consciousness. A teacher has a captive classroom audience, but there are 120 million people in the Bell System classroom, any one of whom can get up and leave when he or she wishes. "The only way you can be sure of making a reasonable dent in the public consciousness is to have what you say so simple that it is easy to understand, and then say it over and over again."

• While the press now and then rumbles against "handouts," it nevertheless prints large amounts of publicity. Perhaps as much as half the news content of the *New York Times* is publicity. What the newspapers collect for themselves consists of unusual things, the abnormalities of life such as murders and accidents. The publicity given to the newspapers and used constitutes the record of ordinary, orderly progress of society and business. This publicity, which the Bell System is excellently set up to distribute, is as important as advertising in communicating with the public.

• Part of the public relations job is to get back to Bell System managers knowledge of what customers and employees think and feel about the telephone business. While getting this information back to management is a more intangible task than sending messages out to the public, it is perhaps more important.

• Within the councils of Bell System management, public relations must act as an advocate for customers. Citing from a book written by one of his former economics professors at Harvard, Page said: "Professor Ripley in his book called *Wall Street and Main Street*, suggested that the corporations have public representatives on the Board of Directors. With all respect to these distinguished bodies, I believe a more effective plan is to have representatives of the public in management, and that is the job of the publicity department. (The publicity department) ought to act all the time from the public point of view, even when that seems to conflict with the operating point of view. It ought to bring to the management at all times what it thinks the public is going to feel about a thing.

• Of the 120 million people in the United States, perhaps only 500,000 are "prime movers," the people who get things done. The prime movers can be given a more complicated message than the masses, a message with more philosophy. "If these key people are thoroughly persuaded, they will effect the result on the rest of the crowd sooner or later."

• It is important that operating department people notify public relations early of any actions they plan to take. Public relations needs time to plan how best to break the news to the public, and to determine if the planned action is in the best interest of the public. The telephone company should not get caught having to make explanations overnight. Organizations informed at the last minute of a planned action by the telephone company might resist it. If told well in advance, the organizations will be more likely to behave in a friendly way,

• The telephone company ought to do things for the public beyond what day-to-day business needs demand. It should, for example, conduct industrial surveys valuable to business and government planners as the Ohio Company did two years earlier. The Ohio Bell business survey, not strictly needed by the telephone business, generated more good will than much of the publicity dealing with telephone service.

The speech makes clear Page's intent to bridge Bell System public relations to the modern concept, where the three major functions are to evaluate public opinion, counsel management and influence public opinion through persuasive communication.[54]

In a presentation a month later, Page called for the associated Bell companies to analyze their ideals and aims, and then write policies (promises to the public) to be advertised in local newspapers as commitments to be met.[55]

Page made his appeal for local institutional advertising by the operating companies to match AT&T's national public relations advertising in a speech not to public relations staffers, but rather, to the Commercial staff of the Bell System. Managers in the Bell System Commercial Depts.—especially the business office managers in each major exchange—were key links in the overall public relations operation. Public relations staffs in the Bell System were concentrated in company headquarters cities like New York, Chicago, Atlanta and San Francisco. The public relations staffs provided guidance to the local managers, who in turn had primary public relations responsibility in their home towns. Employees of other departments such as Traffic (operators) and Plant (installing and maintaining telephones) sat with the local Commercial manager on a home town "local team" committee. In a situation requiring local publicity, someone on the local team might suggest the need for a news release. The Commercial manager would then call Public Relations for help. Public Relations would write the story and send copies to the local manager. The Commercial manger would then deliver the story to local news media. Cultivation of a good working relationship with local news media was the responsibility of the Commercial Dept. representative, although Public Relations might provide guidance.

Walter Gifford's financial policy

ARTHUR PAGE BELIEVED an effective public relations program had to be based on a statement of policy or creed, a promise to the public which the business then sought to fulfill.

On Oct. 20, 1927, AT&T President Walter Gifford provided such a policy for the Bell System in a speech in Dallas, Texas, to what was then called the National Association of Railroad and Utilities Commissioners (NARUC). The organization was composed of members of the Interstate Commerce Commission (ICC), which regulated interstate telephone rates, and members of state utility regulatory commissions.

Arthur Page said in later years of the speech that it represented one of the first instances in which a big business publicly stated the bases on which it planned to serve the public.[56]

The speech was brief—only 11 paragraphs, a little over 1,000 words.

Gifford began by calling for mutual confidence and understanding between public utility commissioners and Bell. Several factors, he said, made it important that telephone management live up to its responsibilities to customers and stockholders. Because ownership of AT&T was diffused (the company then had more than 420,000 investors, none owning more than one per cent of outstanding stock), it was essential that management protect the interests of stockholders. Because AT&T provided service under monopoly conditions, it recognized its obligation to assure that service always be adequate, dependable and satisfactory to users.

"Obviously," Gifford continued in the most important passage, "the only sound policy that will meet these obligations is to continue to furnish the best possible telephone service at the lowest cost consistent with financial safety. This policy is bound to succeed in the long run and there is no justification for acting otherwise than for the long run."

He then discussed what he meant by adequate earnings. He promised that AT&T would not seek speculative profits to distribute as "melons" to stockholders. The company would need enough profit to pay its regular dividend, to provide the best possible service and to assure the financial integrity of the business. Earnings in excess of these requirements, he pledged, would either be spent to enlarge and improve service or be returned to customers as rate reductions.

The rest of the speech briefly recounted the progress of AT&T under 20 years of regulation.[57]

The policy outlined in the speech came to be called internally "the Gifford policy," "the Dallas policy," and "the financial policy." It guided AT&T management for more than two decades. It was a bold policy to announce in 1927, in a period of boom in which most companies were distributing excess profits and the prices of stocks were being driven to dangerously high speculative levels.

Despite the importance of the Dallas speech, it went relatively unnoticed by the mass media. It was too short to appear to be a major new policy announcement. In fact, it wasn't even new. Like most policies, it evolved slowly, a little at a time, over the years. In AT&T's 1925 *Annual Report*, Gifford had said much the same thing. In one passage, he said "In the telephone business, the foundation of good public relations is satisfactory service at the lowest possible rates," and in another, "It is our aim at all times to give the best possible telephone service at the lowest possible cost to the user... There can be nothing inconsistent between our aims and purposes, and the public good...."[58]

What the press didn't realize was that Gifford had more in mind than simply saying in elegant terms what might be translated to read "Regulators, don't limit our profits arbitrarily; give us a chance to be our own watchdogs and we'll give back to customers what we don't need."

Under Gifford's leadership, the vague generalities of the Dallas speech were interpreted into specific policies. AT&T set a rate of return it felt was fair to customers. It established goals to improve every aspect of telephone service. It voluntarily reduced long distance rates. Whether greater rate reductions, more service improvements and a lower rate of return would have resulted from more aggressive regulation is moot.

What is important is that AT&T management translated the Gifford policy into action. The Dallas speech was more than lip service to an ideal. It was another step forward in AT&T's efforts to define its corporate soul.

Several Bell System public relations executives who worked with Page—among them Hale Nelson, an Illinois Bell public relations vice president, and John Shaw, an AT&T assistant vice president—believe Page played a role in drafting the Dallas speech. [59]

Page said the Dallas policy was solely the work of Gifford, and that was probably the case.[60] In support of Nelson and Shaw, some of Page's early statements foreshadowed the Gifford policy. In April 1927, six months before the Dallas speech, he told Bell System public relations staffers that he wanted them to emphasize that excess profits not needed by AT&T to run the business would be returned to customers in the form of reduced rates or service improvements. He asked the public relations staffers in the same presentation to stress in advertising and publicity that there would be no special bonuses or melons for AT&T stockholders.[61]

Whether or not he helped write the Gifford policy which became the keystone of Bell public relations, Page certainly saw the value of it. Immediately after the Dallas speech was given, he made it clear he planned to make the Gifford policy "the fundamental basis of our public relations." He felt confident the pledge would protect AT&T from public attack. Such attacks, he pointed out, usually came because the public didn't like the way a business distributed profits. The Bell System could protect itself from such attacks by promising to return excess profits to customers instead of distributing them as windfalls to stockholders or company insiders.[62]

Page quickly organized Bell System public relations machinery to making various AT&T publics aware of the Dallas commitment.

The personnel staffs of the Bell System held briefing sessions where the policy was explained in simple terms to employees, so that they in turn could pass the policy along to customers. The important role of employees in communicating such messages to the public had been recognized by AT&T at least as early as its 1914-1916 publicity conferences. Managers were told to brief "key people" such as newspaper editors and elected officials in their home towns on the meaning of the policy.[63]

Efforts to inform stockholders of the Dallas policy began at least as early as the spring of 1928, when AT&T's 1927

Annual Report was distributed. The report, which explained the policy, was sent not only to stockholders, but also to a list of influential educators in America which Page had obtained from the Carnegie Corp.[64] Among the educators who replied to the special mailing was corporation critic Dr. Charles A. Richmond, president of Union College of Schenectady, who wrote: "As I understand it, you mean to run your business in such a way that the return to the stockholders will not be excessive but will be sure. Whatever savings are effected will go to the public. If I am right in this, as I believe I am, it seems to me the only sound policy."[65]

Much of AT&T's institutional advertising in some 100 national magazines with a combined circulation of about 15 million was converted to explaining the policy. The institutional ads explained how the Bell System was living up to its promises. One ad gave statistics to show that service was being improved—the average time for handling long distance calls had been reduced from two to one and a half minutes, the number of local calls not completed by customers on the first attempt had been reduced by five percent and the Bell System in the preceding five years had spent $1.8 billion on additions and improvements in its plant. The ad concluded with a promise repeated in many other AT&T ads during the period:

> . . . The American Telephone and Telegraph Co. accepts its responsibility for a nationwide telephone service as a public trust. It is fundamental in the policy of the company that all earnings after regular dividends and a surplus for financial security be used to give more and better service to the public.[66]

Page came to the Bell System with the assurance that he would be given a role in establishing corporate policy in the public interest. The Gifford policy provided such a creed. It guided AT&T management until Page and Gifford retired, at which time gradual erosion began because of a changed business environment.

Building an ethical public relations base

WITH METICULOUS CARE, resisting pressures to spend more money than he thought necessary, Page began to build up the Bell System public relations machinery. Although he was more interested in upgrading the staffs of the associated companies than in building an empire at AT&T's Information Dept., he had by late 1927 selected his principal lieutenants for the parent department.

Thomas Tyson Cook was placed in charge of a section with responsibility for supervising AT&T, Long Lines and Bell Telephone Securities Co. national advertising. The section had a 1927 budget of more than $4.7 million.

William Banning, an assistant vice president, was given the section responsible for publicity, newspaper monitoring, publication of the *Bell System Quarterly* (founded in 1922, and by 1927 AT&T's main employee information organ) and movie preparation and distribution. The Bell System film audience in 1927 was more than 27 million.

William J. O'Connor became responsible for Page's "public relations laboratory," which had the mission of studying the public relations successes and failures of Bell System associated companies, passing along the lessons learned to all public relations staffers.[67]

In addition to establishing new public relations policies, Page had to root out disreputable old ones. In May 1928, he moved to end Bell System participation in public utility information committees and subsidization of a secret propaganda front.

Use of unidentified propaganda fronts is today called "third-party technique." Although legal by Supreme Court decision, use of third-party fronts is unethical under the Public Relations Society of America (PRSA) code, and grounds for expulsion of members found employing them.

Bell System use of front organizations to distribute propaganda dates at least to 1903 when the Publicity Bureau was hired. The Publicity Bureau was attacked for serving as a secret front for railroad propaganda by Ray Stannard Baker in a 1906 *McClure's* article, and again by William Kittle in *Arena* in 1909.[68]

What the Publicity Bureau did for the railroads before it was retained by AT&T it likely did for AT&T while it was retained from 1903 to 1907, but it was not the use of the Publicity Bureau with which Arthur Page was concerned in 1928. The front then being subsidized by AT&T was the news and editorial service of E. Hofer and Sons of Salem, Ore.

The Hofer service began modestly in 1912 as a multigraph story and clipsheet service to country dailies and weeklies in the western United States. In 1922, the agency concluded an agreement with national utility executives. In return for a financial subsidy from the utilities, the agency agreed to distribute propaganda on their behalf nationally. Some 90 utilities, the Bell System among them, began contributing about $84,000 per year to support the Hofer work. [69]

By 1927, the main publications of E. Hofer and Sons were *The Manufacturer* and *Industrial News Bureau*, syndicated to newspapers nationally.[70] In addition, Hofer put out individual multigraphed stories and editorials. In 1927, 12,784 newspapers used Hofer material. These newspapers published about 3.1 million column-inches of Hofer propaganda—the equivalent of about 25,900 standard newspaper pages.[71]

The Hofer editorial matter defended private ownership of utilities, attacked municipal ownership and cooperative systems, criticized government development of electric power (such as Canada's Ontario electric power project, of which American electric power magnates had an almost paranoid fear) and tried to establish the impression that private utilities were mostly owned by small investors.

Had the Hofer service admitted the source of its funding, it could not be called a front operation. It did not. It claimed to be independent. Newspaper editors getting Hofer materials, while normally a cynical lot, were not told it was a paid voice of the electric power and other utilities. When newspapers ran Hofer editorials and news the material was doubly misleading, for in many cases it would appear that the material was the work of local editors.

Although the Hofer operation was large, it was only a small part of a much larger utility propaganda machine put together mainly by electric power firms from 1919 to 1928.

Early in 1919, electric power baron Samuel Insull called together executives of companies he controlled to discuss public relations. From the meeting sprang the Illinois Committee on Public Utility Information, the publicity arm of which was controlled by Bernard J. Mullaney.

Mullaney had done civil defense public relations work for Insull during World War I, when Insull had established Creel Committee propaganda machinery in Illinois. The Illinois Committee became the prototype for other utility information committees, their activities guided by the National Electric Light Assn., later the Edison Electric Institute.[72]

AT&T helped to support the utility information bureaus. At the 1927 Bell System Publicity Conference, Illinois Bell Publicity Manager John Spellman claimed of the Illinois Committee on Public Utility Information that "We started the first committee; we have always had control of it."[73]

While Illinois Bell probably played an influential role in operation of the Illinois Committee, Spellman was surely exaggerating in claiming that Illinois Bell controlled it. Mullaney was Insull's man, not Spellman's. However, Spellman had more than an ordinary interest in the activities of the utility information committees. He had been a member for a few months of a special National Electric Light Assn. committee formed to pressure textbook publishers to give more favorable coverage to investor-owned utilities and less favorable coverage to government-owned operations.

Spellman served as the AT&T representative on the special committee from February to April 1925. Then, to AT&T's credit, several of its executives condemned Bell System participation in the effort to intimidate publishers, and Spellman was told to resign.[74]

In March 1928, under Senate mandate, the Federal Trade Commission (FTC) opened hearings in a sweeping investigation of the privately owned electric power industry in America. The investigators almost immediately focused on the propaganda apparatus the power industry had organized from 1919 to 1928. Alarmed at the critical press coverage of the power industry as a result of the exposure of the propaganda operations, Page in May wrote a circular letter to Bell System presidents saying, "In the last two or three days the papers here and in Washington, and I presume elsewhere in the country, have been full of the Senate Committee's investigation of the state public utility information bureaus. This leads me to raise the question again whether it is wise for the Bell System to be connected with publicity organizations which are not under its control and many purposes of which are not identical with Bell System policy."[75]

After the circular letter, Bell support of the utility committees and Hofer service declined and then ended. According to Noobar Danielian, a Federal Communications Commission staffer during the late 1930s investigation of AT&T, most of the $190,000 or so the Bell System gave to the utility information bureaus was given from 1926 until Page sent the 1928 letter. Danielian says Bell System contributions to Hofer amounted to about $102,000 from 1915 to 1931, with the bulk of the payments made from 1923 to 1928.[76] After 1928, the Bell System pretty much spoke for itself.

Pragmatic policies to promote sale of services

THE GIFFORD POLICY, and policies developed by Theodore Vail before Gifford, were designed to protect Bell System monopoly status. AT&T had gone through an unsettled period of competition when Bell patents expired and did not want to repeat that unhappy and unprofitable experience.

Page in several 1928 speeches detailed how the Bell System could best defend itself against the three objections most frequently raised by the public against monopolies.

The first public objection to monopoly, Page said, was the charge that they were greedy. The best defense against that charge, he felt, was the Dallas policy. One of the early public relations pioneers to recognize the importance of strategic (long-range offensive) over tactical (short-range reactive) public relations, Page said of the Dallas policy:

> It seems to me almost hopeless to endeavor to cor-
> rect the troubles that arise in our public relations by
> running around trying to put salve on each manifesta-
> tion of public displeasure. That means meeting one
> kind of attack here, another kind over there, and be-
> ing continually... on the defensive.
>
> It is for this reason, it seems to me, that a construc-
> tive policy which will forestall and prevent public at-
> tack, is the only answer to the problem, on the theory
> that the best defense is an offence (sic) and that is
> why the affirmative policy of the Dallas speech is so
> important to us... (W)ith that policy almost anybody
> in the Bell System can explain affirmatively what we
> are trying to do....[77]

The second objection to monopoly was the belief it was inefficient, Page argued. The Bell System could best defend itself against that by pointing to intercompany competition— one Bell System company competing against another for the best service indexes. Emphasizing the technological achieve-ments of Bell System research and engineering staffs, espe-cially discoveries of scientists at the Bell Telephone Labora-tories, would also counter the criticism.

The third objection to monopoly, he said, was the public's belief that industries unchallenged by competition became lazy since their profits are guaranteed. The answer to this was an aggressive employee sales effort.[78]

In early 1928, AT&T Vice President Eugene Wilson called for a new approach to employee selling. At the time, the Bell operating companies held occasional sales drives a week or so long to push items such as extension telephones. "You have two ears, why not two telephones?" was an early sales slogan. Wilson now advocated continuous, year-round em-phasis on sales by customer contact employees, with special peak campaign periods.

Page provided a rationale for the selling advocated by Wilson. He argued that aggressive selling was an integral part of socially responsible corporate behavior. The way to counter public belief that monopoly was lazy, he reasoned, was to persuade Bell System employees to enthusiastically sell telephone company wares. He wanted employees to act as though they were in competition with other companies for the consumer dollar. In the process of selling Bell System services, employees would have to become courteous salespersons, for the public does not buy unless wooed through good manners. The increased Bell System politeness would improve good will and be in the public interest.

Emphasis on sales would also make employees listen to what customers said they desired. Employees could pass on to management what customers wanted the Bell System to provide, and management would become more responsive to customer desires. Instead of the Bell System deciding what should be offered to customers, the customers would be making the company responsive to their wishes.

As part of his sales philosophy, Page argued that the time had perhaps come for an end to "basic black" telephone service. While Western Electric offered some 140 different kinds of switchboard cable to the operating companies, the operating telephone companies offered only four telephone instruments to customers—a black desk set, a new black handset (or "French phone"), a black wall set and a black-buttoned intercom system. Customers had little choice in their telephone equipment. A monopoly could not afford to force equipment on the public. Henry Ford had been "forced to make a lady out of his black Lizzie," and it was time for the Bell System to start dressing up its children, offering a greater variety of instruments, perhaps in different colors. Although the introduction of color phones did not follow for many years, the start of AT&T's promotion of horizontal services can be dated from 1928.

Vertical service growth in telephony is expansion in the number of telephone main stations. Up to 1928, AT&T's main emphasis had been on increasing main stations in service—

at encouraging vertical growth by getting homes and offices with no telephones to install them. Horizontal growth is growth in items that supplement main stations, such as extension phones, for which additional charges are levied.

Long distance service is a horizontal growth item. AT&T had promoted long distance for years before Page joined the company. He was innovating, however, when he put a major share of AT&T advertising from 1928 forward behind another horizontal growth item, extension telephones.

The pilot ads for the promotion centered on the comfort and convenience of extra telephones. One ad showed a hostess in evening gown talking on an extension upstairs while she looked down over a balcony at guests in her parlor. The ad said extension phones could save a hostess from the embarrassment of having to talk on the phone in front of guests. Local operating companies were urged to develop similar ads for newspapers in their regions, and to use bill stuffers to promote sale of extensions and other horizontal items.

Page was particularly impressed by a bill stuffer developed by New Jersey Bell to boost sale of the new "French phone." It was being introduced at premium rates as a replacement for the traditional desk set that required a user to hold the receiver to the ear with one hand while grasping base and speaker in the other. The French phone combined receiver and transmitter in a single handpiece.

In January-February 1928, New Jersey Bell sold about 400 of the new telephones per month. Introducing a reduced rate for the French phone jumped sales to 1,200 sets in March. Then the company told customers about the new handsets in a bill insert, and sales jumped to 4,600 sets in April.

Bill stuffers had been in the operating company advertising and public relations arsenal for decades. The successes in New Jersey drove home to Bell public relations representatives the importance of direct mail in selling. The companies were in an ideal position to use it. Bill stuffers could be inexpensively included with monthly phone bills. Most Bell surveys ranked the efficiency of bill stuffers well ahead of newspaper, magazine and radio advertising and publicity.[79]

Another important advertising first was marked in 1928 when AT&T began promoting "Where To Buy It" directories, predecessors of later phone book Yellow Pages. The "Where To Buy It" books were introduced in 700 cities in 1928. They listed national products and trademarks, along with the names and telephone numbers of local dealers handling the brands. The directories were quickly promoted into a lucrative new source of income for the Bell System.[80]

By early 1929, Page had classified Bell System advertising into four categories: (1) ads that informed customers, stockholders and regulators of how AT&T was discharging its trusteeship and of AT&T's ideals, aims, plans and results, (2) ads that told customers how best to use telephone service, (3) ads that asked customers to cooperate with the Bell System by doing things such as notifying the phone company before moving, and (4) ads aimed at sale of telephone services and usage. The first three types of advertising, institutional in nature, paved the way for sales. They made the public friendly to AT&T, happy to see its representatives and ready to listen to them—in short, ready to buy.[81]

Scientific monitoring of public opinion

AT THE BEGINNING and end of a public relations campaign, the practitioner needs information about the opinions of relevant publics. By comparing opinions before and after the campaign, success or failure of the effort can be determined. The feedback can be scientific (surveys conducted under rigorous standards) or nonscientific (mass media clips and transcripts, letters, telephone logs, reports from employees and monitored rumors).

AT&T began monitoring public opinion in 1926. Tests of statistical significance for scientific analysis of opinion polls were developed by Pearson in *The Grammar of Science* in the 1890s. Application of Pearson's tests to opinion measurement is thought to have begun in the 1930s with the pioneering work of George Gallup and Rensis Likert, the latter at the U.S. Dept. of Agriculture. Advances between 1890 and the 1930s are covered in Jean Converse's *Survey Research in the United States.*

Opinion surveying came of age in the Bell System during Page's tenure. He deserves much of the credit for recognizing the need for feedback and encouraging development of systems to gauge the moods of AT&T's publics. Integration of formal feedback systems into the public relations function is among his contributions to public relations practice.

In a 1971 article in *Public Relations Journal*, Prescott Mabon, who worked with Page for many years in the AT&T Information Dept., contended that Page was a major factor in encouraging the development of attitudinal surveys at AT&T.[82] In contrast, John Shaw, who worked directly under Page in 1930, and again from 1944 through 1946, contends that Page viewed the early survey work first of Seymour Andrew and then of Arthur Richardson and C. Theodore Smith with a somewhat amused but skeptical tolerance. Commenting on the Mabon claim that Page encouraged the development of scientific polling at AT&T, Shaw contends:

> ...Pres (Mabon) is correct, of course, in paying these men (Andrew, Richardson and Smith) the tribute of being early pioneers in this field. I was one of those who shared their enthusiasm and was frequently in the position of trying to win Page's support for their programs, not always successfully... Page was usually willing to give us our heads, but to say that he "spurred us on" is overstating the case, I think.[83]

The first customer poll conducted by AT&T appears to be a 1926 study which the firm commissioned the J. David Houser organization to carry out in Detroit. The study predated by about five years the pioneering survey work of Rensis Likert at Agriculture, and by about ten years the early work of George Gallup and Claude Robinson.

In 1929, AT&T commissioned the Houser organization to conduct a second survey, this one in Pittsburgh. The 1929 survey had two goals—first, to determine what proportion of the audience read and remembered AT&T institutional ads, and second, if readership of the ads was related to having favorable attitudes toward the Bell System.

The readership portion of the 1929 survey of 2,500 Bell System customers uncovered much higher retention of AT&T advertising content than Page expected. Seventeen per cent of the respondents were able to remember statements made in specific AT&T ads. An additional 20 per cent, when asked if they remembered specific statements, answered "yes" when their memories were jogged.[84]

Whether or not the Houser survey was able to show if readership of the ads was related to favorable attitudes toward the Bell System is unclear. What was left of the Houser surveys probably retired with C. Theodore Smith.

Page approved the 1929 Pittsburgh study, supporting Mabon's contention that he was ready to advance from reaction to public desires as expressed in letters and newspaper clips to systematic measurement of public opinion.

Page already by 1927 had decided that public relations at AT&T should have two basic responsibilities: first, to act as spokesperson for the executive departments of AT&T through the written word, motion pictures, advertisements and other means, and second, to endeavor to ascertain the public's point of view and to act as advocate for the public's desires within the councils of Bell System management.[85]

In a speech Page made a month before results of the Houser Pittsburgh study were available, he called for the publicity and advertising staffers to develop expertise in forecasting where public opinion would likely be in the future. He wanted them to be able to do that, he explained in the April 1929 Bell System General Publicity Conference speech, so that the System could get itself ready in advance to be in conformity with public opinion when it finally crystallized in a new direction. The speech is laced with examples of how other corporations had accurately predicted trends in public opinion. Page argued that just as other Bell System departments had developed the ability to predict future demands for service, so that equipment could be manufactured and installed in time to meet demand, so also should public relations develop expertise in predicting trends in public opinion.[86]

In 1929-1930, AT&T created a unit in the Chief Statistician's Division to determine how best to apply opinion research techniques to solution of Bell System public relations problems.[87] The research unit was established at the direct request of Page, more evidence in support of Mabon's contention that he actively supported development of attitudinal research. The unit, which gradually evolved into the Business Research Division of AT&T, pioneered in giving the Bell System one of the most advanced attitudinal research operations of any major American corporation.

The preponderance of evidence indicates Page's role in development of opinion polling at AT&T was more than the "amused tolerance" Shaw suggests.

The operating companies follow the leader

UNDER PAGE'S LEADERSHIP, the operating telephone companies upgraded their publicity and advertising operations into full-fledged public relations departments that understood the importance of action in the public interest as essential to building good will.

In the summer of 1929, the New York Telephone Co., crown jewel of the Bell System financial empire, authorized creation of a typical full-service public relations department. The mission statement said the duties of the new department would be "to assist in assuring that no step of any importance affecting the service would be taken by the company without full consideration being given to the public relations significance of the step" and "to study telephone operations from the public viewpoint, working day by day with the departments, making suggestions as to methods and practices, and advising as to the effect that existing or contemplated policies might have on public opinion."[88]

There is no mention in the statement of press agentry,

product promotion or publicity-seeking. Public relations is charged with attending to the state of telephone service, assuring that this service is being provided in the best interests of customers.

The statement provides evidence that the 19th-century press agent ethic, advanced as late as 1927 at the Bell System publicity conference by Ohio Bell, was giving way by 1929 to a modern public relations ethic in the Bell operating companies.

The first Bell System directorships

IN THE FIRST THREE YEARS of his AT&T vice presidency, Page continued to build corporate directorships. In August 1927, he was named president and a director of the Bell Telephone Securities Co., the AT&T subsidiary that promoted sale of AT&T stock around the country. BTSC was created by AT&T to increase its capital flow and diffuse ownership.

In June 1928, Page was elected a director of the Southern Bell Telephone & Telegraph Co., headquartered in Atlanta and serving Kentucky, Tennessee, North and South Carolina, Georgia, Florida, Alabama, Mississippi and Louisiana.[89]

So began a string of directorships on the boards of blue-chip corporations. The appointments show Page was esteemed within the Bell System not only as head of public relations but as a businessman, for the directorships involved responsibilities beyond providing public relations advice.

Page in 1928 resigned his directorship in the Vitaglass Corp.[90] He continued through the period 1927-1929 as a director of the Engineers Public Service Co., and in January 1929 was elected to that firm's executive committee.[91]

The socially responsible businessman

PAGE'S PUBLIC SERVICE activities for philanthropies expanded in 1927-1929. He continued to serve as:

• A director of the American Federation of Arts.

• A director of the British Apprentice Club.

• A member of the Central Council, a vice president, and a member of the executive committee of the Charity Organization Society.

•A director and member of the executive committee of the Roosevelt Memorial Assn.[92]

In addition, he became active during the period in the Leonard Wood Memorial for the Eradication of Leprosy, the American Shakespeare Society and the Educational and Development Fund of the Farmers Federation of Asheville, N.C. He also assumed greater responsibilities with the Long Island Biological Assn.

The American Shakespeare Society sprang into existence in 1926 when fire destroyed the 1879 Shakespeare Theatre at Stratford-on-Avon, England. Briton Archibald Flower, executive director of the Society, mapped a drive to raise $1.5 million in Great Britain and $1 million in America to rebuild the structure and provide an endowment for its operation.[93]

America's bluebloods, members of the *Social Register*, rallied to the cause. Page was named to the executive committee of the Society by April 1927. Other members of the executive committee included public relations pioneer Ivy Lee, Thomas W. Lamont of the House of Morgan, Clarence Mackay of Postal Telegraph, Mrs. Charles Dana Gibson and George Pierce Baker. Honorary officers of the American Society included Elihu Root Jr., Charles Evans Hughes, Robert Lansing, John W. Davis (who had replaced Walter Hines Page as ambassador to Great Britain and then become a presidential nominee) and Frank L. Polk.[94]

In June 1927, Page was elected president of the Long Island Biological Assn., of which he had been a director since 1921.[95] As president, he worked especially to raise money for the institution. Most of the financing came from contributions of people with summer estates like his near Cold Spring Harbor. The Long Island neighbors could afford to make substantial gifts. Most were wealthy investment bankers, Wall Street lawyers, corporation executives and scions.

In November 1927, Page became involved in the work of the Farmers Federation of Asheville, N.C., a cooperative that sought to help improve the economic plight of Blue Ridge Mountain farmers in North Carolina.

The driving force in the Farmers Federation was Chicago minister James G.K. McClure, who went to Appalachia to regain his health after suffering a nervous breakdown. Touched by the poverty of mountain farm families in the Asheville area, he formed the Farmers Federation around 1921 to help develop better strains of livestock and crops, market farm products, provide social outlets for mountain families and support local churches. Funding for the initial venture came from shares in the cooperative purchased by farmers.[96]

In 1927, the Farmers Federation established an Educational and Development Fund to raise money to further the cooperative's work. In November 1927, Arthur Page became president of the new foundation, and also chairman of its New York Committee, a fund-raising arm. Other committees to raise money were established in Philadelphia and Detroit.

Among those active with Page in supporting the Educational and Development Fund were Fairman Dick, with whom Arthur would work in later years to develop public relations campaigns for the railroad industry in America, Thomas J. Watson, founder of International Business Machines, Perry Burgess, who had a fund-raising firm which he abandoned to work full-time for the Leonard Wood Memorial for the Eradication of Leprosy, magazine publisher Henry Luce, auto fortune heir Edsel Ford, newspaper publisher and Associated Press executive Robert McLean, Nicholas Roosevelt and novelist Owen Wister, author of *The Virginian*.[97] Page took considerable interest in the work of the Farmers Federation, and continued to serve as president of the Educational and Development Fund to his death in 1960.[98]

In January 1928, Page was named a trustee and member of the executive committee of the Leonard Wood Memorial for the Eradication of Leprosy (later the American Leprosy Assn.), another charity with a prestigious roster of trustees. The foundation was established to perpetuate the memory of Gen. Leonard Wood, a former American governor-general of the Philippines.

When Page became a trustee of the Leonard Wood organization, his friend Henry Stimson was the American governor of the Philippines, and surely instrumental, along with Perry Burgess, in getting Page involved. Stimson served for a number of years as chairman of the board of the organization, which funded research into leprosy and underwrote a major part of the operation of the massive leprosy treatment center on Culion Island in the Philippines.[99]

Trustee of Vassar, Teachers College and the Jeanes Fund

PAGE CONTINUED in 1927-1929 as a member of the Committee to Visit the Bussey Institute at Harvard.

He also established a scholarship in Walter Hines Page's memory at Harvard. Called the Watauga Fellowship after his father's circle of friends in Raleigh, the scholarship called for him to provide $1,500 per year for five years, with Harvard, Radcliffe, Duke University and the University of North Carolina providing some matching monies and services.

Under the fellowship, a few graduate students from the North were to study at southern schools, and a few graduate students from the South to study at Harvard or Radcliffe. Somewhat upset about the way the scholarship was handled by Harvard, however, and suffering financial reverses because of the Great Depression, Page before the scholarship was fulfilled terminated the fellowship after contributing only $2,500 of the planned $7,500.[100]

He assumed an important new responsibility in November 1928 when he was elected a trustee of Vassar College in Poughkeepsie, N.Y.[101] He served in the post to 1933.

He continued to serve as a trustee of Teachers College of Columbia University. In February 1929, he was named to the executive committee of the board of trustees.[102]

He also continued to serve as president of the St. Bernard's

School Fund board. He kept the St. Bernard's post until 1939, well after his last child had graduated from the school.

In June 1929, Page was elected a trustee of the Negro Rural School Fund-Anna T. Jeanes Foundation, an organization that his father once served as a trustee.[103]

The Jeanes Foundation, which evolved into the Southern Education Foundation, was created in 1907 by Quakeress Anna T. Jeanes, who donated $1 million to be used for improving rural schools serving blacks in the South. At the time Arthur Page joined the Jeanes board in 1929, more than 300 Jeanes teachers were at work moving from school to school to enrich the abysmally inadequate training provided to black youngsters in a segregated southern school system. The salaries of the teachers were paid in part by the Jeanes Foundation, and in part by county school boards. The Jeanes teachers sought to help regular classroom teachers enrich curriculum, and did some teaching themselves of practical subjects such as raising winter gardens and sewing.[104]

Joining the right clubs

THE *NEW YORKER* magazine is noted for making fun in cartoons of octogenarian millionaires sitting in overstuffed chairs in mahogany-paneled private clubs. Funny as those cartoons might be, executives who work in major commercial centers such as New York City know that being selected for membership in the right clubs can do much to enhance their careers.

The New York clubs have a status system. Cleveland Amory quotes a clubman in *Who Killed Society?* as saying: "At the Metropolitan or the Union League or the University, you might do a $10,000 deal, but you'd use the Knickerbocker or the Union or the Racquet for $100,000 and then, for $1,000,000 you move on to the Brook or the Links."[105]

From his last years at Doubleday, Arthur was active in a number of the clubs. He belonged to the University Club of New York, the Metropolitan Club of Washington, the Harvard Club of New York, the Tavern Club of Boston, the Century

Assn. of New York and the St. James's Club of London. In addition, he belonged at various times to prestigious recreational and country clubs such as the Cold Spring Harbor Beach Club, Piping Rock Country Club, New York Yacht Club and the Southside Sportsman's Club.[106]

His membership in the Century is perhaps most worth noting. Many club members were artists, musicians, columnists, lawyers, editors and book-reading corporate executives whose views didn't lean too strongly to the left. The Century was a club heavy with brainpower and wit. Less stodgy and "old-money" than the other clubs, it was the favorite of members of the Council on Foreign Relations, in which Page became a member in 1931. Members in Page's day included Herbert Hoover, John Foster Dulles, Franklin Roosevelt and Averell Harriman to name a few.

Also active in the University Club, Page arranged for a number of speakers there. One was Henry Stimson, governor-general of the Philippines in 1928-1929. Stimson, a charter member of the Council on Foreign Relations, spoke at the club while on leave. The opinion leaders Page invited to hear him included Albert Shaw of the *Review of Reviews*, Ernest Hamlin Abbott of *The Outlook*, Hamilton Fish Armstrong, managing editor of the Council on Foreign Relations's influential *Foreign Affairs* magazine (the editor was Page's favorite history professor at Harvard, Archibald Coolidge), James Mason of the *New York Evening Post* and United Press executive Karl Bickel.[107]

The contacts Page made at the clubs likely had some influence on his thinking. In later life, one of his great interests was in encouraging American schools to do more teaching about and research into the role of freedom in the development of the United States. He was not unique in valuing personal liberty. Ferdinand Lundberg says in *The Rich and the Super-Rich* that talk of "freedom" pervades the clubs. He argues that it is the wealthy who most fear limitations placed on their own freedom by government and the courts, and contends that by preserving freedom in America, people of wealth mostly protect themselves and their own fortunes.

A more current philosophical view holds that some American and world history can be explained as conflict between two camps. One group is composed of the Toquevillians who value patriotism, religious belief and individual freedom. In the other camp are the Gramscians, after Italian philosopher Antonio Gramsci, less privileged people who rely on government to allocate resources fairly and who often are at ideological if not literal war with the privileged classes. Page unquestionably belongs with the Toquevillians.

Regardless of what view one takes of the role individual liberty plays in American history, Page's belief in personal freedom was profound and went far beyond mere lip service. He had a deep and abiding belief that people should be free to pursue their fortunes in a system that does not deprive them of gain by overtaxing them, destroying incentive. He believed it was personal liberty that made America a great country in which to live and a great national power.

While Page was without question an independent thinker, his conversations with other members of the clubs to which he belonged probably reinforced his political views. Membership in the clubs was for the most part right-leaning. The prestigious New York clubs were almost wholly Republican in Page's day, although wealthy Democrats such as W. Averell Harriman and Franklin Roosevelt were tolerated.

Following his father's path, Page politically was a Democrat up to the 1920 presidential election. In 1920, he swung his support to Republican Warren G. Harding. In 1924, he was back in the Democratic camp, a delegate to the Democratic nominating convention. In 1928, his correspondence shows, he supported Republican Herbert Hoover. He supported Republican candidates thereafter to his death.

Page's shift to the Republican camp reveals something about his outlook. As it became increasingly apparent in late 1927 and early 1928 that Catholic Al Smith would get the Democratic presidential nod, he became increasingly a Republican. His opposition to Smith was not based so much on Smith's religion as to what he termed Smith's "courting of foreign-born Democrats"—an allusion to Smith's political base of first-generation Irish-Americans, German-Americans, Jewish-Americans and Italian-Americans. Page feared that Smith, if elected, might reopen the floodgates of immigration closed in 1924 to meet demands from his immigrant supporters, and thus threaten Anglo-Saxon "old stock" predominance in America. In late 1927, he wrote to John Stewart Bryan to say, "If it comes to a choice between Al Smith and a Republican who will stick by the old stock, I am for him." Early in 1928, he wrote to his friend Henry Stimson in the Philippines to express his support for Hoover. Closer to the election, he told Robert E. Blackwell, president of Randolph-Macon College, one of his father's *alma maters*, that he planned to vote Republican.[108] Among other things, Page expressed a hope that the "Solid South" would desert the Democratic camp. Remarkably, it did. Virginia and Page's own North Carolina went Republican in the 1928 presidential election.

Husband, father and friend

DESPITE HIS MANY DUTIES in and outside AT&T, Page found time during the AT&T vice presidency to be husband and father to his family, and a good friend to acquaintances.

In 1927, the year he joined AT&T, his daughter Mollie, oldest of the children, turned 14. Walter H. Page II was 12, Arthur Jr. was 10, and Johnny, the youngest, was 7.

The family spent summers, some weekends and Christmas holidays at County Line. The rest of the year was spent at a residence on 65th St. in New York.

On a typical summer weekend at County Line, Arthur Sr. might spend a Saturday afternoon sailing with his children (he was an ardent yachtsman), teaching the boys to shoot clay pigeons with shotguns (Page liked fine guns, and bought good arms for his sons) or simply watching Johnny play on the lawn with his pet rabbits. The family often spent a part of the summer with Arthur's mother at a summer place near Chocorua, N.H., or vacationing in North Carolina.

During the winter, Arthur and Mollie enjoyed a busy social life, playing bridge with the Bruce Bartons and other friends, dining out or entertaining other couples at the 65th St. home.

About the time Page became an AT&T vice president, he began to build an extensive library in his study at County Line. He bought boxes upon boxes of books on American history, education in the South, business and naval subjects. He particularly liked rare books on sailing in colonial days. He also purchased world literature classics because he wanted his children exposed to the best fiction. A single week might bring the collected works of Goldsmith, Sterne, Bronte, Hardy, James and Dickens to fill the shelves at County Line.

His wife Mollie, in addition to running the Page household, busied herself with various charities. She was active in the women's committees of the Long Island Biological Assn. and the Farmers Federation Educational and Development Fund. Through the Stimsons, she was named president of the Army Relief Society in 1928, remaining active through World War II as the "official mother" of the U.S. Army.

Page devoted considerable time during the early AT&T vice presidency years to keeping his friend Henry Stimson in the Philippines informed on the state of public opinion in America, and acting as Stimson's sometimes public relations representative at home. The manner in which he kept Stimson informed was similar to the service he had provided his father when Walter Page was in England. Instead of writing summaries of American opinion to Stimson, however, Page sent him frequent packets of press clippings.

An emotional letter Stimson sent to Page from the Philippines in the summer of 1928 demonstrates the closeness of the Page-Stimson friendship. After describing his concern for his wife Mabel, who had lost 25 pounds in the heat of the Philippines, Stimson (who had lost 20 pounds himself), said "We think often of you and Mollie... and only the other day in one of our depressed moments, Mabel remarked out of a clear sky, 'How would you feel if the door opened and Mollie and Arthur walked in to talk over things with us.' I replied that it would be like heaven...."[109]

Page sought to represent Stimson on two important matters, the Kiess Bill, which would have given the governor-general of the Philippines greater power over Filipino politicians, and 1928 planks of the Republican and Democratic parties on granting independence to the Philippines.

Page, unable to devote full time to serving Stimson, tried to get him to hire paid public relations counsel in the Philippines and America. Stimson refused, saying American reporters had told him they would interpret such a move as an attempt to propagandize and control the news. However, he allowed Page to hire Pendleton Dudley part-time in the United States to assist in the effort to lobby for the Kiess Bill.[110]

The behind-the-scenes efforts of Page and Dudley in Washington to get the Kiess Bill passed were unsuccessful. American legislators were unwilling to give Stimson the power to appoint department heads of the Philippine government and his own personal advisers without the approval of the Philippine legislature.

Stymied in Washington, Stimson introduced his own version of the Kiess Bill in the Philippine legislature and obtained passage, getting his way in the end.[111]

Stimson opposed the 1928 Democratic platform plank calling for immediate independence for the Philippines and Page denounced it. Page's switch to the Republican party in 1928 may have in part been due to his support for that party's more conservative plank calling for independence for the Philippines at a later date when the native government displayed more ability to govern the country.[112]

In addition to working for passage of the Kiess Bill and to speaking out against the Democratic plank calling for immediate independence for the Philippines, Page also worked in the late 1920s to promote Stimson in America. Among other activities on behalf of Stimson, he arranged for publication by Scribner's of a book Stimson wrote about his work in Nicaragua leading to the Peace of Tipitapa, talked to the Carnegie Corp. about a grant so the book could be published in Spanish and arranged for publication in magazines and newspapers of articles by and about Stimson.[113]

Providing a public relations philosophy

PAGE'S MOST IMPORTANT work during the period 1927-1929 was in providing leadership for AT&T and Bell System public relations staffs.

When he arrived in 1927, AT&T and the associated Bell companies had already developed elaborate systems for:

•Distributing information about the company,

• Influencing opinions of various publics,

• Keeping employees informed through supervisor briefings and printed material,

• Placing institutional and sales-oriented advertising,

• Maintaining memberships in community organizations,

• Building favorable relations with stockholders and other members of the company's financial public, and

• Maintaining cordial relations with higher education (the Bell System held seminars for deans and presidents of the nation's largest engineering schools and universities in 1924, 1925 and 1926).

Rather than starting public relations at AT&T, Page provided a comprehensive philosophy for the role public relations should play in company affairs.

He pragmatically built the philosophy on the concept that good deeds in the public interest had to be the foundation of building good will for the company. The good deeds, he recognized, had to be adequately publicized. But to him, it was the deeds that were important.

The role of public relations in his philosophy was to act as the conscience of the corporation, informing management of what customers, stockholders and employees saw as good deeds and bad deeds. Public relations also had to act as the ears of the company, listening to the various publics to determine what they wanted from the Bell System and to learn what the publics thought to be good deeds.

With this modern public relations philosophy in place, history conspired to test its efficacy. The test came from the

Great Depression which began in 1929. That is the subject of
the next chapter. Page's attendance at the 1930 London Naval conference, and his role in founding the regional cells of
the Council on Foreign Relations is also covered.

ENDNOTES

[1] L.L.L. Golden, "Public Relations: Lessons of History," *Saturday Review*,
July 8, 1967, p. 62.

[2] On Jan. 1, 1926, the Bell System had total assets in excess of $3 billion,
compared to about $2.4 billion for its next closest competitor, U.S. Steel.
The Bell System in 1925-1926 had more than 300,000 employees (including Western Electric), compared to about 250,000 for U.S. Steel. However,
U.S. Steel, General Motors and Standard Oil of New Jersey were all posting
bigger profits than AT&T at the time. See Stuart Chase, "Ten Companies
Reach the Billion Mark," *New York Times*, March 27, 1927, sec. 8, p. 1.

[3] French Strother, "The New Leadership of Business," *World's Work*,
Vol. 52 (June 1926). The story about Gifford applying to Western Electric
thinking it was Westinghouse Electric may be apocryphal.

[4] *Ibid.,* and Walter S. Gifford, "The Changing Character of Big Business,"
World's Work, Vol. 5 (June 1926), pp. 166-68.

[5] Gifford, *op. cit.*

[6] "Who Owns Our Corporations," editorial, *World's Work*, Vol. 52 (May
1926), pp. 11-13, at p. 12.

[7] N.R. Danielian, *A. T. & T.: The Story of Industrial Conquest* (New York:
Vanguard Press, 1939), p. 292.

[8] *Ibid.*, pp. 292-94. See also Arthur Pound, *The Telephone Idea* (New
York: Greenberg, 1926).

[9] *Reminiscences*, pp. 70-72.

[10] *Ibid.*, pp. 16, 70-72.

[11] Letter from Page to Illinois Bell Telephone General Sales Manager
John W. Wolcott, Nov. 24, 1941, in possession of author.

[12] American Telephone & Telegraph Co., *Annual Report* (1921) (1922)
(1924) (1926) (1928) (1941), pp. 14-16, 15-16, 23-24, 3, 3 and inside front
cover respectively.

[13] David F. Houston, "Eight Years with Wilson 1913-1921," *World's Work*,
Vol. 51 (February 1926), pp. 360-360P. Successive installments of the serial
appeared through the September 1926 number.

[14] Correspondence between Page and R.E. Blackwell of Randolph-Macon
College indicates Blackwell regarded Houston, not Gifford, as Page's main
patron at AT&T.

[15] A reproduction of the first advertising flyer prepared by the Bell
Patent Assn. appears in pamphlet, "The Early Corporate Development of
the Telephone," AT&T, July 1964, p. 9.

[16] Letter from Theodore N. Vail to W.A. Leary, Dec. 28, 1883, in Cutlip
and Center, *op. cit.*, p. 67.

[17] Based essentially on pamphlet by Kenneth P. Todd Jr., "A Capsule
History of the Bell System," American Telephone & Telegraph Co. (1972), p.
29; "The Early Corporate Development of the Telephone," *op. cit.*, p. 26;

and L.L.L. Golden, *Only by Public Consent* (New York: Hawthorne Books, 1968), p. 28.

[18] Cutlip and Center, *op. cit.*, p. 83.

[19] Statistics in this paragraph are essentially from Todd, *op. cit.*, p. 30

[20] For an account of Populist demands for government ownership of AT&T, see Alan Raucher, *Public Relations and Business 1900-1929* (Baltimore: Johns Hopkins Press, 1968), pp. 6-7.

[21] Todd, *op. cit.*, p. 32.

[22] The capital assets of American Bell were transferred to AT&T on Dec. 31, 1899. On March 27, 1900, stockholders of American Bell approved the issuance of two shares of AT&T stock for each share of American Bell held. See "The Early Corporate Development of the Telephone," *op. cit.*, p. 26, and Todd, *op. cit.*, pp. 33-34.

[23] Account of Vail's refusal of AT&T presidency and Fish's appointment is based on Danielian, *op. cit.*, and James D. Ellsworth, *The Twisting Trail*, unpublished autobiography, 1936, Mass Communications History Center, State Historical Society of Wisconsin, Madison, Wis., pp. 122-23.

[24] Danielian, *op. cit.*, especially p. 58.

[25] Raucher, *op. cit.*, p. 48.

[26] See especially Scott M. Cutlip, "The Nation's First Public Relations Firm," paper presented at Association for Education in Journalism convention, Syracuse University, Aug. 23, 1965.

[27] Ellsworth, *op. cit.*, pp. 124-25.

[28] See Danielian, *op. cit.*, especially p. 58.

[29] Cited from Prescott C. Mabon, "A Personal Perspective on Bell System Public Relations," pamphlet, AT&T, 1972, p. 2.

[30] Vail's *Annual Report* remarks appear in a collection of Vail's writings, *Views on Public Questions* (New York: private printing, 1917).

[31] Cited from Cutlip paper *op. cit.*

[32] Cited from George Griswold Jr., "How AT&T Public Relations Policies Developed," *Public Relations Quarterly*, Vol. 12 (Fall 1967), p. 8.

[33] *Ibid.*

[34] Ellsworth *op. cit.*, pp. 139-41.

[35] Griswold, *op. cit.*, p. 8.

[36] Todd, *op. cit.*, p. 30.

[37] Ellsworth, *op. cit.*, p. 141.

[38] Griswold, *op. cit.*, p. 10, and Ellsworth, *op. cit.*, pp. 149-50.

[39] Ellsworth *op. cit.*, pp. 152-54; Griswold, *op. cit.*, pp. 10, 12; Todd, *op. cit.*, p. 40; and Raucher, *op. cit.*, p. 55.

[40] Ellsworth, *op. cit.*, pp. 159-62.

[41] Danielian, *op. cit.*

[42] Discussion of work of E.K. Wilson is based essentially on Danielian, *op. cit.*, pp. 318-21.

[43] *Ibid.*

[44] *Ibid.*, pp. 280, 282, 308.

[45] *Ibid.*, pp. 285-86.

[46] Letter from Page to R.E. Mooney, American Telephone & Telegraph Co. historical librarian, June 1, 1955. Ellsworth indicates in *The Twisting Trail* that Vail used the term Information Dept. well before 1922.

[47] *Ibid.*

[48] Arthur W. Page, untitled speech at AT&T General Commercial Conference, June 1927, and Danielian, *op. cit.*, pp. 302 and 304.

[49] Raucher, *op. cit.*, p. 80.

[50] "Telephone Co. To Increase Publicity," *New York Times*, Jan. 4, 1927, p. 31.

[51] Arthur W. Page, untitled speech at Bell System Publicity Conference, Briarcliff, N.Y., April 28, 1927.

[52] Norton W. Long, *The Public Relations Policies of the Bell System: A Case Study in the Politics of Modern Industry*, unpublished Ph.D. dissertation (Cambridge, Mass.: Harvard, 1937), fn. p. 99, and Danielian, *op. cit.*, pp. 310-11.

[53] Arthur W. Page, "What Publicity and Advertising Can Do To Help Operation," *op. cit.*

[54] The three functions of modern public relations practice are delineated in Cutlip and Center, *op. cit.*, p. 6.

[55] Arthur W. Page, untitled speech at AT&T General Commercial Conference, *op. cit.*

[56] Arthur W. Page, *The Bell Telephone System* (New York: Harper and Brothers, 1941), p. 13 ff.

[57] Discussion of the Dallas speech is based on Walter S. Gifford, "A Statement of Policy of the American Telephone & Telegraph Co.," speech before convention of the National Association of Railroad and Utilities Commissioners, Dallas, Texas, Oct. 20, 1927, as reprinted in Addresses, Papers and Interviews by Walter S. Gifford.

[58] American Telephone & Telegraph Co., *Annual Report* (1925), p. 14.

[59] Author personal conversations with Nelson and Shaw.

[60] See, for example, letter from Page to Thomas W. Lamont and Henry James, Oct. 9, 1942, Box 8, Arthur W. Page Papers.

[61] Arthur W. Page, untitled speech at Bell System Publicity Conference, *op. cit.*

[62] Arthur W. Page, untitled speech at Bell System Traffic Conference, Nov. 11, 1927.

[63] Arthur W. Page, "Public Relations," speech at AT&T General Operating Conference, Briarcliff, N.Y., April 28, 1927

[64] Letter from Page to Frederick Keppel of Carnegie Corp., Feb. 15, 1928, Box 1, Arthur W. Page Papers.

[65] Letter to Page from Dr. C.A. Richmond, Box 1, Arthur W. Page Papers.

[66] Cited from Arthur W, Page, "Public Relations and Sales," speech at Bell System General Commercial Conference, June 1928.

[67] Material in this paragraph is essentially from Arthur W. Page, untitled speech at Bell System Traffic Conference, Nov. 11, 1927. The 1927 advertising budget figure is from Danielian, *op. cit.*, p. 314; it disagrees with a figure of $3.5 million for 1927 AT&T advertising mentioned by Page in a June 1928 speech at AT&T's General Commercial Conference.

[68] Ray Stannard Baker, "Railroads on Trial," *McClure's*, Vol. 26 (March 1906), pp. 535-44, and William Kittle, "The Making of Public Opinion," *Arena*, July 1909, as reprinted in Harvey Swados, *Years of Conscience* (Cleveland and New York: World Publishing Co.-Meridian Books, 1962), pp. 399-407.

[69] Ernest Gruening, *The Public Pays... And Still Pays* (New York: Vanguard Press, 1964, first published 1931), p. 189.

[70] Danielian, *op. cit.*, p. 309.

[71] Gruening, *op. cit.*, p. 190.

[72] Gruening, *op. cit.*, pp. 18-21. Gruening's main source of information on the early founding of the Illinois Committee on Public Utility Information was a 1925 article in *Gas Age-Record*.

[73] Danielian, *op. cit.*, pp. 275-76.

[74] *Ibid.*, pp. 277-79.

[75] Letter from Page to E.F. Carter and other Bell System presidents, May 18, 1928, cited from Danielian, *op. cit.*, pp. 276-77.

[76] Danielian, *op. cit.*, pp. 276 and 309.

[77] Arthur W. Page, "Public Relations," speech at Bell System General Operating Conference, May 1928.

[78] For a full delineation of Page's arguments for refuting public objections to monopoly, see "Philosophy of the Business," a speech he made at the Bell System General Plant Conference, October 1928.

[79] Information on Page's rationale for selling as an important adjunct to building customer good will, and on the use of advertising to promote horizontal growth is essentially from Arthur W. Page, "Public Relations and Sales," *op. cit.*

[80] Arthur W. Page, "Public Relations and Sales," *op. cit.*

[81] Arthur W. Page, "Coordination of Sales and Advertising Activities," speech at AT&T General Sales Conference, January-February 1929.

[82] Prescott C. Mabon, "The Art of Arthur Page," *Public Relations Journal*, Vol. 27 (March 1971), pp. 5-9, especially pp. 6-7.

[83] Letter to author from retired Bell System public relations executive John M. Shaw, undated but written shortly after the Mabon article, *op. cit.*, appeared in March 1971.

[84] Arthur W. Page, "Address," speech at 1930 Bell System General Commercial Conference, May 1930, and untitled speech at 1930 Bell System General Operating Conference, May 1930.

[85] Arthur W. Page, "What Publicity and Advertising Can Do To Help Operation," and untitled speech at Nov. 11, 1927, Bell System Traffic Conference, *op. cit.*

[86] Arthur W. Page, "The Problem of Forecasting Public Opinion in the United States," speech at AT&T General Publicity Conference, April 1929.

[87] See especially Kenneth P. Wood, "Understanding Fifty Million Customers," *Public Relations Quarterly*, Vol. 12 (Fall 1967), pp. 17-24, and copy of 1970 letter from C. Theodore Smith to Prescott C. Mabon in possession of author.

[88] Cited from memorandum in John M. Shaw Papers, Mass Communications History Center, State Historical Society of Wisconsin, Madison, Wis., Box 3. This collection hereafter is referred to as the John M. Shaw Papers.

[89] Strahan memorandum and personal 3 x 5 notecards on which Page kept track of his directorships, in possession of author, and hereafter referred to as Page's notecards.

[90] 1947 Page résumé.

[91] Strahan memorandum.

[92] Strahan memorandum; 1947 Page résumé; and Page's notecards.

[93] Letter and accompanying flyer to Page from American Shakespeare Society Campaign Director Paul Franklin, Nov. 9, 1927, Box 1, Arthur W. Page Papers.

[94] Letter to Page from Archibald Flower, April 15, 1927, Box 1, Arthur W. Page Papers.

[95] Strahan memorandum and Page's notecards.

[96] See especially letters from Page to F.R. Keppel of the Carnegie Corp., Dec. 15, 1930, and to Perry Burgess of the Leonard Wood Memorial for the Eradication of Leprosy, Sept. 22, 1933 Boxes 2-3, Arthur W. Page Papers.

[97] Farmers Federation Educational and Development Fund, *Annual Report* (1931 and 1934), and letters from Page to Marshall Field and Henry

Luce, Oct. 31, 1933, Boxes 2-3, Arthur W. Page Papers.

[98] Letter to author from James G.K. McClure Educational and Development Fund Secretary James McClure Clarke, Aug. 4, 1975.

[99] Strahan memorandum and 1947 Page résumé, and letter to Page from Leonard Wood Memorial Executive Secretary H.L. Elias, Sept. 14, 1937, Box 4, Arthur W. Page Papers.

[100] See especially letters from Page to Harvard Professor Edwin Gay, May 21, 1927, May 25, 1927, Feb. 26, 1928, April 24, 1929, June 3, 1929, and Jan. 11, 1932; letter to Page from Harvard President A. Lawrence Lowell, May 3, 1928; letter from Page to Harvard Professor Arthur M. Schlesinger Sr., June 18, 1929; and letters from Schlesinger to Page, June 20, 1929, and April 16, 1930; Boxes 1-2, Arthur W. Page Papers.

[101] "Elected to Vassar Board," *New York Times*, Nov. 18, 1928, and 1947 Page résumé.

[102] Strahan memorandum.

[103] Letter to Page from Jeanes Foundation President Dr. James Hardy Dillard, Nov. 12, 1929, Box 2, Arthur W. Page Papers.

[104] Letter to Page from Dr. James Hardy Dillard, Nov. 12, 1929, and Arthur D. Wright, "Jeanes Teacher," unpublished manuscript, Nov. 23, 1939, Boxes 2 and 6, Arthur W. Page Papers.

[105] Amory passage is quoted from Ferdinand Lundberg, *The Rich and the Super-Rich* (New York: Bantam Books, 1968), p. 310.

[106] According to "A.W. Page Quits Publishers," *op. cit.*, Page in late 1926 was a member of the University Club, Harvard Club of New York and St. James's Club. Other clubs mentioned are from a variety of references.

[107] See Page's letters of invitation to various dignitaries, December 1927 ff., and replies of various individuals invited, Box 1, Arthur W. Page Papers.

[108] Letters from Page to John Stewart Bryan, Oct. 6, 1927, Henry L. Stimson, Feb. 24, 1928, and Dr. R.E. Blackwell, July 7, 1928, Box 1, Arthur W. Page Papers.

[109] Letter to Page from Governor-General of the Philippines Henry L. Stimson, July 28, 1928, Box 1, Arthur W. Page Papers.

[110] Telegram from Page to Henry L. Stimson, March 19, 1928, letters from Stimson to Page, March 24 and March 31, 1928, and letter from Page to Stimson, April 2, 1928, Box 1, Arthur W. Page Papers. Dudley, founder of the Dudley-Anderson-Yutzy public relations agency, had first been retained by Theodore Vail as a public relations consultant to AT&T in the early 1900s. He continued to serve as a consultant to AT&T throughout the Page vice presidency years and thereafter to his death. Page was in contact with Dudley frequently, and it would have been logical for him to suggest that Stimson retain him as a paid consultant.

[111] Letters from Henry L. Stimson to Page, July 28 and Aug. 9, 1928, Box 1, Arthur W. Page Papers.

[112] See especially letter from Henry L. Stimson to Page, June 27, 1928, Box 1, Arthur W. Page Papers.

[113] Letter from Page to Henry L. Stimson, Nov. 14, 1927; letter to Page from "LHF," associate editor at Harper and Brothers, Nov. 14, 1927; letter from Page to Stimson, Dec. 8, 1927; letter from Page to Gen. Frank McIntyre, chief of U.S. Army Bureau of Insular Affairs, July 25, 1928; and War Department cablegram from Stimson to Page, July 11, 1928; Box 1, Arthur W. Page Papers.

[114] Arthur W. Page, "Public Relations," speech at AT&T General Operating Conference, May 1931.

CHAPTER FIVE

Reacting to the Great Depression, 1929-1935

ONE OF THE MOST frenzied financial booms in American history began around the time of the death of President Warren G. Harding in 1923.

During the first years of the boom from 1923 through 1925, stock prices rose, but not excessively. The initial rise in stock prices was a healthy result of sound investment in industry.

From 1926 to late 1929, however, speculation ruled. Stock prices rose to excessively high levels. Speculators of limited means gambled their savings by buying stocks on margin. Unscrupulous financiers fueled the boom. Men like Samuel Insull built holding company empires with watered stock. Some speculators banded together in "investment clubs" to manipulate stock prices to their advantage by buying and selling large blocks of stock, then moving in to make a killing at the expense of others trying to climb on the bandwagon. Harvard economics professor William Z. Ripley referred to the chicanery going on before the bottom fell from the stock market as "honeyfugling, hornswoggling and skulduggery."[1]

As president of the Bell Telephone Securities Co., Arthur Page grew increasingly alarmed at the inflated prices being paid by investors for utility stocks. In December 1927, he wrote to Henry R. Hayes, president of the Investment Bankers Assn. of America, to complain of "reckless selling of public utility properties at absurdly high prices," warning that securities dealers were exposing investors to considerable risk.[2] Within the Bell System, Page warned public relations staffers that a major drop in stock prices could turn the good will of growing numbers of stockholders to animosity.[3]

The big bust came in 1929. On Oct. 23, there was a spectacular drop in stock prices during the last hour of trading on the New York Stock Exchange. The next day, "Black Thursday," prices plunged as 13 million shares, a huge number in 1929, traded on the Big Board. Per-share prices dropped until mid-November, then rose slightly into early 1930. In April of that year, a steady decline in stock prices began. The market reached a rock-bottom Depression low in mid-1932.[4]

Just before Black Thursday, AT&T stock sold at $304 to $310.25 per share. On Oct. 24, the day of wrath, it closed at $272.[5]

The *New York Times* index of selected industrial stocks reached its Depression low of 58, off almost 400 points from the pre-Depression high of 452, in July 1932. AT&T stock hit a low of $69 3/4 a share in the same year. The price of AT&T stock rose gradually in ensuing years, posting a year's high of $187 and a low of $140 in 1937. Prices hovered more or less in the same range through 1940.[6]

Many of the problems with which Arthur Page and Bell System public relations had to cope from late 1929 through 1935 were related to the Great Depression.

AT&T's investor public was less than good-natured about the loss in market value of Bell System securities. Some investors and brokers questioned the wisdom of AT&T management, which several times during the Depression dipped into surplus (the company's savings) to pay the regular $9 dividend. They said AT&T should have reduced the dividend if earnings didn't cover it.

Although AT&T maintained and surpassed service goals during the financial crisis, its relations with customers suffered. One reason was its refusal to lower rates for local service when most other companies were cutting prices.

Employee relations were impaired by layoffs, particularly at the Western Electric Co. Employees of the operating telephone companies who remained on the payroll found their paychecks smaller due to "spread-the-work" policies. People who normally worked a six-day week found themselves working a five-day week instead. Here, public relations staffers were able to use the technique of converting a seeming sin into a virtue by publicizing the humanitarian aspects—keeping people on the payroll by spreading work around, and providing a shorter work week.

The Great Depression led many Americans to lose faith in big business. Hapless victims of the economic system clamored for investigations of the nation's largest firms. AT&T, America's biggest employer and business, became the subject of a number of local probes, and in the last years of the Depression, the target of the first full-scale national investigation of its activities.

During the period 1929-1935, Arthur Page was occupied mainly with helping the Bell System adjust to new realities. He nonetheless found time to attend the 1930 London Naval Conference as an adviser to his friend Henry L. Stimson.

Attending the 1930 London Naval Conference

ARTHUR PAGE'S STATURE within the Bell System grew considerably following his participation in the 1930 London Naval Conference, at which Henry Stimson pressed with limited success for slowing of warship production, particularly by Japan.

The story of how Page came to attend the conclave began when, after his election in 1928, President-elect Herbert Hoover offered Stimson the choice of becoming either attorney general or secretary of state in his cabinet.[7] Stimson opted for the State Dept. job, and prepared to leave Manila for his new post in Washington.

As Stimson transited, Page continued to serve as his confidante and informal public relations aide. In the spring of

1929, Page wrote a flattering article about Stimson's accomplishments that appeared in *Current History* magazine.[8]

In his *Oral Reminiscences*, Page says that soon after
Stimson returned to the United States, he asked Page to become an assistant secretary in the State Dept. In late 1929,
the *New York Times* speculated that Page would be named
successor to Asst. Secretary of State Nelson T. Johnson, who
was to become American minister to China.[9] Page says he
declined for financial reasons,[10] preferring his AT&T salary
to that of a State Dept. officer.

When Stimson asked Page to accompany him as an adviser to the 1930 London Naval Conference, he agreed. He
took a brief leave from his AT&T duties. He and his wife
Mollie were issued diplomatic passports and sailed for London in January 1930.[11]

At the Conference, Page served as Stimson's press relations officer and informal personal confidante. Biographer
Elting Morison notes that Stimson was uncomfortable with
reporters. Feeling that newsmen wanted to know more than
was good for them, the government or the body politic, he
usually told the press little or nothing.[12] Page relieved Stimson
at London of having to answer questions from reporters.

The London Naval Conference opened officially on Jan.
21. That evening, at a 6 p.m. press briefing, Page introduced
a "Mr. Wilson," probably a State Dept. employee who had
been assigned to helping him with press relations. Page said
to the assembled newsmen:

> In the work here, our object has been to try to keep
> the press informed as well as possible on current af-
> fairs and any other questions, and we find that it would
> be easier if there were more of us, and in that circum-
> stance I am particularly happy that Mr. Wilson... is
> going to take it on.
>   ...You will find us both going on with the job of
> trying to be as useful to you as possible, both as to
> current and any other things you would like to know...
> Either one of us will always be available.[13]

Page's early relations with the newsmen were cordial. A few days after the conference began, reporters at one of the press briefings moved a unanimous vote of thanks for the way Page and Wilson were handling news dissemination.[14]

As the conference progressed, however, the press grew critical of the negotiations. Some criticism centered on the alleged failure by Stimson and other American negotiators to keep the State Dept. in Washington and the President better informed.[15]

A treaty was finally signed in London on April 22, 1930. It provided for an extension of the moratorium on capital warship production by Great Britain, America and Japan first hammered out at the Washington Conference of 1922. More importantly, the treaty established quotas for construction by America, England and Japan of smaller ships of the cruiser, destroyer and submarine classes.

Then came further criticism. Some American and British naval authorities objected to provisions giving Japan equality in submarine construction and a bigger ratio of cruisers and destroyers than had originally been envisioned. Other objections were mounted to the treaty's recognition of Japan's primacy in the western Pacific. But perhaps the greatest amount of criticism was directed at the refusal of France and Italy to sign the treaty. Fearing that either fascist Italy or a France afraid of Italy might start major naval construction, Great Britain insisted on an escape clause permitting construction above the allowed quotas if the balance of world naval power was upset by nonsignatory nations.[16]

Page, Mollie and a number of other Americans who had been at the London Conference returned home on the *Leviathan*, one of the first ocean liners equipped with AT&T's new ship-to-shore radiotelephone service.

Back in the United States, Page defended the London Treaty on several occasions. In June 1930, he delivered the commencement address at Vassar, of which he was a trustee. In his speech, he contended that the London Conference (1) continued and strengthened the principle of naval limitation, (2) recorded the utmost confidence between the three largest naval powers, (3) reduced the sizes of the navies of the three largest powers, and (4) gave France and Italy incentive to settle their differences.[17]

Shortly before his death, Page made a final assessment of the accomplishments at London, writing to historian Elting Morison to say, "I agree that it (the London Naval Conference) didn't stop the world sliding into Armageddon. But the real chances to stop the slide were later and it is my feeling that they were far less well handled than the Naval Conference... On paper, the Treaty seemed to contain the Japanese *which was the main purpose of the Conference.*"[18]

Slashing the employee force

WHILE THE LONDON Naval Conference may have delayed an Armageddon of one sort, Page returned to a different Armageddon in America. The country was deep in the throes of the Great Depression. Business floundered. More and more workers were being laid off.

AT&T, which had experienced only growth from the start of the Vail presidency in 1907 forward, suddenly found its fortunes reversed. Formerly complacent customers, investors and employees grew outraged.

The company had regularly made enough to pay its annual $9 dividend and have some profits left over for surplus. In 1929, net earnings available for dividends amounted to $12.67 per share, more than $3 above what was needed to pay the dividend. However, per-share earnings slid in 1930 and 1931 to where they just barely covered the dividend. From 1932 through 1935, the company failed to earn it. In 1934, the worst of the four years, AT&T earned only $5.96 per share.

Despite its inadequate Depression earnings, AT&T was one of the few, perhaps the only major business in America to continue to pay its regular pre-Depression dividend during hard times. Most companies reduced or eliminated dividends. AT&T justified its continued payments on grounds that the

$9 dividend helped buoy up the price of AT&T common stock, thereby protecting investors, many of limited means, and provided a small income for the people who had bought the stock. Critics charged that while it was true AT&T had many small investors, the stockholders who really benefited from the policy were the big banks and institutional investors that owned large blocks of AT&T.[19]

Management had grown accustomed to seeing the number of main telephone stations served by the Bell System grow each year. In 1929, a very good year for growth, the Bell System added 821,000 new mains to the 14,250,000 in service at the end of 1928. In 1930, main station gain dipped sharply to 122,500. Then, in 1931, instead of gaining telephones, the Bell System posted a net loss of 292,000 mains. In 1932, the worst of the Great Depression years for AT&T, some 1.6 million stations were removed from service. A decline of another 630,000 mains was posted in 1933. Then, in 1934, the losses stopped. Thereafter, consistent gains were posted for the remainder of the Depression years. By 1938, all main stations lost in 1931-1933 had been regained, and the company began to set new records for total number of telephones in service.[20]

Bell System employment plummeted during the Great Depression as dramatically as did loss in telephone mains. In 1929, Bell System employment was at an all-time high of 364,000, not counting employees at Western Electric and the Bell Telephone Laboratories. By 1935, the number of workers employed at AT&T and the operating telephone companies had dropped to a Depression low of 244,600, off 33 per cent from 1929.

The employment cuts were the most pronounced at Western Electric and the Bell Labs. In order to meet record demand for telephone service, AT&T by 1929 had built the employee force at the two subsidiaries to 90,500. Most were employed at Western Electric. By 1933, the Depression low for employment at the subsidiaries, only 22,200 workers were left on a payroll, off 74 percent from 1929. Layoffs were greatest among assembly line workers at Western.[21]

To explain the workforce reductions, Arthur Page and other AT&T apologists pointed out that many of the people laid off had been hired as temporary rather than regular employees. Part of the force reduction was accomplished by not replacing employees who died or resigned rather than by forced layoffs. Many regular employees were protected by "spread-the-work" plans. AT&T throughout the Depression resisted demands of customers and regulatory bodies that the company reduce employee wages.[22]

Did AT&T's treatment of labor during the Great Depression conform to the pledge? Arthur Page would have answered emphatically "yes." Government investigator Danielian answered "no" after the FCC investigation of 1935. While much of the Great Depression workforce reduction in the Bell System was accomplished through voluntary resignations and deaths of employees, at least 18,000 Bell System employees went on the relief rolls because they were laid off. Danielian charged that a reduction in the AT&T dividend from $9 to $8 per year during the Depression would have saved $18.7 million per year, enough to have kept the 18,000 on Bell payrolls.[23]

Appeals to reason vs. emotion

For at least a century, persuaders and propagandists have argued about the merits of appeals to emotion versus appeals to reason. The fundamental arguments can be traced back further, to rhetoric teachers in ancient Rome, to the letters of St. Paul crafted in formal rules of rhetoric and to St. Augustine, the Roman rhetorician turned father of the Christian church who argued that the three purposes of rhetoric are to educate/inform, to entertain and to persuade.

In *PR! A Social History of Spin*, Stuart Ewen devotes 24 paragraphs to a presentation made by William Banning at the 1923 AT&T Publicity Conference. Ewen argues that Banning, who favored image over words, marked a break at AT&T from Theodore Vail, who had emphasized educating the public through fact-based explanations in AT&T advertising and publicity. Banning told Bell public relations staffers to instead appeal "to the heart, to the sentiments." Image was more dependable in persuasion than word, Banning said. Words should be subordinate to illustration. Text should trigger feeling above thought.[24]

The trouble with Ewen's argument is that if Banning had any influence at all, it was short-lived. Arthur Page was very much of the Vail school, and it was Page from 1927 to 1946 who was in the driver's seat when it came to AT&T's public relations approach.

In literature, fiction tends to appeal to the emotion, while nonfiction is more likely to appeal to reason. Page came from the nonfiction side of the house at Doubleday. He was a historian, writer and editor interested in the presentation of fact, not in the evocation of emotion.

That is not to say that use of appeals to the higher emotions were anathema to him. AT&T advertising in his tenure was not above portraying as the "typical" AT&T investor a mother figure preparing snap beans. Nor was AT&T advertising above making patriotic appeals during World War II. The annoying shortage of telephone wire at home was because that American fighter plane in the ad illustration, its wing guns blazing, was firing the telephone wire at a Japanese warplane. But when it came to appeals to more base or prurient emotions, keep in mind Page's dislike of the naturalist school of literature.

Coping with a reduced public relations budget

AT&T REDUCED PUBLIC RELATIONS spending during the Depression, but did not gut the function as many companies do during periods of budgetary belt-tightening.

Figures on AT&T's advertising expenditures (exclusive of spending by associated companies) for 1927 through 1935 indicate the general tendency at AT&T to reduce but not eliminate spending on persuasion:[25]

Year	AT&T Advertising Budget
1927	$4,767,869
1928	5,966,675
1929	7,477,108
1930	7,173,279
1931	6,835,876
1932	5,482,858
1933	4,271,731
1934	4,645,217
1935	5,138,567

About half the money in the budget was spent on public relations or institutional advertising, the other half on promoting sale of telephone service. When operating companies argued for eliminating institutional advertising and devoting the full budget to promoting sales, Page argued that any increased revenues resulting from sales advertising would eventually work to AT&T's disadvantage by reducing customer good will. The institutional ads continued.

The social role of the phone came to be emphasized more by AT&T during the Depression. In the first 25 years, AT&T institutional ads had emphasized the importance of the telephone to business, only scantly acknowledging social uses. Male customers were depicted 10 times more frequently than females. Then in 1934, for the first time, an AT&T institutional ad showed two female customers conversing. To countermand public antipathy to emerging chain stores, the institutional ads at this time began to emphasize the local phone operation as a "home town enterprise." During Page's tenure, the institutional ads also became less austere, expanded to full-page and illustrations became the dominant element.[26]

Advertising was the most expensive communications item in the AT&T public relations arsenal. Cuts in the ad budget might be expected during a Depression. Other persuasive items such as corporate films and publicity are not nearly so expensive per person reached. The Bell System might have intensified its use of these. However, AT&T reduced its persuasive efforts across the board during the early Great Depression, until in 1935 it came under fire from an investigation of the new Federal Communications Commission.

The showing of corporate films provides an example. The audience for Bell System films rose dramatically during the early years of the Arthur Page vice presidency, but then declined even more dramatically from 1932 through 1935.[27]

Year	Total Bell System Film Showings	Estimated Audience for Bell System Films
1926	33,211	20,101,904
1927	61,225	27,634,820
1928	86,847	41,228,408
1929	131,696	52,932,769
1930	123,881	60,836,588
1931	146,474	74,074,854
1932	122,483	57,927,242
1933	117,317	48,162,371
1934	97,798	35,376,262
1935	66,856	18,557,313

Page likely had little control over fewer film showings. Local employees showed the films. The reduced workforce was needed to install and repair telephones and handle revenue-producing work, and had no time for showing movies.

Despite fewer film showings, the corporate film continued to be a major persuasive item for AT&T. More than 50 films were produced by AT&T from 1926 through 1935. One Depression-era film is especially worthy of note because of its subtle persuasive appeal.

"Getting Together" was produced by AT&T public relations in response to customer criticism of an extra charge for the new French handset telephone. The premium charge was levied by AT&T not because the new handsets were more expensive to produce and install (they were less expensive), but because the company felt it needed additional revenue and horizontal services provided a convenient source. In "Getting Together," AT&T made no mention of the cost of producing the new telephones or of the reason for the premium charge for them. But the ingenious stop motion and special effects photography of the film, whereby the various parts making up the new phone marched to martial music as they assembled themselves into a complete instrument, left viewers with the impression that the new phones were indeed more complicated and might be expected to be more expensive.[28]

AT&T had a special advantage that permitted it to become the corporate leader in use of film. Through Western Electric, AT&T controlled Electrical Research Products, Inc. (ERPI), which in turn had a near-monopoly on manufacture of equipment used to make and show sound motion pictures. While the leadership of James Ellsworth and Arthur Page helped make AT&T the leading American user of public relations films, AT&T control of ERPI gave it an advantage in development of the genre.

In the area of publicity, AT&T issued regular news releases during 1929-1935. However, the company's main publicity vehicle during the period was a clipsheet, "News and Views of Telephone Service," which superseded an earlier clipsheet called "Telephone Press Service." For the uninitiated, a clipsheet is a printed broadside resembling a small newspaper. Editors are free to clip out stories they like and send them to their own composition rooms for eventual publication. Between 1926 and 1935, AT&T and the associated Bell System companies distributed 1,419,000 copies of "News and Views of Telephone Service" to newspaper and magazine editors.[29]

During the same period, AT&T made at least two studies of the effectiveness of its clipsheet. One of the studies found that in the period March to May 1932, 284 newspapers had used 1,157 items from the clipsheet for a total of 12,525.5 column inches of publicity. The other, examining the use newspapers had made of clipsheet material during the 12 months of 1933, found that 521 newspapers had published a total of 84,800 column inches of clipsheet material.[30] While the column inches of publicity a corporation gets are not a reliable indicator of the amount of good will being built, the studies show AT&T's practice of systematically evaluating public relations devices. The constant evaluation led to considerable sophistication as ineffective techniques were discarded and effective techniques improved.

Page and the modern public relations ethic

ARTHUR PAGE'S PUBLIC RELATIONS philosophy continued to develop in 1929-1935. When Bell System staffers at the 1930 AT&T Publicity Conference asked him to define the proper functions of AT&T's Information Dept., he responded with the following delineation:

1. To be responsible for the spoken, written and picture messages of the company to the public, so that they may accurately picture in the most effective manner the company's character and ideals and practices.

2. To study and analyze the public's reactions to the company's policies and practices as well as all currents of public thought that may affect the company, and keep the executives of the company informed of the public's acceptance of our manner of furnishing service.

3. To present to the operating heads facts and ideas that will help them to give service in the most personal and satisfactory way to the public, and especially to be sure that the principal supervisory operating people have an understanding of the public relations point of view.

4. Initiative, imagination, and foresight are of particular importance in all three of these activities because creating good-will and foreseeing and obviating difficulties—both dependent upon looking into the future—are the main elements of the job.[31]

Page's conception of public relations responsibilities was well in advance of the thinking of most practitioners of the day. There was nothing novel in his charging Bell public relations staffers with responsibility for publicity, but his other three charges were innovative. In a few simple sentences, he assigned three advanced responsibilities—for keeping management posted on the state of public opinion, for advising management how to react to public opinion and for predicting trends in public opinion so that management would be ready for changed future opinion climates.

Page believed that a public relations department had both line and staff responsibilities, a concept that contradicts most textbook theory holding public relations is purely a staff function. As he conceptualized it in a 1931 speech:

> The Public Relations Department does a staff job. It plans, studies, observes and analyses (Page uses the British spelling) the business to see what are the results of its conduct on the public mind, and it advises with the operating departments on the best methods of giving service that is satisfactory to the public.
>
> Besides this staff function the Public Rel(ations) Dept. in the Bell System is responsible for advertising, publicity, motion pictures, speeches, employee magazines, etc. This is an operating function which it is convenient to put under the same head as the public relations staff function.[32]

Page continued during the period 1929-1935 to reemphasize themes he had first conceptualized in 1927-1929. Prominent among these were:

• that good service was the keystone on which to build the Bell System public relations edifice,

• that public relations was the responsibility of every employee, not just the public relations staff,

• that good communication depended not only on outward dissemination of messages, but also on getting feedback from various publics to Bell System management, and

• that employee sales efforts were an integral part of the overall Bell System public relations effort.

Regarding provision of good telephone service, Page continued to argue in the early 1930s for the associated phone companies to provide more varied and better equipment for residence customers, for beautification of telephone buildings, for improved services for rural customers and for removal of unsightly above-ground telephone poles and wires.

Regarding improved rural service and removal of above-ground plant, Page said, "If we wait until the public demands removal of poles along highways, it will cost us more than if we do it gradually and at our own convenience. And if the farmer's service gradually improves, he isn't going to rise in wrath to join the opposition forces."[33]

For the most part, Bell System officials listened sympathetically to Page's arguments. AT&T had a top management structure that appreciated the value of modern public relations. But Page was not always successful in prodding Bell System executives to action. Despite the fact that he and AT&T President Gifford urged introduction of new and more varied residence telephone services, innovations were slow in coming.

Another area where Page had little success was in getting management to allow employees to be more flexible in application of AT&T's rigid practices and guidelines. He argued that during the Great Depression, Bell System employees were better trained than ever, in large part because of increased length of service due to reduced force turnover. That employees had more experience and better training meant that they could be provided greater individual responsibility for interpreting Bell System rules. Flexibility—deciding when rules and practices were inappropriate—would result in better customer relations, he argued.

One of his favorite examples of a situation requiring flexibility involved a case where an installer was sent out to disconnect the telephone of a customer delinquent in payment of his phone bill. The installer found the customer seriously ill and in need of his phone to get help if he grew worse.

Using his judgment, the installer left the phone in service despite company rules and tariffs requiring disconnection.[34] When the ill man recovered, he went first to the phone company, where he paid his bill, saying that although many creditors were pressing him, he wanted to pay the phone bill first because only the phone company had cared about him while he was sick.

Page contended that giving employees greater flexibility would result in more customer good will, favorable news media comment and improved employee morale.[35] His arguments fell pretty much on deaf ears. The Bell System made some progress in giving employees more discretion in applying rules, but routines remained essentially inviolate, and criticism of AT&T as a monolithic monopoly unresponsive to individual needs continued.

Page was much more successful in convincing fellow executives of the importance of keeping employees informed on Bell System policy and the reasons for various routines and practices. He pointed out that in those cases where they had to defend rather than break rules, informed employees would be better able to satisfy customers than employees who could only say, "I don't make the rules, lady, I just do what I'm told."[36]

Page effectively argued that employee face-to-face and telephone communication with customers was of greater importance to building good will for the Bell System than were advertising and publicity in the mass media. In one of his more eloquent statements on the importance of employee communication in building customer good will, he said:

> ...To anyone who has tried other means of reaching the public mind the Bell System employee body appears as a Godsend. They provide a better circulation than can possibly be had by printed matter or radio. In the first place, it has a tremendously wide circulation. Telephone people have millions of contacts a year with the public. Unlike the newspaper and the radio, the employee circulation usually reaches the

public when it is interested in telephone matters. And unlike the press and the radio the employees do not have to merely tell the public something about the telephone, they can tell them what they happen to want to know about it. Moreover, as the employee is not confined to one set message, he can adapt his explanation to the type of person he is dealing with. It is like the difference between telling a story by advertisements and telling the story by a salesman attuned to the person he is talking to.[37]

Page urged that employees be briefed on how to answer questions customers frequently asked. In the early 1930s, he recommended that employees be trained to answer customer queries about why the Bell System refused to lower its service rates when other companies were lowering theirs.

He also objected to the associated company practice of waiting until opposition to a requested rate increase mounted before calling in employees to train them to answer customer objections. Demanding a long-range strategic policy of training employees instead of short-term tactical response, Page said "it seems to me that it would be easier to do it (inform employees) continuously and without pressure—to use our employee contacts to present our case in order to prevent attack rather than wait until it has developed to meet it."[38]

By 1932, Page had concluded employees of the Bell System were the single most important public in the overall AT&T public relations effort. In a speech to conferees at an annual public relations course for employees sponsored by the New York Telephone Co., he said:

... (Y)our public relations are your relations with the public and the relations with the public, you know, occur where our people operating the business come into contact with the public. Our main channel of public relations, therefore, is through the regular lines of the corporation. The people who have the most relations with the public are our operating people below the supervisory level. The consequence is that you have to have an organization completely imbued with the public relations point of view desiring good will of the public, before you can be effective.[39]

Page realized early in the Great Depression that much of AT&T's public relations message output would have to be devoted to coping with public criticism of the telephone company arising from the economic crisis. As America's biggest business, the Bell System was particularly prone to attack by elements in the population who felt "big business" was responsible for the Depression. He decided the way to cope with public discontent was for the Bell System:

1. to provide good service,

2. to rapidly conclude some rate increase cases which had been before public service commissions and in the courts for years,

3. to actively sell telephone service,

4. to stress to the public that the telephone company performed ethically in its business dealings, and

5. to stress the ever-increasing value of service consumers received for each dollar spent with the phone company

The Gifford policy of 1927 had been consciously formulated and publicized to differentiate the Bell System from other big businesses of the day, so that if a public tide of disapproval against big business arose, the Bell System would not be washed away with the tide. Now, during the Great Depression, that policy began to pay off.[40] It became the umbrella under which Page mounted the five-fold public relations defense.

The first element in the defense was continued provision of good service. To demonstrate the importance of good service to overall good will, he was fond of telling an anecdote about a Bell official riding a train from Albany to New York. An important government officer on the train, not realizing he was talking to an AT&T executive, said of the company, "Of course, these fellows are robbers and thieves, but they do know their business." Page used the anecdote to show that the man, like most of the public, respected the excellent service provided by AT&T. As for the allusion to Bell management being made of "robbers and thieves," he said, "that is because the public assumes Bell has the same grasping, greedy and acquisitive attitude they assume other corporations have."[41] The Gifford policy, Page felt, gave AT&T a means of explaining to the public that the telephone company was not as greedy as other businesses. It gave AT&T a chance to argue that it performed ethically and in the public interest.

A problem in making people believe the Gifford policy was real and sincere arose over publicity surrounding a number of requests for rate increases AT&T had filed well before the Great Depression began. These requests for higher rates were still being argued before public service commissions and the courts of various states when the Great Crash came. In the context of the Depression, publicity about the rate increases made it appear the Bell System was greedily looking for more money when other corporations were lowering prices. The rate cases threatened the credibility of the Gifford policy. Consequently, AT&T management decided in 1930 to bring all pending rate cases to speedy conclusions, and to avoid new rate cases for the duration of the Depression.[42]

Employee selling of telephone service remained a key element in creation of favorable public relations. Aggressive selling by employees was supported by AT&T through the Depression. The active hawking of telephone wares probably led to main station loss at the height of the Depression being far less than would have been the case without it.

Another important element in the Bell System's defense during the Great Depression was emphasis on the value of service received per dollar spent by customers. At both the AT&T Presidents Conference and the Bell System Publicity Conference in the fall of 1930, conferees discussed whether or not to launch a publicity campaign emphasizing to customers the low cost of telephone service compared to value received. Page and others concluded the public had no way of knowing absolutely whether Bell System rates were too high, about right or too low.

Independently, Page was conceptualizing how the public used certain broad yardsticks to judge whether or not a price was fair. Early in his Bell career, he decided the public was likely to object to prices if company insiders were caught awarding themselves "melons"—extravagant bonuses, perquisites or stock options—or if the company failed to lower prices during bad times.

Later he concluded the public had three yardsticks for deciding if prices were unreasonable:
- if unwarranted fortunes were made by insiders,
- if dramatic increases in unit prices of a product were initiated without good explanation, or
- if corporate earnings were exceptionally high.

If any of these conditions prevailed, the public was likely to conclude a company was charging too much for its products or services.

Page was aware of the potential public relations damage from failing to reduce rates during the Depression. However, a management decision to hold the line on prices had been made, and the public relations mission became defense of that position.

Page's strategy was to argue through Bell System employees, advertising and publicity that customers would be better served by AT&T giving them more for their dollar at existing rates than from reduced rates.

The important thing, Page argued in establishing the Bell System defense, was to meet public criticism of rates head-on rather than to remain silent. "If we adopt the policy of silence," he warned, "our very silence will condemn us. Other people talk both price and quality. If we talk quality only we shall leave a complete opening for any one who wishes to attack us on price—we almost invite such an attack. And if such an attack comes we shall then have to discuss price, only then we shall be doing it on the defensive."[43]

Page's main public relations emphasis, superseding all other strategy, continued during the period 1929 through 1935 to be based on encouraging corporate performance in the public interest. As he put it in a 1933 speech:

The largest function of public relations in our business... is to turn the searchlight on ourselves and see that we are actually, in every possible way, doing our job in the public interest. In other words, we should try to see in what direction the public interest will lead and where it is going to take us. Then, we want to get there before the public is even aware of what it is going to ask...

It will be a great contribution to the history of the Bell System if we succeed with this work. It is not only delivering messages; it is not merely staying in business; it is demonstrating that large enterprises can be run so intelligently in the public interest that the public will be satisfied and content with their services....[44]

All this may sound like idealistic ranting, but most Bell employees, especially managers on up, believed it implicitly—and therein lay the greatness of the Bell System in its golden age before AT&T was forced to divest itself of its operating companies.

Conversion from Democrat to Republican

PAGE'S POLITICAL PHILOSOPHY, which had taken a Republican bent in 1920 and again in 1928, continued Republican during 1929-1935.

He was philosophically opposed to the candidacy of Franklin Roosevelt and the New Deal reforms Roosevelt initiated after election. He disagreed with Roosevelt blaming big business and Republican political leaders for the Great Depression. He believed, like many of his Long Island neighbors, that Roosevelt was not the man to lead the country out of the Depression. Before the 1932 election, he wrote to Randolph-Macon College President Robert Blackwell saying, "Many people know Franklin Roosevelt personally. Most people know him as governor. Almost no one thinks of him as great, either in character or ability... There may be some poetic justice in putting Mr. Hoover out on the grounds his champions promised that he would continue prosperity. But there is no sense in electing Franklin Roosevelt in the hope he is a genius that can bring it back."[45]

Following Roosevelt's election and the start of New Deal reforms, Page's dislike intensified, due partly to the general dislike of Roosevelt by business leaders, but also to New Deal reforms that cost him several corporate directorships. He disliked the belligerence of Roosevelt Administration agencies such as the Federal Communications Commission toward the Bell System, and he felt the New Deal was destroying freedom in America by taxing away incentive to work and by making individuals dependent on federal welfare.

Two speeches and a second book

PAGE BECAME interested in the sociological implications of the telephone during the early years of the Depression. Two of his speeches deal with the subject.

The first, made in 1932 at the Lowell Institute in Boston, traced a number of changes the telephone had stimulated in American society.[46] The second, made to executives at the Bank of the Manhattan Co. in New York in 1934, dealt with the impact the telephone and AT&T in particular had on America in the past and might have in the future.[47]

The former of the two speeches became a chapter in a book edited by Page and others, *Modern Communication*, published in 1932. The book was the second on which Page's byline appeared, but the least important of the three books he wrote or helped to write in his life.[48]

Joining the AT&T and Rockefeller bank boards

WHEN THE GREAT DEPRESSION began, Arthur Page already held several important directorships. He was serving as president and a director of the Bell Telephone Securities Co. (BTSC), as a director and member of the executive committee of the Engineers Public Service Co. and as a director of the Southern Bell Telephone & Telegraph Co. These directorships, while not as rewarding financially as his base salary at AT&T, were a source of prestige for him.

During the Great Depression, he continued to expand his prestigious corporate directorships. However, New Deal reforms such as the Communications Act of 1934, which prohibited interlocking directorships in communications utilities, cost him several positions.

In March 1931, he was elected a director of AT&T. Now, for the first time, public relations had direct access not only to the president of AT&T, but to the firm's board of directors as well. As a director, he had responsibilities beyond providing a public relations viewpoint to the board. In 1933, he was named a member of the board's Employees' Benefits Committee. The post was of considerable importance, especially when AT&T's employee pension and disability benefits programs came under FCC scrutiny in the late 1930s.[49]

In February 1933, he was elected a director of the New England Telephone & Telegraph Co., one of the associated Bell Telephone companies like Southern Bell, on whose board he continued to sit.[50]

Later in 1933, he lost his position as president and director of the Bell Telephone Securities Co. He resigned both posts in October. AT&T simultaneously dissolved BTSC because management felt new federal laws and regulations on sale of securities made it impossible for the company to continue to sell AT&T stock at telephone offices around the country.[51]

By the time BTSC was dissolved, it had already done its job. In the early 1920s, when BTSC was formed to broaden ownership, AT&T stock was already more widely held than that of any other American corporation. When Page replaced David Houston as president of BTSC in late 1927, AT&T had about 423,000 stockholders. At the end of 1932, ten months before BTSC was dissolved, the number of AT&T stockholders had risen to about 700,000. The broadened ownership diluted the power of individual owners of large blocks such as the J.P. Morgan investment bank. In addition, BTSC had provided a flow of capital to the Bell System.

The reasons AT&T stopped selling its stock at local telephone offices are complex. Part of the problem was BTSC's promotion of AT&T securities on the installment plan. Early in the Great Depression, BTSC had to extend installment deadlines because many investors, especially Bell System employees, were unable to pay. In June 1933, BTSC suspended installment sales of securities pending clarification of the new Federal Securities Act.[52] When it appeared likely that installment sales of securities were forbidden by the new law (a misguided interpretation), AT&T dissolved BTSC, and Arthur Page lost the first of several directorships to the New Deal.

In August 1933, Page became president, treasurer and a director of the Aberdeen Co., a small firm with $20,000 capitalization that he formed with his brother Ralph and Herbert L. Bodman of the Produce Exchange of New York City to grow peaches in North Carolina.[53]

In March 1934, he was elected a director of the Chase National Bank of New York (later the Chase Manhattan and then J.P. Morgan Chase), a position of considerable prestige.[54] At the time he was elected, the bank was at a critical juncture. While perhaps not Rockefeller-controlled, it was certainly a Rockefeller-influenced bank. In early 1933, Winthrop Aldrich, who had married into the Rockefeller family, was named chairman of the board, replacing as chief executive officer Albert H. Wiggin, who retired.

It was Aldrich who broke the Wall Street domination of the House of Morgan (Morgan Guaranty Trust, 23 Wall Street) by recommending to the Roosevelt Administration financial reforms which undercut Morgan power.[55] Upon his election in early 1933, Aldrich moved almost immediately to restructure control of the Chase by paring its board of directors from 72 to 36 members. Page became one of the 36. He and Aldrich were both directors of AT&T when Page was elected to the Chase board.[56]

Shortly before he became a director of the Chase, it was plagued by two serious public relations problems. The first involved disclosure in the press of a $100,000 per year pension Chase directors had voted to Albert Wiggin at of his retirement. Wiggin declined to accept the pension after public objections to it arose.[57] The second problem centered on disclosure in 1933 hearings of the Senate Banking and Currency Committee of financial irregularities at the Chase. In early 1934, shortly before Page was elected a director, the bank's board reacted to criticism by appointing a board committee to investigate the charges of the Banking and Currency Committee, with Elihu Root Jr., a director of AT&T, named to serve as legal counsel.[58]

Aldrich was receptive to advice on public relations, and as years went by, came to respect Page's judgment more and more. By 1947, when Page retired from AT&T, Aldrich retained him at $25,000 per year as a public relations and business counsel to the Chase.

In 1935, Page was forced to resign his directorships of New England Bell and Southern Bell. Under provisions of the Communications Act of 1934, he had petitioned the FCC for permission to retain these directorships plus his directorship of AT&T. The FCC interpreted the Communications Act to prohibit all cross-directorships in the telephone industry, including directorships of officers in a parent company on the boards of subsidiaries. In December 1935, his petitions denied by the new FCC, Page resigned his Southern Bell and New England Telephone directorships.[59] The New Deal thus cost him two more directorships.

Carnegie Corp. trustee and other charities

PAGE ADDED prestigious new directorships in various philanthropies in 1929-1935.

In March 1934, he was elected a trustee of the Carnegie Corp. of New York, which sponsored some projects of its own, but acted mainly at the time as a funding arm for other Carnegie charities.

Steel magnate Andrew Carnegie established the Carnegie

Corp. in 1911 with a grant of $150 million. It was the first great American foundation, the prototype for many others that followed such as the Rockefeller Foundation (1913), the Duke Endowment (1924), the Ford Foundation (1936) and the Lilly Endowment (1937).[60]

The Carnegie Corp. was established both to provide funding for charities which Carnegie had established earlier in his life and to fund new projects. The charities Carnegie established earlier included public libraries, the Carnegie Institute of Pittsburgh, the Carnegie Institute of Technology (later Carnegie-Mellon University), the Carnegie Trust for the Universities of Scotland, the Carnegie Institution of Washington, D.C., the Carnegie Hero Fund, the Carnegie Foundation for the Advancement of Teaching and the Carnegie Endowment for International Peace.[61]

Until his death in 1919, Andrew Carnegie served as president of the Carnegie Corp. The board consisted of the heads of five other Carnegie charities, plus Carnegie's financial and personal secretaries.

In 1922, the board amended the foundation's charter to permit addition of seven outside trustees to the board.

In 1923, Frederick P. Keppel became president. The foundation then had income of about $6 million per year to spend. However, it had long-term financial obligations of about $40 million, mostly to other Carnegie charities. Carnegie and his early board had been overly generous in committing anticipated revenues.

When Arthur Page became a trustee in 1934, the Carnegie Corp. had little income available for new projects. By 1958, when he resigned as a trustee, large sums had come available for new projects as existing commitments were fulfilled. Rather than commit the new revenues to other Carnegie charities, the board began to fund innovative projects.[62]

In 1932, Page had made arrangements for Carnegie Corp. President Keppel to publish a commissioned biography of Andrew Carnegie. The biography was written by Burton Hendrick and published by Doubleday, Doran.[63]

In November 1934, a few months after he was elected a

trustee, Page was named to the Carnegie board's Finance Committee, which was headed by Russell Leffingwell of the House of Morgan.[64]

Page's work for the Charity Organization Society of New York became particularly important during the Great Depression. In addition to continuing as a vice president and member of the executive committee of the society, he was active on two special committees. He served with Ogden Mills on a special committee on unemployment insurance. The final report of this committee took a liberal stance, urging that COS go on record favoring unemployment insurance so long as it was established at the state rather than national level. The report proved unpopular with businessmen serving as the controlling hierarchy of COS.[65] Second, Page devoted long hours to a special Emergency Unemployment Relief Committee which operated semi-independently but in coordination with COS to cope with unemployment in New York City.[66]

In October 1931, Page was named to the COS Committee on the School of Social Work. This committee, with Columbia University, directed operation of a pioneering school to train social workers and study welfare needs in America.[67] Page held other COS assignments in the period 1929-1935, and was involved in raising funds for the organization.

Also in 1931, he became a member of the prestigious Council on Foreign Relations, the main think tank for American foreign policy, and a favorite meeting ground for the inner circle of the Eastern establishment. Incorporated in 1921, the Council was merged from two groups. One was composed of academics and diplomats assembled in 1917-1918 by Walter Lippmann on the advice of Col. Edward House to provide guidance on options for a postwar peace to President Woodrow Wilson. The other was a group of international businessmen organized by Elihu Root Sr., who had been President William McKinley's secretary of war and Theodore Roosevelt's secretary of state. Awarded the Nobel Peace Prize in 1912, Root served as president of the Carnegie Endowment for International Peace from 1910 to 1925. The Coun-

cil created in 1921 from these groups, while including business leaders, academics and diplomats, was top-heavy with
Wall Street lawyers and investment bankers. Page was an
appropriate candidate, having been an outspoken internationalist during and after World War I, the press officer for
the London Naval Conference and offered high office in the
State Dept. At the time he was elected, John W. Davis served
as president.[68]

In December 1935, he added another prestigious office
when he was elected a trustee of the Metropolitan Museum
of Art in New York.[69]

Page in 1929-1935 remained active in organizations he
had joined earlier. Among those in which he retained office
or expanded his activities were:

- *The American Federation of the Arts.* Remained
a director at least through March 1934.[70]
- *American Leprosy Assn.* Continued as a trustee
and member of the executive committee.[71]
- *American Museum of Natural History.* Expanded
his involvement, begun as a Roosevelt Memorial Assn.
trustee, by serving on two museum committees. One
committee worked to expand paid museum memberships, the other oversaw publication of the museum's
Natural History magazine.[72]
- *British Apprentice Club.* Continued as a director,
and in May 1932 was elected treasurer.[73]
- *Farmers Federation Educational and Development
Fund.* Continued to serve as chairman of the fund and
as chairman of its New York Committee.[74]
- *Long Island Biological Assn.* Continued as president. Survival of the laboratory was threatened by a
shortfall in operating capital due to the Great Depression. He devoted much of his attention to finding new
sources of funding.[75]
- *Negro Rural School Fund-Anna. T. Jeanes Foundation.* Continued as a director of the organization. In
1931, he was elected chairman of the Finance Com-

mittee, and became responsible for investing the organization's money. Return on foundation investments at the time had dropped precipitously. Some of the real estate it owned was providing a low return, and dividends on stocks had declined because of the Depression. In addition, contributions by the General Education Board dropped from $84,500 in 1928-1929 to $66,300 in 1930-1931. The General Education Board subsidies were to decline even more to $36,600 in 1932-1933. Page resisted pressure from Jeanes Fund President Arthur Wright to launch a general public fund-raising drive, and instead set about to totally revamp the foundation's investment portfolio. Under his guidance, investments were diversified. Real estate and New York City bonds were sold, and revenues reinvested in common and preferred stocks and municipal bonds. The strategy eventually paid off, but for several years after Page took charge of the Finance Committee, survival of the Jeanes Teacher program was touch-and-go. The short-run factor saving the program was increased subsidization by the General Education Board after 1933 until Jeanes Fund investment return began to improve.[76]

• *Roosevelt Memorial Assn.* Continued to serve as a trustee and member of the executive committee.[77]

Serving Vassar, Bennington, Columbia and Harvard

PAGE REMAINED a trustee of Vassar until 1933, when his term expired.[78]

In June 1934, he was elected a trustee of Bennington College in Vermont, an innovative school for women that his daughter Mollie was attending. Either simultaneously with his election or a short time later, he was named chairman of the Bennington board of trustees.[79] He was soon deeply involved in raising money for the school.

He had been a trustee of Teachers College of Columbia

University since 1928, shortly after William Russell was elevated from acting to permanent dean. Russell's distinguished deanship lasted to 1949, and made him one of America's preeminent authorities on education.

Correspondence between Page and Russell shows how much the two respected one another. In 1929, Page was named to the executive committee of the Teachers College board. In 1931, he became vice chairman of the board, a post he retained to 1959.[80]

Near the end of 1929-1935, Page's service to Harvard also began to expand.

To 1930 he served as a member of the Committee to Visit the Bussey Institute at Harvard.

In 1931, AT&T President Walter Gifford was elected to a six-year term as an overseer of Harvard. Page himself ran unsuccessfully for overseer in 1929 and 1933, placing 14th and then eighth in the elections. He was eventually elected in the 1950s.[81]

In 1934, he became a member of two Harvard alumni committees, one the Committee to Visit the Harvard University Press, the other the Committee to Visit the Department of History.[82]

In 1935, he became active in two much more important committees discussed in the next chapter, Harvard's Three Hundredth Anniversary Fund Committee, and a special committee formed to assist in revamping the Harvard School of Dental Medicine.[83]

The Walter Hines Page School of International Relations began operation at Johns Hopkins in 1930, while Arthur was at the London Naval Conference. Although the Page School trustees with whom Arthur Page had worked were unable to raise the $1 million Johns Hopkins wanted, the university decided to activate the school anyway when given assurances that at least $50,000 per year would be available to support the venture for a minimum of three years. John V.A. MacMurray, a former American minister to China, was named to head the new Page School.[84]

Although Arthur was not a trustee of the Page School, he

took a strong interest in its affairs. A number of letters between him and MacMurray are in his papers. Much of the correspondence deals with MacMurray's requests that Page arrange for donation of materials from the London Naval Conference for use as a resource at the Page School MacMurray also lobbied for Page to use his influence with Henry Stimson, Herbert Hoover's secretary of state, to get State to invite the Page School to study relations between America and the Soviet Union.[85]

In addition to his work for Bennington, Vassar, Harvard, Teachers College and the Page School at Johns Hopkins, he continued to serve in 1929-1935 as a member of the board of directors and president of the St. Bernard's School Building Fund.[86]

A private fortune isn't essential

C. WRIGHT MILLS has written of the American "power elite," and other pundits have exhaustively covered what constitutes "the Eastern" or the "WASP (white Anglo-Saxon Protestant) establishment." By 1935, while perhaps not a prince of power himself, Page was moving in ever more lofty circles. If not classifiable as a member of the establishment, he was certainly close to being one.

The various corporate boards on which he sat, the philanthropies and educational institutions he served, the government service he performed and the clubs of which he was a member put him in frequent touch with powerful Americans such as President Franklin Roosevelt, Secretary of State Stimson, Carnegie Corp. head Frederick Keppel, financier Henry James, AT&T President Walter Gifford, lawyer Elihu Root Jr., International Business Machines head Thomas J. Watson, publisher Henry Luce and other influentials such as Ogden Mills, John W. Davis, Carter Glass, Henry Morgenthau, Adolph Ochs of the *New York Times*, Col. Edward M. House and George Foster Peabody.

Arthur Page moved in influential circles, and his advice

was valued by his friends, but he lacked one prerequisite for true membership in the power elite—a personal fortune that made him not as merely rich, but super-rich. Although information on Page's financial circumstances is sketchy for 1929-1935, his personal correspondence makes it clear he did not consider himself wealthy during the Great Depression. Despite a more-than-adequate salary from AT&T, and the money he had obtained by selling his Doubleday, Page stock when he left the publishing house, he indicates in his letters that he felt hard-pressed to meet financial commitments.

In January 1931, he transferred $360,000 to trusts for his children. That transaction may have involved a good share of the capital he acquired from sale of the Doubleday, Page common stock.

In 1933, at the time of the bank holiday declared by President Roosevelt, he spent a considerable sum to protect the Page family name in North Carolina after the Page Trust Co. in Aberdeen closed for good. According to son John H. Page, his father also spent a large sum of his own money to help relatives in North Carolina whose property was threatened by debt. Between the transfer of assets to the trust for his children, and the money spent to protect the Page family name and property in North Carolina, Page may have had no large amount of capital left by 1934.[87]

That he, without legal obligation, would spend his own money to pay creditors of the Page Trust Co. and lienholders on Page family property provides an example of how highly he valued a good family name. There is no axiom of public relations that says "Persons who value their reputations will work to maintain good reputations for their employers," but perhaps there should be.

ENDNOTES

[1] See Samuel Eliot Morison, *The Oxford History of the American People* (New York: Oxford University Press, 1965), pp. 935-40.

[2] Letter from Page to Henry R. Hayes, Dec. 20, 1927, Box 1, Arthur W. Page Papers.

[3] Arthur W. Page, "The Problem of Forecasting Public Opinion in the United States," *op. cit.*

[4] Morison, *op. cit.*, p. 940.

[5] Financial pages, *New York Times.*

[6] John M. Blum, Bruce Catton, Edmund S. Morgan, Arthur M. Schlesinger Jr., Kenneth M. Stampp and C. Vann Woodward, *The National Experience* (New York: Harcourt, Brace and World, 1968), p. 661; Morison, *op. cit.*, p. 940 and *New York Times* financial pages.

[7] Elting E. Morison, *Turmoil and Tradition* (Boston: Houghton Mifflin, 1960), p. 302.

[8] Arthur W. Page, "Henry L. Stimson—A Character Sketch," *Current History*, Vol. 30 (April, 1929), p. 7.

[9] "Arthur W. Page Mentioned for Post of Minister to China," *New York Times*, Nov. 15, 1929, p. 1.

[10] *Reminiscences*, p. 56.

[11] Letter from Page's secretary to Donald Wilhelm, Jan. 9, 1930, and letters to Arthur W. and Mollie Page from State Dept. official R.B. Shipley, Sept. 28 and 30, 1933, Boxes 2-3, Arthur W. Page Papers.

[12] Elting Morison, *op. cit.*, p. 337.

[13] Transcript of press conference, Tuesday, Jan. 21, 1930, 6 p.m., in Records Group 43, London Naval Conference, 1930, National Archives and Records Service, Washington, D.C., cited here from Raleigh, *op. cit.*, p. 98.

[14] *Ibid.*, Tuesday, Jan. 28, 1930, 12 noon, cited from Raleigh, *op. cit.*, p. 99.

[15] Elting Morison, *op. cit.*, p. 338, contends that Under Secretary of State Joseph Cotton was not always certain of what Stimson was doing at London, and that Charles G. Dawes felt Stimson did not do enough to keep President Hoover informed.

[16] Blum *et al.*, *op. cit.*, pp. 666-67.

[17] Arthur W. Page, "The Meaning of the London Conference," *Vassar Quarterly*, Vol. 15 (July 1930), pp. 137-41.

[18] Letter from Page to Elting Morison, Oct. 1, 1959, Box 60, Arthur W. Page Papers.

[19] For a particularly virulent criticism of AT&T's dividend policy during the depression, see Danielian, *op. cit.*, pp. 200-21.

[20] Data on telephone main station loss and gain during the Great Depression is from American Telephone & Telegraph Co., *Annual Report* (1929 through 1941).

[21] Workforce data is from American Telephone & Telegraph Co., *Annual Report* (1929, 1933 and 1935), pp. 26, 18, and 22 respectively. Figures are rounded to nearest hundred.

[22] Arthur W. Page, *The Bell Telephone System, op. cit.*, pp. 66-74, and letter from Page to Edwin M. Clark, general plant manager of Bell Telephone Co. of Pennsylvania, June 3, 1940.

[23] Danielian, *op. cit.*, pp. 216-17, 221.

[24] Stuart Ewen, *PR! A Social History of Spin* (New York: Basic Books/HarperCollins, 1996), pp. 192-96.

[25] Advertising budget figures are from Danielian, *op. cit.*, p. 314.

[26] Arthur W. Page, "Address," speech at AT&T General Commercial Conference, May 1930, and Roland Marchand, *Creating the Corporate Soul:*

The Rise of Public Relations and Corporate Imagery in American Big Business (Berkeley: University of California Press, 1998), p. 72-84.

[27] Danielian, *op. cit.*, p. 340.

[28] *Ibid.*, pp. 302-03.

[29] *Ibid.*, p. 308.

[30] *Ibid.*

[31] Letter from Page to all Bell System presidents, Nov. 8, 1930, in possession of author.

[32] Arthur W. Page, "Public Relations," speech at Bell System General Operating Conference, May 1931.

[33] *Ibid.*

[34] *Ibid.*

[35] Letter from Page to Bell System presidents, Nov. 8, 1930, *op. cit.*, and Arthur W. Page, "Address," speech at Bell System General Commercial Conference, May 1930.

[36] Arthur W. Page, "Public Relations," speech to Bell System General Operating Conference, May 1931.

[37] *Ibid.*

[38] *Ibid.*

[39] Arthur W. Page, "Talk on Public Relations," speech at New York Telephone Co. Public Relations Course, March 28, 1932.

[40] See Arthur W. Page, "Public Relations," speech at Bell System General Operating Conference, May 1930.

[41] *Ibid.*

[42] *Ibid.*

[43] Arthur W. Page, "Public Relations," speech at Bell System General Operating Conference, May 1931.

[44] Arthur W. Page, "Our Public Relations Today and the Outlook for the Future," speech at New York Telephone Co. Public Relations Course, December 1933.

[45] Letter from Page to R.E. Blackwell, July 29, 1932, Box 2, Arthur W. Page Papers.

[46] Arthur W. Page, "Social Aspects of Communication Development," lecture at the Lowell Institute, Boston, Jan. 26, 1932.

[47] Arthur W. Page, "The Telephone—A Coming Industry," speech to employees of the Bank of the Manhattan Co. sponsored by the Junior League of New York City, November 1934.

[48] Arthur W. Page *et al.*, *Modern Communication* (Cambridge, Mass.: Houghton Mifflin, 1932).

[49] Strahan memorandum, and American Telephone & Telegraph Co. pamphlet, "Directors and Officers of American Telephone & Telegraph Co. from Incorporation," Aug. 9, 1951, p. 6.

[50] Strahan memorandum and Page's notecards.

[51] Letter from Page to board of directors, Bell Telephone Securities Co., Oct. 17, 1933, Box 68, Arthur W. Page Papers.

[52] See "Employee Stock Subscriptions," *New York Times*, March 22, 1930, p. 31, "Rules for Extensions on Stock Payments Eased," *ibid.*, Sept. 8, 1932, p. 29, and "Suspends Installment Sales until Federal Securities Act Is Clarified," *ibid.*, June 7, 1933, p. 31.

[53] Strahan memorandum.

[54] Memorandum to Page from AT&T officer R.H. Strahan, Dec. 9, 1935, in possession of author; letter from Page to Engineers Public Service Co. President D.C. Barnes, March 7, 1934, Box 5, Arthur W. Page Papers; and

letter to Page from Gardner B. Perry of Northwest Bancorporation, March 21, 1934, Box 3, Arthur W. Page Papers.

55 "A.H. Wiggins Resigns as Chairman; W.W. Aldrich Likely Successor," *New York Times*, Dec. 22, 1932, p. 1; "W.W. Aldrich Elected Chairman," *ibid.*, Jan. 12, 1933, p. 25; and Lundberg, *op. cit.*

56 "Directors Cut from 72 to 40," *New York Times*, April 6, 1933, p. 1, and "Stockholders Vote To Cut Directors from 72 to 36," *ibid.*, May 17, 1933, p. 23.

57 "A.H. Wiggins Testifies Board Voted Him $100,000 Annually for Life," *ibid.*, Oct. 18, 1933, p. 1, and "He Gives It Up," *ibid.*, Oct. 28, 1933, p. 1.

58 "Committee of Directors Appointed To Investigate Irregularities," *ibid.*, Jan. 10, 1934, p. 1.

59 Page's notecards.

60 Waldemar A. Nielsen, *The Big Foundations: A Twentieth Century Fund Study* (New York: Columbia University Press, 1972), pp. 22, 31, 34-35.

61 *Ibid.*, pp. 33-34.

62 *Ibid.*, pp. 31-40. See also memorandum from Henry S. Pritchett to Frederick P. Keppel, Dec. 6, 1933, Box 3, Arthur W. Page Papers. Pritchett says eight rather than seven outside trustees were added.

63 See correspondence between Page and Frederick P. Keppel beginning June 2, 1932, Box 2, Arthur W. Page Papers.

64 Strahan memorandum, and letter to author from Carnegie Corp. Secretary Florence Anderson, Aug. 5, 1975.

65 Letter from Page to Samuel Crowther, June 15, 1939, and attached "Report on Unemployment Reserves as Submitted to Executive Committee Charity Organization Society," Nov. 14, 1934, Box 5, Arthur W. Page Papers.

66 See especially letter from Page to Harry Field, Dec. 4, 1930; letter from Prof. Philip Cabot of Harvard to Page, Oct. 21, 1931; and letter from Page to August P. Belmont of Emergency Unemployment Relief Committee, Oct. 25, 1932; all in Box 2, Arthur W. Page Papers.

67 Strahan memorandum and 1947 Page résumé.

68 Letter to author from Council on Foreign Relations Vice President and Secretary John Temple Swing, Oct. 20, 1975, and Peter Gross, *Continuing the Inquiry: The Council on Foreign Relations from 1921 to 1996* (New York: Council on Foreign Relations, 1996), cited from web site.

69 Page's notecards, and letter to author from Metropolitan Museum of Art Assistant Archivist Ms. Frances G. Oakley, July 29, 1975.

70 The last reference to Page's directorship in the American Federation of the Arts the author was able to find appears in "Arthur W. Page, Our New Director," *The Chase* (employee magazine of the Chase National Bank), March 1934.

71 Strahan memorandum and 1947 Page résumé.

72 Strahan memorandum and Page's notecards.

73 Strahan memorandum.

74 Strahan memorandum and letter to author from James G.K. McClure Educational and Development Fund Secretary James McClure Clarke, *op. cit.*

Documentation for Page's increasing involvement in fund-raising can be found scattered in the Arthur W. Page Papers.

76 See especially Negro Rural School Fund-Anna T. Jeanes Foundation, *Annual Report* (April 28, 1932), p. 25; Minutes of the Board of Trustees, Negro Rural School Fund-Anna T. Jeanes Foundation, April 28, 1932; letter from Page to Jeanes Fund President Arthur D. Wright, June 2, 1932; letter

from Page to Spencer Trask and Co. executive C. Everett Bacon, Jan. 22, 1935; and Negro Rural School Fund-Anna T. Jeanes Foundation, *Annual Report* (1934); all in Boxes 2-3, Arthur W. Page Papers.

[77] Strahan memorandum.

[78] 1947 Page résumé.

[79] *Ibid.*, and Strahan memorandum.

[80] Information on specific offices Page held as a trustee of Teachers College is based on Strahan memorandum and telephone conversation between author and Ms. Judy Suratt, assistant to the president of Teachers College, Columbia University, Oct. 21, 1975.

[81] See especially letter to Page from Harvard Alumni Assn. General Secretary Henry C. Clark, November 1932; letter from Page to Clark, Nov. 28, 1932; letter to Page from *Le Figaro* (Paris) correspondent Morton Fullerton, April 22, 1933; and letter from Page to Fullerton, May 3, 1933; all in Boxes 2-3, Arthur W. Page Papers. Page's record in the 1929 and 1933 elections is in letter to author from Robert Shenton, an officer of Harvard College, Nov. 20, 1975.

[82] Letter to Page from Harvard Board of Overseers Executive Committee Chairman Henry James, June 30, 1934, Box 3, Arthur W. Page Papers.

[83] 1947 Page résumé.

[84] "Fund Pledged for Starting Page School," *New York Herald Tribune*, Feb. 15, 1930, and "Funds Assured for Page School," *New York Times*, Feb. 15, 1930.

[85] Letter from J.V.A. MacMurray to Page, March 11, 1930; letter from MacMurray to Page, March 25, 1931; letter from Page to AT&T President Walter Gifford, Feb. 28, 1931; letter from MacMurray to Page, June 9, 1931; telegram from MacMurray to Page, Oct. 3, 1931; letter from Page to MacMurray, Dec. 1, 1931; and other correspondence; all in Box 2, Arthur W. Page Papers.

[86] 1947 Page résumé.

[87] Letters to author from Arthur W. Page Jr., Aug. 19, 1975, and from John H. Page, Nov. 11, 1975.

CHAPTER SIX

The FCC Investigation Years, 1935-1941

A THREAT to AT&T's reputation arose in 1935 when the new Federal Communications Commission (FCC) launched a comprehensive Special Telephone Investigation. Although the investigation concluded in 1939, its after-effects persisted to 1941, presenting significant public relations challenges to Arthur Page and the Bell system public relations staffs.

The FCC's predecessor in regulating AT&T at the national level was the Interstate Commerce Commission (ICC), which was given authority to regulate interstate telephone rates by the Mann-Elkins Act of 1910.

The ICC proved a desultory regulator at best. In not one instance from 1910 to 1934 did it order AT&T to reduce long distance rates. There were rate reductions, but all were due to AT&T asking permission to reduce its own rates.

Public sentiment for more rigorous regulation of rates grew during the Great Depression. People found it hard to understand why telephone rates were not lowered when other companies were reducing their prices.

It's axiomatic in public relations that public outrage often results in government investigations. Intervention—new laws and controls on business—usually follows the investigation. That AT&T was not immune to investigation and more stringent regulation became apparent in April 1931, when a Congressional committee that investigated AT&T issued its report. The *Preliminary Report on Communications Companies*, informally called the Splawn Report, charged there was little if any formal federal regulation of the telephone industry. Americans were entitled to know if they were being overcharged for their phone service, whether or not they were satisfied with the quality of that service, said Splawn.

Before the Splawn Report was published, President Franklin Roosevelt asked Congress to place the communications industry under regulation by a single federal agency. Congress responded with the Communications Act of 1934, which created the FCC and empowered it to regulate the telephone, broadcasting and telegraph businesses in America.

On March 15, 1935, the 74th Congress adopted Public Resolution No. 8 empowering the FCC to undertake a comprehensive investigation of the telephone industry.[1]

Responsibility for conducting the Special Telephone Investigation was given to the Telephone Division of the FCC. Commissioner Paul A. Walker was placed in charge of the investigation, for which Congress appropriated $1.5 million.

AT&T reacts to investigation

AT&T INITIALLY SAID of the Special Telephone Investigation that it continued to welcome regulation as always. Soon after the investigation was announced, AT&T President Gifford answered a reporter's question by saying, "In a business as extensive as ours which so vitally concerns so many people, the public has a right to the fullest information as to how its affairs are conducted. We therefore have no objection to investigation by properly constituted authorities at any time. We have no skeletons in the closet to be exposed."[2]

As the investigation dragged on, the FCC uncovered some irregularities—call them bones in the closet, if not full skeletons. AT&T became increasingly combative. The reason given for the change was that the FCC was unfair in denying it an opportunity to present its own testimony during hearings, and for refusing to allow its lawyers to cross-examine

FCC witnesses. Many AT&T executives felt the FCC was engaging in a witch-hunt to destroy big business. The company summarized its position in its 1937 *Annual Report*, published immediately after conclusion of formal FCC hearings:

> ...(The inquiry) has been one-sided throughout. The Company was denied not only the right to cross-examine investigation witnesses and to be heard in its own behalf, but was denied the right to have included in the record written material which it had prepared and considered necessary to point out serious and important errors affecting most of the investigators' reports...[3]

Errors notwithstanding, Commissioner Walker's Telephone Division did a monumental job of analyzing AT&T. Tens of thousands of pages of testimony and statistics were accumulated. The FCC questioned long distance rates; the relationship of AT&T to its operating companies; the relationship of AT&T to its Long Lines Dept. and the Western Electric Co.; AT&T's license contracts with subsidiaries; the stranglehold Western Electric's Electrical Research Products, Inc. (ERPI) had on the sound motion picture business; the way in which AT&T used patents, especially those developed by the Bell Telephone Laboratories, to control competition; massive expenditures to enhance public relations and influence local and national government officials; and administration of company pension and disability benefit funds.

As a result of the investigation, the FCC and AT&T negotiated a set of long distance rate reductions. The reductions were the most significant result of the probe.

From 1926 to 1930, AT&T had of its own volition asked the ICC to approve long distance rate reductions resulting in estimated savings to customers of $11 million annually. From 1930 to 1935, AT&T held the line on interstate long distance rates. Not until 1935 and 1936, the first years of the FCC investigation, did AT&T again offer to reduce long distance rates. In these two years, AT&T asked for and received permission from the FCC to introduce rate reductions estimated to save customers $8 million annually. The reductions were by volition of AT&T, without formal negotiations.[4]

The FCC felt the profits of AT&T's Long Lines Dept. were still too high in comparison to earnings of the operating telephone companies. It entered into negotiations with AT&T for further reductions. As a result, AT&T introduced reductions in 1937 designed to saving long distance customers $12 million annually, and another $19.5 million beginning in 1940-1941.[5]

Had the FCC in fact uncovered evidence at the national level, where ICC regulation had been weak, that AT&T was making more money than it should? Arguably no. In 1937, AT&T Long Lines earnings were 7.48 percent of assets. That was in line with the average rate of return being earned by the operating telephone companies whose rates were regulated by supposedly more aggressive state public service commissions. In 1937, nine of the Bell System operating companies earned less than six per cent on assets; seven earned between six and seven per cent; ten earned between seven and eight per cent, in the same range as Long Lines; and one earned more than eight per cent. Had the FCC not ordered the $12 million rate reduction in January 1937, Long Lines earnings in the year would have been a bit higher than 7.48 per cent.[6]

The Gifford policy, foundation of AT&T public relations from 1927 forward, was an appeal for government to let AT&T regulate itself. While the FCC investigation of Long Lines rates provided some evidence that in the absence of strong regulation AT&T would maximize profits where it could, the evidence uncovered was hardly profound. Still, the FCC had reason to be suspicious of AT&T's intentions.

The FCC investigation prodded AT&T's public relations staff to reexamine how well the Bell System was living up to its commitments to the public. The company became a little more open and honest. In its 1936 *Annual Report*, it listed a few subsidiaries that had not appeared before—the Christian-Todd Telephone Co. subsidiary of Southern Bell, the Tri-State Telephone and Telegraph Co. and Dakota Central Telephone Co. subsidiaries of Northwestern Bell, the Nassau Smelting and Refining Co. subsidiary of Western Electric, the 195 Broadway Corp. subsidiary of AT&T, responsible for the company's headquarters building, and the Empire City Subway Co. subsidiary of New York Telephone.[7]

Despite some irregularities uncovered by the probe, AT&T emerged from the investigation relatively unscathed. Page deserved some credit for that. Shortly before the FCC sent its final report to Congress, his old roommate from the Lawrenceville School, Ike Kampmann, sent him a clipping from the *San Antonio Evening News* that said:

> ...American Telephone and Telegraph has weathered the exhaustive investigation of its affairs by the Federal Communications Commission in a manner to arouse the envy of beleaguered electric utilities. The F.C.C.'s heaviest guns have failed to disturb its equilibrium or dent its armor.
>
> Keen New York analysts ascribe three reasons for A.T.&T.'s virtual immunity to "political attack." First is that, unlike electric utilities, it can and does follow a single-minded and coherent policy. Second, the government cannot very well threaten to set up direct competition for the telephone company. Third and most important, it has a beautiful system of public relations, including skillful use of institutional advertising and a huge list of stockholders.
>
> The man most responsible for this happy state of affairs is Vice-President Arthur W. Page... Mr. Page has been with American Telephone for 10 years and what he says about public relations goes—with Walter Gifford and everybody else.[8]

On April 1, 1938, FCC Commissioner Walker sent his proposed report to Congress, specifying that it was *his* proposed report and not the final report of the full FCC. On Oct. 25, the FCC gave AT&T 30 days (extended to 40 days) to reply to Walker. In its response, AT&T contended the opportunity for reply was not an adequate substitute for the opportunity denied it during the hearings to present its own evidence and cross-examine witnesses. The brief charged the hearings were unfair and incapable of producing reliable conclusions, and that the proposed report was "incorrect, incomplete and contained unsound recommendations."[9]

In June 1939, the FCC transmitted a watered-down version of Commissioner Walker's proposed report to Congress as its final report.[10] Congress was not receptive to the recommendations. It avoided action on the single most dangerous recommendation, that AT&T be made to divest Western Electric. The Justice Dept. with antitrust enforcement powers also disregarded the recommendation.[11]

Page writes his last book

THREE BOOKS, one by Page himself, grew directly from the FCC investigation of AT&T.

Horace Coon's *American Tel and Tel* is superficial. In contrast, Noobar Danielian's *A. T. & T. The Story of Industrial Conquest* is a scholarly indictment of the Bell System by a Harvard professor who left teaching to serve on the Special Telephone Investigation staff. The book so upset Page that he wrote his third and final book, *The Bell Telephone System*, as a point-by-point refutation of Danielian's allegations.

Danielian gave examples of what he thought unethical behavior uncovered by the FCC probe. He described a dozen cases of a Bell operating company using paid advertising to buy the favor of newspaper editors. In a letter urging Bell public relations vice presidents to read the book, Page said it showed:

1. Something of the philosophy of those who believe that regardless of how an enterprise is conducted, large enterprise is too dangerous for the country to have.

2. Also, particularly in the chapter on public relations, how isolated indiscretions—even if they have to
be collected over a 25-year period, and even if they
are contrary to the actual operating practices—can be
used to build up a case damaging to reputation.[12]

Page's *Bell Telephone System* is an exercise in damage
control, a tightly reasoned argument for corporations to perform in the public interest and a cogent rationale for the
importance of public relations to big business success.

Prescott Mabon says Page finished the book in about six
weeks.[13] Letters Page wrote to clear portions of the manuscript indicate he worked on it for more like three months.[14]

The book was published in 1941 by Harper. Because Page
had written it on company time, he assigned all royalties to
AT&T.

The book wasn't a runaway best seller, but it did get to
the public. AT&T bought large quantities, first of the
hardbound edition, and then of a cheaper softcover version,
for distribution to shareholders, employees, libraries, people
in the mass media and other opinion leaders.

Most of the book deals with AT&T policy and with the
company's performance during the period 1925 through
1940 in meeting its public promises. Data is presented to
support Page's contentions that the Bell System during the
15-year period had provided ever-better telephone service
at reasonable cost, that employees had been provided just
and reasonable wages and other benefits such as shorter
hours and pensions and that investors had been treated fairly.

Other portions of the book deal with a defense of AT&T
control of Western Electric and the Bell Telephone Laboratories, which the FCC had challenged.

Three chapters are devoted to the FCC investigation and
federal and state regulation of the telephone industry. Ob-
jecting to the manner in which the FCC investigation had
been conducted, Page summed up the reasons why AT&T,
which normally welcomed regulation, had objected strongly
to the FCC inquiry:

This was a most unusual proceeding for a business that had long advocated and lived with regulation. But there were two compelling motives to register every possible objection to the methods of the investigation.

Character is an asset of a business. Reputation affects the customers, the stockholders, and the employees. The method of the investigation, far from tending to improve service or economy, was calculated to create discord, destroy morale and frighten investors. The Bell System would have been derelict in its responsibilities had it not protested.

In the second place, the people who make up the Bell System are citizens of the United States with standing in their various communities. They have children and friends like other people and their reputations mean something to them. They have, therefore, every reason for deep seated personal resentment when an agency of the Government which they help to support, sets out to attack their characters.[15]

Page valued his reputation and AT&T's. He grew incensed when his reputation or his company's was questioned. Citizen Page had worked to build a life of service to others and a personal reputation beyond reproach. He worked at AT&T to encourage all employees to give the corporation a similar reputation. In a chapter of his book dealing with Bell System public relations, he referred back to his days as editor of the *World's Work* to justifying the public relations function, saying, "It seemed to me then, as it does now, that all business in a democratic country begins with public permission and exists by public approval. If that be true, it follows that business should be cheerfully willing to tell the public what its policies are, what it is doing, and what it hopes to do."[16]

Page had first used the sentence "All business in a democratic country begins with public permission and exists by public approval" in a 1939 speech to railroad executives.[17] The sentence became a common slogan in the utterings of Bell System public relations executives after it was included in *The Bell Telephone System*. Better than perhaps any other single statement by Page, it summed up the keystone premise of his public relations philosophy.

The Bell Telephone System contains other important elements of Page's philosophy. He makes it clear in the book that he regarded publicity as of greater importance than advertising in keeping the public informed.[18]

He wrote a persuasive, not an objective book. Two deletions made in the manuscript before publication show that the public relations vice president was the author.

One of the deletions occurs in what is otherwise a verbatim reprint of Walter Gifford's 1927 NARUC speech in the book. The speech appears as it was delivered except for deletion of a few lines. The passage deleted is one in which Gifford had quoted Harvard Business School Professor Philip Cabot praising the Bell System. In *A. T. & T.*, Danielian pointed to a cozy relationship between AT&T and Cabot extending back to the early 1920s. Page realized that including the reference to Cabot in the reprinted Gifford speech might be embarrassing to Cabot and to AT&T.[19]

Another deletion occurs in the chapter on big business ethics.[20] As a case to show the Bell System observed its stated policy of refusing to pay graft to politicians, Page had planned to tell the story of how the Bell System had declined to make a political contribution demanded by Louisiana demagogue Huey Long. Immediately after the Bell System refused to cave in to the shakedown demand, Louisiana regulators ordered a reduction in Southern Bell rates in the state. It would have been far less expensive for Bell to make the political contribution. Southern Bell objected to inclusion of the material. Huey Long's forces were still strong in his home state.[21] Page substituted several less explosive examples of minor political figures unsuccessfully trying to shake down AT&T.

While Page skirted the issues of Cabot and Huey Long, he made head-on attacks on several charges and allegations raised by Danielian and the FCC.

Both the FCC and Danielian alleged that the Bell System used newspaper advertising to influence the attitudes of editors and publishers. Danielian charged that Bell companies used newspaper advertising not only to create good will among readers, but to dispense patronage to editors and publishers who favored AT&T editorially, and to buy the good will of hostile newspapers. Page countered that newspaper advertising was controlled by the Bell operating companies. All instances the FCC had uncovered of an operating company using advertising to buy good will instead of to inform had occurred over a 15- to 20-year period in the territory of a single operating company, he said. He doesn't name the company, but it was Southern Bell. He added that the instances uncovered were in direct violation of clearly stated AT&T policies for advertising by subsidiaries.

Arguing that the operating companies advertised in almost all newspapers published in their territories, with no discrimination on the basis of the editorial stance of the papers toward the Bell System, Page pointed out that the policy of the Bell System for more than 20 years had been to avoid attempts to control the press by giving or withholding advertising.[22] Summing up his own attitudes towards the use of advertising to influence publications, Page said: "It is perfectly clear that no business, big or little, has a right to live in a democracy if it bases that right on the practice of corrupting the press."[23]

Resurrecting AT&T's brief participation in the electric industry's public information bureaus in the late 1920s, Danielian criticized bureau attempts to propagandize schoolchildren. Page countered in *The Bell Telephone System* by restating the Bell policy of going to schools only by request. "It is unquestionably good for the telephone industry to have the oncoming generation know how to use the telephone and understand the physical forces back of it," he said. "On the other hand, the Bell System does not want to ask the public schools to spend the public's money for preliminary sales work for it. As a result, the program adopted is to furnish printed matter or speakers or demonstrations or movies within reason when the school authorities ask for them."[24]

Page had resisted pressures within the System for more

aggressive school relations. In an internal memo written more than a year before publication of *The Bell Telephone System*, he said:

> It seems clear to me that within reason it is our duty to furnish the schools at their request with information about the business as we do other groups. But I think it essential that it be done only at their request. I am clear that we do not want to press anything on the schools, nor offer them anything, nor instigate any request from them.
>
> Within reason what they ask for on their own initiative let's give them when we can. Beyond that let's leave them alone.[25]

Page's school policy stayed in effect until after his retirement in 1946. Then pressures developed within AT&T's board for Bell participation in a postwar program launched by industrialists to provide "economic education" to American schoolchildren. Steering a careful course, John Shaw and other public relations staffers mapped a more intensive school relations program while avoiding the "economic education" tack being taken by many firms.[26]

To refute the Danielian charge that Bell used propaganda fronts, Page noted that it was System policy to clearly identify the source of all publicity it released, to do its own talking directly to the public and not to pay other people or other firms to talk for it.[27] He added that the Bell System spent slightly less than one per cent of total operating revenues on public relations and paid advertising.[28]

The Bell Telephone Hour

FROM 1908 FORWARD, the main outlet for AT&T's national advertising was the mass circulation magazine. In April 1940, "The Bell Telephone Hour," AT&T's first attempt to influence the public through network radio, went on the air.

Planning for the program began at the 1930 Bell System Publicity Conference. There, John Shaw was asked to explore the possibilities of radio. He submitted a report in 1931 recommending that Bell sponsor a national show. From then until 1939, however, the recommendation remained in limbo.

One reason the recommendation wasn't immediately implemented is that Bell executives couldn't agree on how best to use radio. Some felt AT&T should sponsor a national program on behalf of the operating companies, while others felt the operating companies should sponsor their own programs on local stations. There was also disagreement on the type of program that would be most in keeping with telephone company character.

Probably the biggest obstacle, however, was resistance to Bell radio advertising by the company's N.W. Ayer and Son advertising agency.[29] After Shaw submitted his 1931 memorandum on a national show, Ayer advised AT&T to wait until radio developed further, and until it could find a program that would "reach the maximum mass audience without descending to sordid depths."[30]

The FCC's final report to Congress in 1939 may have been the factor that precipitated action from AT&T and Ayer. In the report, the FCC said:

> The Bell System does comparatively little advertising by radio, despite the fact that it is one of the beneficiaries of radio broadcasting through the leasing of circuits for program transmission service. The reasons, as stated by one of its advertising agents, for the Bell System's failure to advertise more extensively over radio are twofold: first, such advertising would direct the public's attention to the amount of money being spent for advertising purposes, and second, the probable adverse effects upon the established goodwill of newspaper editors.[31]

A few months after the FCC report was issued, Page ordered AT&T Information Dept. staffer Tommy Cook to coordinate with N.W. Ayer the production of six sample musical programs including commercials to be played for the approval of Bell System executives.[32]

By March 1940, Page was writing to Bell System presidents to say that negotiations had been concluded with NBC's Red Network for coast-to-coast airing of the weekly "Bell Telephone Hour." N.W. Ayer was to handle production of the weekly broadcasts, budgeted at $950,000 for the first year.[33]

Soon on the air, the show, a half-hour long despite its name, presented musical fare ranging from classical selections to familiar favorites, with emphasis on semiclassical and classical music. A 57-member orchestra assembled from the New York Philharmonic, the Metropolitan Opera and other sources performed selections. Donald Voorhees conducted the orchestra. The initial lead male and female vocalists were James Melton and Francia White.[34]

Cook was self-confessedly "scared stiff" of the assignment because he knew little about classical music. He was nonetheless placed in charge of coordinating "The Bell Telephone Hour" with producer N.W. Ayer.[35]

The audience was as large as might be expected for a classical music show on network radio. By the end of the first 20 weeks the program had been on the air, its Crossley ratings had crept into the 6.0 range, meaning about six million Americans weekly were listening to it. By the winter of 1940-1941, when prime time audiences were larger, the ratings jumped into the 10.0 to 11.0 range, making the "Telephone Hour" one of the more popular of the eight musical programs being aired on network radio. However, the Crossleys for the show never came close to the average 39.0 ratings being enjoyed by Jell-o's "Jack Benny" program.

Although the Crossleys for the "Telephone Hour" did not set listenership records, Arthur Page was satisfied with the program. He knew that audiences for classical and semiclassical to "pop" music shows were heavy with literate, affluent, opinion-leading Americans. The program was dignified, in keeping with the type of reputation (or "image") the Bell System wished to communicate. Content of the program was noncontroversial. Only about one per cent of the fan mail generated by the program was critical of it or the Bell System. Finally, even during the summers, when Crossleys for the "Telephone Hour" regularly dipped into the 6.0 area, the cost per 1,000 persons reached was only $2.77, compared to a cost of $3.29 per 1,000 impressions for AT&T's magazine advertising.[36]

Keeping employees informed:
emphasis on supervisors

PAGE CONTINUED in 1935-1941 to stress the importance of an informed employee body to Bell System public relations.

The main mass medium used by the Bell System to inform employees continued to be the magazine. By 1940, all the Bell System companies were publishing them for employees. Many had been using magazines for decades.[37] AT&T and the operating companies also used pamphlets, employee bulletins, internal newspapers and other print media to keep employees up-to-date.

Page realized that mass media alone were insufficient to keep employees informed. Under his guidance, public relations staffs developed an efficient program whereby themes covered in employee mass media were reinforced in small-group discussions led by first-line supervisors. By 1940, this formal employee discussion program had been in operation for years.[38] According to Page, the sessions were held not to convince workers how well off they were, but to give employees an interest in the business for which they worked.[39]

When public relations pioneer Glenn Griswold asked Page for his opinion of a pamphlet Griswold produced for Studebaker employees, Page responded, "The pamphlet you sent seems terse, convincing and informative, - a good pamphlet. Our experience has been that informative pamphlets are a fundamentally useful means of reaching employees but they are not very effective unless they are used as a means of discussion between the first line of supervision and the rank and file of employees. We feel that discussion added to reading is essential to any real effectiveness...."[40]

Page saw an additional advantage in employee-supervisor discussion sessions. Because employees could ask questions at the meetings, such as the one held with employees each year for supervisors to discuss the AT&T *Annual Report*, supervisors felt obligated to study before such sessions so that they would be prepared to answer questions likely to come up. Thus supervisors became particularly well informed on current issues facing the Bell System.[41]

Showmanship enters into
AT&T displays and special events

BELL SYSTEM USE of displays and exhibits became increasingly sophisticated in the 1930s. The pseudo-event tradition started by Alexander Graham Bell with his early "live call" meetings in the 1870s and expanded by Jim Ellsworth from 1908 to 1926 grew to maturity during the tenure of Arthur Page in 1927-1939.

The "Weavers of Speech" exhibit at the 1933 Century of Progress Exposition at Chicago, in which live operators at work were highlighted by overhead spotlights, attracted critical acclaim and marked AT&T's growing sophistication in entertaining the public at events that attracted large crowds. The Chief Statistician's Division carefully measured the impressions and reactions of visitors.

AT&T in 1939 opened its crowd-pleasing displays at the New York World's Fair and San Francisco Golden Gate International Exposition. At New York, 50-foot-high panels depicting a lineman and an operator at work greeted visitors as they entered the AT&T exhibit. That same year, in cooperation with Illinois Bell Telephone, AT&T was putting the finishing touches on its permanent display at Chicago's Museum of Science and Industry.

The Bell System's exhibit at the New York World's Fair drew about eight million visitors in the summer of 1939.

One of the most popular displays there and at San Francisco was a device called the "Voder." With 14 keys and pedals, the Voder, when played by a trained operator, could synthesize human speech.[42] The New York and San Francisco exhibits also featured the placing of some 60,000 long distance calls by visitors while another 2 1/2 million spectators listened. The Bell System gave free hearing tests to some two million visitors at the two locations, and later analyzed 500,000 of the tests at the Bell Telephone Laboratories in order to develop a profile of the hearing characteristics of the American population.[43] By the time the second season for the two expositions had concluded in 1940, some 20 million visitors had passed through the two Bell System displays at New York and San Francisco.[44]

By 1940, even the humble telephone open house, which had been a staple in the Bell System public relations arsenal for some 20 to 30 years, had taken on a plating of showmanship. The open house had begun with invitations to customers to come in to see the local phone company's central office switchboard in operation. Gradually, visitors were permitted to see more and more of the central office, until the open house evolved into a tour of all local phone facilities. By 1940, subscribers were being shown not only the entire central office, but elaborate displays such as "Hear Your Telephone Voice" as well. The crowd-pleasing displays were shipped from town to town as needed.[45]

Arthur Page felt that limited Bell System participation in national expositions was good business, but he also recognized that national displays were expensive. He turned down many invitations for Bell System participation at national gatherings.[46] The local telephone open houses, however, he felt to be well worth the money spent.

AT&T financial relations: envy of big business

THE AT&T FINANCIAL RELATIONS program was the envy of big business in America from the 1920s through the 1940s. Although relations with stockholders, bondholders, banks and investment houses were the ultimate responsibility of AT&T's Treasury Dept., Page's public relations staff played an important role in guiding the program.

The AT&T Treasury Dept. handled actual release of materials such as letters to stockholders. The Information Dept. wrote the form letters and other messages, and was responsible for assuring that the messages left the desired impressions of AT&T.

From around 1929 through the 1940s, AT&T's messages to the financial public consisted of five basic items: a welcoming letter sent to new stockholders; a booklet entitled "Some Financial Facts," updated annually and sent to new stockholders and members of the financial community; annual reports; quarterly earnings statements sent with dividend checks; and a letter of regret sent to stockholders who disposed of their stock.[47]

In addition to these standard communications, AT&T on occasion sent special messages to the financial public. In the late 1930s, for example, AT&T included a notice offering stockholders various pamphlets published by the company with its quarterly dividend checks.[48]

All the publicity and goodwill material would not have created favorable opinion of AT&T in the financial community had the company's earnings performance been poor. Even during the Great Depression, when AT&T failed to earn its $9 dividend, it continued to pay the dividend by taking money from surplus, its "savings." Reliably paying the dividend gave AT&T a reputation for being the safest stock on Wall Street in which to invest. Further, the company had a reputation in the investment community for being one of the best managed in America.

Page played a major role in developing AT&T's financial policies. He was among the executives who argued for an increased ratio of stock to bonded indebtedness. As president of the Bell Telephone Securities Co. and in the years thereafter, he saw that policy implemented. In 1920, AT&T raised only 53 per cent of its new capital from stock sales.

The remainder of its new capital came from sale of bonds, and to a minor extent, from bank loans. By 1940, AT&T was raising 69 percent of its new capital by stock sales, and Page continued to argue for the higher ratio.[49]

Page was among the management leaders who called for a higher rate of return on assets for the Bell System during 1935-1941. Although Walter Gifford in outlining his financial policy at Dallas in 1927 did not mention the specific rate of return AT&T would seek as acceptable, the figure aimed at in the late 1920s was five per cent. By the late 1930s, AT&T was seeking a rate of return on assets in the seven per cent range. In a memo to public relations staffer Doug Williams, Page laid the five per cent figure to rest, saying "...(T)here is one thing I don't want to do any more, although I was responsible for it before, and that is, I don't want to ask any questions or do anything at any time which might imply that 5 per cent. is enough to run this business on, for the simple fact is that it isn't."[50]

Old AT&T public relations staffers sometimes contend that public relations "went to hell in a basket" after Arthur Page and Walter Gifford retired following World War II. They argue that after the Page-Gifford retirements, the Dallas policy was gradually eroded as new officers pursued ever-higher rates of return for AT&T. But the rate of return the Bell System was already seeking in the late 1930s and the Page memorandum to Doug Williams make it obvious that pursuit of greater profit—erosion of the Dallas ideal—was already under way while Page and Gifford were still on watch.

Sticking to telephone business

PAGE'S BELIEF that AT&T should always speak for itself, and not use outside spokespersons, extended to the frequent invitations AT&T received to participate in propaganda campaigns aimed at persuading the public of the benefits of "free enterprise," "democracy," "freedom" and the like.

Many of Page's letters turn down invitations for AT&T to

participate in such propaganda efforts. He declined a 1940 invitation for AT&T to sponsor a series of radio broadcasts on "What Is Democracy, Anyhow?" by writing "If we use the stockholders (sic) money to talk to the public I think we must confine our talk to those subjects to which our stockholders have designated us to act i.e., the telephone business. I don't think we can use their money to promote Democracy, Religion or the Ten Commandments. Those things are more important than telephony, but we are not chartered to work in those fields."[51]

He particularly kept AT&T out of right-wing promotions of "free enterprise." While defense of free enterprise is certainly a legal right of businesses, participation in such efforts has all too often in American history made big business look foolish because the rhetoric of such campaigns is scoffed at by citizens, or simply ignored.

A clear public relations ethic

PAGE BY 1935-1941 HAD DEVELOPED a clear-cut view of the role public relations should play in corporate affairs.

At the 1938 Seventh International Management Conference in Washington, he delineated four elements necessary to a successful business public relations program.

First, he said, the business had to have a top management that had analyzed its overall relations with the publics it served, and which was constantly on watch for changes in public desires.

Second, the business needed a system for informing all employees of the general policies and practices of the company.

Third, it needed a system for giving contact employees the knowledge they required to be reasonable and polite, and the incentive of knowing that these qualities counted in their pay and promotion.

Fourth, it needed a system for getting employee and public questions and criticisms back to management so that management could adjust the corporation to make it conform to public desires.[52]

The speech does not list publicity as a prerequisite, but Page acknowledged that businesses had to inform customers through employee contacts, advertising, publicity, speeches and other messages.

In 1942, he added face-to-face and mass media communication as a fifth prerequisite for effective corporate public relations programs.[53] He treated the publicity function, regarded by some practitioners even today as an end-all, as an afterthought, and then only as one part of the overall function.

A theme stressed often by Page in this period is the need for business to constantly adjust itself to the changing desires of society. In 1938 he said, "The task which business has, and which it has always had, of fitting itself to the pattern of public desires, has lately come to be called public relations."[54]

In several cases, he compared the problem of business to American colonists convicting British Governor Hutchinson of Massachusetts of "treason" against a state that did not yet exist outside the minds of the Sons of the Revolution. He argued that the American public treated big business just as the colonists had treated Hutchinson. The public could convict a business in its mind of not having done something in the past that the people at some future time decided it should have done. He warned New York Telephone employees in 1938, "... (T)he public convicts the business of not having performed... before it was told (to act). The only safeguard for those of us in a large business, therefore, is to keep a pretty careful watch on the way people's minds are running, figure out the coming public attitudes, what the public decisions are likely to be—and then be ready for them. We must try not to be in the position of being convicted of treason. We must obey the rules even before they are passed."[55]

Another theme in several of Page's 1935-1941 speeches is that public relations can't be used as a cloak or cosmetic to mask failure to perform in the public interest. No amount of cosmetic publicity or advertising would for long delude the public, he warned. In one of his more pointed refutations of cosmetic public relations, he said to New York Telephone executives, "In discussing our public relations... I don't want to make it appear that we are talking about a cloak, or a special method... I am not talking about stage management. I am... talking about character. The thing we are trying to do is to be the kind of employees who want to serve the public, who want to be friends with their neighbors, who have a pride in their own profession... and who want to see that this profession is held in high esteem by other people because it deserves to be...."[56]

Again in 1938, he warned managers, "Publicity is an important part of public relations, but in business as in most human affairs, what you do is more important than what you say. It is always possible to make a good statement on a good set of facts, but no more in business than in politics can you fool all the people all the time, and if you expect to stay in business long, an attempt to fool even some of the people some of the time will end in disaster."[57]

Page clearly understood that public opinion played a critically important role in corporate survival. At any time, he explained at the Seventh International Management Congress, hostile public opinion could be converted into controls on business—new laws, federal regulation through various commissions or the ultimate control, withdrawal of patronage by consumers. [58]

The American public, he contended, was afraid of big business for two main reasons: it feared concentration of power, and it disliked the arrogance big business sometimes showed. The answer, he argued, was for big business to avoid abuse of power, showing the public it could be reasonable and polite. If big business failed to placate the public, he warned, the public would restrict corporate freedom. Then corporations whose freedom was restricted, such as the railroads, lost their power to serve in the public interest. The result was a vicious cycle of ever-poorer performance, more public hostility and increased limits on corporate power.[59]

"The political test comes down to this," Page said in another of his judgments. " If the reputation of big business is good enough for the public, no one representing the public—whether in press, politics, or any other capacity—will be hostile to it. Because of the ordinary human suspicion of size, big business will always be closely scrutinized. It will have to be a better citizen than if it were smaller. It will have to be good enough to have public confidence. Many people feel that there isn't a possibility of getting to such a state. But certainly there is no reason to believe that good public relations are impossible until business, by and large, has put the same thought and effort on the subject that is put on research, production and selling."[60]

By 1935-1941, Page was showing an increased optimism at progress being made in attitudinal research both within the Bell System and by outside polling firms, although he recognized that research results were imperfect.

In a 1938 speech, he said measurement of opinions of Bell System customers pointed to four important conclusions.

First, Americans almost universally believed Bell System service to be good.

Second, the public by and large suspected that the charges for service were too high. The suspicion about rates was due to lack of knowledge of the cost of providing telephone service. As a remedy, he pointed to a before-and-after study of customer attitudes conducted by Bell of Pennsylvania in which opinions about the cost of service were much more favorable after customers had attended a telephone open house and seen how telephone people and complex equipment were teamed to serve them. The results convinced him that telephone open houses were worth the expense.

Third, data indicated that the more customers knew about the Bell System, the better they liked it.

Fourth, people in higher income groups tended to know more about the Bell System than people in lower economic brackets. Knowledge of the Bell System was particularly low among people in the bottom economic brackets—who often did not have telephones.[61]

Decades ahead of other public relations professionals, Page was especially concerned about the attitudes toward the Bell System held by low-income groups. He called for a thorough examination of Bell System relations with black American and other low-income ethnic groups. Because of the New Deal, he felt, the "underprivileged third" in American society had more impact on public opinion in the 1930s than it had had in the past. He was convinced the influence of low-income Americans was likely to continue, and that the Bell System for practical if not humanitarian reasons needed to improve its relations with the disadvantaged.[62]

Although Page was far-sighted in calling for improved relations with low-income groups, little action resulted in response to his plea. It took the race riots of the 1960s to shake AT&T into effective affirmative action.

Perhaps the most eloquent speech Page made in the period 1935-1941 was entitled "Industrial Statesmanship." It was delivered before executives of the Chesapeake and Ohio Railway Co. in 1939.

The opening of the speech, noteworthy for the philosophy it outlined, delineated how Page felt the public would move to control business if unhappy with it.

All business begins with public permission and exists by public approval. The public permission takes the form of charters, licenses and legal authorizations of one kind or another. Public approval is generally represented by reasonable profits, reasonable freedom of action and a few kind words. A lack of public approval is expressed in a good many ways—laws, regulations, commission rulings, investigations, public hostility and most vital of all, by a lack of patronage. The purpose of public relations is to deserve and maintain public approval....[63]

Page believed that actions in the public interest were far more important than publicity in creating good will for business. In "Industrial Statesmanship," he made one of his earliest references to his belief that public relations was "90 per cent doing, and only 10 per cent talking about what was being done." That aphorism became, through widespread repetition, the Bell System definition of public relations. In the speech, he said:

> ...In my opinion, the conduct of a big business in a democracy consists of 90 per cent. of what is done and 10 per cent. or thereabouts in explaining it, but I still think that 10 per cent. is a vital part of the enterprise. If what the business is doing is not in the public interest, the more explaining the worse the result. But even if the policies are such as commend themselves to the public, the public is generally too busy with its own affairs to know about them unless they are set forth.
>
> Public relations, therefore, is not publicity only, not management only; it is what everybody in the business from top to bottom says and does when in contact with the public....[64]

Under fire from New Deal reforms at the time, corporations across America were showing an increased interest in public relations as a way of coping with government pressures. Because AT&T had one of the oldest and most effective public relations operations in the country, many businesses turned to Arthur Page and the Bell System public relations staffers for advice and guidance on how to set up their own public relations operations.

In 1937, Page estimated that the number of businessmen asking AT&T for public relations advice had doubled or tripled since 1932. To meet demand for information on the subject, he had the "Industrial Statesmanship" speech printed. After 1939, when he received requests for information, he usually included the pamphlet with his reply.[65]

That the Bell System appreciated Page's performance is perhaps best evidenced by his salary increases.

He started at AT&T in 1927 at $35,000 per year. By 1938,

his salary had climbed to $67,500. While that may seem small by 21st-century standards, it made him the fourth most highly paid officer at AT&T. His salary was surpassed only by those of President Gifford ($209,350), Vice President Charles P. Cooper ($102,699) and General Counsel Charles M. Bracelen ($75,000). [66]

Hostile to the New Deal

PAGE, A BELIEVER in individual freedom, resented what he regarded as restrictions on liberty imposed by President Franklin Roosevelt's New Deal reforms.

Many letters in the Page Papers reveal his anglophiliac confidence in the superiority of the British system which he thought to have few specific rules on individuals and corporations, but severe penalties for violations of the rules. That, he was sure, was preferable to the New Deal's laying down many rules and regulations that kept some individuals and corporations from antisocial behavior, but also kept many more individuals and corporations from performing socially responsible acts.[67]

Page resented having to give up corporate directorships for no good reason. He was in constant contact with others who opposed the Roosevelt reforms—top management of AT&T, the directors of the various corporations on whose boards he sat, his social contacts. To attribute Page's dislike of the New Deal to self-interest or the attitudes of acquaintances alone, however, would be wrong.

Arthur Page's children argue that their father's convictions stemmed from his own reflections and strong personal belief in individual liberty, not from the influence of others or a desire to be accepted by others. Page's son John Hall says:

Dad was always first an independent citizen of the United States. No group or organization owned him. He was willing and capable of stating where he stood

and why and living by the consequences. Part of being
a citizen in his view was appropriate involvement in
his country's or his area's concerns. He would never
accept the proposition that he was first an "A.T.T. man"
or a "Chase man." He was Citizen Page first. He was
contemptuous of those of old wealth who were not involved, or of the steel men or automobile men, etc.,
who were just that and couldn't see beyond their pa-
rochial horizon... (P)erhaps his colleagues in A.T.T. influenced his change from being a Democrat to a Republican. To the extent that he and they were subject
to the same perceptions, this might be true. But (don't
imply) he did so to be more acceptable to that group,
(for) I am sure that was not the case.[68]

Page believed freedom made it possible for him to achieve
status and affluence on his own abilities. And while it may
be argued that his father gave him his start in life at the
World's Work magazine, Walter Page had nothing to do with
Arthur's success after he left Doubleday in 1926. He wanted
others to have the same chances in life that he had seized.

Page summed up his feelings about federal economic planning and increased taxation in 1938 when he said, "Now I
think we are trying the centralized planning in a large number of fields in which we have little experience—under the
general philosophy that if no one is allowed to get rich all
will be better off. Personally I don't believe that for I think
that in a country where the opportunity to get rich is banned
the fate of the poor will be bad...."[69]

When Franklin Roosevelt was elected to an unprecedented
third term in 1940, Page wrote waspishly to Hugh Gibson in
England: "We have, I think, just demonstrated that five billion dollars of bread and circuses is patronage enough to
re-elect any one over tradition." He felt America was moving
toward a stratified European form of society in which a large
bureaucracy, a semi-planned economy, restricted initiative
and heavy taxation would all be necessary to maintain a permanent class of unemployed individuals.[70]

Joining the Continental Oil and Westinghouse boards

IN JANUARY 1937, Page was elected a director of AT&T's Long Lines Dept., a subsidiary responsible for overseeing all interstate long distance telephone operations.

In 1938, the New Deal, which had already cost Page directorships in New England Telephone and Southern Bell, exacted a third directorship from him. New federal regulations on cross-directorships convinced him to resign from the Engineers Public Service board.

He more than compensated for the loss within a year by joining the boards of the Continental Oil Co. (later Conoco) and Westinghouse Electric.

Page was not strictly obligated to resign his Engineers Public Service Co. directorship. Under provisions of the Public Utility Holding Company Act passed early in the New Deal, all directors of utility holding companies had to indicate if they were officers, directors or partners in any banks, trust companies, investment banks or banking associations. In compliance with the law, Page declared he was a director of Engineers Public Service (an electric and natural gas holding company) and a director of the Chase National Bank. He then filed a petition with the Securities and Exchange Commission to remain a director of both companies.

Before the petition was acted upon, the Supreme Court ruled that the Public Utility Holding Company Act's prohibition of cross-directorships in holding companies and banks was legal. Page wrote immediately to Engineers Public Service President Donald Barnes to resign his directorship and from the executive committee. Barnes tried to persuade Page to reconsider, pointing out that a director could still petition for exemption from the cross-directorship prohibition. Page replied that he did not want to ask the federal government for any special favors. His resignation from Engineers Public Service became effective Dec. 31.[71]

In December 1938, he was elected to the board of the 195 Broadway Corp., which oversaw operation of AT&T's headquarters building in downtown New York.[72]

In September 1939, he was elected a director of Continental Oil.[73]

The same day he was elected to the Conoco board, he wrote to Westinghouse Electric President A.W. Robertson to say he was grateful for having been offered a Westinghouse directorship, but that he felt his many corporate and outside responsibilities would keep him from doing a good job if he accepted. His protestations went unheeded. He was elected to the Westinghouse board in December 1939. He accepted the position, but concerned about a possible conflict of interest, wrote a letter saying that as a Westinghouse director he would neither try to sell AT&T services to Westinghouse nor Westinghouse services to AT&T.[74]

In November 1941, Page was named a director of the Bell Telephone Co. of Canada, in which AT&T held a minority stock interest.[75]

Not long before, he had made several visits to America's northern neighbor to speak before prestigious groups and confer with Canadian government officials. In 1938, he had traveled to Canada with several Carnegie Corp. trustees to brief members of the Seigniory Club on the activities of the Carnegie British Dominions and Colonies Fund in Canada. On that trip, he and Mollie spent two days at Government House in Ottawa so he could confer informally with Lord Tweedsmuir, governor-general of Canada.[76]

The corporate directorships served to entrench his position as a member of the establishment.

Page was in regular contact with other members of the establishment through the clubs of which he was a member, through government assignments he accepted, through boards of trustees of educational institutions on which he sat, through the boards of great philanthropies on which he served, through the policy- and report-making bodies such as the Council on Foreign Relations of which he was a member and through the corporate boards on which he sat.

Consider the outside directors in 1940-1941 with whom Page came in contact through just the AT&T board:

• Winthrop Aldrich, chairman of the board of the Chase

National Bank, director of the Metropolitan Life Insurance Co. and Westinghouse Electric and trustee of the Rockefeller Foundation.

• Charles Francis Adams, treasurer of Harvard from 1898 to 1929, and Secretary of the Navy from 1929 to 1933.

• James F. Bell, chairman of the board of General Mills, director of Northwestern National Bank and Trust and the Pullman Co..

• Lewis H. Brown, president of the Johns-Manville Corp., director of Bankers Trust Co. of New York, Mutual Life Insurance Co. and Pacific Southwest Railroad

• David A. Crawford, president of the Pullman Co., director of Armour and Co., Continental Illinois National Bank and Trust, Montgomery Ward, Harris Trust and Savings Bank of Chicago and West Virginia Coal and Coke Corp.

• John W. Davis, a lawyer, onetime Democratic presidential nominee, former ambassador to the Court of St. James's, a director of Guaranty Trust Co. of New York (the House of Morgan) and Mutual Life Insurance Co..

• W. Cameron Forbes, a former governor-general of the Philippines, a former ambassador to Japan and director of the Old Colony Trust Co. of Boston.

• G. Peabody Gardner, director of General Electric, Old Colony Trust Co., Amoskeag Co., Boston Fund, Eastern Steamship Lines and First National Bank of Boston.

• Barklie Henry, director of the Texas Co. (later Texaco) and United States Trust Co.

• Thomas I. Parkinson, president of Equitable Life Assurance Society and trustee of the Rockefeller Foundation.

• Elihu Root Jr., lawyer, director of Fiduciary Trust Co. of New York and Mutual Life Insurance Co., and trustee of the Carnegie Corp.

• Tom K. Smith, president of Boatmen's National Bank of St. Louis and director of the Wabash Railway Co..

• Myron C. Taylor, a former U.S. representative to the Vatican and chairman of U.S. Steel, director of the New York Central Railroad, U.S. Steel, the Atchison, Topeka and Santa Fe Railway, First National Bank of New York and Mutual Life

Insurance Co., and a trustee of the Metropolitan Museum of Art.

• Samuel A. Welldon, vice president of the First National Bank of New York, and director of the Bigelow-Sanford Carpet Co., Northern Pacific Railroad and Wilkes-Barre Corp.

• Daniel Willard, president of the Baltimore and Ohio Railroad and a director of the Mutual Life Insurance Co.

• S. Clay Williams, chairman of the board of R.J. Reynolds Tobacco and a director of the Security Life and Trust Co.[77]

If, in his capacity as a trustee of the Carnegie Corp., he wanted to solicit some help from the Rockefeller Foundation, on whose board Winthrop Aldrich served, Page could approach Aldrich before or after a regular AT&T board meeting, a Chase National board meeting, or a Westinghouse board meeting. More likely, of course, such contacts would be arranged outside the board meeting, perhaps by a phone call or at lunch at one of the clubs.

The picture becomes more complicated when the names of all the individuals with whom Page was in regular contact are considered. A few hundred names stand out as belonging to members of the establishment who called upon one another regularly because they respected one another's judgment and intelligence.

Page did not belong to this elite group because of personal wealth. He belonged mainly because of the positions he held with various organizations. He was also a member, however, because others respected his wisdom. Examples abound in the Page Papers of other powerful individuals seeking out his advice—and of young men on the way up seeking his counsel, for he deeply enjoyed helping the young.

People sought out Page for advice because of his common sense. Edward M. Block, who became AT&T's public relations vice president in 1975, and later, founder of the Arthur Page Society, recalls having once asked another AT&T vice president of public relations, Walter Straley, what had made Arthur Page such a good public relations man. Straley's reply was that Page had not been a good public relations man—he had simply been a very wise man.[78]

Myrdal and the 'American Dilemma'

PAGE'S MOST SIGNIFICANT philanthropic work in 1935-1941 was for the Carnegie Corp. With Henry James, he helped to arrange for investment of Carnegie Corp. assets (about $100 million) to be overseen by J.P. Morgan and Co. With other directors, he participated in the decision in 1938 to fund (Karl) Gunnar Myrdal's pioneering study of blacks in American society which signaled a new direction in Carnegie Corp. philanthropy. He helped to find a replacement for retiring Carnegie President Frederick Keppel and to provide a research grant to the new Joint Army and Navy Committee on Welfare and Recreation.

The Carnegie Corp.'s relations with the House of Morgan date to at least 1929, well before Page became a director. In 1929, Carnegie Corp. directors approved retaining J.P. Morgan and Co. as financial counsel. At the time, Russell Leffingwell, a partner in the Morgan firm, was a Carnegie trustee and chairman of its Investment Committee. Leffingwell made it clear in correspondence with Carnegie President Frederick P. Keppel that he was aware of the ethical dangers in making the House of Morgan an investment counsel while he was a trustee.[79]

From 1929, when Morgan was first retained as financial consultant, through 1935, the importance of the House of Morgan as investment agent for the Carnegie Corp. grew. In 1933, Morgan handled none of the Carnegie Corp.'s preferred stock transactions, and only 2.8 percent of its bond purchases and sales, but acted as agent in 92.5 percent of the Carnegie Corp.'s common stock transactions. By 1935, Morgan handled 47.9 percent of all Carnegie bond transactions, 59.9 percent of all preferred stock sales and purchases and 99.7 percent of all common stock transactions.[80]

In 1936, the members of Leffingwell's Carnegie Corp. Investment Committee were Arthur Page, financier Henry James, Frederick Keppel and financier Frederick Osborn. That same year, Page and James drafted a recommendation that the Carnegie board designate the House of Morgan as sole agent for investment of Carnegie Corp. funds.[81] Only Dr. Nicholas Murray Butler, president of Columbia University and a longtime Carnegie Corp. trustee, objected. Congress had announced plans for an investigation of the great philanthropies in America, and he did not want to be on record approving a lucrative investment contract to a bank that had several trustees on various Carnegie boards.[82]

While there is no evidence in his papers that he played other than a minor role in the funding of Gunnar Myrdal's pioneering study of black Americans by the Carnegie Corp., Page was aware of the project and interested in it.

With the Myrdal study, the Carnegie Corp. began funding research into sociological problems. Until then, Carnegie Corp. projects—even those that were innovative—were restricted to studies in noncontroversial areas. When the Carnegie trustees funded Myrdal's work, the charity began paying for research designed to seek ways for America to come to grips with the deep political, economic and social problems confronting the nation's society.[83] Other major American philanthropies noted the new tack the Carnegie Corp. was taking, and the more adventurous began to imitate its course.

Myrdal assembled a distinguished project staff and then returned to Sweden, leaving organization of the research to Prof. Samuel A. Stouffer of the University of Chicago. By the time the research staff was disbanded in the autumn of 1940, some 20,000 pages of manuscript were in first or second draft, and the job of selecting papers for publication began.

In the spring of 1941, Myrdal returned to America and began writing with Richard Sterner and Arnold Rose what became the landmark two-volume *An American Dilemma: The Negro Problem and American Democracy*.[84] By the time *Dilemma* was published in 1944, Frederick Keppel, who deserves much of the credit for arranging the funding, had retired as president of the Carnegie Corp. He wrote the forward to the work, cautiously justifying Carnegie involvement in exploration of social issues so long as the foundation's role was nothing more than making facts available to the public, and not an attempt to mold public opinion in favor of one course of action or another.[85]

Although the *Dilemma* project was a monumental work that cast the Carnegie Corp. in the role of pioneer, the agency's trustees made little effort to attract praise for the study by touting its innovativeness. By 1944, the trustees were too busy with World War II duties to devote much attention to the Myrdal work.

One aspect of Carnegie Corp. involvement in the World War II effort is particularly relevant to the career of Arthur Page. Frederick Osborn, a Carnegie Corp. trustee and Wall Street man who had served with Page on the Carnegie Investment Committee, in 1941 accepted appointment as a brigadier general in the Army. Henry Stimson, who became Franklin Roosevelt's Secretary of War in 1940, made Osborn chief of the Army's Morale Branch. Among other duties, Osborn headed a new Joint Army and Navy Committee on Welfare and Recreation. Arthur Page would soon be named to head that agency and guide it through the duration.

The purpose of the Joint Army and Navy Committee (JANC) was to coordinate the activities of civilian agencies such as the American Red Cross, United Service Organizations (USO) and Citizens Committee for the Army and Navy working at or near military installations.[86] In late 1941, Carnegie Corp. trustees approved a $200,000 grant for JANC to create experimental recreation programs for the men and women in America's rapidly mobilizing fighting forces, for meeting special racial needs of men in arms and to design programs to improve the morale of citizens entering the military.

When the grant was made, Page was serving as a committee of one to find a replacement for Carnegie President Keppel. Efforts to find a successor had begun in the spring of 1940. Between then and the summer of 1941, Page unsuccessfully championed Frederick Osborn, Whitney Shepardson and Henry Wriston to replace Keppel. With Keppel's retirement fast approaching, the trustees finally agreed to a compromise in the summer of 1941. They named Walter Jessup, who had been serving as president of the Carnegie Endowment for the Advancement of Teaching, to Keppel's job with the clear understanding that they could replace him after giving six months' notice. Page held a private luncheon at his AT&T office to give Jessup an opportunity to meet the Carnegie trustees.[87]

Page devoted considerable time to the Metropolitan Museum of Art, of which he became a trustee in late 1935. Between then and America's entry into World War II in late 1941, he served on eight different Metropolitan committees.[88]

From 1938 to 1942, he chaired a special committee to expand paid museum memberships. The committee, reconstituted several times, included Nelson Rockefeller, Henry S. Morgan, Roland Redmond, Vanderbilt Webb, Robert A. Lovett, Elihu Root Jr., William Church Osborn and Thomas J. Watson. Page did little with the committee until he was embarrassed by a mass mailing to 14,000 prospective members that produced only $305 in revenue, not enough to cover even the mailing costs. He then asked Harry Batten, president of AT&T advertising agency N.W. Ayer & Son, to prepare a master plan for recruiting new members and keeping old ones.[89]

In preparing his recommendations for "repackaging" the Metropolitan, Batten called for advice from Francis Henry Taylor, director of the Worcester, Mass., Art Museum. Taylor, who was being considered for the directorship of the Metropolitan, wrote to Page to say he thought a national membership drive was in order for the museum, but that he had some definite ideas about the need for an internal reorganization before a drive was conducted. Taylor came to New York and was entertained by Page and the members of his special committee in the spring of 1940. Soon thereafter Taylor was named director of the Metropolitan.[90]

Early in 1941, Taylor rejected the membership drive plan prepared by N.W. Ayer at Page's request. Taylor said he preferred to have membership activities run by the museum's internal staff rather than by an outside agency. Page accepted Taylor's recommendation, and his membership committee was reconstituted to oversee the work of the museum staff. The committee issued a final set of recommendations in February 1941, but did little thereafter.[91] Page lost interest after Taylor rejected the Ayer plan. The ensuing membership drive led by Taylor and his staff was a lackluster affair.

Page considerably expanded his involvement with the Anna T. Jeanes Foundation-Negro Rural School Fund in 1935-1941. His attitudes regarding Afro-Americans, like those of most white Americans of southern heritage at the time, were not particularly enlightened. He believed blacks lowered standards wherever they resided. In a 1936 letter to Carnegie Corp. head Frederick Keppel about possible funding for the Jeanes program, written a year before he became chairman of the Jeanes board, he said: "I think it is a fact that the standard of living, of education, of political life or any other measurement you want to make is lower the more Negroes there are in the community, not only amongst the Negroes but amongst the whites that have contact with them as well."[92]

He regarded blacks as the greatest handicap hindering the progress of American society. To him, they were "the white man's burden," firstly because "whites had brought the blacks to America," and secondly "because (the black American) isn't responsible and responsibility must rest somewhere."[93]

Like many Americans with a southern heritage, Page believed in segregation. He also believed in improved educational opportunities for black Americans. His efforts in support of the Jeanes Foundation can in part be attributed to his feeling a responsibility to follow in his father's footsteps on the Jeanes board. He also believed, patronizing as the view might be, that working through the Jeanes organization to improve education for blacks in the segregated school system helped to fulfill the white American responsibility to Americans of African ancestry.

In his letter to Keppel cited above, Page argued that the Jeanes Foundation was better equipped than any other in America to improve education in a segregated black school because its outlook wasn't "muddied by the hallucinations about the Negroes' contributions to culture..."[94]

In May 1936, a few months after he had written the letter to Keppel, Page was elected chairman of the Jeanes Foundation board. He replaced George Foster Peabody, who became honorary chairman. The annual budget of the foundation at the time was about $196,000.[95]

Page and Jeanes Foundation President Arthur Wright began work on a proposal to merge the Slater Fund, headed by Dr. Albert Shaw of the *Review of Reviews*, into the Jeanes Foundation. At a meeting in New York in early 1937, the boards of the two foundations formed a committee to work out details.[96] Immediately after the merger was approved, the General Education Board slashed its annual gift to the foundation from $67,500 to $25,000. The Carnegie Corp. made an emergency donation of $6,000, but the foundation was forced to drastically curtail operations. Existing Jeanes teachers were kept on the payroll, but funding for new teachers, county training schools for black teachers, experimental schools and other programs had to be eliminated.[97]

Merger of the Slater and Jeanes Funds was completed by the end of 1937. The merged organization was renamed the Southern Education Foundation (SEF). Page served as chairman of the SEF board from 1937 to 1945, and as a member of its executive committee from 1941 to 1945.[98]

Much of Page's work for the SEF consisted of improving its precarious financial position. Under his leadership, and over the strong protests of Arthur Wright, the SEF operating budget was slashed from $150,000 in fiscal 1937-1938 to $104,000 in fiscal 1938-1939. At the same time, SEF investments were overhauled by the Investment Services Dept. of the Chase National Bank. By 1940, annual income from investments had risen to about $110,000 annually, with other money available from outside sources.[99]

No sooner had Page guided the SEF through the financial crisis than he had to face another emergency. Arthur Wright collapsed of a cerebral hemorrhage.[100] While he was recuperating, Page and Leslie Snow, a member of the SEF Finance Committee, ran the foundation while clerks tried to figure out the accounts from ledgers which, it was discovered, were in total disarray. Wright had more or less run the foundation out of his head.

After that crisis had passed, Page tried unsuccessfully to resign from the foundation but couldn't find a suitable successor.[101]

Other charities with which Page continued to work in 1935-1941 included:

• *The Charity Organization Society.* Continued to serve as a member of the Society's Central Council, as a vice president and as a member of its executive committee to April 1939. When COS merged with another large charity in New York and changed its name to the Community Service Society, Page served as a member of the new organization's board from 1939 forward, and as chairman of its committees to oversee the work of the Institute of Welfare Research and the School of Social Work in New York.[102]

• *New York Committee on Planned Parenthood.* Became a member of the committee in 1938 after a friend insisted.[103]

• *Council on Foreign Relations.* Active member in 1935-1941. He helped to get a $50,000 Carnegie Corp. grant in 1937 used by the Council to expand beyond New York. The money was used to form eight regional units in the nation's largest cities called Committees on Foreign Relations.[104] Page was one of the driving forces behind the expansion.[105]

• *English-Speaking Union.* Occasionally active. John W. Davis was president.[106]

• *Farmers Federation Educational and Development Fund.* Continued to serve as president of the Fund, and also as chairman of its New York money-raising committee. The more influential members of Page's New York Committee during the period were Winthrop Aldrich, John W. Davis, Fairman Dick, Cleveland Dodge, Thomas J. Watson and Henry Luce.[107]

• *Greater New York Fund.* Named a director of the sponsoring committee by Chairman James G. Blaine in early 1938. This agency sought to raise money to be divided among a number of New York City charities. [108]

• *International Chamber of Commerce.* Served as a member of the Chamber's American Committee during the period.[109]

Page's *pro bono* service set a corporate social responsibility example for other AT&T executives. However, he so extended himself that he had to reassess his volunteer service. He was less active in 1935-1941 in:

• *The Roosevelt Memorial Association.* Resigned as a trustee and member of the executive committee in October 1936, saying he no longer had the time to adequately serve the organization.[110]

• *The British Apprentice Club.* Resigned as secretary and treasurer in January 1939, but continued to take an interest in the organization. In later years, he involved members of his family.[111]

• *Leonard Wood Memorial for the Eradication of Leprosy.* Resigned from the executive committee in December 1940, and as a trustee in April 1941.[112]

• *Long Island Biological Assn.* Resigned as president in late 1940 and was replaced by Dr. Robert Cushman Murphy, a Long Islander employed as Lamont curator of birds at the American Museum of Natural History. Page was elected a vice president, director and member of the executive committee of LIBA. He remained active in fund-raising. Plans were well under way at the time for merging LIBA and the Carnegie Institution Genetics Station under joint directorship, a reorganization Page had long advocated.[113]

In service to higher education

IN *PRO BONO* service to higher education, Page served as chairman of the Bennington College board of trustees to 1941, several years after his daughter Mollie graduated.[114]

The main concern of the board while Page headed it was with finding new money for Bennington. While he helped to raise dollars, he wasn't convinced that funding scholarships for girls whose parents lacked the means to send them to Bennington was wise. He felt private schools like Bennington were draining good students from the less expensive state universities by providing them scholarships and that

Bennington might be making the scholarship girls unhappy by putting them in an environment where they had to compete socially with girls from well-to-do families.[115]

Page's children remember him as a Jeffersonian Democrat, but he was also something of a closet Hamiltonian aristocrat.

He continued to serve in 1935-1941 as vice chairman of the board of trustees of Teachers College at Columbia, where he oversaw investment of the Teachers College endowment. In 1936, the Finance Committee of which Page was a member transferred responsibility for investment of the endowment to the Chase National Bank, of which he was a director. He had served as a member of the Teachers College Finance Committee since 1923.

Investment responsibility for Teachers College endowment money did not move to the Chase until shortly after Page became a director of the bank. In fairness, the endowment fared well under Chase guidance. Despite an overall decline in the stock market after 1936, and the fact that Teachers College spent some of its endowment outright, income increased from $266,000 in 1936 to $275,000 in 1940.[116]

Until 1935-1941, Page's involvement with Harvard was confined to serving on several visiting committees and to twice running for overseer. Then his involvement expanded.

In 1935-1936, he served as a member of the prestigious Harvard Three Hundredth Anniversary Fund Committee. During the Harvard tercentenary fund drive, he also served on a Special Committee on a New Plan for Research for the Harvard School of Dental Medicine, and arranged some major funding for the school. In 1939-1940, he served in addition as a vice president and director of the Harvard Alumni Assn.[117]

The goal of the Harvard tercentenary drive was $25 million. In addition to serving on the steering committee which ran the drive with assistance of the John Price Jones Organization, Page directly sought contributions from among the more affluent of the 11,000 or so Harvard alumni living in the New York City area. Among those with whom he worked in the effort were Learned Hand, Thomas W. Lamont, Henry James, J.P. Morgan *fils,* Henry Francis DuPont, Samuel Welldon, Walter Gifford, Elihu Root Jr., Fairman Dick, George Whitney, Winthrop Aldrich, Kermit Roosevelt, Walter Lippmann and Cass Canfield.[118]

In connection with the Three Hundredth Anniversary Fund, Harvard sought $3.4 million to revamp its Dental School into a School of Dental Medicine subordinate to the Harvard Medical School. Dental students in an accelerated five-year program were to earn not only the traditional D.M.D. (dentistry) degree, but an M.D. (doctor of medicine) as well. Purpose of the program was to train periodontal disease researchers. Training of mere dental practitioners was to stop.

Page was a principal on the committee assigned to raise the $3.4 million. He was directly involved in obtaining pledges of $650,000 from the Carnegie Corp., $400,000 from the Rockefeller Foundation and $250,000 from the John and Mary Markle Foundation.

In 1940, just before the School of Dental Medicine opened, a flurry of criticism from practicing dentists erupted. The dentists did not like the idea of dental training under the control of doctors who have traditionally treated dentists as poor cousins. The American Dental Assn. attacked in a 1940 editorial in its *Journal.* Despite the lack of popular support among dentists, Harvard opened the School of Dental Medicine with nine students in the fall of 1941, and by 1944 had completely phased out traditional training of dentists.[119]

Page's involvement in School of Dental Medicine funding is noteworthy for several reasons. First, it shows the power to raise large sums of money that he already had by the late 1930s. Second, it shows that, although he was normally an empathic individual able to foresee and head off public relations problems, he was not infallible. He was caught completely by surprise by the criticism targeted at the Harvard project, having failed to recognize the jealousy between the dental and medical professions.

He served during much of 1935-1941 on the overseer Committee to Visit the Harvard University Press. Among the more noteworthy members of the committee were Roy Larsen of *Time* magazine, John Cowles of Cowles Communications and Sen. Henry Cabot Lodge.

In 1938, Page ran a third time for election as a Harvard overseer. He was unsuccessful, but his prestige among alumni was obviously growing. He ran seventh in the field, compared to having placed 14th in 1929 and eighth in 1933.[120]

In late 1939, the Harvard Alumni Assn. named Page a vice president.[121] After Harvard's *Alumni Bulletin* created public relations problems for Harvard President James B. Conant, Page recommended changes in editing of the publication and in the manner in which the editor reported to Conant.

Soon after the Alumni Assn. appointment, Conant asked Page to chair an Advisory Committee on Public Relations. Page helped to select Calvert Smith to serve in Conant's five-man cabinet with direct responsibility for advising Conant on public relations.[122]

After Smith was appointed to Conant's cabinet, Page occasionally advised both on public relations matters such as a controversy among alumni touched off by Harvard's brief appointment to the faculty of left-wing British philosopher Bertrand Russell. Page approved Smith's plan to make Russell immediately available to the press for interviews after he arrived in Cambridge, saying "I agree that when there is bad news the thing to do is get it out first. I think your strategy and the war and the (presidential political) campaign will submerge Russell unless there is a piece of bad luck or he ranges to play the fool."[123]

Last cruises of the Rampage

EXCEPT FOR YOUNGEST SON John, Arthur Page's children graduated from Harvard and Bennington in 1935-1941, going on to work, or in the case of Mollie Jr., to marriage.[124] In 1938, Mollie Jr. married Anderson Hewitt, who built a distinguished career in the advertising industry. The newlyweds lived briefly in San Francisco before moving to Chicago.

Arthur and Mollie Sr. made several trips to England between 1935 and the 1939 outbreak of World War II. Often the Page children traveled separately to Europe with friends in the same period, and in a few cases, met their mother and father briefly in England.

The period 1935-1941 was one of frequent summer cruises for the Pages aboard the family's sailing yacht *Rampage*. Arthur Page joined the New York Yacht Club, a watering place for a segment of New York high society, not so much for the prestige of belonging, but because membership was the only way for him to buy the *Rampage*. The boat belonged to a class of sailing vessels sponsored by NYYC, and couldn't be purchased by a nonmember. Page was not very active in the club, aside from perfunctorily serving several terms on its Library Committee. According to his son John, father Arthur was not a great sailor, but got considerable enjoyment from watching his children sail the boat.[125]

Even before the start of World War II in the late summer of 1939, the careers of Page's children began to interfere with the family's summer cruises aboard the *Rampage*. Sons Walter Hines II and Arthur Jr. exempted themselves from the crew in 1939, the first to begin work at the Morgan investment bank (of which he became president in 1971), and the second, an ensign in the Naval Reserves, to serve for the summer aboard a Navy destroyer. Daughter Mollie by the summer of 1939 had not only a husband to care for, but as well an infant daughter, Mollie Cary, the first of Arthur Page's grandchildren.

His family crew gone, Page scuttled tentative plans to take the *Rampage* to Swedish waters in the summer of 1939, and instead entered the boat in a race from Marblehead to Halifax, Nova Scotia. He returned leisurely via Cape Sable and the New England coast.

Page received the first news of the calamitous events in Europe over newly installed radio equipment on the *Rampage*. The yacht was at sea when Hitler invaded Poland, leading Great Britain to declare war on Germany. The Ivison Macadams, Page friends in England, told him by radiotelephone that they were sending their children to America for safety. Page then used the radio equipment to arrange for his secretary and others to meet the children in New York.[126]

In the fall of 1939, Arthur Jr. joined White, Weld and Co., an investment house handling many of the financial chores for the Southern Education Foundation which his father headed. Son John, youngest of the Page brood, entered Harvard as a freshman that same fall and, to his father's delight, played center on the freshman football team.[127]

Page's sons all chose service in the U.S. Navy, perhaps influenced by summers on the *Rampage*, perhaps because Navy officer ranks were populated by the elite. They had taken Navy Reserve Officer Training Corps courses at Harvard.

In June 1941, Arthur Jr. left his job with White, Weld to go on active duty with the U.S. Navy at Trinidad. Two months later, son Walter accepted a commission as an ensign in the Navy. Eventually son John, who completed his sophomore year at Harvard in 1941, and even son-in-law Anderson Hewitt, ended up in Navy blue.

The summer of 1941 was the last in which the *Rampage* remained in Page family hands. During the first few months of the summer, son John used the boat as a floating dude ranch in Canadian waters. In late August, Arthur and Mollie Sr. commandeered the vessel for a loafing cruise down the Maine coast. A short time later, Page sold it.[128]

Page joins John Hill's 'Wise Men'

IN NOVEMBER 1938, John Wiley Hill, cofounder of the Hill and Knowlton public relations firm, held an informal dinner at his apartment for a small group of the most prestigious public relations counselors in America. James Selvage helped Hill draw up the invitation list. The members of the group decided to meet monthly thereafter to discuss whatever matters were on their minds. Pendleton Dudley, another pioneer and a friend of Page, became secretary for the group, membership in which was by invitation only. Somewhat tongue-in-cheek, an early member suggested that the group call itself the "Wise Men," and the name stuck.

John W. Hill did not recall when asked before his death if Arthur Page was at the organizational meeting in 1938. Dudley and Selvage, who might have known, were already dead. But Hill did recall with certainty that Page was an early member and that he remained active until the 1950s.

Hill remembers Page as one of the star members of the group, seldom disposed to talk, preferring to listen, but capable of captivating the others with his eloquence when he did speak. "It was hard to get him to talk," Hill recalled. "But once he started speaking, no one wanted him to stop because he could express himself so well."

Early members of the prestigious group, along with Hill, Page, Dudley and Selvage, included Paul Garrett, who organized the public relations function at General Motors in the 1930s, pioneer counselor Tommy Ross, and Verne Burnett, who moved from a career in food processing public relations to founding his own agency.[129]

In touch with the leading public relations professionals of the nation through the Wise Men, Page corresponded with many leaders in his field, and met them at social and business functions. During the period 1935-1941, Page:

• Corresponded with Bruce Barton about the implications of technological unemployment for the American economy,[130]

• Carried on correspondence with Frank R. Schell, who had served as director of public relations for Thomas A. Edison, Inc., from 1928 to 1938, and then opened his own agency.[131]

• Wrote to public relations pioneer William H. Baldwin, then with Baldwin and Beach, about a variety of topics.[132]

• Appeared with Paul Garrett at a weekend seminar at Harvard on public relations. Professor Cabot of the Graduate School of Business, an old friend of AT&T and of Page, conducted the seminar.

• Briefed a group of public relations executives from oil companies such as Standard Oil and Texaco on what modern public relations entailed.[133]

• Discussed with Pendleton Dudley the best method of placing an article about Allied war debts in the *Reader's Digest* as Dudley wished to do.[134]

• Provided guidance to Rex F. Harlow, president of the American Council on Public Relations, on development of that professional society.[135]

• Tried to help James L. McCamy, assistant to the secretary of agriculture, find a director of information for the department. He recommended William Wesley Waymack, the Pulitzer-winning editor of the *Des Moines Register & Tribune*. Waymack got away before McCamy could hire him, and Morse Salisbury was hired instead.[136]

• Advised Curtiss-Wright Aircraft President Guy Vaughan on public relations, suggesting that Vaughan retain Ivy Lee and T.J. Ross or Baldwin, Beach and Mermey or Pendleton Dudley as a public relations consulting agency.[137]

Stimson becomes FDR's war secretary

As WAR BROKE OUT in Europe in 1939, President Roosevelt's secretary of war was the isolationist Harry H. Woodring, who had taken pride in 1938 in not putting the B-17 "Flying Fortress" bomber into production. By 1940, as Kai Bird points out in his excellent biography of John J. McCloy, the Wall Street bankers and lawyers who dominated the Council on Foreign Relations wanted Woodring out.

COFR members had reached the consensus that it was time for the United States to replace Great Britain and its empire as the world's leading power, and Woodring was in the way. Frank Altschul of the Lazard Freres investment banking firm, a director of COFR, and Thomas Lamont of J.P. Morgan started a campaign to replace Woodring with Henry L. Stimson. Woodring was encouraged through a ploy to resign.

In June 1940, as Republican delegates gathered in convention to nominate Wendell Willkie to run against Franklin Roosevelt, who was seeking his third term, FDR offered the job to Stimson.[138] Stimson's acceptance set the stage for Arthur

Page's distinguished wartime service. From the Japanese attack on Pearl Harbor on Dec. 7, 1941, to Page's retirement from AT&T, the nation was preoccupied with fighting World War II and building a postwar peace. Page himself went to Europe for the Normandy invasion, and returned to participate in the release of information on the atomic bomb. These and other things are covered in the next chapter.

ENDNOTES

[1] Discussion of events leading up to the Special Telephone Investigation is based on information in *Final Report of the Telephone Rate and Research Dept.* (Washington, D.C.: Federal Communications Commission, June 15, 1938, pp. 3-7. This document hereafter is referred to as *TR&RD Final Report.*

[2] Cited from Page, *The Bell Telephone System, op. cit.,* pp. 171-72.

[3] American Telephone & Telegraph Co., *Annual Report* (1937), pp. 9-10.

[4] Long Lines rate reduction figures for 1926-1936 are from *TR&RD Final Report,* p. 9.

[5] *Ibid.,* p. iii; letter from Page to Bell System presidents, March 15, 1940, in possession of author; and American Telephone & Telegraph Co., *Annual Report* (1941), pp. 12-13.

[6] See *TR&RD Final Report,* pp. 88-89.

[7] American Telephone & Telegraph Co., *Annual Report* (1936), p. 14.

[8] Unheadlined editorial from *San Antonio Evening News,* attached to letter to Page from Ike S. Kampmann, May 3, 1937, Box 14, Arthur W. Page Papers.

[9] American Telephone & Telegraph Co., *Annual Report* (1938), pp. 10-11.

[10] That AT&T protested far less about the final FCC report than it did about Walker's earlier proposed report provides evidence that it regarded the final report as far less threatening to it.

[11] War clouds looming in Europe probably saved AT&T from having to face Congressional or Justice Dept. action aimed at forcing it to spin off Western Electric. The defense manufacturing capabilities of Western Electric were great. AT&T itself was essential to national defense. But the 1939 FCC recommendation that AT&T divest itself of Western Electric came back to haunt AT&T. The Justice Dept. moved unsuccessfully in 1949 to force divestiture. It filed another action in 1974 that eventually led to the breakup of the Bell System.

[12] Letter from Page to all Bell System public relations vice presidents, Nov. 13, 1939, in possession of author.

[13] Mabon, "The Art of Arthur Page," *op. cit.,* p. 7.

[14] The three-month timespan is based on letters Page wrote to AT&T directors on Dec. 19, 1940, and another letter to Southern Bell Telephone & Telegraph Co. President J.E. Warren, March 12, 1941, all in possession of author.

[15] Page, *The Bell Telephone System, op. cit.,* p. 173.

[16] *Ibid.*, p. 154

[17] Arthur W. Page, "Industrial Statesmanship," speech at public relations conference of the Chesapeake and Ohio Railway Co., White Sulphur Springs, Va., October 27, 1939.

[18] Page, *The Bell Telephone System, op. cit.*, p. 154.

[19] *Ibid.* The deletion is marked by an ellipsis.

[20] *Ibid.*

[21] Letter from Page to Southern Bell Telephone and Telegraph President J.E. Warren, March 12, 1941 *op. cit.*

[22] *The Bell Telephone System, op. cit.,* pp. 159-161.

[23] *Ibid.*, p. 161.

[24] *Ibid.*, p. 162.

[25] Memorandum from Page to AT&T public relations executive Douglas Williams, March 14, 1940, in possession of author. Williams was responsible for coordinating Bell System educational relations.

[26] The Bell System assigned responsibility for reviewing its school relations program to John M. Shaw in the late 1940s after AT&T director James Bell, chairman of the board of a large Minneapolis food manufacturing firm, encouraged AT&T to participate in a program his company had initiated. See John M. Shaw Papers, late 1940s and early 1950s.

[27] Page, *The Bell Telephone System, op. cit.,* pp. 161-62.

[28] *Ibid.*, p. 158.

[29] Ralph K. Martin, "John M. Shaw, 1930-1947," unpublished University of Wisconsin term paper, Jan. 14, 1969, in possession of author, and memorandum by John M. Shaw, "Notes on Ayer Memorandum of November 1951 re: TV Program," Nov. 23, 1951, Box 3, John M. Shaw Papers. The latter is hereafter referred to as "Notes on Ayer Memorandum."

[30] "Notes on Ayer Memorandum."

[31] Cited from Page, *The Bell Telephone System, op. cit.*, p. 156.

[32] Memorandum from Page to AT&T Asst. Vice President T.T. Cook, Nov. 10, 1939, in possession of author.

[33] Circular letter from Page to J.J. Robinson and other Bell System presidents, March 13, 1940, in possession of author.

[34] John M. Shaw special report, "Bell System Radio Program 'The Telephone Hour,'" April 1940, pp. 6-9, in Box 3, John M. Shaw Papers.

[35] Letter to author from retired AT&T Assistant Vice President T.T. Cook, Aug. 13, 1970.

[36] Data on Crossley ratings and "Bell Telephone Hour" fan mail is from report, "A Review of the Telephone Hour April-September 1940," Box 3, John M. Shaw Papers, and a circular letter from Page to all Bell System presidents, Jan. 30, 1941, in possession of author.

[37] Letter from AT&T public relations executive William P. Banning to Weirton Steel Co. executive Jack Meagher, Oct. 30, 1940, in possession of author.

[38] Letter from Page to Dr. David Spence Hill, Oct. 11, 1939, in possession of author.

[39] Letter from Page to J. Thomas Baldwin, Nov. 25, 1940, in possession of author.

[40] Letter from Page to Glenn Griswold, Feb. 4, 1941, in possession of author.

[41] Letter from Page to D.H. Hartwell, April 11, 1941, in possession of author.

[42] American Telephone & Telegraph Co., *Annual Report* (1938 and 1939),

pp. 11 and 10 respectively.

43 *Ibid.*, (1939), p. 10.

44 *Ibid.*, (1940), p. 11.

45 Letter from Page to Henry Dreyfuss, May 7, 1940, in possession of author.

46 Letters from Page to William M. Kirby, April 1, 1940, and to Henry W. Leeds, Sept. 4, 1940, in possession of author. They are among a number of letters Page sent to individuals who had asked for the Bell System to participate with exhibits in national trade fairs and expositions declining the invitations.

47 Letter from Page to Northrop Clarey of the Standard Oil Co. of New York (Socony-Mobil), Nov. 9, 1939, in possession of author.

48 *Ibid.*

49 Page's position favoring an increased ratio of stock to bonded indebtedness set him somewhat at odds with a number of other members of top AT&T management. Some AT&T managers argued that it was cheaper to issue bonds, paying interest for a period of time, and then calling the bonds back in, than it was to pay dividends on stock forever. Walter Gifford agreed with the Page position. Page's philosophy on stock versus bonded indebtedness, outlined in many memos, is perhaps best set forth in an internal AT&T memorandum, June 1940, in possession of author.

50 Memorandum from Page to Douglas Williams, Oct. 18, 1940, in possession of author.

51 Letter from Page to Dr. Charles Fleischer, March 29, 1940, in possession of author.

52 Arthur W. Page, "Fundamentals of a Public Relations Program for Business," speech at Seventh International Management Congress, Washington, D.C., Sept. 20, 1938.

53 Arthur W. Page, "Some Remarks on Public Relations," speech to members of the Institute of Life Insurance, New York City, Dec. 2, 1942.

54 Arthur W. Page, "Fundamentals of a Public Relations Program for Business," *op. cit.*

55 Arthur W. Page, "Public Relations Today and the Outlook for the Future," speech at New York Telephone Co. public relations course, December 13, 1937.

56 *Ibid.*

57 Arthur W. Page, "Fundamentals of a Public Relations Program for Business," *op. cit.*

57 Arthur W. Page, "Fundamentals of a Public Relations Program for Business," *op. cit.*

59 *Ibid.*

60 *Ibid.*

61 *Ibid.*

62 *Ibid.*

63 Arthur W. Page, "Industrial Statesmanship," *op. cit.*

64 *Ibid.*

65 Allusion to increased requests from executives for information about AT&T public relations is from Arthur W. Page, "Public Relations Today and the Outlook for the Future," *op. cit.*

66 Salary figures are from Danielian, *op. cit.*, p. 90.

67 See, for example, letter from Page to Charles F. Speare of the North American Newspaper Alliance, March 7, 1941, in possession of author.

68 Letter to author from John Hall Page, Nov. 11, 1975.

[69] Letter from Page to Frederick L. Allen of *Harper's* magazine, June 15, 1938, Box 68, Arthur W. Page Papers.

[70] Letter from Page to Hugh Gibson, Nov. 8, 1960, Box 7, Arthur W. Page Papers.

[71] Letter to Page from D.C. Barnes, Jan. 18, 1938; letter from Page to Barnes, Jan. 19, 1938; Securities and Exchange Commission Form U-17-3 completed by Page and dated Feb. 17, 1938; letter to Page from AT&T executive C.W. Kellogg, March 29, 1938; letter from Page to Barnes, Oct. 31, 1938; letter to Page from Barnes, Nov. 9, 1938; and letter from Page to Barnes, Nov. 14, 1938; all in Box 5, Arthur W. Page Papers.

[72] Page's notecards.

[73] *Ibid.*

[74] Letter from Page to A.W. Robertson, Sept. 20, 1939; letter to Page from Westinghouse Electric Secretary C.M. Pomeroy, Dec. 14, 1939, Boxes 5-6, Arthur W. Page Papers, and letter from Page to Westinghouse Electric executive Albert L. Hoffman, Jan. 18, 1940, in possession of author.

[75] Page's notecards.

[76] Letter from Page to Lord Tweedsmuir, Feb. 3, 1938, and letter to Page from Comptroller of the (Canadian) Governor-General's Household Eric Mackenzie, Feb. 10, 1938, Box 5, Arthur W. Page Papers.

[77] List of AT&T directors and offices held is extracted from eight pages of copy prepared by Arthur Page for inclusion in *The Bell Telephone System*. The draft copy is in possession of author.

[78] Telephone conversation with Edward M. Block, Oct. 14, 1975.

[79] See especially letter from Russell Leffingwell to Frederick P. Keppel, Feb. 14, 1929, in Box 4, Arthur W. Page Papers.

[80] Letter to Page from Russell Leffingwell, Aug. 3, 1936, Box 4, Arthur W. Page Papers.

[81] *Ibid.*

[82] Letter from Nicholas Murray Butler to Frederick P. Keppel, Oct. 20, 1936, attached to letter from Keppel to Page, Jan. 5, 1937, Box 4, Arthur W. Page Papers.

[83] Nielsen, *op. cit.*, p. 39 ff.

[84] See especially Gunnar Myrdal, "The Negro in America Memorandum," attached to letter to Page from Frederick P. Keppel, March 12, 1940, and "Memorandum on the Status of the Negro Study," attached to note from Keppel to Page, July 10, 1941, Boxes 6-7, Arthur W. Page Papers.

[85] See Nielsen, *op. cit.*, p. 39.

[86] Letter from Samuel E.M. Crocker, associate executive director of Joint Army and Navy Committee on Welfare and Recreation, to Frederick P. Keppel, attached to letter from Keppel to Page, Sept. 15, 1941, Box 7, Arthur W. Page Papers.

[87] See especially letter from Page to Russell Leffingwell, March 26, 1940; letter from Page to Dr. Nicholas Murray Butler, May 1940; undated list of possible successors to Frederick Keppel which Page used as a "scratch list" in discussions with other Carnegie trustees; letter from Page to Elihu Root Jr., June 6, 1941; and letter from Page to Butler, July 7, 1941; Boxes 6-7, Arthur W. Page Papers.

[88] Page served as a trustee of the Metropolitan from Dec. 16, 1935, to his death in 1960. The various Metropolitan committees on which he served during this period (the eight committees with which he was involved from 1935 to 1941 can be extrapolated from the list), were: Auditing Committee, 1937 to 1948; Committee on the American Wing, 1936 to 1945; Committee

to Consider the Proposed Budget, 1948; Committee on Educational Work, 1936 to 1945; Committee on Far Eastern Art, 1937 to 1945; Finance Committee, 1947 to 1948; Committee on the Library, 1936 to 1945; Committee on Prints, 1943 to 1945; Committee on Vacancies on the Board of Trustees, 1943 to 1945; Special Committee on Membership (chairman), 1939 to uncertain date; New Committee on Membership (chairman), 1941 to 1942; Nominating Committee, 1944 to 1945; Special Committee to Survey Museum Finances (chairman), 1939 to 1940; Trustee Visiting Committee to the Dept. of Public Relations, uncertain date to 1960; Special Trustee Committee on Staff Publications (chairman), 1953 to 1960. Letter to author from Metropolitan Museum of Art Assistant Archivist Ms. Frances G. Oakley, July 29, 1975.

[89] See letters to Page from H.W. Kent, Jan. 11 and 20, 1939; letter from Page to Vanderbilt Webb, Nov. 10, 1939; letter to Page from Kent, Dec. 7, 1939; letter from Page to William Church Osborn, Dec. 27, 1939; letters from Page to Nelson A. Rockefeller, Webb, Elihu Root Jr., Robert A. Lovett and Osborn, March 19, 1940; and letter to Page from Harry Batten, March 20, 1940, all in Boxes 5-6, Arthur W. Page Papers.

[90] See especially letter from Francis Henry Taylor to Page, March 19, 1940, and letters from Page to Nelson A. Rockefeller, Vanderbilt Webb, Elihu Root Jr., Robert A. Lovett and William Church Osborn, same date, Box 6, Arthur W. Page Papers.

[91] See especially letter from Francis Henry Taylor to Page, Jan. 8, 1941, with attached 13-page memorandum on new membership drive; letter from Page to Henry S. Morgan, Jan. 13, 1941; letter from Metropolitan Museum Vice-Director Horace H.F. Jayne to Page and others, Jan. 21, 1941; and "Report of the Committee on Membership," Feb. 18, 1941, attached to letter from Taylor to Page, same date; Box 7, Arthur W. Page Papers.

[92] Letter from Page to Frederick P. Keppel, Jan. 2, 1936, Box 4, Arthur W. Page Papers.

[93] *Ibid.*

[94] *Ibid.*

[95] "Minutes of the Negro Rural School Fund/Anna T. Jeanes Foundation," May 20, 1936, Box 4, Arthur W. Page Papers.

[96] Letters to Page and Dr. Albert Shaw from Arthur D. Wright, June 11, 1936, and "Minutes of Joint Meeting -Slater and Jeanes Boards January 14, 1937," Box 4, Arthur W. Page Papers.

[97] Letter to Page from Arthur D. Wright, Feb. 1, 1937, and letter to Page from Carnegie Corp. Secretary R.M. Lester, March 15, 1937, Box 4, Arthur W. Page Papers.

[98] Letter to Page from Frederick M. Eaton, April 28, 1937, and letter from Page to Edward A. Oldham, Jan. 18, 1938, Boxes 4-5, Arthur W. Page Papers, and 1947 Page résumé.

[99] "Minutes," meeting of Southern Education Foundation Finance Committee, March 21, 1940, Box 6, Arthur W. Page Papers.

[100] Letter from Mrs. Arthur D. Wright to Leslie Snow, July 21, 1940, Box 6, Arthur W. Page Papers.

[101] See especially letter from Page to Arthur D. Wright, Dec. 3, 1940; letter from Wright to Page, Jan. 6, 1941; and letter from Page to Robert O. Purves, Sept. 23, 1941; Box 7, Arthur W. Page Papers.

[102] 1947 Page résumé.

[103] Page's notecards. Mrs. Willis Wood insisted he participate.

[104] Page was a trustee of the Carnegie Corp. from 1934 to 1958. During

that period, the Carnegie Corp. gave $1,815,624 to the Council on Foreign Relations. Letter to author from Carnegie Corp. Secretary Florence Anderson, Aug. 5, 1975. See also Grose, *Continuing the Inquiry: The Council on Foreign Relations from 1921 to 1996, op. cit.*

[105] See especially letter from Page to Carnegie Corp. President Dr. Walter A. Jessup, April 27, 1942, Box 8, Arthur W. Page Papers.

[106] Letter to Page from Mrs. F. Huntington Babcock, Nov. 1, 1938, Box 4 or 5, Arthur W. Page Papers.

[107] See especially "Report of 1938 Expenditures, Educational and Development Fund of the Farmer's (*sic*) Federation, Asheville, N.C." in Box 5, Arthur W. Page Papers. See also letter to Page from James G.K. McClure, Sept. 13, 1937, Box 4, Arthur W. Page Papers.

[108] Page's notecards.

[109] *Ibid.*

[110] *Ibid.*, and Strahan memorandum.

[111] *Ibid.*

[112] Letters between Page and Leonard Wood Memorial Executive Director Perry Burgess, Nov. 11, 1939, Nov. 4 and Dec. 11, 1940, and April 22, 1941, Boxes 6-7, Arthur W. Page Papers.

[113] Page's notecards; letter from Page to University of Texas President Homer P. Rainey, Jan. 22, 1941, Box 7, Arthur W. Page Papers; and Cold Spring Harbor Laboratory, *Annual Report* (1974), p. 95.

[114] 1947 Page résumé.

[115] See especially letter from Page to Mrs. George S. Franklin, Feb. 3, 1933, Box 3, Arthur W. Page Papers.

[116] Letter to Page from Chase National Bank executive Wilton A. Pierce, Nov. 22, 1940 Box 7, Arthur W. Page Papers

[117] Based essentially on Page's notecards.

[118] See especially typed manuscript, "Harvard 300th Anniversary Fund," Feb. 15, 1935; letter to Page from John Price Jones, April 28, 1936, with attached John Price Jones Organization plan for publicizing Harvard Tercentenary Celebration and Three Hundredth Anniversary Fund; Boxes 3-4, Arthur W. Page Papers.

[119] See especially letters between Page and Harvard Dental School Dean Dr. Leroy M.S. Miner, May, 1936, and Feb. 5, 6 and 7, 1941; letter to Page from John and Mary Markle Foundation Vice President Archie S. Woods, March 26, 1936; letter to Page from Harvard Board of Overseers Assistant Secretary Jerome D. Greene, May 26, 1938; letter from Frederick P. Keppel to Prof. S.A. (probably meant for S.E.) Morison of Harvard College, Nov. 20, 1939; letter to Page from Harvard Medical School Dean Dr. C. Sidney Burwell, Dec. 18, 1939; and note from Charles Dollard of the Carnegie Corp. to Page transmitting to Page a memorandum entitled "Harvard School of Dental Medicine," Dec. 19, 1941; all in Boxes 4-8, Arthur W. Page Papers.

[120] Letter to author from Robert Shenton, secretary to the corporation, President and Fellows of Harvard College, Nov. 20, 1975.

[121] Letter to Page from Henry C. Clark, Oct. 10, 1939, Box 5, Arthur W. Page Papers.

[122] Letter to Page from James B. Conant, Feb. 2, 1940, and letters from Page to Donald K. David, March 12 and 29, 1940

[123] Letter from Page to A. Calvert Smith, Oct. 7, 1940, Box 7, Arthur W. Page Papers.

[124] John Hall Page completed his years at Harvard after 1941. In one of those ironic repetitions of history, he, like his father, was temporarily ex-

pelled from Harvard. Probably with his own experience in mind, Arthur Page did not show the notice from Harvard to son John until the end of the Christmas holiday season. John's "eviction notice" turned out to have been due to a clerical error, and like his father earlier, he was quickly reinstated. Letter to author from John Hall Page, Nov. 11, 1975.

125 *Ibid.* Letters regarding Page's chairmanship of the New York Yacht Club Library Committee are sprinkled throughout the Page Papers.

126 Letter from Page to friend Sven Salen in Sweden, July 28, 1939, and telegrams to Page from the Ivison Macadams in England, Aug. 25 and 31, 1939, Box 5, Arthur W. Page Papers.

127 Based essentially on letters from Page to J.S. Harrold and Hugh Gibson, Nov. 22, 1939, and Nov. 8, 1940, Boxes 6-7, Arthur W. Page Papers.

128 See especially letters from Page to Henry C. Corbett and Gardner B. Perry, June 21, 1941, and Aug. 6, 1941, Box 7, Arthur W. Page Papers.

129 Discussion of Arthur Page and the Wise Men's Club is based mainly on telephone interview with Hill and Knowlton Executive Committee Chairman John W. Hill, Aug. 1, 1975. See also George F. Hamel, "John W. Hill, Public Relations Pioneer" (Master's thesis, University of Wisconsin-Madison, 1966), pp. 229-31.

130 Letter to Page from Bruce Barton, May 16, 1938, Box 5, Arthur W. Page Papers.

131 Letter to Page from Frank R. Schell of Frank R. Schell and Associates, Aug. 9, 1938, Box 5, Arthur W. Page Papers.

132 Letters to Page from William H. Baldwin, March 24, 1939, and Jan. 27, 1941, Boxes 5 and 7, Arthur W. Page Papers.

133 Letter from Northrup Clarey of Standard Oil to Page, Dec. 27, 1939, Box 6, Arthur W. Page Papers.

134 Letter from Page to Pendleton Dudley, Jan. 23, 1940, Box 6, Arthur W. Page Papers.

135 Letter to Page from Rex F. Harlow, March 23, 1940, Box 6, Arthur W. Page Papers.

136 Letters to Page from James L. McCamy, Dec. 19, 1940, and Jan. 21, 1941, Box 7, Arthur W. Page Papers.

137 Letter from Guy Vaughan to Page, April 15, 1941, and Page's reply, April 25, 1941, Box 7, Arthur W. Page Papers.

138 Kai Bird, *The Chairman: John J. McCloy, the Making of the American Establishment* (New York: Simon & Schuster, 1992), pp. 108-113.

CHAPTER SEVEN

World War II through Retirement from AT&T, 1941-1946

ARTHUR PAGE DEVOTED much of his time during World War II to assisting in the war effort. He performed important missions assigned to him by his old friend and neighbor Henry L. Stimson, who headed the War Dept. for the duration.

He made two wartime trips to Europe at Stimson's request, one to oversee troop information for the Normandy invasion, the other to resolve some Army personnel problems, particularly a clash between Gen. George S. Patton and the staff of armed forces newspaper *Stars and Stripes*. He devoted many hours to heading the Joint Army and Navy Committee on Welfare and Recreation from 1942 to 1946.

In connection with his work for the War Dept., Page wrote what was surely the most widely published news release of his life. The story went out to the world at 11 a.m. Washington time on Monday, Aug. 6, 1945. The words were written by Page for President Harry S Truman, who at the time was returning from the Potsdam Conference aboard the cruiser *U.S.S. Augusta*. The Truman statement began:

Sixteen hours ago an American airplane dropped one bomb on Hiroshima, an important Japanese Army base. That bomb had more power than 20,000 tons of TNT. It had more than two thousand times the blast power of the British "Grand Slam" which is the largest bomb ever yet used in the history of warfare.

The Japanese began the war from the air at Pearl Harbor. They have been repaid manyfold. And the end is not yet. With this bomb we have added a new and revolutionary increase in destruction to supplement the growing power of our armed forces. In their present form these bombs are now in production and even more powerful forms are in development

It is an atomic bomb. It is a harnessing of the basic power of the universe. The force from which the sun draws its powers has been loosed against those who brought war to the Far East.

Before 1939, it was the accepted belief of scientists that it was theoretically possible to release atomic energy. But no one knew any practical method of doing it...

We have spent $2 billion on the greatest scientific gamble in history—and won.[1]

On the other side of the international date line, three American B-29 bombers had flown the six-and-a-half-hour trip from Tinian to Hiroshima. The lead plane, the *Enola Gay*, carried an atomic bomb nicknamed "Little Boy." Measuring 10 feet long and a little over two feet in diameter, and weighing some 9,000 pounds, "Little Boy" detonated on Aug. 6 at 8:15 a.m. Hiroshima time (7:15 p.m. Aug. 5 Washington time). The two chase bombers recorded what they could of the damage.

Upon landing at Tinian, Lt. Col. Paul Tibbetts of the *Enola Gay* was awarded the distinguished service cross, then the nation's second-highest award for valor. Tibbetts described the mission succinctly: "Saw city, destroyed same." That was understatement. Of the 245,000 to 350,000 people living in the Hiroshima environs, some 40,000 of them military personnel, 120,000 to 170,000 were casualties—70,000 to 100,000 killed immediately, 50,000 to 70,000 seriously injured in the initial blast. Radiation would over time maim and mutilate tens of thousands more.

In early 2000, a panel of journalists at the Newseum in

Alexandria, Va., selected the atomic bomb as the top news story of the 20th century. The biggest story of the 20th century was also one of the most managed.

On the day Hiroshima was incinerated, Acting Press Secretary Eben Ayers, a Roosevelt press aide who stayed on at Truman's request, read Page's 1,160-word news release to a dozen or so reporters at the White House. Just before the story was shuttled from the Pentagon to the White House for release, the War Dept. revised the lead sentence to name the target city and specify the hours since the bomb exploded. The words "an important Japanese Army base" were added to the lead to justify the selected target. The revisions were probably made by Gen. Leslie Groves, director of the Manhattan Project, or at his orders by a staffer.

Minutes after Ayers gave newsmen the release, it was being taken down over the telephone by a dictationist at the Washington Bureau of United Press, predecessor of United Press International. Like many American newsmen, Chiles Coleman, manning the UP Washington desk that morning, had trouble comprehending the magnitude of the story. As the dictationist tore the story from her typewriter and handed it to him, he glanced at the words. Then he tried to envision the explosion of 20,000 tons of TNT. The impact of the story began to register. As the story started to clatter out on the UP trunkwire, he realized that the death of elderly Progressive Sen. Hiram Johnson would not be the day's top story.

Reporters covering the story were initially given only the Truman announcement, plus a 7,500-word statement by Secretary of War Stimson and a Pentagon news item saying an impenetrable cloud of dust and smoke over Hiroshima prevented an accurate assessment of damage. Americans got their first information about the bomb from radio broadcasts and afternoon daily newspapers on Aug. 6th.

Several hours after the Truman and Stimson materials were handed out at the White House, the Pentagon released 14 background articles about the bomb, most of them by William L. Laurance, science reporter of the *New York Times*. He was the only reporter who had been at the Trinity site.

His stories appeared in morning dailies on Aug. 7, under his byline in the *New York Times*, but rewritten in many a.m. dailies under other bylines.

The Potsdam Conference, held in East Germany near Berlin, concluded on Aug. 1. Secretary of War Stimson, invited only reluctantly by Truman to Potsdam and then snubbed by him there, flew back to Washington two days before the end. Truman flew to England where he had lunch with King George VI on *H.M.S. Renown*, and then departed from Plymouth Roads on the *U.S.S. Augusta* for the return to America.

Aboard the *Augusta* at lunchtime on Aug. 6, Truman received a coded message from Stimson telling him about Hiroshima: "Results clear-cut successful in all respects. Visible effects greater than in any test." A second message confirmed the detonation time. "This is the greatest day (or 'thing,' depending on which source you believe) in history," a jubilant Truman is said to have told the sailors.

The *Augusta* arrived at Norfolk at dinner time on Aug. 7, and Truman was back at his desk in Washington on the morning of the 8th.[2]

The story of how Page became privy to one of the best-kept secrets in American history is told later in this chapter.

Keeping up morale of the fighting forces

THE JOINT ARMY and Navy Committee on Welfare and Recreation of World War II grew out of World War I experience, when morale services for men in arms were exclusively provided by civilian agencies like the Young Men's Christian Assn. After the war, Raymond Fosdick, who had been responsible for coordinating these organizations, recommended that in the future the Army take responsibility for many of the morale services that had been provided by civilian agencies. Secretary of War Newton Baker agreed.

In 1940, when expansion of the American military machine began, the only morale services available to those in uniform were libraries and the Army Motion Picture Service.[3]

In January 1941, Carnegie trustee Frederick Osborn was called to Army uniform as a brigadier general to build troop morale services. Initially named the Morale Branch, his command was soon renamed the Special Service Division.

The Army at this time also created a War Dept. Committee on Education, Recreation and Community Service to coordinate military and civilian morale services for soldiers. Osborn headed the committee composed of both civilians and military officers.[4] Within a month after it was formed, a turf war erupted. Although the Navy and Federal Security Agency agreed to participate, FSA Administrator Paul V. McNutt's office was irked by the War Dept.'s invasion of its responsibility.

In February 1941, Secretary of War Stimson, Secretary of the Navy Frank Knox and FSA Administrator McNutt submitted a memo to President Roosevelt outlining what they thought their respective troop welfare responsibilities should be. The War Dept. agreed to be responsible for morale services at Army bases. The Navy said it would care for welfare programs at its installations. The Federal Security Agency claimed sole responsibility for federal and civilian morale services in communities adjacent to military installations.[5]

Roosevelt approved the memorandum. Representatives from the Navy and FSA joined Gen. Osborn's committee, and it became the Joint Army and Navy Committee on Welfare and Recreation, or JANC. In October 1941, General Osborn stepped down as chairman of the committee and was replaced by Fowler V. Harper, an Indiana University law professor serving as deputy chairman of the War Manpower Commission and as a member of the National War Labor Board.[6]

Arthur Page, who had exchanged several letters with Osborn about Army morale in the early 1940s, became actively involved in JANC in May 1942, when he was asked to head one of the blue-ribbon subcommittees formed by JANC to deal with various morale problems. Page was asked to chair the JANC Subcommittee on Radio. He accepted the position, and became a special consultant to the Secretary of War, a title he held for the duration.[7]

Page's subcommittee was assigned the mission of making recommendations on how the military could best deliver popular radio entertainment and news programs to troops at home and in combat zones abroad. Page held the first meeting of the group at his AT&T offices in May 1942. Among those present were John Reber of the J. Walter Thompson advertising agency (one of the nation's largest radio program producers), Davidson Taylor, standing in for CBS chief William Paley, and Ralph Starr Butler of General Foods, one of the nation's largest radio program sponsors. Members of the subcommittee endorsed Army plans to make radio programs available through short-wave broadcasting and through massive distribution of records to be played on phonographs provided to individual troop units.[8]

The Subcommittee on Radio oversaw a program to entertain and inform troop units. Early in the war, it:

• Urged the military to stop asking sponsors to furnish free recordings of popular radio shows and instead pay for pressings provided to troops.[9]

• Recommended that the Armed Forces Radio Service (AFRS) be formed in the Army Signal Corps to originate news, troop information and entertainment programs.[10]

• Called for construction of larger rebroadcasting transmitters and the issuance of more powerful shortwave receivers to American forces in Europe and North Africa. Early in the war, American forces in these theaters were listening to stronger signals from the BBC and German transmitters.[11]

• Recommended, following a visit of subcommittee member Niles Trammell of NBC to North Africa, that more attention be given to news on AFRS. Lt. Gen. Mark W. Clark had complained to Trammell that his Fifth Army was getting too much entertainment and not enough information.[12]

• Urged the use by AFRS of more powerful transmitters in the Pacific Theater, where armed forces were getting a better signal from Radio Tokyo than from the Pentagon voice.[13]

Page's work for the Subcommittee on Radio was prelude to more important duties with the War Dept. In July 1942, Gen. Osborn asked Page if he would take over the chairmanship of JANC, permitting Fowler Harper to resign and attend to other duties. In August, the Secretaries of War and Navy made the request formal, and Page accepted.

Through early 1942, JANC was concerned with placing recreation and welfare programs at military installations and with coordinating civilian agencies that provided leisure-time activities for the military in communities near bases. By late 1942, JANC was more concerned with maintaining troop morale through information and education programs. Page used his skills as a communicator to oversee programs designed to get American troops in a fighting frame of mind.

Page's appointment as chairman of JANC was announced by the War Dept. in early December 1942.[14] The committee was then operating on a fiscal-year budget of $80,000 provided by the Army and Navy.[15] In addition, a special Committee of Trustees on Experimental Programs subordinate to JANC had additional money from the Carnegie Corp. to fund studies into troop morale.

When Page became JANC chairman, the committee had 11 civilian members, four military members and three paid staffers. Perhaps the best-known civilians were Rockefeller Foundation head Raymond Fosdick, Sinclair Oil Chairman Sheldon Clark (who also headed the Navy League) and Charles P. Taft, assistant director of the Office of Defense Health and Welfare Services.

Page conducted much of his business through JANC Secretary Francis Keppel, the son of retired Carnegie Corp. Executive Director Frederick Keppel.[16]

JANC held some 50 meetings during the war. Among its accomplishments, the committee:

• Oversaw the most extensive troop information and education program in American military history.

• Allowed the Army and Navy to exchange information on what each was doing in the morale area.

• Kept peace (most of the time) between the American Red Cross and United Service Organizations (USO), the major civilian troop welfare agencies, between which there was considerable rivalry.

• Inspected hundreds of military installations and made recommendations for improving morale at them.

• Made recommendations for improving morale services for minority troops, particularly black Americans and women, and played a role in desegregation of domestic recreational facilities for military personnel.

• Assisted from 1943 forward in demobilization planning.

Page's powers of diplomacy were put to severe test in his efforts to maintain peace between the Red Cross and USO.

The Red Cross had established a precedent for providing welfare services to military personnel in World War I.

A formidable competitor was created in 1941 when the USO was formed to coordinate the military service programs of the YMCA, YWCA, National Catholic Community Service, Salvation Army, Jewish Welfare Board and National Travelers Aid Society. Chester Barnard, the brilliant president of the New Jersey Telephone Co., an AT&T subsidiary, was named to head the USO, which conducted a $10 million fund drive to finance its operations. In addition to providing leisure-time opportunities for soldiers and sailors in towns near military installations, the USO had an affiliate, Camp Shows, Inc. Headed by Thomas J. Watson of International Business Machines, Camp Shows provided vaudeville and other live entertainment for U.S. military personnel.[17]

In early 1942, the USO asked for permission to establish clubs in England, and to eventually expand into other overseas zones where U.S. troops were stationed. The military, wishing to deal with as few private agencies as possible, restricted the USO to operating only in the U.S.A., Hawaii, Panama, Newfoundland, Bermuda, the Caribbean, South America and parts of Alaska. The Red Cross was given sole permission to coordinate civilian services in the North African, European and Pacific Theaters, where troop concentrations would eventually be densest. Heaping insult on injury, the military said the USO should stage its camp shows at Red Cross clubs in the major combat zones.[18]

Page made it clear in a vexed letter to Gen. Osborn that he felt the USO had a right to feel angry.[19]

Raymond Fosdick deserves much of the credit for restoring a temporary truce between the Red Cross and USO in early 1943. He persuaded John D. Rockefeller Jr. to send letters to USO Chairman Barnard and American Red Cross Chairman Norman Davis urging them to reconcile their differences, which they did.[20]

The feud between the two agencies broke out again in 1944. The new conflict erupted when Navy Secretary James Forrestal asked the YMCA and Catholic Charities, members of the USO, to put their properties in the Philippines and China under jurisdiction of the Red Cross until the end of the war. The two charities protested. Chester Barnard released them from their agreement not to function in the Pacific.

In an angry letter to Asst. to the Secretary of War Harvey Bundy, Page said Barnard's action resulted from mishandling of the matter by the military. He warned that military commanders in the Pacific might soon be dealing with a multiplicity of civilian agencies if the Pentagon did not move quickly to repair the damage. The military engineered a compromise whereby the YMCA and Catholic Charities were permitted to take back control of their former properties in just-liberated territory, but civilian welfare operations elsewhere had to continue under jurisdiction of the Red Cross in the Pacific to the end of the war.[21]

Another sensitive area for JANC was in regard to blacks and females in the Army and Navy.

In June 1940, unable to sweet-talk A. Philip Randolph of the Brotherhood of Sleeping Car Porters into calling off a planned 100,000-black march on Washington, President Roosevelt signed an executive order banning discrimination in defense industry employment because of "race, creed, color or national origin."

Although black leaders and civil rights advocates from then on pressured for fair treatment of blacks in the armed forces, the United States in World War II deployed the largest racially segregated military force in the nation's history. By the time Japan surrendered, almost 700,000 blacks were in the segregated U.S. Army around the world, and another

167,000 were serving in the Navy. More than 19,000 blacks ultimately served in the Marine Corps. [22]

Although an amendment to the Selective Service Act of 1940 stipulated that selection of volunteers and draftees was not be based on "race or color," the act gave military departments unlimited discretion in developing their own standards. The upshot was a defense establishment that was largely segregated until July 1948, when President Truman desegregated the armed forces with Executive Order 9981.

The Army policy that prevailed for most of the war was issued by President Roosevelt just before the 1940 election. In an interpretation of the Selective Service Act, he ordered the War Dept. to maintain the same proportion of blacks in the military as in the general population, at the time 10 percent. However, the policy also stipulated that for purposes of troop morale and defense preparations, the War Dept. would not "intermingle colored and white enlisted personnel in the same regimental organizations."

The Army from 1941 to 1943 held that the military should not be a laboratory for social experimentation. Integration might hurt unit efficiency and create racial friction. In a 1942 memo to Gen. Osborn, Arthur Page reflected the prevailing attitude. In his opinion, he said, a solution to the race question "is not a military matter and any effort to make it so will neither further the cause of the Negro, solve the problem, nor advance America's cause in the war."[23]

The Navy and Marine Corps were at first able to avoid the race problem by accepting only white volunteers except for the most menial tasks. As the war progressed, the needs of all military branches for manpower led to increased reliance on the draft and to more blacks in uniform.

In response to racial problems in the Army, Secretary of War Stimson in 1942 created the Advisory Committee on Negro Troop Policies chaired by Asst. Secretary John J. McCloy. Black ranks swelled by the draft led to more racial pressures and to the gradual reform of policies.[24]

Although Page was not in sympathy with the aggressive efforts by blacks to win concessions, other members of JANC were. Fred Hoehler of the American Welfare Assn. called for better treatment of Afro-Americans following a visit in the fall of 1942 to Ft. Huachuca, Ariz., an almost all-black post. In mid-1943, Townsend Hoagland called for better treatment of blacks at Alaskan installations he had just visited.[25]

As the number of blacks in the military swelled, segregation led to morale problems in black units and an increasing number of racial incidents at domestic Army posts. In the first half of 1943, there were racial incidents at Camp Van Dorn, Miss.; Camp Stewart, Ga.; March Field, Calif.; Fort Bliss, Texas; Camp Breckinridge, Ky.; and San Luis Obispo, Calif.[26]

Among other actions, McCloy ordered JANC to investigate desegregation of domestic recreational facilities—theaters, post exchanges and canteens. Social scientist Donald Young of the University of Pennsylvania was assigned to develope plans for better integrating uniformed blacks into the military machine. He spent two days a week at the JANC offices at the Pentagon until mid-1944, when he resigned, charging that the Army was falling far short of its potential for utilizing black soldiers.[27]

The recommendations of the McCloy Committee to better utilize black soldiers domestically and abroad were grudgingly and far from universally implemented by Army leaders. The Army adjutant general signaled progress when he issued a March 1943 letter that all personnel, regardless of race, were to be given equal opportunity to enjoy recreational facilities at each Army post, camp and station. More was accomplished in July 1944 when Army Adj. Gen. James A. Ulio issued a memo to all commanding generals reiterating the 1943 order, and specifically stipulating that post exchanges, transportation facilities and motion picture theaters were to be available to all regardless of race. The Ulio memo helped to resolve a particular problem, blacks having to wait before boarding trucks between bases and buses to local communities until whites were aboard, resulting in blacks having to stand on the bus or wait for the next vehicle. [28]

The ordered desegregation did not go unchallenged by JANC. Page recruited James G. Hanes, chairman of the board

of the Hanes Hosiery Mills of North Carolina, to inspect morale and recreational facilities that had been desegregated
in the Jim Crow states of Georgia, Alabama, North and South
Carolina. Hanes forwarded his final report to JANC in the
spring of 1944 while Page was in England. Page upon returning brought the report up for approval at a JANC meeting so
it could be forwarded to the secretaries of war and navy. Dr.
Channing Tobias, the black member of JANC representing
the YMCA National Council, vehemently objected to a section calling for resegregation of recreational facilities at southern military installations. Hanes contended both blacks and
whites he had interviewed had expressed a desire for such
segregation. JANC members voted to forward the report as
Hanes had written it, but only after Gen. Osborn had attached
a cover letter disavowing the call for resegregation.[29]

In an effort to better understand the welfare and morale
needs of women in the armed forces, Page recruited Sarah
Gibson Blanding, dean of the College of Home Economics at
Cornell University, to look into problems facing females in
military branches such as the WAACs (the WACs after Sept.
1, 1943), WAVES, WASPS and SPARS.[30] She began her work
soon after a public spate of criticism regarding the morale of
women on active duty with the Army WAACs branch.[31] In a
report issued about a year after her appointment to JANC,
she called for efforts to improve attitudes toward women in
the military and to end the impression that women in uniform were not welcome at USO clubs.[32]

As chairman of JANC, Page acted as overseer of a monumental public relations program aimed at educating and informing the armed forces and maintaining the morale of
troops. The various branches of the armed forces of course
did the work, but JANC provided guidance and necessary
approvals. The final report of Page's committee gives some
idea of the magnitude of the programs JANC supervised.
Among other things:[33]

- The military ran a motion picture distribution syndicate involving 1,100 Army and 550 Navy theaters in
  the United States, and the showing of Hollywood films

wherever troops were stationed overseas, from jungle clearings to aboard ships.

• The Armed Forces Radio Service by the end of 1945 was distributing 120,000 transcriptions of popular radio programs monthly. In addition, AFRS was doing its own broadcasting over 177 of its own transmitters and another 54 foreign-owned stations, originating 4,400 hours of shortwave programming per week from New York and San Francisco.

• By the end of the war, USO Camp Shows had sent some 700 professional entertainment units overseas, and another 500 units had performed in the United States. An estimated 155 million troops had seen the shows. Millions more had seen "soldier and sailor" shows staged with uniformed personnel.

• The military had organized athletic leagues around the world, providing coaches and equipment to players.

• Some 62 million books were furnished to troops by the end of the war, and magazines were being sent out to reading rooms at home and abroad at the rate of 120 million copies per year.

• The Army organized the U.S. Armed Forces Institute (USAFI), an educational facility headquartered at Madison, Wis., with branches during the war in London, Rome, Anchorage, Brisbane, Manila, Cairo, New Delhi, Puerto Rico, Panama and New Caledonia. Through USAFI, more than a million servicemen and women enrolled in courses in hundreds of subjects.

• The military produced a wide variety of films for training and morale purposes. Most notable for their troop indoctrination purpose was a series of films called "Why We Fight," designed to explain why America was at war. A number of other orientation films, including Donald Young's "The Negro Soldier" were also produced.

• *Stars and Stripes*, the daily newspaper published by the military for fighting forces, by the end of the war was publishing 1.2 million copies per day in Europe, 200,000 copies per day in the Mediterranean and 70,000 copies per day in the Pacific. Weekly editions were published in other areas.

• *Yank* magazine, another part of the military morale effort, had risen by 1945 to a circulation of 2.4 million copies per week.

• News maps published by the War Dept. to update American forces on progress of fighting in the various theaters rose to a circulation of 60,000 copies domestically and 130,000 copies overseas by war's end.

Page continued to head JANC through 1946, overseeing production of its final report and supervising the postwar planning of the Army and Navy to continue welfare, recreation, troop education and information programs for personnel not yet discharged from active duty.

In early January 1947, he recommended dissolution of JANC to Secretary of War Robert Patterson who had succeeded Stimson.[34] Because Secretary of the Navy Forrestal did not wish the committee totally disbanded, a successor organization not headed by Page and with which he was only marginally involved was appointed. The successor organization faded away in 1949.[35]

Preparing fighting forces for the Normandy Invasion

IN THE SPRING of 1944, some three million men were being prepared in England for Operation Overlord, the proposed Allied invasion of the European mainland.

On June 6, an armada of 5,000 ships began unloading the first contingent of 176,000 men on the beaches of Normandy. Fighting men, support troops and materiel were poured into the foothold that had been established. In July, one British, one Canadian and two American columns broke out of the Cherbourg Peninsula, beginning an offensive that would end, following the Battle of the Bulge, in the collapse of Germany.[36]

The American forces that would participate in Overlord had to be mentally prepared. On April 5, 1944, Page departed for England on a secret 100-day mission for the secretary of war. His main assignment was to oversee indoctrination of the American invasionary force.

Col. Oscar N. Solbert, chief of morale and special services for the European Theater of Operations, had overall responsibility for troop information, education and morale. Page was sent to assist him, particularly in getting troop commanders to cooperate in information and education efforts.

As he had in World War I, Page declined a commission in World War II. He went to England as a civilian, with the assimilated rank of colonel, knowing he would be better able to work with Solbert if he neither outranked nor underranked him.[37]

Page stayed in Europe for more than three months, through D-Day and long enough after to make a visit to Cherbourg on the continent.

He helped Col. Solbert and his staff coordinate information provided to the invasionary force through *Stars and Stripes, Yank*, daily broadcasts of the Army News Service (ANS), Army films and newsreels and troop information meetings. He prepared schedules of what was to be said to soldiers each week, sat in on military staff meetings as emissary of the secretary of war and wrote the statement to be given to soldiers as they embarked for the Normandy beaches.[38]

As he had stressed face-to-face supervisor-employee communication at AT&T, Page stressed to Solbert and invasion force commanders the importance of Army mass media messages (such as those in *Stars and Stripes*) being discussed by officers face-to-face with their enlisted men. Despite the resistance of some commanders to troop information sessions, orientation materials were issued to commanders along with orders to cover the topics with their men.[39]

In remarks to AT&T's Information Dept. after returning from England, Page explained what he had done:

> We spend considerable time and effort trying to persuade the people in the Bell System—in print and otherwise—to be courteous and polite... This was the same

process in the Army in exactly the opposite direction. The job there was to persuade the men in the Army to be anything but polite to the Germans.

Now, the method was to have a pamphlet for discussion by the officers with all the men once a week, an inset in the daily paper once a week, a radio program which gave the same picture over the radio once a week, plus plugs all through the week and occasionally *Yank*, the Army weekly magazine, would help out when it could. All of that was directed so that if the fellows missed it at one count they got it on the rebound somewhere else .

...(W)e took things Hitler had said and explained them in G.I. language... We had men from the First Division tell their experiences in Italy—all translated into G.I. language. There were some generals who did not like it but actually it had an effect on the men. I was very much surprised because as you know, in our work here it takes a long time to get an idea to percolate. This was very different. When the marshalling area was closed off... from contact with everything outside, two things happened—attendance at church went up 300%, and attention to what was printed went up about the same....[40]

From D-Day forward, the troop orientation job became one of keeping soldiers informed, particularly on the lessons being learned in combat. *Stars and Stripes* became the main vehicle for rapidly informing troops of combat lessons. For the first few days after the beachhead was established, the staff continued to print the paper in London, with copies shipped to France. Soon after the invasion, however, the staff moved to the Cherbourg foothold on the continent, where firsthand information was more readily available, and began printing a continental edition of the newspaper there.[41]

Page recognized the effectiveness of combat information printed in *Stars and Stripes.* "After the first three or four days of the invasion the Germans tried the same old 'white flag' trick and offered to surrender, but when our men went up to get them they were shot down," he related to AT&T employees. "The men wounded in that were interviewed and it was printed in the paper. About four days later a G2 officer asked if we would not please write how to take prisoners safely. They... had not taken any in the last few days."[42]

While in London, Page developed a liking for Maj. Arthur Goodfriend, who wrote for *Stars and Stripes* and handled other troop information duties. Goodfriend, in later life a controversial employee of the U.S. Information Service, and author of *The Twisted Image*, a book critical of USIS programs in India, earned Page's respect because he kept up-to-date on G.I. vernacular by periodically donning a private's uniform and slipping into combat units with replacements.[43]

Soon after D-Day, Page made a brief trip to the Cherbourg peninsula before returning home.[44] At Cherbourg he liberated a bottle of French brandy that he never got to enjoy. He left the bottle in a suitcase in a railroad locker in New York while he went on to Washington to report on what he had seen and heard in England and France. When he was finally able to reclaim the suitcase, he found the bottle had exploded, ruining both the vintage and his clothes.[45]

Back in the United States, Page took several actions aimed at improving morale among European troops. He:

• Urged Pentagon officers to use a lighter hand in ordering material into *Stars and Stripes*. Civilian war correspondents were protesting Army interference with what was supposed to be a voice written by enlisted men for enlisted men.[46]

• Smoothed over another controversy between the Red Cross and USO, this one involving whether or not the USO should he permitted to send mobile cinema units to entertain troops in Europe. Page over Red Cross objections got permission for the USO to send the units.[47]

• Assisted in getting war correspondent and humorist Bill Mauldin permanently assigned to the European edition of *Stars and Stripes*.[48]

• Intervened to prevent *Stars and Stripes* from being taken away from the Army's Information and Education Division and placed under control of the Army Bureau of Public Relations. Page argued that *Stars and Stripes* should be a morale vehicle, not a means for propagandizing troops and planting publicity favorable to the military.[49]

Second mission to Europe

IN EARLY FEBRUARY 1945, Page left America for a second wartime visit to Europe, this one to Paris, which had been liberated from German control.[50] He was on another mission for the War Dept., ostensibly to review Army radio operations in Europe, but in reality, to troubleshoot problems at the G.I. newspaper *Stars and Stripes*.

Col. Solbert had asked that Page be sent back to the European Theater to resolve a conflict that had erupted between the War Dept. and the editorial staff of *Stars and Stripes*. By 1945, the editorial staff, headed by maverick Maj. Arthur Goodfriend, believed it should have complete freedom from the War Dept. to decide what went into the newspaper. That resulted in several clashes.

The most publicized fight was between *Stars and Stripes* staffer Bill Mauldin and Third Army Commander Gen. George S. Patton. Patton believed in "spit-and-polish" military discipline. He objected to "Willie and Joe," the disheveled, unshaven and extremely popular G.I. cartoon heroes Mauldin drew for *Stars and Stripes*.

While the conflict between Patton and Mauldin is familiar history, a less well-known incident led Gen. Osborn (who by 1945 was in charge of the Army's Information and Education Division) to ask Page to tactfully fire Goodfriend as editor of the European edition of *Stars and Stripes*.

The incident that angered Osborn involved Goodfriend obeying rather than refusing to take orders about the content of *Stars and Stripes*. Undersecretary of War Robert Patterson had asked Goodfriend to write an editorial for *Stars and Stripes* that he could use as ammunition in Congress to lobby for a bill the War Dept. wanted enacted. Goodfriend wrote the editorial. Staffers at *Stars and Stripes* went to civilian war correspondents and complained that the editor was taking orders from the Pentagon. A critical story moved from Europe on the Associated Press wire, discrediting any political value the Goodfriend editorial might have had in Congress.[51]

Page wrote at least two letters to Osborn from France arguing against dismissing Goodfriend. On the surface, Osborn appeared mollified. He wrote to Goodfriend congratulating him on his promotion to lieutenant colonel, and telling him not to worry about the flap over the editorial, but in his private correspondence with Page, he remained adamant about the need to remove Goodfriend. Page too could be stubborn. He finally persuaded Osborn that the wisest course would be to let Goodfriend stay on.[52]

While in France, Page laid the groundwork for a policy aimed at freeing *Stars and Stripes* from interference of War Dept. officials such as Patton and Patterson. Shortly after Page left the European Theater to return home, Gen. Dwight D. Eisenhower, supreme Allied commander in Europe, issued a letter ordering that *Stars and Stripes* was to be free from all interference from anyone but him personally. Objections from commanders to content of the newspaper were to pass through him.[53]

A second outcome of Page's visit to Paris was a reorganization resulting in troop orientation programs being placed under direct control of an officer on Eisenhower's personal staff. Field commanders had been shirking their duty to keep soldiers informed. The officer made it clear that troop information and education was a command responsibility.[54]

Mauldin and Patton met informally at Patton's headquarters soon after Page returned to America and declared a temporary cease-fire in their battle of wills. The truce was soon broken when Mauldin again attacked Patton,[55] who might have taken a lesson from Boss Tweed of Tammany Hall. Tweed didn't care what was written about him since the electorate didn't read, but "hated them damned pictures" of him drawn by cartoonist Thomas Nast.

Privy to Manhattan Project secrets

PAGE BECAME INVOLVED in the Manhattan Project, the
super-secret program for development of S-1 (the atomic
bomb), shortly before a prototype of one of the two versions
of the bomb was successfully tested at the Trinity Site near
Alamogordo in New Mexico.

In March 1945, after returning from Paris, he began planning a trip to the Pacific Theater to review morale and troop
information activities. On March 29, he cancelled the trip.
Secretary of War Stimson had asked him to conduct an immediate review of the Army Public Relations Office.[56]

On April 6, the *New York Times* reported Page had been
called to full-time duty as a consultant to Stimson to work
with Maj. Gen. Alexander Day Surles, chief of the War Dept.'s
Bureau of Public Relations. The *Times* conjectured that his
duties would involve preparing plans for informing the public on redeployment of American forces to the Pacific and
eventual demobilization.[57] *Business Week* said Page's job
would be "to refine the Army's usually heavy-handed public
relations techniques" in acquainting the public with the hard
facts of redeployment of troops from Europe to Asia.[58]

Page completed his study of the Bureau of Public Relations in early June, recommending sweeping changes in organization discussed later in this chapter.[59] He also reviewed
Army plans to inform the public of redeployment of troops
to the Pacific for the final struggle against Japan.

On June 11, he asked Stimson to relieve him of full-time
duty and let him return to AT&T.[60]

Although he had completed his mission, Stimson asked
him to stay on. It was then, Page recalled later, that he learned
the real reason he had been called to active duty. Stimson
wanted someone he could trust near him to talk about the
atomic bomb. As Page put it in his *Reminiscences*:

> He had a great conscience about whether he ought
> to use this doggoned thing or not, and if so, how. What
> he wanted to do was to have somebody he could talk it

over with... (W)e'd been together so much, I think he just liked to talk this thing over, and that's what it was all about.

He had a committee which was advising him about the bomb. They didn't meet very often. I met with them once or twice. It had George Harrison and Jimmy Byrnes and various people on it. But when he really got down to it, the Colonel had to make up his mind and do the recommending to the President. So he decided to use the bomb, where you use it, and how you use it.

...It was very distressing to me, not because I had any question about what you do about weapons you've got when you're fighting. I didn't have half as much conscience about it as he did. But it is really a most bothersome thing to have something on your mind you can't talk to anybody about....[61]

In his biography of Stimson, Elting Morison provides much the same account. While Stimson was deliberating use of the bomb, he wanted someone constantly at his side to listen, "someone that he knew he could trust, that had no stake in the game." He could have used Harvey Bundy, George Harrison or John McCloy of his staff for this, but all three had a stake in the bomb. Bundy received his first briefing on the Manhattan Project (so named because its original offices were in Manhattan) in late 1941. Harrison was responsible for monitoring final development of the weapons. McCloy, who believed an invasion of Japan was unnecessary, was drafting the Potsdam Declaration for President Truman. He wanted to include a warning about the bomb and an assurance that Emperor Hirohito would be permitted to retain his throne after Japan surrendered. Stimson supported both of these provisions. Truman, influenced by Byrnes, cut both from the final draft.[62]

Vice President Harry S Truman had become president on April 12, 1945, when Franklin Roosevelt died. As a senator in 1944 he was only vaguely aware of a secret weapon project.

Immediately after Truman was sworn in on the evening

of April 12, Stimson gave him a sketchy warning about the bomb. The same evening, Stimson began plans to create an Interim Committee to advise the new president on its use. A week later, Gen. Leslie Groves gave Truman a thorough briefing on the Manhattan Project.

Page was first told about the Manhattan Project around the time the Interim Committee was formed. This Committee was headed by Stimson himself. Members in addition were Harvard President James Conant, Massachusetts Institute of Technology President Karl T. Compton, Carnegie Institute President Vannevar Bush, Undersecretary of the Navy Ralph A. Bard, Asst. Secretary of State William L. Clayton, Stimson's special assistant on S-1, George L. Harrison, and Jimmy Byrnes, who succeeded Edward Stettinius as secretary of state and was Truman's man on the committee.

The obvious reference Page makes in his *Reminiscences* to attending meetings of the Interim Committee make it certain he knew about Manhattan and S-1 by May 1945 since the Interim Committee held its only meetings on May 9, 14, 18 and 31. For certain, he was present with the eight members at the May 31 meeting when final recommendations were formulated. Other non-members present were Generals Leslie Groves and George C. Marshall; Harvey Bundy; and Scientific Advisory Panel members Robert Oppenheimer, Enrico Fermi, Arthur Compton and Ernest O. Lawrence.

Although Navy Undersecretary Bard had reservations, members unanimously endorsed use of the atomic bomb, without warning, as soon as possible, against a target that would make a "profound psychological impression." Jimmy Byrnes, who had told Truman what he knew about the bomb the day after Stimson provided the initial information, now bypassed Stimson and carried the Interim Committee recommendations directly to Truman, who concurred. It remained for Stimson to make his personal recommendation to Truman, which he did on July 6.

When Page refers to the 78-year-old Stimson's "great conscience" about using the bomb, he may be referring to Stimson's personal thought processes or to the impact on

Stimson of an emotional letter sent just before Hiroshima by an engineer named Brewster. The letter discussed the implications for the future of civilization of "loosing the whirlwind." However, Stimson, renowned for his honesty and decency, was also then concerned about ongoing firebombings of Japan, and Page may be alluding to Stimson's heightened sensitivity to the unprecedented destruction the atom bomb would unleash. While Stimson never actually opposed the use of the bomb, John McCloy recalled in later years that Stimson lay awake at night considering the consequences of using it on cities the size of Hiroshima and Nagasaki.

Despite reservations, Stimson like Truman was committed to the bomb as a way to end the war before the great loss of life that would certainly occur on both sides if American troops had to invade the Japanese mainland. Stimson and Truman remained committed during the Potsdam Conference, where they first received news of the successful July 16 test near Alamogordo, N.M. There was little if any indecision on the part of either that the bomb was going to be used to bring a quick end to the war in the Pacific—and to justify the expenditure of $2.6 billion on its development.

Although Page knew after the successful Trinity Site test of the plutonium bomb (there was never any doubt that the uranium-235 bomb would work) that the Pacific war would likely be over sooner than most War Dept. officials believed, secrecy kept him from stopping preparation of troop information materials—films, *Yank* articles and such—that the War Dept. Bureau of Public Relations was frantically producing.

Page saw J. Robert Oppenheimer, the brilliant physicist selected by Gen. Leslie Groves to shepherd the bomb from concept to reality, immediately after the successful pre-dawn test of the "gadget" at Alamogordo. He recounted with amusement how Oppenheimer, who had lost 30 pounds from a combination of stress and an attack of chicken pox, and who was back to smoking five packs of cigarettes a day, had bet before the test that it would not be successful because he didn't trust the implosion detonating mechanism.[64]

Page was nearly correct in predicting the date the war in

the Pacific would end. On July 18, two days after Trinity, he wrote to George Harrison of the Interim Committee to say, "I would think that by the 15th of August the destruction of Japan will be sufficient materially and psychologically to justify the President in saying to the Japanese that as natural forces are evidently on our side and as we have no intention of destroying their people or their religion they might well capitulate to the power of the universe..."[63] Harrison had by this time cabled Stimson at Potsdam to tell him of the successful test, although the detailed report of Gen. Leslie Groves's staff on the test at the Trinity site did not arrive by courier at Potsdam until July 21. Page's words about "not destroying their religion" indicate he was of the impression Emperor Hirohito would be permitted to remain on the throne after Japanese surrender, a stipulation that as noted Truman took out of the Potsdam Declaration.

Stimson was asked to prepare an announcement on use of the bomb for President Truman and another for himself. Stimson's 7,500-word statement was written by an Army officer, probably Lt. Col. Charles T. Arnett who served on the War Dept. Special Staff in 1943-1946.[65]

About two months before Hiroshima, William Laurance of the New York Times had written a draft statement for President Truman. James Conant of the Interim Committee thought it flowery, detailed, exaggerated and phoney. Committee members recommended that a completely new version be prepared. Page, asked to write the new version, used the 7,500-word Stimson statement to prepare a more condensed and dramatic statement for Truman. The new draft had the cadences, simplicity, brevity and impact that AT&T had used over the years to make its institutional ads effective. The announcement was at once powerful, easy to read, understandable and (for Americans) upbeat. Page says in his Reminiscences that Truman made only a few changes.[66]

On July 25, nine days after the Trinity test, President Truman directed the Army Air Force to deliver the first bomb as soon as weather permitted after Aug. 3. Additional bombs were to be used thereafter as they became available. Truman on July 26 issued the Potsdam Declaration, an ultimatum, warning Japan to surrender or suffer "prompt and utter destruction." The same day, the *U.S.S. Indianapolis* unloaded the uranium core for "Little Boy" at the Tinian B-29 base.

The first paragraphs of the statement Arthur Page prepared to announce the first military use of the bomb are at the beginning of this chapter. The statement went on to warn the Japanese that, "If they do not now accept our terms, they may expect a rain of ruin from the air, the like of which has never been seen on the earth."

However, even after the more powerful plutonium-239 implosion bomb nicknamed "Fat Man" was dropped a little off target on Nagasaki, some Japanese military leaders still opposed surrender. Emperor Hirohito fortunately intervened and insisted that the government accept defeat. The Japanese agreed to the Potsdam ultimatum on Aug. 10, a day after Nagasaki, and surrendered *almost* unconditionally (the emperor was to remain) on Aug. 14. Aug. 15 was celebrated in the United States as V-J Day, and the surrender was formally signed on the battleship *Missouri* on Sept. 2.

President Truman would state later in life, when asked about his decision to use the atomic bomb, that he had never lost any sleep over it. "The final decision of where and when to use the bomb was up to me," he said. "Let there be no mistake about it. I regarded the bomb as a military weapon and never had any doubt that it should be used."

What Harry Truman said in later years may well have been true. Books have been written about whether or not the bomb was actually needed and about the morality of its use. There was never any hesitation in Truman's resolve to use the weapon. However, at the time he made his decision, he complained of terrible headaches that dragged on for days. As for having "a conscience" about it, as Page says Stimson did, Truman ordered on Aug. 10 that a third bomb that would become available for use in a few days not be used without his direct orders. The thought of wiping out one more city and "all those kids" was too ghastly for the feisty World War I artillery commander.

Helping to develop Pentagon public relations machinery

THROUGHOUT WORLD WAR II, Page played an important role in influencing the military's public relations operations.

When AT&T executive Carroll Bickelhaupt early in the war went to the Army Signal Corps as a colonel, Page advised him to make the Signal Corps appear "interesting, a good outfit" that "has the most know-how in the Army," a branch of the military that served as "a source of knowledge," "the line of command," "the signal of success." [67]

He advised Joel E. Harrell, a special consultant to the Civilian Personnel Division of the Army's Services of Supply, on how to use communication, staged special events and incentives to improve productivity of American factory workers. [68]

In November 1944, Page created a committee to advise the Army on public relations. The group, which included Frank McCoy of the Foreign Policy Assn. and Harry Batten of N.W. Ayer, met with War Dept. officials Harvey Bundy, Maj. Gen. Alexander Surles (a World War I veteran and later tank commander at Fort Knox who headed Army public relations throughout World War II) and Chief of Staff Gen. George C. Marshall to discuss public relations problems. [69]

Page's report on Army plans for informing the public of troop redeployment to the Pacific and demobilization led the Secretaries of War and Navy to ask him to study public relations in the two main combat arms, and make recommendations for more efficient organization.

He completed the study of Navy public relations first, in April 1945. In his report, he noted that while the Navy was using more than 30 separate media to reach sailors, its efforts were largely uncoordinated. He recommended:

• Assignment to Adm. Nimitz's staff of an officer of the rank of captain or above, widely respected by his fellow officers, to coordinate Navy public relations.

• That this officer oversee the activities of six chiefs of different Navy public relations operations such as press relations and sailor information and education.

• That all naval officers be made aware of the importance of the information and education function to creating a good public reputation for the Navy, and

• That public relations be taught to all midshipmen at Annapolis.[70]

About a month later, Page submitted to the Secretary of War a more elaborate memorandum calling for reorganization of Army public relations. In this second advisory, Page stressed the need for the Army to convince the public that it was a servant of the people, reasonable and public-minded.

Noting that Army career officers looked on public relations assignments with disdain, Page called for a program to change attitudes. He recommended that the Army begin assigning some of its best career officers to public relations, promote the officers who performed well and make public relations training part of every officer's education. He called for appointment of a three-star general to coordinate three separate Army public relations efforts fragmented under two-star generals—Maj. Gen. Surles's Bureau of Public Relations, Maj. Gen. Osborn's Information and Education Division and Maj. Gen. Wilton B. "Jerry" Persons' Legislative and Liaison (lobbying) Division.[71]

An ad hoc committee consisting of Page and six major generals met to discuss Page's Army proposals. The committee made a final report in September 1945, calling for adoption of all of Page's recommendations. That final report, generally called the "Page Report," is recognized as the keystone of public relations programs of the modern U.S. Army.[72]

The first steps to reorganize Army public relations in accord with Page's recommendations were announced by the War Dept. later the same month.[73] In December 1945, Lt. Gen. J. Lawton Collins, the three-star general Page had requested to coordinate Army public relations, assumed his duties as Army Chief of Information.[74] In early 1946, the Army opened its Information School to train personnel in public relations techniques, rounding out implementation of the recommendations in the Page Report.[75]

For his work in helping to establish the Army Information School at Carlisle Barracks, which evolved into the Defense Information School (DINFOS) at Ft. Benjamin Harrison, Page earned the honorary titles of "Father of the Army Information School" and "Chairman of the Board of Regents." He was one of the lecturers to the first graduating class at the school in 1946, and lectured on public relations at a number of succeeding classes.[76]

Soon after becoming Army Chief of Information, Gen. Collins, widely respected by other officers for his combat performance, asked Page to recommend someone to study Army public relations. Page suggested Jack Lockhart of the Scripps-Howard newspaper chain, who completed his appraisal in the summer of 1946.

One section of Lockhart's report sums up Page's public relations philosophy in words that might have been Page's own: "...If the Army is good, the story will be good—and public relations will be good. If the Army is bad, the story will be bad and the results bad. In the end, public opinion about the Army reflects what the Army itself is. That is the whole secret of Army public relations."[77]

By the end of World War II, Page had become a well-known figure at the Pentagon, a man courted by generals and admirals. A subordinate at AT&T, Doug Williams, said, "He had the ear of the boss (Secretary Stimson) and... could get to see the boss easier than most. So pretty soon, generals and admirals and government officials of various levels of importance used to visit his office and pour out their troubles and use him as an intermediary...."[78]

Although Page may have been a gateway to Stimson, when the Colonel resigned as Secretary of War after the Japanese surrender the parade of military officers to Page continued. By late 1945, he had won the confidence and respect of many who continued to ask for his advice.

For his work for the War Dept.—especially for heading the Joint Army and Navy Committee, for his two special missions to Europe and for helping to prepare the publicity on the atomic bomb— Page was awarded the Medal of Merit by President Truman on Jan. 12, 1946.[79]

PUBLISHER, PUBLIC RELATIONS PIONEER, PATRIOT   257

Other government service

PAGE WAS INVOLVED in several other government projects during World War II.

In a telegram to Atty. Gen. Francis Biddle in late December 1941, he said he was performing a one-month mission for "Colonel Donovan's organization," a reference to William "Wild Bill" Donovan's Office of the Coordinator of Information. COI was the predecessor of the Office of Strategic Services (OSS), America's clandestine intelligence service in the European Theater during the war. Donovan, a millionaire Wall Street lawyer, earned the nickname "Wild Bill" for his exploits during World War I with the "Fighting Irish" 69th Division, in which he rose in rank from private to colonel. The telegram for obvious reasons does not say what Page was doing for Donovan.[80]

From the late fall of 1942 to 1946, Page served as chairman of the executive committee and of the board of United Seamen's Service, an agency financed by the National War Fund to supervise pension and survivor benefits for men employed in the Merchant Marine. One of Page's last official acts in this capacity was to establish a $400,000 contingency fund to operate the agency until the pension fund could again become self-sustaining from member contributions.[81]

In 1943, he served on the Advertising, Publicity and Sales Promotion Committee of the Second War Bond Drive of the Treasury Dept.'s War Financing Committee. Winthrop Aldrich of the Chase National Bank headed the drive.[82]

In 1944, he briefed executives of the Bureau of the Budget in the Executive Office of the President on public and personnel relations theory, an indication his renown was beginning to spread beyond War Dept. circles.[83]

A few months after the war ended, Page worked with writer John P. Marquand on a statement for President Truman announcing some of the secret work on biological warfare conducted during the war. The Truman statement was to clear the way for the new president of the University of Wisconsin, bacteriologist Edwin B. Fred, to brief the National Academy of Sciences on the work his War Research Service had done.[84] Page's work for Truman was at War Dept. request.

In April 1946, Page became a director of the Panama Railroad Co., which operated the U.S. government's railway in the Canal Zone, a steamship line and telephone concession. He was one of the War Dept. appointees to the board. Among other directors with whom he served were Harvey Bundy, one of Col. Stimson's most loyal supporters and aides during the war, and Col. George R. Goethals. Board meetings were held at the organization's headquarters in New York. Page, who had a lifelong interest in railroads dating to his boyhood experience with the Aberdeen & Asheboro, remained on the Panama board until early 1949.[85]

Campaigning for a postwar "pax Americana"

ARTHUR PAGE'S FATHER Walter, in his appeals for President Wilson to abandon neutrality and enter World War I on the side of the Allies, had been an internationalist.

Cast in his father's image, and guided by Henry Stimson, Arthur Page too was an internationalist. He became so during his World's Work years. His reading of the letters of George Washington immediately after World War I for evidence that Washington favored foreign alliances also evidences his early interest. He nurtured this interest through conversations with Council on Foreign Relations and Foreign Policy Assn. members such as Allen and John Foster Dulles and Frank McCoy. He was most active in the Council on Foreign Relations, helping to fund creation of the regional cells of that organization, which by 1946 had grown from eight to 25. He was familiar with the workings of the Foreign Policy Assn. through his friendship with Frank McCoy and because the Carnegie Corp., of which he was a trustee, was a major source of funds for the FPA.

Page's interest in American foreign policy led him to occasional attempts to influence the U.S. Dept. of State.

He did a considerable amount of campaigning from 1943

to 1946 for development of a postwar American foreign policy that would minimize the role of any new international peace-keeping body and maximize the roles of the United States and Great Britain in enforcing a postbellum "*Pax Americana-Britannica.*" He sought to make his views known through contacts with his friends in the State Dept., through influencing reports of the Council on Foreign Relations and Foreign Policy Assn. and through letters to influential senators and congressmen he knew.

In addition to calling on the State Dept. to lead the way in postwar peacekeeping efforts, Page also sought to influence State to intensify its domestic information efforts. He believed that an informed U.S. citizenry would support an aggressive American role as international peacekeeper.

By late 1942, Page had concluded that the end of the war in Europe would probably find the Russian Army facing American and British forces in Berlin, with the United States forced to accept Stalin's dominance in Eastern Europe. He decided that the only workable American foreign policy in such a situation would be a balance-of-power system in which the United States would deal on a day-to-day basis with Russia using tolerance, fairness, and above all, power.[86]

In a memorandum he prepared for Sen. Kenneth S. Wherry of Nebraska in 1943, Page stressed the importance of avoiding a postwar policy whereby America delegated responsibility for peacekeeping to an international court or league.

"I propose," Page said, "that it be a national policy that the President of the United States report to the Congress on the state of world peace as he does on the state of the nation, and that he and the Secretary of State not wait for a war to go abroad to meet with the heads of other states." To be effective, he added, such a policy would require that the people of America be kept informed on international decisions so that the president and Senate would be acting with the approval of the people.[87]

In the spring of 1943, Page began to articulate his views for a postwar peace. His Long Island neighbor John Foster Dulles had been working for two years as chairman of a task force studying alternatives for a durable postwar peace. Foster asked Page's reactions to the conclusions of the group before they were made public. Page told Dulles he had no confidence in trying to build peace through an international league (the United Nations) such as proposed. He added he would not oppose an international organization if the United States moved independently to set up a global network of sea and air bases to enforce world peace.[88]

Just before Foster Dulles went to the San Francisco meetings that established the United Nations, Page told him he felt the United States should establish a postwar *pax Americana* paralleling the balance of power situation Great Britain created to assure world tranquility up to 1914. "I know it was... called imperialism, power politics and worse names," he wrote. "But, there were... things to be said for it."[89]

Page believed that to maintain peace, America had to maintain a strong postwar Army and Navy. He supported a postwar draft, and provided guidance in 1945 to officials of the War and State Depts. on how to effectively lobby for a universal military training (UMT) law. Without one, he feared the armed forces would be demobilized after victory. He urged Foster Dulles, at the time taking part in the San Francisco talks, to support the UMT bill.[90] He also worked with publications such as DeWitt and Lila Wallace's *Reader's Digest* to create articles that would shape public opinion in favor of postwar conscription.[91]

Although suspect of the United Nations, he served on a New York committee that helped officials of the fledgling international organization find a permanent site for its headquarters. Secretary General Trygve Lie personally thanked him for his help.[92]

Guiding wartime AT&T public relations

THE PUBLIC RELATIONS problems facing the Bell System during the war and immediately after were as great as those the company faced during the Great Depression.

Long distance lines, already overtaxed at the beginning of the war because of a surge of calling generated by defense mobilization, became even busier as the war progressed. Price controls retarded earnings, so that several times during the war AT&T again failed to earn its $9 dividend.

Because materials such as copper were needed for the war, the company was unable to build new telephone plant. Even if raw materials like copper had been available, it's unlikely Western Electric would have been able to help, for its facilities were needed to manufacture materials needed for the war effort. The number of customers waiting for telephone service climbed first into the hundreds of thousands, then into the millions. AT&T, which had prided itself on providing ever-improved service to customers, now found itself with service indexes slipping badly, and having to crowd customers on party lines. AT&T needed the sympathetic understanding of its customers.

People unfamiliar with public relations work may think of it as martini luncheons, courting celebrities and staging publicity stunts. In reality, public relations is a tough communications job in which face-to-face and mass media messages must be teamed to produce sympathetic public opinion for an institution.

Confronted with the wartime emergency and gradual erosion in public good will, AT&T's Information Dept. and the public relations staffs of the associated companies sought public cooperation and understanding. Advertising, publicity and employee communication with customers were teamed to persuade customers that the national interest required them to make only essential long distance calls so war-related messages could go through.

AT&T's efforts to get the public to hold down long distance traffic were intensified at the request of the Board of War Communications in mid-1942. Efforts were expanded to include newspaper, magazine and radio advertising, bill inserts, coin phone card notices, posters, window displays, streetcar and bus cards, booklets, leaflets, imprints on customer bills and bill envelopes, blotters, employee bulletin board notices and letters to heavy users of long distance service.[93]

Such work is not glamorous. The main requirements for persuading the public in such situations are an ability to write simple, easily understood messages, and a willingness to pay attention to detail so that no opportunity to communicate a message is overlooked.

Although Page had advised pioneer public relations counselor James Selvage against riding on patriotic fervor in paid advertising, the Bell System's national advertising during the period of the war often stressed patriotic themes in an effort to evoke sympathy. A typical magazine ad showed an American fighter plane, its six wing guns spitting flame, with text headlined "He's firing telephone wire at a Zero." The copy explained that copper was needed for the war effort and couldn't be used to build new telephone lines, and asked citizens to help by making only essential long distance calls.[94]

In 1943, Page played a role in ridding the Bell System of one of its public relations problems, the Electrical Research Products, Inc. (ERPI) subsidiary of Western Electric.

The FCC had criticized AT&T during its telephone investigation for alleged efforts to control the sound motion picture business through ERPI. In 1942, William Benton of the Benton and Bowles advertising agency, which had taken over the Encyclopaedia Britannica organization, learned that ERPI was for sale. Wishing to establish a Britannica educational film service, and knowing that ERPI was the largest producer of such films in the nation, Benton in mid-1943 entered into talks with Page and Western Electric Vice President Kennedy Stevenson. Late in the year, Benton purchased ERPI and renamed it Encyclopaedia Britannica Films, Inc.[95]

As AT&T's public relations chief, Page oversaw the company's charitable contributions policy, which changed dramatically toward greater generosity immediately after the war. Within two weeks after Pearl Harbor, Page recommended an AT&T contribution of $500,000 to the American Red Cross—one per cent of the national goal of $50 million.[96] He advocated major AT&T giving to the National War Fund. But there he drew the line, continuing to oppose AT&T gifts to colleges, religious organizations and pressure groups.[97]

When Mrs. W. Averell Harriman, heading the Navy Relief Society, asked for an AT&T contribution, Page declined. He noted that AT&T had refused to give to the Army Relief Society which his wife Mollie headed.[98] Within a few months, however, he changed his mind, and both the Army and Navy Relief Societies received gifts from AT&T.[99]

AT&T's policy on corporate giving remained essentially conservative. In 1943, Page explained the policy in a letter:

> The charters of our companies generally specify that we are to use stockholders' money for the communications business and things allied to it.
>
> They do not provide that we advance adult education, reform the political structure, beautify the landscape, or do a lot of other things which are good in themselves and which have a considerable part in making the United States the best country in the world.
>
> However, the stockholder does give to these enterprises direct. He didn't authorize us to act as his almoner, but only to make his money serve the public in the telephone business.
>
> We do, however, give to the Red Cross, and National War Fund on the basis that they are so universally accepted that our stockholders would overwhelmingly agree.
>
> We give to the Y.M.C.A. and hospitals and community chests on the basis that they are services used by our employees and are, therefore, a legitimate business expense.
>
> We try to keep the list of the kinds of things we give to small and clean and logical and then we try to give quickly and cheerfully where we give at all.[100]

This policy, which disarmed charges that AT&T sought to buy public favor by widespread giving, would be liberalized within a few years. In 1946, Congress passed a law to encourage corporate philanthropy by allowing tax advantages for gifts of up to five per cent of net profits. Page was skeptical of the change in government attitude, recalling that only a few years earlier federal regulatory agencies were complaining about large corporations "buying public favor by large donations."[101] Ever capable of adjusting to changing times, however, Page in the last years of his life helped to liberalize philanthropic policies at AT&T and the other corporations on whose boards he sat.

He continued in these years to encourage research into customer attitudes, although he had as much faith in good human judgment as he did in survey results when it came to decision-making. In the summer of 1942, Page sent Bell System public relations executives the results of the first large-scale study of customer attitudes made in wartime, noting that customers seemed as friendly as in the prewar period.[102]

Perhaps the most significant development in attitudinal surveying at AT&T during the Page vice presidency occurred in 1946, shortly before he retired. In that year, AT&T introduced its Customer Attitude Trend Survey (CATS), regularly polling 5,000 customers nationwide.

By 1949, all Bell System operating companies had adopted the survey in their own territories, and a steady stream of results permitting AT&T to identify changing trends in customer sentiment began to flow to company headquarters. The survey remained the main tool in AT&T's efforts to obtain feedback from customers until 1966, when it was abandoned in favor of even more intensive and frequent attitudinal measurement systems, the Service Attitude Measurement (SAM) and Telephone Service Attitude Measurement (TELSAM) instruments.[103]

Another significant development in Page's final years in the AT&T vice presidency was a renewed emphasis on customer and employee films.

By 1946, the Bell System was spending ten times as much annually on corporate film production as it had been before the war, and had developed more effective techniques for reaching audiences. A series of conferences in the fall of 1946 informed associated company public relations staffs of how best to use the AT&T Motion Picture Division.[104] The Army's use of films for indoctrination during the war had not escaped Page's attention. In the summer of 1946, AT&T commissioned Pathéscope Pictures, which had made many Army morale films, to shoot a movie aimed at restoring telephone operator interest in the "spirit of service." The Bell System's "voice with a smile" had developed a bit of a snarl during the wartime deterioration in service. The result, a film entitled "The Big Day," was released in August 1946.[105]

The "Bell Telephone Hour" had also come of age by 1946. The program had the highest listenership ratings of any musical show on network radio, although its ratings were still well below those of comedy and drama shows.[106]

Much of Page's work from 1944 forward was devoted to organizing public sentiment in favor of higher earnings for AT&T. Perhaps the main mission of Page's public relations staff from 1944 through his retirement was to argue for a more adequate level of earnings for the Bell System operating companies and AT&T itself. By 1944, it was abundantly clear to AT&T management that wartime earnings were inadequate to finance the huge construction job that would be necessary immediately after the war to provide service to the millions of customers on waiting lists for telephones.[107] Although executives at the nation's biggest corporation were afraid to even whisper the truth, the pressures—customer demand for construction and inadequate earnings to finance it—were sufficient, if management was not careful, to drive AT&T into bankruptcy. The subject of how AT&T coped with held orders, and went about finding new capital, is covered in the next chapter.

Freedom becomes a fetish

PAGE'S PUBLIC RELATIONS philosophy had already been developed by 1940. The themes that he covered in his speeches, letters, and published writings in 1941-1946 can be found in his earlier work. He became a bit more eloquent in expressing his ideas. That's the only real difference.

The theme of freedom threads through much of Page's thinking about public relations philosophy in this period.

As he saw it, people throughout history had feared large institutions—the church, government, big business—because they tended to restrict individual liberty. If a business inspired confidence in people, he felt, the people would not fear it, and would give it considerable freedom. If the public lacked confidence in a business, on the other hand, citizens would restrict its freedom through regulation or other means. The irony was that in restricting the freedom of a business, the public also restricted that business's ability to serve in the public interest. When an enterprise was so restricted by regulation that it couldn't do anything bad, it usually couldn't do anything good either. "Real success," Page said in a speech to the Life Insurance Institute in 1942, "both for big business and the public, lies in large enterprise conducting itself in the public interest and in such a way that the public will give it sufficient freedom to serve effectively."[108]

Page believed a great deal but not total freedom should be given to business. He would point out that AT&T was happy to be regulated, giving up a degree of its own freedom in return for the right to serve without competition.[109] He felt that regulation had been good for AT&T, as it had been for the insurance industry, but that the same regulation had been bad for other industries such as banking and railroads.[110]

Page's deep belief in freedom for individuals and institutions helps to explain his dislike of labor unions, which he saw as a threat to management's freedom to run a business in the public interest.

Pres Mabon, one of Page's trusted lieutenants at AT&T public relations, felt Page had a blind spot regarding unions. As he puts it:

> ...I would say that his natural temperament, his boundless faith in personal freedom and his instinct not to accept the contrary, perhaps limited his under-

standing of unionism and the permanence of union power...

...(I)f there was a hole somewhere in Arthur Page's thinking, I would locate it here. He simply did not understand that the unions were not going to go away.[111]

In opposition to the Mabon view, John Shaw, another close Page compatriot, thinks Page's assessment of unions was sounder than the view most American managers held. Page, says Shaw, recognized that perpetual bargaining between management and unions would destroy freedom. "In supinely accepting in the early thirties the restrictive provisions of the Wagner Act, management catapulted into power a host of Hoffas and Biernes whose objectives are anything but the service to the public that was the essence of all Page's philosophy," Shaw contends.[112]

Page saw unions as a threat to the efficiency of corporations, and therefore a threat to the common good. He felt unions restricted management's freedom to reward good workers and punish bad ones. A believer in threats and rewards, he clearly stated his views in a 1944 letter:

> There are two main incentives that affect people in an organization: Rewards and punishments. The chance to rise by energy and ability. The chance to be fired for sloth and stupidity...
>
> In order to prevent abuse and unfairness all kinds of restraints are built up, union rules... etc. They increase rather than decrease unfairness, for they all tend to level down... They definitely set limits to the effectiveness of management.
>
> We used to think that a man's right to chuck a job and go elsewhere was a fundamental defense against a bad boss, but with the growth of the idea that a man has a vested right in a job and security the minute he is hired, that defense is hardly considered of value now... (T)he rewards and punishments have considerably lost their effectiveness.[113]

Page had confidence in the ability of America's management class to run business and the country in the best interests of individual citizens. He felt federal New Deal reforms had hampered management's ability to pull the country out of the Great Depression. He felt even more strongly that government efforts to manage industry during World War II were another stumbling block for "the managing class in this country, on which after all depends the winning of the war."[114]

Despite his dislike of federal bureaucracy, Page never fell into the trap of advocating an open fight against encroaching government which ensnared many corporation executives during the years Franklin D. Roosevelt occupied the White House. He disliked the policies of "that man," the establishment's code phrase for Roosevelt, but in later years attributed the Bell System's survival during the New Deal years to its remaining aloof from the general fight of big business against Roosevelt.[115]

By 1941-1946, Page had a considerably more advanced concept of what public relations was than his earlier and somewhat simplistic definition of it as "90 per cent doing and 10 per cent talking about it." In a 1942 speech he said:

> Public relations... is not publicity only, not management only; it is what everybody in the business from top to bottom says and does when in contact with the public...
>
> The task which business has, and which it has always had, of fitting itself to the pattern of public desires has lately come to be called public relations.
>
> Public relations in this country is the art of adopting big business to a democracy, so that the people have confidence that they are being well served and at the same time the business has freedom to serve them well.[116]

John J. McCloy, Henry Stimson's Undersecretary of War during World War II, who worked closely with Page on Army matters, attests to Page's maturity of outlook:

I thought Mr. Page a very wise counselor not only on public relations, but generally... I remember sitting in on many occasions when Stimson asked him for his advice in connection with his public relations matters in the War Department. He always believed in playing things with a low key, but usually with more effect because they were pitched in low key. He not only knew the mechanics of public relations, but he had a proper philosophy in regard to them. Stimson deeply respected his judgment as did I. He was not given to public relations gimmicks and he gave his advice on the basis of wise, knowledgeable appraisals.[117]

Adding Kennecott Copper and
Prudential Insurance directorships

PAGE MADE SEVERAL important additions to his corporate directorships in the period 1941-1946.

In February 1943, he was elected a director of the Kennecott Copper Co., which operated a huge open-pit mine in Utah, and of the firm's Chilean subsidiary, Braden Copper.[118] Kennecott was a child of the Guggenheim mining interests backed by J.P. Morgan. The company got its start exploiting a mountain of almost pure copper in Alaska—see the next chapter. AT&T was one of the nation's biggest consumers of copper. Copper telephone wire was the staple for signal transmission.

In March, he was named a director of the Prudential Insurance Co. of America, headquartered in Newark, N.J.[119]

Page as well was increasing his influence on the Chase National Bank and Westinghouse Electric boards at the time. In January 1942, he was elected to the Chase National executive committee, and in April 1944, he was named to the Westinghouse executive committee.[120] He remained a director of AT&T and of Continental Oil.

In 1946, Page's last year in the AT&T vice presidency, he reshuffled his directorships in various AT&T subsidiaries. In

February, he was elected to a new term on the board of the
Southern Bell Telephone & Telegraph Co. He had served on
the board from 1928 to 1935. In May, he resigned from the
board of the Bell Telephone Co. of Canada. On Dec. 31, 1946,
his last full day of employment with the Bell System, he resigned as chairman of the board of AT&T's Long Lines Dept.
and as chairman of the board of the 195 Broadway Corp.[121]

Precious little time for charity

PAGE'S WORK FOR the War Dept., together with the demands
of his jobs at AT&T, left him little time in 1941-1946 for the
charities in which he was interested. But aside from resigning his posts in New York's Community Service Society and
the Southern Education Foundation, he retained his major
philanthropic directorships and added more.

New Carnegie Corp. President Walter Jessup made only
minor demands on his board of trustees during the war.
Jessup devoted much of his time to a thorough review of the
Corporation's grants and investments during the preceding
30 years. Carnegie largesse took no dramatic new directions
during his administration. Most grants made were to
war-related causes such as the American Red Cross, USO, Joint
Army and Navy Committee on Welfare and Recreation and
similar undertakings.[122]

After only two and a half years in office, Jessup died un-
expectedly in 1944. His death touched off a battle over naming a successor. The struggle pitted Carnegie board chairman Nicholas Murray Butler, who advocated Brown University President Henry Wriston, against most of the outside
Carnegie trustees who regarded Wriston as "too controversial." Russell Leffingwell, who with the strong support of Dr.
Vannevar Bush led the outside trustee opposition to Wriston,
at one point campaigned for Page to be named as successor
to Jessup. The trustees finally elected Devereaux Josephs, an
investment banker who was a trustee of the Carnegie Corp.
and active in several of its branch institutions.[123]

Nielsen contends the major accomplishment of the Josephs presidency was establishment of the Educational Testing Service at Princeton shortly after the end of the war.[124] However, it was during Josephs' tenure that Carnegie greatly expanded its funding of studies of American international relations, a direction Page had urged it to take.

In the 15 years before Jessup was named president of the Carnegie Corp., it gave some $450,000 in grants to various international affairs foundations such as the Council on Foreign Relations, the Institute of Pacific Relations and the Foreign Policy Assn.[125] This limited funding continued at an unaccelerated pace during the Jessup presidency. Arthur Page took particular interest in grants to the Council on Foreign Relations, which by 1943 had established 17 of the regional councils he had advocated, and which had a membership of more than 600.[126]

The funding of international relations studies was greatly stepped up during the Josephs presidency. By November 1945, Josephs had placed before Carnegie trustees a proposal for spending $1 million per year on programs aimed at making the American public aware of the national responsibility to exercise world leadership.

Dr. Butler objected to the proposal on the grounds that such studies and programs were more appropriately the responsibility of the Carnegie Endowment for International Peace than of the Carnegie Corp., but other trustees paid him little heed.[127] By 1947, the funding of international relations programs and studies had become one of the two major goals of the Carnegie Corp., the other being the funding of studies into ways to improve domestic government institutions.[128]

In January 1946, the Carnegie trustees took two important actions. They elected Russell Leffingwell chairman of the board, replacing Dr. Butler. Second, they changed the makeup of the board, which had been composed of nine outside directors and six heads of Carnegie philanthropies. The board voted that as the heads of the Carnegie philanthropies retired, they would be replaced by outside directors.

Only the president of the Carnegie Corp. proper was to retain a seat, and then only as an *ex officio* member.[129]

On being elected chairman of the Carnegie board, Leffingwell resigned as chairman of the Finance Committee. Arthur Page was named to replace him, now responsible for oversight of investment of the institution's millions.[130]

When the Corporation trustees voted to remove heads of other Carnegie philanthropies from their board, they also adopted a policy of no further grants to the other Carnegie charities except in exceptional circumstances. That freed money for the Corporation to move in bold new directions. The purging of the board cleared spaces for new trustees. In June, General of the Army George C. Marshall was elected a trustee to fill the first vacancy created.[131]

To further encourage innovation, Carnegie began in 1946 to hire out-of-the-box thinkers for key positions. John W. Gardner joined the staff from the Marine Corps and Office of Strategic Services to supervise program proposals. Pendleton Herring was hired from Harvard to supervise a proposed program to educate Americans on foreign relations. Whitney Shepardson, a director of the Council on Foreign Relations and ex-O.S.S. officer who in 1919 had been Col. House's aide at Versailles, was hired to head the British Dominions and Colonies Fund. Oliver Carmicheal was lured from Vanderbilt University to head the Carnegie Foundation.[132]

Page added a *pro bono* directorship in December 1942 in which he took considerable interest for the remainder of his life. He was elected one of the five trustees of the American Historical Assn. In 1953, he became chairman of the board of trustees, an office he held to his death in 1960.[133] The main duty of the trustees was to oversee the Society's investment portfolio, amounting in 1944 to about $230,000 in capital returning $5,000 annually, but considerably more by the time of his death.[134]

Because of more pressing duties, and because, in his words, he had "gotten out of touch" with changing concepts of welfare in America, Page in 1943 resigned all his offices in the Community Service Society of New York. At the time, he was on four CSS committees, two overseeing the New York School of Social Work and the Institute of Welfare Research. AT&T President Walter Gifford, heading CSS, accepted Page's resignation reluctantly. Among many letters expressing regret that Page was leaving CSS was one from General Motors public relations chief Paul Garrett, who headed the CSS public relations committee on which Page had been serving.[135]

Page resigned all offices in the Southern Education Foundation in January 1945, leaving on a negative note. During the Great Depression, he had opposed Arthur Wright's wish to conduct a major fund-raising drive for the foundation. In 1944, Wright informed Page that he had hired George Ketcham, a former employee of the Hampton Institute, to supervise a fund-raising effort. Wright invited Page to a New York banquet to launch the effort.

Page said he was not eager to help raise money until SEF developed a plan for spending new funds. He was more blunt in a letter to Robert Purves, whom he had tried to recruit to replace him as SEF chairman. He told Purves he didn't think Wright's operation was worth any more money than was already being spent on it. He also objected to what he mistakenly thought was an attempt by Wright to spend the $700,000 in capital appreciation that had accrued from investment of the Peabody, Jeanes and Slater Funds. Above all, he had come to believe that the Jeanes Teacher program had outlived its usefulness, and that the $100,000 or so per year in revenue the Southern Education Foundation had to spend could be put to better use funding studies of new programs that could be financed by other philanthropies. Feeling he was out of step with the other trustees, and irked at the direction SEF was taking, Page resigned all offices in early 1945.[136]

Other charities involving Page in 1941-1946 included:

• *Farmers Federation Educational and Development Fund.* Continued as chairman of the fund and of its New York Committee. By 1943, the fund was spending more than $50,000 per year in support of various Farmers Federation programs. Among the major contributors were the Carnegie Corp. and Alta Rockefeller Prentice.[137]

• *Metropolitan Museum of Art.* Remained active as a trustee. In late 1945 and 1946, he chaired a public relations committee that oversaw a fund-raising and publicity program run by the John Price Jones Organization in conjunction with the Museum's 75th anniversary.[138]

• *Greater New York Chapter, American Red Cross.* Named a member of the Citizens Committee that supervised 1942 fund-raising. In 1943, he was named to a committee that oversaw 1944 fund-raising. In April 1945, in recognition of his work, he was named an honorary member of the board of the Red Cross's New York War Fund.[139]

• *Beekman Street Hospital.* Chaired a committee to raise funds from commerce and industry for this New York hospital in 1943.[140]

• *Legal Aid Society of New York.* Served at the request of Irving S. Olds on the steering committee for the Society's fund-raising operations in 1944 and 1945. The Society provided legal counsel to people with little financial means.[141]

• *Long Island Biological Assn.* Continued to serve as a vice president and director. LIBA was engaged in significant war-related research. Among other things, the laboratory personnel produced aerosol delivery systems for penicillin and investigated means of combating chemical and bacteriological agents that might be used in warfare.[142]

• *Sportsmanship Brotherhood.* Evidence is sketchy, but Page appears by 1941-1946 to be serving as a director of this pet project of his Long Island neighbor John Perry Bowditch. The agency sought to promote ideals of sportsmanship in amateur and professional athletics.[143]

• *Thomas A. Edison Centennial Committee.* Served in 1946 on a committee formed to recognize the 100th anniversary of the birth of the inventor of the electric light and other appliances. The celebration was held in early 1947. C.F. Kettering headed the committee. Henry Ford, who had been a friend of Edison, served as honorary chairman.[144]

• *New York Botanical Gardens.* Served on the Committee of Sponsors for the institution's 50th anniversary celebration, headed by John W. Davis and Joseph R. Swan.[145]

Higher education and building the postwar peace

PAGE'S INTEREST IN foreign relations and the shaping of a durable postwar peace led to his involvement as a charter trustee of the Foreign Service Educational Foundation (FSEF), established in 1943 to fund advanced international relations training for career diplomats.

In 1942, Page was involved with the Diplomatic Affairs Foundation, funding arm for the Fletcher School of Law and Diplomacy operated at Medford, Mass., by Harvard and Tufts Universities.[146] Halford Hoskins, dean of the Fletcher School, involved Page in the efforts of Congressman Christian Herter and Paul Nitze of the State Dept. to sever Fletcher School ties with Harvard and Tufts and open a new school in Washington. While plans for the new school were being laid, Page tried to tie it to the Walter Hines Page School of International Relations at Johns Hopkins. Hoskins gently fended Page off, saying the new school would be happy to work in cooperation with Johns Hopkins, but not subordinate to it.[147]

In late 1943, Page was elected a trustee of the Foreign Service Educational Foundation.[148] The roster of charter trustees, in addition to Page, included Herter; diplomats Joseph Grew, William Clayton and Robert Bliss; Harvard President James Conant; Special Asst. to the Secretary of State Thomas Finletter; New York Life President George Harrison (of the Interim Committee on S-1); Time/Life Chairman Henry R. Luce; General Electric President Charles Wilson; Brown University President Henry Wriston; and Hugh Wilson, a Versailles generation diplomat who in World War I was first secretary at America's Embassy in Berne when young Allen Dulles was posted there by his uncle Bert Lansing.[149]

To fund the new school, FSEF trustees sought contributions of up to $10,000 from the nation's largest multinational corporations. Page worked specifically on gifts from Westinghouse, Kennecott Copper and the Chase National Bank. Funding obtained, the ` opened its doors to students in the fall of 1944. Page served as an FSEF trustee to at least 1946.[150] In 1950, after difficulty in raising funds, SAIS finally did affiliate with Johns Hopkins and its Walter Hines Page School of International Relations as a graduate division. The Washington campus was named in honor of Paul Nitze.

Arthur Page maintained contact with the Page School at Johns Hopkins through 1941-1946. He became more active after 1944, when Page School Director Owen Lattimore returned from wartime duties. In addition to seeking for SAIS to affiliate with Johns Hopkins, Page sought Rockefeller Foundation and Carnegie Corp. funding for a Johns Hopkins seminar to study alternative solutions for building a postwar peace.[151]

As for Harvard, in 1942 he chaired the nominating committee of the Harvard Alumni Assn., recommending among other things that Joseph Grew be elected president.[152] He served on the Committee to Visit the Harvard University Press to 1942, when he declined reelection, saying he was too busy with War Dept. and AT&T duties to serve.[153] He worked from 1941 to 1944 on a special Harvard committee studying alternatives for more efficient placement of graduates.[154]

He continued throughout the period to serve as vice chairman of the board of trustees of Teachers College.[155]

Club memberships

PAGE CONTINUED in 1941-1946 to belong to various prestigious clubs. In the New York area, he remained a member of the Harvard Club, the Century Club, the Down Town Assn., the New York Yacht Club (he wasn't very active after selling the *Rampage*), the Piping Rock Country Club and Cold Spring Harbor Beach Club. He remained a member of the Tavern Club of Boston, the Metropolitan Club of Washington and the St. James's Club in London.

After reading a draft of this manuscript, Page's sons Arthur Jr. and John cautioned against assuming that their father was a sophisticated club man. Arthur W. Page Jr. said: "As a general subjective comment, I feel you give an impression that my father was something of a polished, socially conscious, aristocrat and club man. He wasn't; he was a democrat as opposed to an aristocrat."[156] Son John Hall Page wrote:

> I think you overemphasize and misunderstand the position of clubs in Dad's life. Firstly, some of the clubs you mention just don't qualify as exclusive centers of great thought. For instance, the Harvard Club of New York is not very important, exclusive, nor does it represent a meeting place of great minds. The fact is that while it is legally a private club and members must be voted on, any Harvard University graduate is eligible, and unless he is totally disreputable, he is admitted... The New York Yacht Club is another case... But more to the point is the reality that people with like interests get together whether at a club or not... What was significant is that Dad had the respect and friendship of certain people. Where they met to talk was incidental and, frankly, I would guess that most meetings were not at a club.[157]

Page's sons knew their father well, and their perceptions are valuable in interpreting the importance of clubs in their father's life. At the same time, Peter Schrag, among other writers about the power elite, identifies the Century Club, the Harvard Club of New York City, the Piping Rock Country Club, Down Town Assn. and Metropolitan Club as favorite haunts of the establishment.[158]

I do agree emphatically with his sons that it was wisdom and not club memberships that made Arthur Page establishment.

Planning for retirement

As early as 1945, Page began planning to retire from AT&T, and to spend his remaining years as a business consultant.[159]

In early July 1946, Keith McHugh was named to replace

Page as vice president in charge of the AT&T Information Dept.[160] Page stayed on for six months to guide McHugh though the change in command.

On Jan. 1, 1947, Page formally retired as public relations vice president of AT&T. He was 63 years old at the time. He had served the Bell System for 20 years.

Retirement is an inappropriate word for the final years of Page's life, from 1947 through 1960. In his last 14 years, he successfully established a third career as business and public relations consultant, earning more per year in retirement than he had while actively employed by AT&T. In addition, he devoted considerable time to functioning as a warrior in the Cold War.

ENDNOTES

[1] Text of statement of President Harry S Truman announcing first use of the atomic bomb against Japan, *New York Times*, Aug. 7, 1945, p. 4.

[2] Background color on release of atomic bomb publicity is from Chiles Coleman, United Press International, "That Day They Announced the Atomic Bomb," *Wisconsin State Journal*, July 26, 1970, sec. 6, p. 1. Background color on dropping of the bomb and reaction of principals is from J. Perry Leavell Jr., *Harry S. Truman* (New York: Chelsea House, 1988), pp. 13-18; Robert J. Lifton and Greg Mitchell, *Hiroshima in America* (New York: Avon Books, 1995), pp. 1-39; and Maj. Gen. Charles W. Sweeney with James A. and Marion K. Antonucci, *War's End: An Eyewitness Account of America's Last Atomic Mission* (New York: Avon Books, 1997).

[3] Raymond B. Fosdick, "The Leisure Time of a Democratic Army," *Survey Graphic*, June 1942, pp. 280-85, and draft of speech entitled "Special Service," probably by or for Brig. Gen. Frederick H. Osborn, Nov. 3, 1942, the latter in Box 10, Arthur W. Page Papers.

[4] News release by War Dept. Public Relations Branch, Jan. 9, 1941; memoranda from Gen. George C. Marshall to Secretary of War Henry L. Stimson, Dec. 11 and 23, 1940; and letter from Page to Brig. Gen. Frederick Osborn., Jan. 5, 1941; all in Box 7, Arthur W. Page Papers.

[5] Memorandum from the Secretary of War, the Secretary of the Navy and the Federal Security Administrator to the President, "Outline of Respective Responsibilities of the War Department, the Navy Department and the Federal Security Agency in Connection with Leisure-Time Activities for Military and Naval Personnel," Feb. 8, 1941, Box 7, Arthur W. Page Papers.

[6] News release by War and Navy Depts., "Joint Army and Navy Committee on Welfare and Recreation Is Organized," Feb. 12, 1941, Box 7, Arthur W. Page Papers, and Raleigh, *op. cit.*, p. 110.

[7] For further information on Page's appointment as chairman of the Joint Army and Navy Committee's Subcommittee on Radio, see telegram

from Francis Keppel to Page, May 4, 1942; letter to Page from JANC Chairman Fowler V. Harper, May 4, 1942, with attached authorization for formation of Subcommittee on Radio; note to Page from his secretary, Margaret Phelps, May 5, 1942; and telegram to Page from Fowler V. Harper, May 6, 1942; all in Box 8, Arthur W. Page Papers. Page was variously called a "special consultant" and "expert consultant" during the war.

[8] Joint Army and Navy Committee on Welfare and Recreation Subcommittee on Radio, Minutes of Meeting of Members, July 30, 1942, attached to letter to Page from Francis Keppel, May 25, 1942, Box 8, Arthur W. Page Papers. Similar minutes hereafter are referred to as JANC Subcommittee on Radio Minutes of Meeting.

[9] JANC Subcommittee on Radio Minutes of Meeting of July 30, 1942, attached to letter to Page from Francis Keppel, Aug. 13, 1942, Box 8, Arthur W. Page Papers.

[10] Memorandum from Maj. Arthur C. Farlow to Brig. Gen. Frederick H. Osborn, Aug. 22, 1942, with attachments, Box 8, Arthur W. Page Papers.

[11] Untitled memorandum to Page from "W.C.P.," Jan. 31, 1944, Box 10, Arthur W. Page Papers.

[12] Letter to Page from John F. Royal of NBC, Feb. 28, 1944, with three attachments, Box 10, Arthur W. Page Papers.

[13] Untitled memorandum to Page from "W.C.P.," op. cit.

[14] War Dept. news release, originally dated for release Nov. 21, 1942, but superseded by a corrected copy dated for release Dec. 4, 1942, Box 8, Arthur W. Page Papers.

[15] Letter to Page from Francis Keppel, Aug. 8, 1942, Box 8, Arthur W. Page Papers.

[16] "Report of Fowler V. Harper to the Secretaries of War and Navy and the Federal Security Administrator," Oct. 27, 1942, and letter to Page from Secretary of War Henry L. Stimson, Nov. 11, 1942, both in Box 9, Arthur W. Page Papers. Late in the war, John Russell, whom Page had known as a Harvard administrator, replaced Francis Keppel.

[17] See especially "Report of Fowler V. Harper to the Secretaries of War and Navy and the Federal Security Administrator," op. cit., and Raleigh, op. cit., p. 116.

[18] See especially letter to USO President Chester Barnard from Secretary of the Navy James Forrestal, July 3, 1944, Box 11, Arthur W. Page Papers.

[19] Letter from Page to Brig. Gen. Frederick Osborn, Nov. 30, 1942, Box 9, Arthur W. Page Papers.

[20] Letter from Raymond B. Fosdick to Page, Jan. 14, 1943, Box 9, Arthur W. Page Papers.

[21] Letter to Chester Barnard from Secretary of the Navy James Forrestal, July 3, 1944, op. cit.; letter from Page to Harvey H. Bundy, Aug. 4, 1944; letter to Page from Asst. Secretary of War John J. McCloy, Aug. 17, 1944; letter to Page from Chester Barnard, Sept. 15, 1944, with attached letters from Barnard to the Secretaries of War and Navy; letter from Page to Harvey H. Bundy, Jan. 18, 1945; letter to Page from JANC Executive Director John M. Russell, March 15, 1945, with attached letters from Page to Chester Barnard and Red Cross official Richard F. Allen; and Joint Army and Navy Committee on Welfare and Recreation, Minutes of Meetings of Members, 1942-1946, meeting of Sept. 18, 1945; all in Boxes 11 and 12, Arthur W. Page Papers. Hereafter, minutes such as those mentioned in the last citation are referred to as Minutes of Joint Army and Navy Committee Meeting of (date).

[22] Bernard C. Nalty and Morris J. MacGregor, eds., *Blacks in the Military: Essential Documents* (Wilmington, Delaware: Scholarly Resources, 1981), pp. 103, 133.

[23] Martin Binkin and Mark J. Eitelberg with Alvin J. Schexnider and Marvin M. Smith, *Blacks and the Military* (Washington, D.C.: The Brookings Institution, 1982), pp. 19-26; memorandum from Page to Brig. Gen. Frederick Osborn, Oct. 9, 1942; and letter from J.T. Sheafor to Mr. Welch regarding Detroit protest speech of A. Philip Randolph, Sept. 30, 1942, Box 8, Arthur W. Page Papers.

[24] Neil A. Wynn, *The Afro-American and the Second World War*, Rev. Ed. (New York & London: Holmes & Meier, 1993), p. 27, and Nalty and MacGregor, *op. cit.*, p. 116.

[25] Letters to Page from Fred K. Hoehler, Sept. 4 and 29, 1942, Box 8, Arthur W. Page Papers, and Minutes of Joint Army and Navy Committee Meeting of July 20, 1943, Box 10, Arthur W. Page Papers.

[26] Nalty and MacGregor, *op. cit.*, pp. 104, 121.

[27] Memorandum from John J. McCloy to Page, Nov. 14, 1943, attached to letter to Page from JANC Administrative Asst. Doris Goss, Nov. 15, 1943, Box 10, Arthur W. Page Papers, and letter from Special Consultant to the Secretary of War Donald Young to JANC Secretary Doris Goss, May 3, 1944, Box 11, Arthur W. Page Papers.

[28] Nalty and MacGregor, *op. cit.*, pp. 126-27, and Wynn, *op. cit.*, pp. 27-28.

[29] Letter to Page from R.M. Hanes of Wachovia Bank and Trust Co., April 23, 1943, attachments B and C to Minutes of Joint Army and Navy Committee Meeting of Feb. 2, 1944, and Report of James G. Hanes on Visits to Southern Military Installations, undated but probably issued April 21, 1944, all in Boxes 9, 10 and 12, Arthur W. Page Papers; and Minutes of Joint Army and Navy Committee of Aug. 2, 1944, Box 11, Arthur W. Page Papers. In fairness to Hanes, a War Dept. survey at the time found that as many as 40 per cent of blacks in the Army thought segregated post exchanges were a good idea, 12 per cent were undecided and only 48 per cent thought them a poor idea. Wynn, *op. cit.*, p. 28.

[30] Letter to Page from Raymond B. Fosdick, Jan. 8, 1943; note from Page to Francis Keppel, Jan. 11, 1943; and letters from Page to Sarah Gibson Blanding, Jan. 20 and Feb. 15, 1943; Box 9, Arthur W. Page Papers.

[31] Letter to Page from Francis Keppel, June 28, 1943, Box 9, Arthur W. Page Papers. See also Julie A. Rhoade, "Special Delivery," *American Legion* magazine, January 2001, pp. 34-35.

[32] Minutes of Joint Army and Navy Committee Meeting of June 28, 1943, Box 9, Arthur W. Page Papers.

[33] Description of armed forces morale and troop information activities is from "Recommendations and Report to the Secretaries of War and Navy from the Joint Army and Navy Committee on Welfare and Recreation," May 1, 1946, Box 13, Arthur W. Page Papers. See also earlier drafts of this final report in Page Papers, and Raleigh, *op. cit.*, pp. 130-31.

[34] Letter from Page to Secretary of War Robert P. Patterson, Jan. 3, 1947, Box 14, Arthur W. Page Papers.

[35] Raleigh, *op. cit.*, pp. 133-34.

[36] Statistics are from Oscar Handlin, *America, A History* (New York: Holt, Rinehart and Winston, 1968), pp. 907-09.

[37] Letter to Page from Maj. Gen. Frederick Osborn, June 1, 1944, Box 11, Arthur W. Page Papers.

[38] Statement of Maj. Gen. Frederick Osborn on Page's assignment in England in Minutes of Joint Army and Navy Committee Meeting of May 3, 1944, Box 11, Arthur W. Page Papers.

[39] Page's report on his activities in Europe are in Minutes of Joint Army and Navy Committee Meeting of Aug. 2, 1944, and Arthur W. Page, "Notes on Informal Talk by Arthur W. Page to Members of Information Dept. on His Return from London," July 19, 1944, both in Box 11, Arthur W. Page Papers. The latter is hereafter referred to as "Notes on Informal Talk."

[40] "Notes on Informal Talk," *op. cit.*

[41] *Ibid.*

[42] *Ibid.*

[43] *Ibid.*

[44] Minutes of Joint Army and Navy Committee Meeting of Aug. 2, 1944.

[45] Letter from Page to Col. Oscar N. Solbert, July 19, 1944, Box 11, Arthur W. Page Papers.

[46] *Ibid.*

[47] Letter from Page to Col. Oscar N. Solbert, July 19, 1944, and letter from Solbert to Maj. Gen. Frederick Osborn, July 21, 1944, Box 11, Arthur W. Page Papers.

[48] Letter to Page from Col. Oscar N. Solbert, Aug. 3, 1944, and letter to Page from Maj. Gen. Frederick Osborn, Aug. 12, 1944, Box 11, Arthur W. Page Papers.

[49] Letter from Page to Maj. Gen. Frederick Osborn, Aug. 22, 1944, with attached letter from Col. Oscar N. Solbert to Page, Aug. 16, 1944, and letter to Page from Osborn, Aug. 24, 1944, Box 11, Arthur W. Page Papers.

[50] Official orders issued by Army Adjutant General's Office, Feb. 6, 1945, and letter to Page from Maj. Gen. Frederick Osborn, Feb. 8, 1945, Box 12, Arthur W. Page Papers.

[51] Letter from Maj. Gen. Frederick H. Osborn to Page, Feb. 10, 1945, Box 12, Arthur W. Page Papers. See also coverage in the *New York Times*, Feb. 8, 1945, and *New York Herald Tribune*, Feb. 9, 1945.

[52] See especially letters from Maj. Gen. Frederick H. Osborn to Page, Feb. 19 and 22, 1945, and letter from Osborn to Lt. Col. Arthur Goodfriend, Feb. 19, 1945, Box 12, Arthur W. Page Papers.

[53] Letter to Page from T/5 Francis Keppel, March 17, 1945, Box 12, Arthur W. Page Papers.

[54] Letter from Page to J. Walter Thompson executive Arthur Farlow, March 28, 1945, Box 12, Arthur W. Page Papers.

[55] Letter from Page to Lt. Col. Arthur Goodfriend, April 4, 1945, Box 12, Arthur W. Page Papers.

[56] See especially letter to Page from Lt. Col. Harry A. Berk, March 28, 1945, and letter from Page to Lt. Col. Robb Winsborough, March 29, 1945, Box 12, Arthur W. Page Papers; and *Reminiscences*, pp. 57-58.

[57] *New York Times*, April 6, 1945, p. 8.

[58] "For Diplomacy," *Business Week*, April 14, 1945, p. 34.

[59] *Reminiscences*, p. 58.

[60] Memorandum from Page to Secretary of War Henry L. Stimson, June 11, 1945, Box 12, Arthur W. Page Papers. See also Raleigh, *op. cit.*, pp. 155-56.

[61] *Reminiscences*, pp. 58-59.

[62] Elting Morison, *op. cit.*, p. 618; Kai Bird, *The Color of Truth McGeorge Bundy and William Bundy: Brothers in Arms* (New York: Simon & Schuster, 1998), pp. 83-84; and Kai Bird, *The Chairman: John J. McCloy, the Making of the American Establishment*, pp. 240-268.

[63] Letter from Page to George L. Harrison, July 18, 1945, Box 12, Arthur W. Page Papers.

[64] *Reminiscences*, p. 59.

[65] Raleigh, *op. cit.*, p. 160, identifies Arnett.

[66] *Reminiscences*, p. 60. See also letter from Page to Gavin Hadden, Dec. 29, 1954, Box 39, Arthur W. Page Papers.

[67] Letter from Page to Col. C.O. Bickelhaupt, April 23, 1942, Box 8, Arthur W. Page Papers.

[68] Letter to Page from Joel E. Harrell, May 3, 1942, Box 8, Arthur W. Page Papers.

[69] See especially letter from Page to Asst. to the Secretary of War Harvey Bundy, Box 11, Arthur W. Page Papers.

[70] Arthur W. Page, "Memorandum for the Secretary of the Navy," April 19, 1945, Box 12, Arthur W. Page Papers.

[71] Memorandum marked "Draft," May 23, 1945, attached to letter from Page to Maj. Gen. Frederick H. Osborn, July 5, 1945, Box 12, Arthur W. Page Papers, and Raleigh, *op. cit.*, pp. 168-71.

[72] Raleigh, *op. cit.*, pp. 171-72.

[73] Letter to Page from Brig. Gen. Luther Hill, Oct. 1, 1945, with attached War Dept. news release dated Sept. 28, 1945, Box 12, Arthur W. Page Papers.

[74] Raleigh, *op. cit.*, p. 174.

[75] *Ibid.*, pp. 164-66.

[76] *Ibid.*, pp. 162-66.

[77] U.S. War Dept., *The Lockhart Report*, by Jack H. Lockhart, Box 13, Arthur W. Page Papers.

[78] Letter to author from retired Bell System executive Douglas Williams, Aug. 21, 1970.

[79] "Citation to Accompany the Award of the Medal for Merit to Arthur W. Page," Jan. 12, 1946, Box 81, Arthur W. Page Papers.

[80] Telegram from Page to Atty. General Francis Biddle, Dec. 31, 1941, Box 8, Arthur W. Page Papers, and Nelson D. Lankford, *The Last American Aristocrat: The Biography of Ambassador David K. Bruce* (Boston and New York: Little, Brown & Co., 1996), pp. 124-31.

[81] Letter from Page to Cdr. Paul Hammond, Oct. 12, 1942, and letter to Page from J.F. McTyier, general business manager of United Seamen's Service, Sept. 26, 1947, Boxes 8 and 16, Arthur W. Page Papers. See also 1947 Page résumé.

[82] Letter from Page to Donald Wilhelm, Sept. 1, 1943, Box 10, Arthur W. Page Papers, and Page's notecards.

[83] Letters to Page from Donald C. Stone of Bureau of the Budget, Aug. 2 and Sept. 18, 1944, Box 11, Arthur W. Page Papers.

[84] Letter from Page to Cdr. W.B. Sarles, Oct. 16, 1945, Box 12, Arthur W. Page Papers.

[85] Page's notecards, and Panama Railroad Co., *Annual Report* (1945), Box 12, Arthur W. Page Papers.

[86] Letter from Page to Johns Hopkins President Isaiah Bowman, Dec. 31, 1942, Box 9, Arthur W. Page Papers.

[87] Arthur W. Page, memorandum entitled "A Plan to Maintain Peace and Order in the World," March 25, 1943, Box 9, Arthur W. Page Papers. See also letter from Page to Sen. Kenneth S. Wherry, March 26, 1943, and Wherry's reply, March 29, 1943, also in Box 9.

[88] Letter to Page from John Foster Dulles, March 8, 1943, and Page's

reply, March 9, 1943, Box 9, Arthur W. Page Papers.

[89] Memorandum dated Aug. 21, 1944, attached to letter from Page to John Foster Dulles, same date, Box 11, Arthur W. Page Papers.

[90] Letter from Page to John Foster Dulles, May 23, 1945, Box 12, Arthur W. Page Papers.

[91] Letter from Page to Maj. Gen. A.D. Surles, Aug. 9, 1945, Box 12, Arthur W. Page Papers.

[92] Memorandum from Page to United Nations Consultants Committee officer Huntington Gilchrist, Jan. 4, 1946, and letter to Page from Trygve Lie, Feb. 28, 1946, Box 13, Arthur W. Page Papers.

[93] American Telephone & Telegraph Co., *Annual Report* (1942), p. 6, and letter from Page to Ethel M. Kurth, July 7, 1942, latter in possession of author.

[94] The ad appears in *Survey Graphic*, Oct. 1942, p. 402

[95] Sidney Hyman, *The Lives of William Benton* (Chicago: University of Chicago Press, 1969), p. 273.

[96] Letter from Page to Bell System public relations vice presidents, Dec. 19, 1941, in possession of author.

[97] See especially letter from Page to Bell System presidents, Dec. 18, 1941; letter from Page to New York Federation of Churches President Theodore Fiske Savage, Dec. 23, 1941; and letter from Page to Bell Telephone of Canada executive C.F. Sise, Nov. 1, 1943; first two in possession of author, last in Box 10, Arthur W. Page Papers.

[98] Letter from Page to Mrs. W. Averell Harriman, Feb. 11, 1942, in possession of author.

[99] Letter from Page to Bell System presidents, May 11, 1942, in possession of author.

[100] Letter from Page to James W. Irwin of the National Dairy Products Corp., Dec. 14, 1943, in possession of author.

[101] Letter from Page to Gordon Gray of Piedmont Publishing, May 7, 1946, Box 13, Arthur W. Page Papers.

[102] Letter from Page to Bell System public relations managers, June 12, 1942, in possession of author.

[103] See Kenneth P. Wood, "Understanding Fifty Million Customers," *op. cit.*, pp. 18-21.

[104] American Telephone & Telegraph Co., "Report of Conferences on Film Distribution Procedures," September or October 1946, Box 3, John M. Shaw Papers.

[105] Pathéscope Pictures, "A Plan for Action," July 1946; notes by John M. Shaw for use by Keith S. McHugh at 1946 Bell System Presidents Conference; both in Box 3, John M. Shaw Papers.

[106] Memorandum to Page from Bell System Asst. Vice President James W. "Joel" Cook, January 1946, Box 13, Arthur W. Page Papers.

[107] See especially memorandum from Page to Bell System public relations executive Prescott C. Mabon, Nov. 19, 1944, Box 12, Arthur W. Page Papers. In this document Page details how he wanted the campaign for higher rates orchestrated.

[108] Arthur W. Page, "Some Remarks on Public Relations," speech to members of the Institute of Life Insurance, New York, Dec. 2, 1942. (Pamphlet.)

[109] Arthur W. Page and Keith S. McHugh, "What Should a Business Do about Public Relations," *Advertising and Selling* (October 1946), pp. 41-42 ff.

[110] Arthur W. Page, "Looking Forward," speech at annual meeting of

Assn. of Life Insurance Presidents, Dec. 2, 1943

[111] Mabon, "The Art of Arthur Page," *op. cit.*, p. 9.

[112] Letter to author from John M. Shaw, *op. cit.*

[113] Letter from Page to Northwestern University Professor Marshall Dimock, Oct. 19, 1944, Box 11, Arthur W. Page Papers. There is more evidence to support the Shaw view of Arthur Page's attitudes toward unions than to support the Mabon view.

[114] Letter from Arthur Page to his brother Ralph Page, March 31, 1942, Box 8, Arthur W. Page Papers.

[115] Letter from Page to Bell Telephone Co. of Canada executive C.F. Sise, Nov. 1, 1943, *op. cit.*

[116] Arthur W. Page, "Some Remarks on Public Relations," *op. cit.*

[117] Letter to author from John J. McCloy, Dec. 5, 1975.

[118] Page's notecards. Page was elected to both the Kennecott and Braden Copper boards on the same day, Feb. 16, 1943.

[119] Letter to author from Prudential Insurance Co. News Service Manager James A. Longo, July 18, 1975.

[120] Page's notecards.

[121] Page's notecards, and letters to Page from Southern Bell Secretary Payton W. Greene, Feb. 28, 1946, and Bell Telephone of Canada executive G.H. Rogers, May 23, 1946, Box 69, Arthur W. Page Papers.

[122] See especially Nielsen, *op. cit.*, pp. 40-41.

[123] Letter from Nicholas Murray Butler to Carnegie Corp. staffer Robert M. Lester, July 21, 1944; letter from Butler to Page, July 24, 1944; letter from Page to Butler, July 27, 1944; letter from Dr. Vannevar Bush to Russell Leffingwell, July 25, 1944; letter from Leffingwell to Bush, July 28, 1944; letter from Page to Frederick H. Osborn, Aug. 7, 1944; letter from Leffingwell to Page, Oct. 2, 1944; letter from Leffingwell to Butler, March 7, 1945; letter from Butler to Leffingwell, March 10, 1945; and letter from Leffingwell to Page, April 30, 1945; all in Boxes 11-12, Arthur W. Page Papers.

[124] Nielsen, *op. cit.*, p. 41.

[125] Nathaniel Peffer, "Memorandum on Carnegie Corporation Grants in the Field of International Relations," April 17, 1942, attached to letter to Page from Carnegie Corp. President Walter A. Jessup, Box 8, Arthur W. Page Papers.

[126] *Ibid.*, and letter from Percy W. Bidwell of the Council on Foreign Relations to Page, May 10, 1943, with attachments; letter from Page to Walter A. Jessup., April 27, 1942; letter to Page from Jessup, May 9, 1942; and letter to Page from Roger Burlingame, May 13, 1943; Boxes 8-9, Arthur W. Page Papers.

[127] See especially letter from Carnegie Corp. President Devereaux Josephs to Page, Nov. 19, 1945, with attached exchange of correspondence between Josephs and Dr. Nicholas Murray Butler, Box 12, Arthur W. Page Papers.

[128] Nielsen, *op. cit.*, p. 41.

[129] *Ibid.*, p. 40, and letter from Devereaux Josephs to Page and other trustees, Jan. 4, 1946, Box 13, Arthur W. Page Papers.

[130] Letter to author from Carnegie Corp. Secretary Florence Anderson, Aug. 5, 1975, and letter to Page from Russell C. Leffingwell, March 1, 1946, with attachments, Box 13, Arthur W. Page Papers.

[131] Letter from Page to Gen. George C. Marshall, June 5, 1946, Box 13, Arthur W. Page Papers. There was no public announcement of Marshall's appointment, ostensibly to avoid upsetting a delicate mission to China he had been assigned to make.

[132] Memorandum from Devereaux Josephs to all Carnegie Corp. trust-

ees, Feb. 18, 1946, Box 13, Arthur W. Page Papers.

[133] Page's notecards; 1947 Page résumé; letter to Page from American Historical Assn. Executive Secretary Guy Stanton Ford, Jan. 11, 1943, Box 9, Arthur W. Page Papers; and e-mail to author from Pillarisetti Sudhir, managing editor, *Perspectives*, American Historical Assn., Jan. 17, 2001.

[134] Letters to Page from John Fiske of Fiduciary Trust Co., Sept. 12 and 14, 1944, Box 11, Arthur W. Page Papers.

[135] See especially letter from Page to Community Service Society board chairman Walter S. Gifford, March 26, 1943; letter to Page from Charles Burlingham, June 11, 1943, with attached excerpt from minutes of Community Service Society board meeting of May 26, 1943; and letter to Page from Paul Garrett, May 1, 1943; all in Box 9, Arthur W. Page Papers.

[136] See especially letters from Page to Arthur D. Wright, Jan. 18, 1944; from Page to Robert 0. Purves, Feb. 14, 1945; from Page to Leslie Snow, Dec. 5, 1944; from Page to Warren Kearney, Dec. 8, 1944; and from Kearney to Page, Dec. 27, 1944; in Boxes 10 and 12, Arthur W. Page Papers. See also 1947 Page résumé and Page's notecards.

[137] See especially letter to Page from James G.K. McClure, Dec. 28, 1943, and Farmers Federation Educational and Development Fund, Minutes of Meeting of Board of Trustees, Dec. 15, 1943, in Boxes 8 and 10, Arthur W. Page Papers.

[138] See especially John Price Jones Organization, "A Plan of Publicity and Public Relations for the Metropolitan Museum of Art," October 1945, Box 13, Arthur W. Page Papers. Box 13 also includes Page's letters of invitation to join the committee. They were sent to public relations counselor Earl Newsom, Paul M. Hollister of CBS, broadcaster Lowell Thomas and *Newsweek* editor and publisher Malcolm Muir, among others. James M. Cecil, president of Cecil and Presbrey, served as vice chairman of Page's public relations committee.

[139] Page's notecards.

[140] *Ibid.*

[141] See especially letters to Page from Irving S. Olds, Jan. 25, 1944, and Jan. 11, 1945, Boxes 68-69, Arthur W. Page Papers.

[142] See especially memorandum by Lt. Col. Harold A. Abramson entitled "Tentative Year-Round Plan for the Biological Laboratory, Cold Spring Harbor, for the Years 1946-1956," Jan. 30, 1946, and manuscript by Abramson entitled "Research on War Projects" attached to letter from Dr. M. Demerec of Long Island Biological Assn. to LIBA board chairman Dr. Robert Cushman Murphy, May 22, 1946, Box 69, Arthur W. Page Papers.

[143] See especially letter to Page from John Perry Bowditch and Dan Chase, July 18, 1945, Box 12, Arthur W. Page Papers.

[144] See letter from C.F. Kettering to Page, Dec. 27, 1945, and Page's reply, Jan. 3, 1946, Box 69, Arthur W. Page Papers.

[145] Page's notecards.

[146] Letter to Page from Carnegie Corp. executive Charles Dollard, July 9, 1942, and letter from Page to William Phillips, July 10, 1942, Box 8, Arthur W. Page Papers.

[147] Letter to Page from Halford Hoskins, July 31, 1942; letter to Page from Dr. Henry M. Wriston, July 26, 1943; letter from Page to Halford Hoskins, July 27, 1943; letter from Hoskins to Page, July 29, 1943; letter to Page from Congressman Christian Herter, Aug. 16, 1943; letter from Page to Herter, Aug. 18, 1943; letter to Page from Hoskins, Aug. 20, 1943; and letter from Page to Hoskins, Aug. 24, 1943; Boxes 8-10, Arthur W. Page Papers.

[148] Letter to Page from Christian Herter, Nov. 10, 1943, Box 10, Arthur

W. Page Papers.

[149] Foreign Service Educational Foundation, Minutes of First Meeting of Board of Trustees, Nov. 20, 1943, and pamphlet, "Proposals with Reference to a Center for the Advanced Study of International Affairs under the Auspices of the Foreign Service Educational Foundation," *ca.* December 1943, both in Box 10, Arthur W. Page Papers.

[150] Letters to Page from Congressman Christian Herter, Jan. 14 and Sept. 27, 1944, Boxes 10-11, Arthur W. Page Papers, and Page's notecards.

[151] See especially memorandum from Johns Hopkins President Dr. Isaiah Bowman to Page, Dec. 4, 1944; letter from Page to Bowman, Dec. 8, 1944; letter and memorandum from Bowman to Page, Jan. 4, 1945; letter from Page to Bowman, Jan. 29, 1945; letter to Page from Rockefeller Foundation head Raymond B. Fosdick, Feb. 2, 1945; and letter from Page to Bowman, Feb. 5, 1945; Box 12, Arthur W. Page Papers.

[152] Letter from Page to Harvard Alumni Assn. President Charles Warren, April 9, 1942, Box 8, Arthur W. Page Papers.

[153] See especially letter to Page from Harvard Board of Overseers Secretary Jerome D. Greene, Box 8, Arthur W. Page Papers.

[154] 1947 Page résumé.

[155] *Ibid.*, and Page's notecards.

[156] Letter to author from Arthur W. Page Jr., Oct. 23, 1975.

[157] Letter to author from Walter H. Page II, Nov. 11, 1975.

[158] Peter Schrag, "America Needs an Establishment," *Harper's Magazine,* Vol. 251 (December 1975), pp. 51-58.

[159] See, for example, letter from Page to Edward Pulling, Oct. 15, 1945, Box 69, Arthur W. Page Papers.

[160] Letter from Page to Maj. Gen. A.D. Surles, July 3, 1946, Box 13, Arthur W. Page Papers.

CHAPTER EIGHT

Consultant and Philanthropist, 1947-1960

P AGE'S ANNUAL AT&T salary in 1946 was $75,000. His retirement pension came to $12,116 per year.[1]

In the spring of 1946, well before his retirement, he concluded agreements whereby AT&T and the Chase National Bank beginning in 1947 would each pay him $25,000 per year as a consultant. That added $50,000 per year to his retirement income.[2]

Page made the consulting arrangements with Walter Gifford of AT&T and Winthrop Aldrich of the Chase National. Both men were soon to serve terms in London as ambassadors to the Court of St. James's—Gifford appointed by President Truman, and Aldrich named by President Eisenhower to succeed Gifford. Although Gifford and Aldrich left their respective employers, Page's consulting fees continued, the one from AT&T to his death in 1960, and the one from the Chase National to 1956, when it was gradually reduced in amount to only $5,000 per year by 1960.[3]

In addition to his pension and the $50,000 in annual retainers he had negotiated with AT&T and Chase National, Page had other sources of income. He was paid regular fees for attending meetings of corporate boards and their executive and special committees. The director fees in the 1940s usually came to only $100 or so per meeting attended, but considerably more was paid to Page for serving on executive committees of the boards. Of greater importance, he gradually built up a list of corporations and institutions that paid him regular retainers or fees. It seems reasonable to assume that, at least through 1956, he made more per year as a consultant than the $75,000 annually he had been paid at AT&T.

While his duties as a consultant and corporate director took time, he had more hours to devote to the nonprofit institutions in which he was interested.[4]

Page's consultancy years began in the latter half of 1946, after Keith McHugh had been named his successor. In the autumn of 1946, he traveled to Chile with Kennecott Copper President E. Tappan Stannard to negotiate settlement of a communist-led strike. When he returned from Latin America in late 1946, he occupied an office suite on the tenth floor of the Wadsworth Building at 46 Cedar St. in New York. He leased the office from Chase National Bank, and for a time, his telephone was patched into Chase National's switchboard.[5]

His third career as a consultant was as studded with accomplishment as were his careers with Doubleday and AT&T.

By the consultancy years, Page was a senior member of the best and the brightest of the Eastern establishment. Like other members, he did his share in guiding American government, helping to set foreign policy, overseeing large corporations, helping higher education and serving great and powerful foundations. He had a winter home in the area of New York that Theodore H. White calls "the Perfumed Stockade," an area peopled by members of the establishment.[6] Like many other members, he shuttled from New York to Washington, Boston and other American power centers in order to meet his various responsibilities.

He spoke often in these years of liberty in America, and was fond of comparing freedom in this nation to the lack of freedom in other countries. The theme that unified the Eastern establishment from the Great Depression through World War II and the Cold War was universal support of "freedom." Almost to a man (for this was a time before the feminist movement), the establishment was Republican, in part because the Republican Party was seen as the one that promised the most freedom from government intervention in the operation of business and the most freedom for an individual to achieve his or her destiny with a minimum of government constraint.

Unlike many members of the establishment who merely paid lip service to the ideals of freedom, Page did something about it. He actively intervened to promote liberty. He took dynamic action on the side of democracy in two world wars. After World War II, he played a major role (with the Central Intelligence Agency) in the founding of Radio Free Europe, the goal of which was freedom for the nations of the Central European shatter zone. He got Carnegie Corp. funding for the Center for the Study of Liberty in America at Harvard.

The theme of freedom is prominent in the last years of Arthur Page. He felt government from the New Deal forward had eroded individual and corporate freedom to the detriment of society. He summed up his feelings simply in a letter to Continental Oil President Clint McCollum, saying in thanks for some Texas cantaloupes, "I look forward to cutting the melons, especially as one doesn't have to give the meat of these to the government and eat the rind."[7]

Establishing the consultancy

WHEN PAGE OPENED his office on Cedar St., he intended to do only limited consulting for firms other than AT&T and the Chase National. When fellow AT&T director Myron Taylor, chairman of U.S. Steel, suggested that he also become a consultant to that firm, Page politely declined, saying he wanted to consult only for the firms and industries with which he was most familiar.[8] By the 1950s, however, he had broadened his client list, and at the request of John Hill of Hill and Knowlton, did some consulting for the American Steel Institute.[9]

Although his list of clients gradually expanded, he never sought to build a full-service public relations or business consulting firm. His staff throughout the consultancy years consisted only of a secretary—at first, Marguerite Phelps, who followed him from AT&T, and then Ethel Betts.

His office was not imposing. One feature was a large table piled high with books, magazines, reports and manuscripts. He would tell visitors that the table contained things he ought to read. When the piles became so high they threatened his safety, he would clear the table and start piling it anew.[10]

One of the first outside consulting jobs he accepted was for the Weyerhaeuser Timber Co., which felt the U.S. Forest Service was interfering with its ability to do business. He visited the firm's headquarters in the Pacific Northwest. On returning to New York, he sent President J. Philip Weyerhaeuser Jr. a list of recommendations that he thought would lead the Forest Service to give the firm greater freedom. He also tried unsuccessfully to persuade Weyerhaeuser to open a new line of credit at the Chase National Bank.[11]

Page had contacts during the early consultancy period with Col. Sosthenes Behn, organizer of the International Telephone and Telegraph Co. (later the ITT conglomerate), for which his brother Frank then worked, and with Douglas Stewart, president of the Quaker Oats Co., whom he advised on employee incentive plans.[12]

By 1951, Page was a retained consultant to Kennecott Copper in addition to AT&T and Chase National, and was doing regular work for the Mayo Clinic, Pennsylvania Railroad and New York's Consolidated Edison Co.[13] He also advised the Symington-Gould Corp., which made heavy metal castings for the railroad industry, on how best to meet the stinging attacks of labor after passage of the Taft-Hartley Act.

Director of and consultant to AT&T

As a consultant to AT&T, Page attended many company meetings. At the annual Bell System public relations conferences, he would reflect on the directions America seemed to be taking as currents tugged the nation's leaders one way and another. Sipping bourbon or Scotch whiskey in the evenings, he would talk informally about whatever was troubling the public relations staffers.

Page usually captivated an audience with his soft-spoken, colloquial way of interpreting current events. At the 1947 Bell System Public Relations Conference, he began his analysis of the American scene with some homespun reflections on Arthur M. Schlesinger Sr.'s theory of cycles in history, adding his own observation that the nation seemed to be entering a new conservative cycle. Before going to the meeting at Seaview, N.J., Page had checked with the elder Schlesinger to be sure he agreed.[14] He went on, with some relish, to share with the conferees his view that many Roosevelt New Dealers were losing top posts in the Truman government. As he put it, "The topside of the FCC's getting to be Christian, but you still have some heathens at the bottom. These have a deep-seated animus against business success. They're not as common as they were." He then commented on how he thought the Gifford financial policy applied to 1947. His basic message was that AT&T needed better earnings, and the company needn't be ashamed to make a profit. "You know," he remarked, calling for public relations to win public support for better AT&T earnings, "the Bell System established the only fully developed public relations department in modern industry, set up at the policy level where you can help direct the course of events."[15]

Page knew the Bell System needed more money to cope with postwar problems. When a big company like AT&T complains that its earnings are inadequate, the public is likely to be skeptical, suspecting greed and not need as the motive. But in 1946 and 1947, AT&T was facing serious financial problems. Associated companies were scurrying about seeking rate increases they had not been able to get during the period of wartime price controls. Without more money, AT&T could not finance the record construction program needed to meet postwar demand, and it could not satisfy the demands of labor which had grown militant following relaxation of wartime controls on wages.

The need for construction of telephone facilities was acute. Immediately after the war ended, about two million people were on waiting lists for phone service. By 1947, 1.9 million people were still waiting. As fast as the company built new lines and central offices, new requests for service went on the waiting lists. To make matters worse, facilities available to customers who did have telephones were overloaded.[16]

Part of Page's solution to the problem was to see that Bell System employees were kept hard at work putting in new telephone plant as fast as Western Electric could manufacture it. The other part was to assure that employees were trained to face customer irritation with the utmost politeness and sympathy. As he put it, "neither impatience nor irritation can make much headway against a solid front of customer courtesy."[17] Employees were taught to answer angry customers with rational, courteous answers, and never lose their own tempers. A soft answer to dissipate wrath remained for years the common response of Bell System employees to customer irritation, as many a person who tried to provoke one of "Ma Bell's" employees to anger will attest.

AT&T stockholders posed another public relations problem in the postwar years. AT&T required vast injections of capital to finance construction. Until the operating companies were able to drive through local rate increases, money from earnings was inadequate. As late as 1947, AT&T failed to earn its $9 dividend, although it was paid as usual. Some of the money was raised by issuing new common stock, much of it sold through employee stock purchase plans. Perhaps the most popular instrument was the convertible debenture, a form of bond which the owner, after a set period of time, can convert to common stock. Use of convertibles, along with sale of conventional bonds, changed AT&T's debt ratio (the ratio of bonds to stock) from 30 per cent bonded indebtedness at the end of the war to 50 per cent by 1950. Some stockholders complained that AT&T common stock was being watered by overuse of convertible debentures. Others complained that a day of reckoning would come when AT&T had to pay back the principal on bonds that had not been converted to common stock. Much of Page's consulting at this juncture was devoted to advising management on how to maintain AT&T's reputation in the financial community as "America's soundest investment."[18]

Page also counseled AT&T executives on how to cope with the problems of labor grown militant in the postwar years. Although agreements between Bell System companies and labor unions can be traced to at least 1898, it was not until 1918, while AT&T was under wartime federal control, that Postmaster General Burleson issued a bulletin saying telephone employees had the right to bargain with their employers individually or collectively through unions. According to labor historian Jack Barbash, AT&T moved immediately after World War I to short-circuit adversary unions by creating company unions. The docile company unions were characteristic until 1939, when, after the National Industrial Recovery Act of 1933 and the Wagner Act of 1935 paved the way, employees organized the National Federation of Telephone Workers (NFTW). It was the predecessor of the Communications Workers of America (CWA) and International Brotherhood of Electrical Workers (IBEW). Impetus to the growth of NFTW came in 1941, when the National War Labor Board (NWLB) ordered Southern Bell to dismantle its company union, clearing the way for NFTW organization in the South, and eventually elsewhere. Another major victory for labor came in 1945, when the NWLB established a national telephone commission that gave the NFTW authority to bargain nationally with AT&T instead of regionally with the Bell System operating companies.[19]

There were several threatened and actual strikes by Bell System workers during World War II, all small in scale. Big strikes began immediately after the end of the war. The first postwar strike, against Illinois Bell, began in November 1945. The concessions won by the Illinois Bell workers were noted by other Bell System unions around the country, and a rash of strikes occurred in 1946. All were local in scope.[20]

Then, at 6 a.m. on April 7, 1947, the first national strike of telephone workers began. The issues involved were more complex than more pay. At the core of the dispute was a head-on clash between AT&T management and the NFTW over whether the union would bargain locally with Bell System operating companies, or nationally with AT&T. AT&T management, which wanted bargaining conducted locally, emerged the winner.[21]

Through all the turmoil of AT&T's stand against the union's desire to bargain nationally, Page remained firm, not in the belief of some that the union had to be crushed, but in his own belief that an alert and sympathetic management could head off strikes before they began. Strikes did not have to occur, he believed. "The American Rolling Mills didn't have 'em," he wrote to successor Keith McHugh in 1947. "Standard of New Jersey didn't have 'em. They may be the work of devils but they are not Acts of God and therefore inevitable." He asked McHugh to make it clear to the Bell System presidents that having or not having strikes was their responsibility. They, he said, should use the power of persuasion when strike threats loomed. "(W)hen you want to persuade people, you talk to them," he told McHugh. "If it is a hard job you start early and give yourself plenty of time."[22]

On Feb. 18, 1948, Walter Gifford left the AT&T presidency to become chairman of the board. Leroy A. "Lee" Wilson, an exceptionally conscientious and tough manager who had spent much of his career with Indiana Bell, replaced him. On the same day Gifford left the AT&T presidency, Page resigned as a director, his place on the board taken by Wilson.[23]

Although Page left the AT&T board, his $25,000-per-year consulting job continued. He remained a director of Southern Bell, which in 1948 won rate-case victories in the courts of Mississippi and Georgia of great significance to the entire Bell System.[24]

In October 1949, Page resigned from the Southern Bell board. The next month, when Lee Wilson became president of AT&T, Page was reelected to the AT&T board. At the time of the reelection, he was also named for the first time to the AT&T executive committee.[25] The assignment greatly increased his influence on the board. In addition, by the early

1950s the executive committee was worth another $5,000 per year in income for him. Other members of the executive committee serving with Page, in addition to AT&T President Wilson, were Winthrop Aldrich of the Chase National, long-standing Page friend John W. Davis, Charles F. Adams, Elihu Root Jr. and Samuel Welldon.[26]

When the AT&T board ruled in late 1950 that retired AT&T executives could not serve on the board for more than three years after retirement, the directors specifically exempted Page from the provision with a qualifier that said the rule applied only to retired executives who had served continuously on the board from retirement. Page's service as a director had been interrupted from 1948 to 1949.[27]

In May 1951, the strain of command took its toll on the hard-working Wilson, who had been devoting all available energy to improving AT&T's financial position. He collapsed.

The pressures Wilson had faced during his presidency were immense. In later years, talking with John Paige of the Wisconsin Telephone Co., Arthur Page credited Wilson with having saved the Bell System from financial collapse. Driving himself to exhaustion, firing or retiring associated company presidents unable to get rate increases through state public service commissions, Wilson had made great strides in restoring the Bell System to solvency.[28]

As the days dragged on into the early summer of 1951, Wilson lay incapacitated, the Bell System without a chief executive. Pressures grew within management and the board for the naming of a replacement. The board of directors, not knowing if Wilson would recover or die, was reluctant to act.[29]

Board Chairman Walter Gifford, serving as the American ambassador to Great Britain, wanted Cleo Craig named acting president of AT&T. Page carried that wish to the AT&T executive committee. On June 27, the executive committee elected Craig to the post. The next day, Wilson died.[30]

On July 2, the full AT&T board, the visage of Theodore N. Vail staring down sternly from a portrait on the boardroom wall at 195 Broadway, voted to remove the word "acting" from Craig's title as president. At the meeting, Page, Winthrop

Aldrich and Elihu Root Jr. staved off a halfhearted attempt by James Bell to get Vannevar Bush named to the presidency instead of Craig. It was Bush who stopped the move, saying lightheartedly that he "was not a candidate for the office, would not run if nominated and would not serve if elected."[31]

It was at about this time that Arthur Page acquired increased renown as a letter writer. His father had acquired considerable fame, much of it posthumously, for his skill as an eloquent letter writer. Arthur's fame came not so much for writing the flowery prose that had characterized his father's letters, but for his ability to write clear, concise, persuasive business letters.

In 1952, the Pacific Telephone & Telegraph Co. published in pamphlet form an exchange of letters between Page and PT&T President Mark Sullivan, most of the pamphlet consisting of a long memorandum by Page on how to write effective business correspondence. The pamphlet, entitled "An Experiment in Business Letter Writing," is probably still tucked away in some executive desk drawers. In it, Page called for managers to forget all letter-writing formulas, business jargon, stilted words and rules of grammar. He called on them to say as simply and directly as they could whatever they had to say as though talking to someone face-to-face.

Page, who never had high regard for formal grammar nor cared greatly about spelling, summed up his feelings about dictionaries and grammar books in the pamphlet:

> William Shakespeare wrote without benefit of dictionary or grammar. In fact, he wrote 100 years before either existed for the English language. And yet he wrote well. The first dictionary was published in 1775 and the first English grammar in the United States in 1765. There have been dictionaries ever since but they never quite catch up with the English language for it is a living, growing thing changing all the time. A dictionary is a useful thing but the letter writers of the Pacific Company are more apt to know the local meaning in the Pacific area of any simple word than a dictio-

nary published ten years before in New York or London. If you have to use the dictionary much, the man who receives the letter will probably have to use it even more, which he will not like.

...The Constitution of the United States and probably all the political papers of its time, including the writings of Jefferson, Madison and Chief Justice Marshall were written by people who had never studied any English grammar.

I suspect that most people pay more attention to grammar than is good for their writing, for the grammar writers have thought up various rules which they had no right to do for they do not own the language. It is free for anyone to use. It is a tool anyone may shape for himself to gain the ends he has in mind. If you use language so that it is an easy, pleasant and effective transmitter of your thoughts, you need not bother about the rules. But if your language varies from the good usage of the time and neighborhood, so that it calls attention to itself rather than the thought it is conveying, it defeats its purpose. Formal or overly grammatical language is not effective nor is slang before it is generally accepted into the language.[32]

Page regarded the election of Dwight Eisenhower in 1952 as propitious for the Bell System. At the AT&T Public Relations Conference in 1954, he rhapsodized over the changes the Eisenhower administration had worked in its first year. Controls on materials and prices had been removed, clearing the way for expedited AT&T construction. Regulatory agencies had grown less hostile; the FCC had allowed an important interstate rate increase. There were fewer employee strikes in 1953 than any other postwar year, an event Page attributed to labor no longer having a "back door entrance" to the White House. A budget deficit created by the Truman administration defense spending had been pared, and inflation retarded. The stability of the world appeared to Page to be improving. And the administration, he felt, was doing what it could to refinance the national debt. Page was sure that Eisenhower had ushered in a new economic climate in which business could prosper.[33]

An issue that preoccupied Page as a director of AT&T and other corporations from the mid-1950s forward was the age of corporate directors. He became interested in the issue when 66-year-old Edward L. Ryerson, chairman of Inland Steel and a director of five other corporations, charged that the biggest corporations in America were losing ground to competitors because their boards were controlled by old men. In early 1953, Ryerson resigned from the board of Northern Trust, explaining that he was stepping aside to make room for appointment of a younger director.[34]

In late 1954-early 1955, AT&T's executive committee took action to remove the oldest directors from a board that was becoming dominated by elderly men. The executive committee passed a resolution that no new directors under 72 should be appointed to the board, and that the ten directors on the board 72 or over—including Page—should be retired in stages from 1956 through 1959. Page was appointed to make unpleasant but necessary visits to the first two directors affected, W. Cameron Forbes, 86, who had been on the AT&T board since 1919, and Myron Taylor, 82, who had been serving since 1929. Page called on the men in Miami and Nassau. Following his visits, the AT&T board approved the executive committee resolution.[35]

In 1956, the AT&T presidency passed for a third time to a new man. In September, Cleo Craig became chairman of the AT&T board, and Frederick Kappel, a tough, sometimes temperamentally explosive executive, became the president.[36] Under the rough-hewn Kappel, the conservative financial policy of no dividend increases and no stock splits that had prevailed from 1921 forward was abandoned. In 1959, AT&T stock was split three shares for one, and the dividend per share increased to $9.90 per pre-split share.[37] The change was popular with stockholders, who approved the 1959 stock split by 99.1 per cent.[38] Further stock splits and dividend increases followed.

Another issue confronting AT&T in the late 1950s that concerned Page as a director and a consultant was the 1958 Celler Commission probe. The investigation resulted in charges that AT&T was operating a monopoly through Western Electric, that the company had used its influence with the Defense Dept. to head off Justice Dept. antitrust action, that AT&T was profiteering in its contracts with the Defense Dept. (in 1958, AT&T was the nation's third-largest defense contractor) and that the Bell System had undue influence in the Defense Dept. The last allegation was based on the fact that 35 AT&T executives had served in key Defense Dept. posts during the Eisenhower Administration. In 1958, 14 of these executives were still in strategic appointive posts.[39]

On Dec. 16, 1959, in keeping with the policy that he had helped formulate to remove older men from the AT&T board, Page resigned his AT&T directorship, but continued as a consultant to the company. Except for the brief interruption from 1948 to 1949, Page's tenure on the board had been continuous from 1931.

Last years of service to the Chase National Bank

THE CHASE NATIONAL BANK in 1950 was among the more popular with corporate America. In that year, fully 405 of the 500 largest corporations in America did some business with Chase.[40]

Page's most important work for Chase, aside from counseling Winthrop Aldrich and other executives, was to serve on the bank's executive committee from 1953 to 1955, and chair the bank's personnel committee from 1951 to 1955.[41]

The board personnel committee Page headed oversaw the Chase National's liberal employee benefits program. Following a survey of Chase employee attitudes toward fringe benefits in the fall of 1952, Page participated in management planning for an employee information program to explain a vastly revised benefits program introduced in 1953.[42]

His service as a director of the Chase ended in 1955. In

the spring of that year, stockholders of the Chase National and of the Bank of the Manhattan Co. approved merger of the two financial institutions. At the time of the merger, the Chase National had deposits of more than \$5.3 billion, and the Manhattan had deposits of almost \$1.5 billion.[43]

Page was dropped from the board of the new Chase Manhattan Bank. However, he was appointed a member of the Chase Manhattan's Trust Advisory Board in April 1955, a post he held to his death in 1960.[44] He continued as a consultant to the Chase Manhattan, although his annual retainer was considerably reduced from 1956 forward.

Confronting the communist unions in Chile

THE STORY OF Kennecott Copper, incorporated in 1915, began 14 years earlier in 1901, when Stephen Birch, with the financial backing of Henry O. Havemeyer of the sugar refining trust, secured promising copper properties in Alaska. Dan Guggenheim caught wind of the find, and sent the top assayer of Guggenex, the Guggenheim family holding company, to Alaska to investigate. In the remote wilderness above Kennecott Creek, the assayer found a mother lode of millions of tons of ore that assayed an unbelievable 70 to 75 per cent pure copper. Dan Guggenheim arranged financing through J.P. Morgan, and thereby Morgan got an interest in the find and the Guggenheim family got the capital to develop it. Through the Guggenheims, the new mining syndicate eventually acquired the Utah Copper Co., which owned a massive copper lode at Bingham Canyon, Utah, and a rich copper mine high in the Chilean Andes which had been started by William Braden. By the time Kennecott Copper was incorporated in 1915, the syndicate also controlled mining properties in New Mexico, Arizona and Nevada in addition to Utah Copper and the Braden Copper operation in Chile. It was the Kennecott bonanza lode in Alaska, however, that was the core business until it played out. The Alaska lode was the richest copper deposit in the world. The great porphyry deposits of Utah and Nevada, which would come into dominance after the Kennecott lode played out, assayed only two to three per cent copper.[45]

As the exploitation of Alaska by the Guggenheim-Morgan interests developed, with acquisition after acquisition by the syndicate, cartoonists created two monster polar bear-Eskimo figures called Guggenmorgan and Morganheim that were often portrayed in various stages of devouring Alaska.

In late 1946, when Arthur Page started his consultancy, Edmond A. and Solomon R. Guggenheim represented the Guggenheim family interests, and George Whitney and Charles O. Dickey represented the Morgan interests. Another prominent member of the Kennecott board, Alfred P. Sloan, had spent his active business career with General Motors.[46]

The main Kennecott properties in 1946 were the Bingham Canyon open pit mine near Salt Lake City, Utah, and the El Teniente mine of Braden Copper in Chile. Copper from the mines was processed by Kennecott's Magma mill near the Great Salt Lake and the Sewell plant in Chile.

Page brought his public relations and business sagacity to the Kennecott board. In addition, he had cross-directorships in corporations of interest to Kennecott. AT&T, of which he was a director, was one of the nation's largest users of copper. About two years after Page joined the board, Kennecott entered into a joint oil exploration venture with Continental Oil, of which Page was also a director. When Wolverine Brass, a competitor of Kennecott's Chase Brass subsidiary, lured away a contract to provide the plumbing fixtures for the new Prudential Insurance building, Page wrote a circumspect letter of complaint to Prudential, of which he was a director, and the plumbing fixture contract went back to Chase Brass.[47]

In late 1946, Page traveled with Kennecott President E. Tappan Stannard and another director, Medley G.B. Whelpley, to Chile. There the three negotiated with leaders of the communist labor union which had gone on strike at the Braden Copper Co.'s Sewell processing plant, located in the Andes below Braden's huge El Teniente mine.

The crisis in Chile began when the Sewell labor syndicate, dominated by the Chilean communist popular front, refused to accept the same terms of an agreement Kennecott had reached with three other Chilean unions and went on strike in November. The strike coincided with elections in Chile. In the elections, Radical candidate Gabriel González Videla, whose party had the support of Chilean communists, captured the presidency.[48] González formed a cabinet that contained some communist ministers and some members of the opposition Liberal party.

The strike was still under way when Page, Stannard and Whelpley flew to Chile to try to hammer out a settlement on terms as favorable as possible to Kennecott. It quickly became apparent to the trio that they were playing from a weak hand. The labor union leaders held the trump cards.

In Chile, González and his Radical ministers, especially the minister of labor, tried to pressure the Kennecott officials (Yankee "imperialists," as González called them) into accepting arbitration of the strike. The Kennecott team resisted, maneuvering through officials of the opposition Liberal and Conservative parties. Their efforts were fruitless. In early December, the Kennecott officials faced a choice between agreeing to arbitration or having their property seized and placed under government control. Page, Stannard and Whelpley knew the Chilean government lacked the capital and expertise to run the Braden property for long. They also realized that government seizure could lead to hostile inspection of Braden's financial records, to damage to Sewell machinery during government control and to possible permanent confiscation. On Dec. 10, the three representatives agreed to arbitration of all but a few of the 14 demands of the strikers. With an arbitration order issued, work resumed at El Teniente and Sewell on Dec. 10.[49]

In an untitled manuscript in the Page Papers dated Jan. 17, 1947, almost certainly written by Page, the author recommends that Kennecott take two actions. First, Kennecott should demand that the State Dept. recall Ambassador Bowers, who allegedly had invited "the chief Communist of South

America as a guest at our Embassy" and who was "an admirer of Jeffersonian and Jacksonian democracy... rather friendly toward radical commotion and allergic to big business." Second, the author advised Kennecott to pressure American financial institutions making development loans to Chile to consider denial of further loans until a more favorable climate for American investment in Chile arose.[50]

Page believed America should use its economic muscle to pressure foreign nations into accepting American investment. In letters he wrote after returning from Chile, he called on powerful friends—such as John J. McCloy, who after his World War II service in the War Dept. had become president of the International Bank for Reconstruction and Development—to deny loans to inflation-plagued Chile until the González regime became more receptive to American investments.[51]

Many of Page's friends were in sympathy with his pleas for America to use economic pressure on other nations. In late 1946, Winthrop Aldrich chaired President Harry Truman's Special Committee on Foreign Loans and Allied Matters. Undersecretary of State for Economic Affairs William Clayton was paving the way for the World Bank to take over the foreign loan responsibilities of the Roosevelt Administration's Export-Import Bank. Aldrich's committee called for Clayton's office to make it World Bank policy to refuse loans to foreign nations that refused to welcome American investment.[52]

Page called after returning from Chile for propaganda efforts by the American government and by Braden Copper to combat the propaganda of the communist-led Chilean unions. He especially sought a way to counter the influence of the communist daily newspaper *El Siglo*, which had a smaller circulation than many of the Santiago dailies, but published more pages than any Chilean daily except *El Mercurio*. *El Siglo* was especially potent in labor camps, where communist union members used intimidation to keep vendors from selling newspapers other than the party organ.[53]

Kennecott's problems in Chile were somewhat alleviated in 1948 when the Chilean government, under considerable

American pressure, outlawed the communist party and removed 30,000 voters with communist affiliations from vot-
ing roles.[54] Kennecott still faced a discriminatory rate of exchange for dollars to pesos and ever-increasing taxes in Chile.

In 1948, Kennecott President E. Tappan Stannard intensified diversification into fields other than copper mining. The
firm expanded its oil exploration venture with Continental
Oil, concluded an agreement with New Jersey Zinc to begin a
titanium mining venture in Canada and opened negotiations
with a South African consortium which eventually led to
Kennecott's involvement in gold-mining in that nation.[55]

In 1949, Page helped to find a successor for Kennecott
President Stannard. In the summer of 1948, Solomon
Guggenheim, who funded the great Guggenheim Museum of
modern art in New York, had recommended hiring Climax
Molybdenum President Arthur D. Storke to replace Stannard,
who was due to retire. Storke had only been on the Kennecott
payroll a few days when he and Stannard flew to Canada to
inspect the new Kennecott-New Jersey Zinc titanium mine.
The plane crashed killing Stannard, Storke and another
Kennecott executive.[56]

After the accident, Page wrote to Edmond Guggenheim,
the largest private stockholder in Kennecott (who had
dropped out of Guggenheim Brothers in 1923 to protest the
sale by his uncles of the giant Chiquicamata mine in Chile to
Anaconda), to suggest several possible new presidents. One
of the men he recommended was Charles R. Cox, the
58-year-old president of Carnegie-Illinois Steel. The Kennecott
board named Cox president in December 1949.[57]

As a public relations consultant to Kennecott, Page advised Presidents Stannard and Cox. He introduced them to
leading Washington officials. He counseled executives on the
institutional advertising campaign the company initiated in
1949 with the Cunningham and Walsh advertising agency.
He advised officials of both Kennecott and Braden Copper
on how to cope with public relations problems through use
of corporate films and employee information. He assisted in
writing Kennecott annual reports, and helped plan special

events such as entertainment for the president of Chile when he visited the United States.[58]

Charges of Central Intelligence Agency intervention in the internal affairs of Chile during the regime of Salvadore Allende in the early 1970s—a regime that nationalized Kennecott properties in Chile—raise the question of whether Kennecott ever sought help from the CIA, and if so, when. Allen Dulles, an OSS officer during World War II, was a Page friend and neighbor. In 1950, W. Bedell Smith had called Dulles back to government service first as director of Plans and then as deputy director of the CIA. A letter in the Page Papers from Page to Dulles in 1952 indicates Page had recently met with Dulles to discuss a matter affecting Kennecott interests—a matter which, according to the letter, had since been referred by Kennecott President Charles Cox to President Truman through Secretary of Commerce Charles Sawyer.[59] The letter does not state the nature of the matter Page discussed with Dulles on behalf of Kennecott.

In 1951-56, Page helped reshape Kennecott's contributions policy.

In the spring of 1951, Mrs. Learned Hand wrote asking him for a substantial donation to the Foreign Policy Assn. from Kennecott.[60] He answered that he couldn't recommend a gift because the Foreign Policy Assn. hadn't worked to benefit Kennecott and its employees, and he couldn't be sure a donation would be acceptable to all stockholders. He indicated, however, that his own philosophy of corporate philanthropy was liberalizing. He recognized that public opinion was coming to support the idea that corporations should give more to worthy causes. They were giving more to charity because of tax advantages and because they knew that inflation had eroded the charitable capacity of the nation's traditional social betterment agencies. His main reservation, he said, was that he believed corporate giving should be on the basis of some reasonable principle, and his conscience kept him from recommending a gift from Kennecott to the Foreign Policy Assn. because he hadn't yet decided what principles should guide Kennecott giving.[61]

A few months later, Page urged Kennecott President Cox to establish an educational and welfare foundation to receive a portion of Kennecott's excess profits and channel them in subsequent years into charity.[62]

By 1952, Page had changed his thinking about corporate giving. Earlier he had favored gifts only to organizations that provided tangible benefits to Kennecott, such as local community chests which directly helped employees. Now he was willing to liberalize that view so long as Kennecott directors carefully considered whether or not a gift made a major contribution to improving overall public welfare.[63]

In 1953, Page was selected to chair a new Kennecott board committee to develop a company policy on philanthropy and advise the full board on specific donation requests.[64]

In June 1953, the New Jersey Supreme Court ruled in the case of A.P. Smith v. Ruth F. Barlow, *et al.*, that a corporation had considerable freedom to make contributions to charity. Although confined to New Jersey, the case had an important national effect, clearing the way for expanded corporate philanthropy just as federal tax incentives had done. Page was familiar with the decision. [65] He soon carried recommendations for expanded giving to the Kennecott board.

Although Page after 1953 was willing to recommend contributions to charities to which Kennecott had not earlier contributed, he did not become profligate. When David O. McKay, president of the Church of Jesus Christ of Latter-Day Saints, which wields prodigious power in Utah, asked Kennecott for a hefty contribution to help build a replica of the Old Salt Lake Theatre on the campus of the University of Utah, Page objected. He thought the gift, if made, could create a precedent whereby the Mormon hierarchy would come to count on Kennecott for automatic contributions to any causes the church undertook. He recommended that Kennecott pledge $61,000 conditional upon the church first raising $425,000 from other sources. The Kennecott board approved a donation of $250,000, considerably in excess of what Page had advised.[66]

Overall, Kennecott expanded its giving between 1954 and

1957, particularly increasing its generosity to higher education. The firm's contributions rose from $379,000 in 1954 to $903,000 in 1957. Then, in 1958, a bad earnings year, contributions dropped to $526,000. Page recommended in 1959, shortly after leaving the Kennecott board, that contributions be held to $700,000 per year, regardless of how much went into the Kennecott Foundation, with unexpended surplus to be used in years when earnings were lean.[67]

Page played a role in introducing a mandatory retirement age of 72 for Kennecott directors. In early 1957, he wrote to Alfred Sloan about setting a mandatory retirement age, noting that AT&T and U.S. Steel had initiated such rules. Sloan said he felt such a policy, if adopted by Kennecott, should not apply to directors already on the board (Sloan) or to directors with large blocks of Kennecott stock (the estate of the by then deceased Solomon Guggenheim, and still living directors Edmond Guggenheim and Henry Havemeyer *fils*) but suggested that Page bring up the matter at the next board meeting.[68]

Page was named to chair a special committee to explore the matter of mandatory retirement age. The committee hammered out a schedule for retiring all directors 72 and older by 1960. The schedule was approved by the Kennecott board, although a few directors affected by the policy—especially Henry Havemeyer—objected.[69]

Although Page was not scheduled to retire under the new policy until 1960, he sent Kennecott President Cox his letter of resignation in May 1959. He was feeling the effects of age, he explained, and growing increasingly reluctant to travel.[70] At about the same time, he resigned from Continental Oil and the Carnegie Corp. for the same reasons.

Shortly after Page left the Kennecott and Braden Copper boards, his son Walter H. Page II became a Kennecott director. When Walter in 1971 became president of Morgan Guaranty Trust, he was still on the Kennecott board.[71] Well after that, Kennecott assets passed to a British company, Rio Tinto Plc., becoming Rio's Kennecott Holdings Corp., Kennecott Energy & Coal and Kennecott Utah Copper subsidiaries.

Public relations consultant to Conoco

THE CONTINENTAL OIL CO., of which Page became a director in 1939, was one of the companies created when Standard Oil was broken up by trustbuster Judge Kennesaw Mountain Landis during the Taft Administration. By 1947, Continental was a dynamic, growing firm ranked in the top 15 petroleum companies in America in terms of gross operating revenue and net income.[72]

In late 1947, L.F. "Clint" McCollum, one of Standard of New Jersey's bright young men, was lured away to become president of Continental.[73] Page and McCollum became friends, and Page's influence on the Conoco board correspondingly increased. During much of the period 1947 to 1958, Page had another ally on the Continental board in George Whitney of Morgan Guaranty Trust, chairman of the Conoco executive committee.

Page met the traditional responsibilities of a Continental director. In 1948, he successfully argued over the objections of board chairman James J. Cosgrove for an increase in the Continental dividend to $4. From 1950 to 1957 he served on George Whitney's committee which reviewed executive salaries, and from 1957 to 1958 he chaired the committee.[74]

Page was the public relations expert on the Continental board. Although he refused an invitation from Clint McCollum in 1951 to become a paid public relations consultant to the company,[75] his influence on the development of Conoco's public relations philosophy was nevertheless extensive.

Page often talked about public relations and its role in the modern corporation to Conoco executives and at meetings of the board of directors. In an April 1951 speech he made to the Conoco board—a speech given a day earlier to a group of Continental executives in Texas—Page outlined the fundamental reason he felt that Conoco needed a public relations program:

> The Continental Oil Co. was chartered by public authority on the assumption that it would serve the

public's needs for petroleum products. The theory was that its self-interest would insure its activity and competition would keep its products and services and its prices satisfactory

...(P)ublic authority can at any time limit its functions, its methods or abolish it altogether.

So we, like all other companies, live by public approval and roughly speaking, the more approval we have the better we live.

This is the fundamental reason for seeking public approval.

The fundamental way of getting it is to deserve it.

For a long time business men figured that if they produced goods at a price that the public would buy that was ample evidence that they deserved and had public approval.

But it turned out not to be as simple as that.

Business found it could lose public approval by having trouble with labor, by being unpopular in its home town, by using selling methods that didn't suit the government, and by an infinite number of other things, some of them seemingly quite harmless.

So it has become generally accepted that a Corporation must be a good citizen in all kinds of ways besides a good producer and distributor.[76]

Page believed in the solid building of good will among customers, stockholders, employees and government. He was skeptical of flamboyant aspects of public relations, deploring press agentry, the glitter of cosmetic public relations and "show business" tricks. But he liked pseudo-events such as first-call ceremonies, ground-breakings and anniversaries.

Page took a particular interest in Conoco's public relations campaign to publicize the firm's 75th (Diamond) Anniversary. In late 1949, when planning began, he asked Clint McCollum to put down on paper the exact objectives Conoco hoped to accomplish with the observance. When McCollum sent his list to Page in early 1950, Page recommended that

Conoco retain either Selvage and Lee or Verne Burnett and Associates to assist with the effort. Continental retained Verne Burnett as the primary agency for the celebration, and the George Kirksey firm of Houston to help.[77]

When Continental executives opposed a Burnett recommendation for a detailed employee attitude survey as part of the planning for the anniversary celebration, Page sided with the agency, but wrote to Verne Burnett to say, "I think (the attitude survey) is a tool that is less precise than some and I don't want (Continental executives) to expect more than they will get out of it."[78]

He recommended that Burnett and Conoco go further than both had proposed in the employee education component of the campaign. Page wanted more attention paid to economic education of employees. He wanted to tell employees how inflation could erode the value of their pensions, and urge them to set up their own separate savings and investment programs to provide for their retirements.[79]

He was skeptical of the component aimed at stockholders, saying he had never seen any substantial results from superheated efforts aimed at stockholders "except prizes from financial writers and the public relations fraternity."[80]

He was also skeptical when Burnett hired a song-writer to produce a ballad for the anniversary, saying he couldn't envision Conoco truck drivers marching around to a company song. He relented somewhat when he learned that Burnett had hired Elizabeth Lomax to write the ballad. Doubleday, Page had published her first book of Western ballads when Page was still with the firm, and, he told Burnett, "this ancient memory softens my brain some."[81]

Page was able to see through the surface showmanship of the celebration and recognize that beneath the glitter lay substantial value—the campaign was likely, he felt, to make Conoco employees better disposed toward their company, and the attendant publicity was likely to make Conoco's marketing efforts more successful.[82]

Realizing that good employee relations were essential to the building of a successful public relations program, Page championed an employee incentive plan at Conoco in 1951-1952. The plan ultimately adopted, involving stock options for executives and a company-matched savings plan for rank-and-file employees, was not as liberal as the plan Page had hoped to see adopted.[83]

Page was involved in Conoco's philanthropic policies. In the fall of 1951, Continental President McCollum called for the firm to establish a foundation with $1 million to make gifts to education. Page endorsed the decision, suggesting that Conoco develop a specific policy to guide gift-giving, and then place responsibility for overseeing largesse in the hands of Conoco executives in local communities.

Continental Vice President and General Counsel Lloyd Thanhouser opposed establishing a foundation. He recognized that because of tax advantages the $1 million would only cost Continental $230,000 in profits, but felt that the company had no business funding education or other charities.[84] Nonetheless, Conoco developed a policy for its philanthropy and the firm's contributions budget was expanded. Page served as a member of the Contributions Committee.[85]

In 1956, Thanhouser reversed his position on corporate contributions and issued a memo establishing a liberal program. He recognized that Conoco's aid to higher education had fallen behind that of other corporations, and that the firm's philanthropy lacked coordination and planning. The memo outlined plans for forming a committee on financial aid to education to oversee the new program,[86] which implemented the recommendations Page had made in 1951.

As he had at AT&T and Kennecott, Page campaigned at Continental Oil for a mandatory retirement age for directors. Within weeks after suggesting that Conoco adopt such a policy, he himself resigned from the Conoco board in 1957.[87] McCollum ignored the resignation letter. A year later, Page again resigned. Now 74 years old, he said he could no longer do all the things a director should do. His resignation was finally accepted in November 1958. One of his last acts was to make arrangements for AT&T Executive Vice President Eugene McNeely to replace him on the Continental board.[88]

One of the tributes Page received for his service on the Continental board came from Philip Lauinger, president of the *Oil and Gas Journal* in Tulsa, who wrote: "I always looked upon you as a knowledgeable man who understands people and their reactions to a remarkable degree, and I regard you as the chief stabilizing influence on the board."[89]

The Prudential and Westinghouse boards

PAGE RESIGNED from the board of the Prudential Insurance Co. in January 1955. During his final years on the board, he served on the Auditing Committee from 1951 to 1953, on the Committee on Dividends from 1951 to 1953 and on the Committee on Salaries from 1951 to 1953. He was still serving as chairman of a board committee on Prudential's triennial audit and on a special Committee on Committees of the Board at the time of his resignation.[90]

Page remained on the Westinghouse Electric board and a member of the executive committee until his death in 1960.[91]

The indirect interlocking director

IN 1951, PAGE was a subject in a Federal Trade Commission (FTC) report on indirect interlocking directorships.

The 500-page report, issued in March, warned Congress that the nation's 1,000 largest manufacturing concerns were linked by a web of common directors. The Clayton Act prohibited directors from sitting on the boards of competing corporations such as Westinghouse and General Electric, the FTC noted, but did not prohibit directors of competing corporations from meeting on neutral ground. A director of General Electric and a director of Westinghouse might both serve as directors of the Chase National Bank, meeting on that board to hatch common strategies. Such indirect interlocking directorships, the FTC argued, were legal but posed a threat to competition.[92]

Arthur Page is mentioned several times in the report as an interlock between the Chase National Bank, AT&T, Continental Oil and Kennecott Copper. The FTC was particularly concerned about the Chase National's ties to the petroleum industry, noting that in addition to holding large blocks of oil company stocks in trust for the Rockefeller family, the Chase had on its board four men (Page was one of them) who were also directors of large oil companies.[93]

Soon after the FTC report was issued, an official in the Justice Dept. Antitrust Division published an article in the *Yale Law Journal* calling for a new statute and revision of the Clayton Act to prohibit persons from holding directorships in more than one corporation with assets over $60 million.[94]

In June 1951, Sen. Hubert H. Humphrey introduced a bill designed to implement the *Yale Law Journal* recommendations. Because directors of banks and common carriers were exempted from the provisions, the Humphrey bill, had it become law, would have permitted Page to remain a director of the Chase National, AT&T and one other company.[95]

Lawyer Thanhouser of Continental Oil called the FTC report a "product of bureaucratic boondoggling" by "socialist-minded FTC probers." Referring to the study as "the Spider Web Report," Continental Oil President McCollum, knowing the power of the oil lobby in Congress, correctly predicted the bill would die in committee.[96]

In helping to organize opposition to Senate Bill 1659, Page argued that the Humphrey bill was a direct attack on size and would deny large companies the service of directors with experience in big enterprise. The bill would prevent officers of big companies from serving on the boards of other big companies where they could get useful experience, he noted, and would result in big companies having boards made up largely of their own executives.[97]

Page felt it was an "Alice in Wonderland" idea to think directors of one company joined boards to meet directors of other companies to hatch conspiracies. If such conspiracies were to be hatched, he pointedly argued, the conspirators would break the law in secret, not at a board meeting.[98]

The organized opposition to the Humphrey bill was effective. The bill died in the Senate Judiciary Committee.[99]

Getting reinvolved in book publishing

PAGE FOUND SEVERAL opportunities during his consultancy years to become reinvolved in book publishing.

In 1946-1947, he helped arrange for publication of Henry Stimson's memoirs. Stimson had resigned as secretary of war on Sept. 21, 1945, and then collapsed at his Highhold estate. A month later, he suffered a massive coronary occlusion. At about this time, James Van Toor of Farrar and Rinehart asked Page to encourage a Stimson autobiography.[100] Stimson remained ill through the winter. By the spring of 1946, he regained his health, and Page began discussing three books with him, an autobiography, a biography and a volume of edited diaries and other papers.

Page discussed the proposed autobiography with Harvey Bundy, suggesting Hawthorne Daniel for the collaborator. Bundy independently talked to War Dept. historian Rudolph Winnacker, and they suggested to Stimson that McGeorge "Mac" Bundy, Harvey Bundy's third son, write the book. Mac Bundy, later a Harvard dean, advisor to Presidents Kennedy and Lyndon Johnson and Ford Foundation head, had been an admiral's aide during the war. On returning, he took a junior fellowship at Harvard. He had proved an able writer of articles for *The Atlantic*, was free to work on the project and was the son of a trusted Stimson aide. Cass Canfield, an editor at Harper & Brothers, assured Page that Bundy was the right man for the job. It surely didn't hurt that Mac (like his brother Bill and father Harvey) and Stimson had both been elected members of the prestigious Skull and Bones secret society at Yale. He moved into the little red cottage on Stimson's Highhold estate and began work.[101]

Before completing the book, Bundy collaborated with Stimson on writing a *Harper's* magazine article defending the Hiroshima and Nagasaki bombings. The article was suggested by James Conant of Harvard. Stimson is said to have had more last-minute qualms and doubts about publishing it than about any other article by him in his lifetime.

On Active Service in Peace and War, Stimson's autobiography written with the 28-year-old Bundy, was published in 1948. It quickly became a Cold War primer on internationalism for the establishment, teaching the doctrine of promptly meeting threats to democracy with military force. In addition to arranging publication of the book with Cass Canfield of Harper and Brothers, Page handled details for serialization in the *Ladies' Home Journal.*[102]

In November 1946, Page became a charter member of the editorial advisory board of the new Executive Book Club, organized by public relations pioneer Bronson Batchelor, along with Dr. Claude Robinson of the Opinion Research Corp. and John P. Syme of the Johns-Manville Corp.

Members of the editorial advisory board helped to select books on economics and management theory for offerings as club selections. Members of the board in addition to Page included Henry Hazlitt, financial editor of *Newsweek*; Fowler McCormick, chairman of the International Harvester Co.; Stanley Resor, president of the J. Walter Thompson advertising agency; Alfred P. Sloan, chairman of General Motors; and Dr. Henry Wriston of Brown University.[103]

Page approved republication of Professor Louis M. Hacker's classic *The Triumph of American Capitalism* because he felt the book would help young executives understand that America's economic system was the best servant for attaining the twin goals of freedom and opportunity for individuals. He approved publication of Henry Chamberlain's *European Cockpit*, noting that "A man can't be a good executive in this era if he does not think in world terms."[104] He recommended against Robert Wood Johnson's *Or Forfeit Freedom* as a club selection on the grounds that Johnson (of the Johnson & Johnson medical supply company) permeated the book with the same critical attitude that he had expressed when part of the Ordnance Dept. and chairman of the Smaller War Plants Corp. during the late years of World War II. "His

viewpoints are irritants to a good many in the business community," he said, "not so much because of what he said but
because of his 'holier than thou' attitude." Page advised
against selection of James Farley's *The Roosevelt Years* saying, "Farley tells the story of his connection with the government without mention of the public welfare, but only of par-
tisan and personal political rewards."[105]

Henry Stimson died in 1950. Page and McGeorge Bundy
were named trustees of his papers, and given the mission by
his widow of selecting an author to write a posthumous biography. They chose MIT historian Elting E. Morison, nephew
of noted Harvard historian Samuel Eliot Morison. His family
ties made him comfortable among the power elite. Page had
known him at least as early as 1945, when Morison was editing the correspondence of Theodore Roosevelt, and Page had
provided some of his own materials to him through Hermann
Hagedorn of the Roosevelt Memorial Assn. Both Bundy and
Morison were members of the Friday Night Supper Club, a
group of a dozen or so Cambridge intellectuals who got together on the first Friday of the month to gossip and discuss
matters of far-ranging mutual interest.[106]

Page was delighted with Morison's work. He wrote him in
1959, before the manuscript was published, to say, "Being a
Trustee to get a scholarly book written about a person you
care about is as hazardous as having a portrait painted. I
shall never do it again. I have done it twice, once with
Hendrick, writing the life of my father, and now with you,
writing the life of Henry L. Stimson. Each to me is an outstanding success. I'll take no more risks with a perfect score.[107]

Morison's biography, *Turmoil and Tradition: A Study of
the Life and Times of Henry L. Stimson,* was published by
Houghton Mifflin in 1960.[108]

Center for the Study of Liberty

PAGE PLAYED an important role in the late 1950s in arranging
funding by the Carnegie Corp. for an important publishing

project, the Center for the Study of Liberty in America. The Center was founded at Harvard in 1958 under the direction of historian Oscar Handlin. It performed its mission of encouraging publication of scholarly works on the history of freedom in America until academic year 1969-1970, when funding expired and the operation was absorbed by Harvard's Charles Warren Center for Studies in American History.[109]

During its life, the Center for the Study of Liberty arranged publication of more than 20 major works, including Bernard Bailyn's *Origins of American Politics* (Pulitzer Prize, 1968), Leonard W. Levy's *Origins of the Fifth Amendment* (Pulitzer Prize, 1969) and Richard L. Bushman's *From Puritan to Yankee: Character and Social Order in Connecticut, 1690-1765* (Bancroft Prize, 1968).[110]

Page had wanted for decades to get scholars to study and write about the role played by individual liberty in the shaping of American society. The story of the Center, which did that, began near the end of Page's life.

In 1957, he learned that Paul Buck of Harvard had a similar interest, and had been planning a project at Harvard to study the national history of freedom. Excited, Page discussed the project with John W. Gardner of the Carnegie Corp., who pursued the matter with Buck. Buck recommended that Oscar Handlin be named to head the project. Page agreed to find funding in addition to the $400,000 the Carnegie Corp. ultimately committed. The Carnegie Corp. made an initial grant of $200,000 in December 1957, and the Center for the Study of Liberty was activated in early 1958.[111]

In arranging funding for the Center, Page did much to accomplish his long-standing goal of encouraging the academic world to pay greater attention to "what the people did when they were free rather than what the government did in inspiring their activities."[112]

In June 1960, shortly before his death, Page joined the Woodrow Wilson Foundation Sponsors Committee overseeing publication of the Woodrow Wilson Papers by a committee headed by Dr. Arthur S. Link.[113] That was his final effort in publishing.

The Eisenhower Cabinet Report on Transportation

IN 1954, PAGE co-authored with Fairman Dick, a railroad financing specialist with the firm of Dick and Merle-Smith, a booklet entitled "A Plea for the Return of the Railroads to a Healthy Economy." The booklet, widely distributed to leading government officials, was heavy with data. It argued that American railroads had earned an average of only 3.62 per cent on assets from 1921 through 1947, and that the Interstate Commerce Commission (ICC) should allow the railroads a return of seven per cent if they were to remain solvent.[114]

In April 1954, Nelson Rockefeller, Milton Eisenhower and Arthur Flemming recommended to President Eisenhower that national transportation policy should be reexamined. In July 1954, Eisenhower created a Cabinet Committee on Transport Policy and Organization chaired by Secretary of Commerce Sinclair Weeks. The committee, which included several other cabinet members and high-ranking government officials, was ordered to report back to the President with recommendations for revitalizing transportation in America by Dec. 1, 1954.[115]

Secretary Weeks asked Page to organize a working group to prepare a report on domestic rail, truck and barge transport. Page accepted and formed a committee of himself, transportation law specialist George Roberts of Winthrop, Stimson, Putnam and Roberts, Columbia University Professor of Transportation Ernest W. Williams, General Foods Vice President Arthur C. Schier, Union Carbide Vice President Charles H. Beard, Fairman Dick and Charles L. Dearing of the Brookings Institution. Dearing was a special consultant on transportation matters to the Secretary of Commerce and had co-authored a 1949 book, *National Transportation Policy*, which called for modernization of federal regulation of railroads.[116] The group held no formal hearings, but invited written briefs from the railroad, trucking and inland waterway industries.

The group presented its recommendations to the Cabinet Committee in November 1954. The most explosive central recommendation of the report was a call for the government to free railroads from ICC rate regulation. The report also recommended that the railroads be allowed to engage in the trucking business, that the government eliminate special taxes of 10 per cent on rail passenger and three per cent on rail freight charges and that the government engage in basic research for the railroads in areas such as development of coal-fired gas turbine locomotives.[117]

Between completion of the working group report in November and early December, Page rewrote the report. The final result, Cabinet Paper 6, met some objections from the Bureau of the Budget and was ready for presentation to President Eisenhower on Dec. 8, 1954.[118]

A storm of controversy erupted after the report was made public. The trucking and barge industries and a number of newspapers charged that the report was a "sellout" to the railroads. The Justice Dept. raised serious objections to some of the recommendations and forced a redraft in which several proposals were watered down. Enabling legislation, introduced in the Senate by George Smathers, Warren Magnuson and John Bricker, and in the House by J. Percy Priest, died in committee in 1955.[119]

Why did Page, pragmatic and wise, make a frontal assault on the ICC that had little if any chance of success? E. Hornsby Wasson, an AT&T executive who knew Page well, provides a logical answer:

...After several months of intense study by himself and his colleagues, Arthur came up with a set of recommendations to be presented to the President and his Cabinet... Prior to presenting his findings, he asked a number of us to sit with him to go over his recommendations. I was one of the many present, and one of his recommendations was to abolish the Interstate Commerce Commission. I remember quite well taking strong issue with this on the premise that it was unrealistic and had no chance of being... passed by Congress. Arthur's reaction was immediate and decisive. He realized that such a bill had no chance of passage, but it would do several things. Mainly, it would shake up the ICC so that it would bear down in cleaning up its backlog. In addition, he said if... a bill was introduced, it would stand no chance of passage, but in subsequent sessions of Congress watered down bills would be introduced and one would eventually pass....[120]

Page's assessment was perceptive. In 1958, Sen. Smathers introduced a new, diluted version of the bill he had originally introduced in 1955. This bill passed, and was signed into law by President Eisenhower in August.

The bill enacted did not abolish ICC regulation of interstate transportation, but it prohibited the ICC from holding the rates of one carrier artificially high to protect another (the railroads complained their rates were being held high to keep them from competing with trucks) and removed the three per cent federal tax on rail freight charges. The legislation included provisions beneficial to the railroads not recommended in the original Page report.[121]

Heading the New York-New Jersey Rapid Transit Project

PAGE'S EXPERIENCE with the Presidential Advisory Committee on Transportation Policy and Organization led him to another project involving improvement of the mass transit system serving residents of New Jersey who worked in New York.

In September 1955, Page became project director at $30,000 per year of the Bi-State Metropolitan Rapid Transit Commission. His job was to organize a team of consultants to recommend an improved commuter transit system for metropolitan New York.

When he accepted the job, rail commuting between New York and New Jersey was deplorable. Some 150,000 commuters from New Jersey bedroom communities poured into New York each workday. The suburban railroads that carried the commuters were losing $13 million per year on the traffic. Because the commuter lines were losing money, they did little to improve service. Of the 1,300 or so passenger cars in service, only about 30 were modern, and only 150 were air-conditioned. Most of the dilapidated coaches had been made in the 1930s.[122]

The legislatures of New York and New Jersey in 1954 authorized a Bi-State Metropolitan Transit Commission to study the problem and recommend solutions. Almost $1 million was provided by the two states and the New York Port Authority for the study.[123]

Allen Hubbard of New York, a member of the Transit Commission, proposed that Page be hired as project director. Page began work on Oct. 1, 1955. He had a paid staff of four in addition to himself.[124] He retained seven consultants and consulting firms to conduct studies. Although he had estimated the project would take a year, several consultants were late in delivering their reports. The final report was ready in mid-May 1957.[125] It made four recommendations:

• Create a Bi-State Rapid Transit District to supervise an improved mass transit service between New York City and the surrounding area.

• Direct the new Bi-State District to improve suburban rail service by buying new cars, building new rail stations and other facilities and supplementing rail service with buses in areas where rail service was not conveniently available.

• Extend the New York City rapid transit system into some new areas of New Jersey, especially by construction of a new closed-loop mass transit system into New Jersey via two new tunnels under the Hudson River.

• Cover any deficits from operation of the new system with tax levies in New York and New Jersey, with New Jersey residents paying the lion's share.[126]

The estimated initial cost of implementing the recommendations was $400 million. It was further estimated that the system would have an annual operating deficit of $12 million, which would have to be covered by taxes.[127]

Although public reaction to the report was favorable, the proposals died of politics and inertia. One of the consulting firms had proposed a more elaborate $600 million improved system that a majority of the Bi-State commissioners came to favor over Page's recommended $400 million system.[128]

The Transit Commission finally recommended that as a first step the proposed Bi-State Transit District be created. New York passed enabling legislation, but New Jersey lawmakers balked. They feared New Jersey would end up paying for a system that mainly benefited New York.[129] With creation of the Bi-State District stalemated, the Metropolitan Rapid Transit Commission expired in March 1959.

Page's work led ultimately to watered-down improvements, subsidized by New York and New Jersey.[130]

Defending the Girl Scouts from the American Legion

PAGE CONTINUED in the consultancy years to devote much of his time to *pro bono* service.

In January 1947, he met with Mrs. Paul (Constance) Rittenhouse, national director of the Girl Scouts of America, to discuss Girl Scout public relations. He later met with Girl Scout Public Relations Director Anne New, providing advice on several matters.[131] In May 1947, he became a member of the Girl Scouts National Advisory Council.[132]

In 1954, he became embroiled in a controversy with elements of the American Legion who alleged that the *Girl Scout Handbook* contained anti-American material. The fracas began in August, when the American Legion in Illinois passed a resolution withdrawing its Girl Scout support. The Illinois Legion's Anti-Subversive Commission charged that the 1953 edition of the *Girl Scout Handbook* gave "the United Nations and one-world citizenship precedence over American citizenship" and that the Girl Scout magazine had recommended writings by "pro-communist" authors.

Months before the controversy arose, Girl Scout officials had begun revising the *Handbook* to meet objections that had been raised by more than a few Americans suspicious of this nation's support of the United Nations. Already set in type when the Legion brouhaha arose in Illinois, the changes included addition of the full text of the Bill of Rights of the Constitution, addition of three stanzas of the "Star-Spangled Banner," renaming of the "One World" merit badge to "My World," elimination of a quiz game about the United Nations and the striking out of sentences such as "You are preparing yourself for world citizenship."

Wire services, broadcast media and magazines such as *Newsweek* picked up the story. Most of the news coverage was pro-Girl Scout and anti-Legion. Herblock, for example, drew a devastating cartoon showing fat and aging Legionnaires hiding in bushes spying on young Girl Scouts gathered around a campfire, and the *Chicago Sun-Times* headed one of its editorials with a comment that had been shouted at the Illinois Legion convention, "How silly can you get?"

Girl Scout leadership feared the Illinois resolution would be debated at the national American Legion convention, sparking further controversy. They called on Page for his advice. He recommended making judicious contacts to head off any debate pro or con. The ploy worked. Debate on the Illinois resolution was stifled at the convention. Scout leaders were even successful in getting Georgia delegates (the Girl Scout movement was born in Savannah) to drop a resolution expressing confidence in the Girl Scouts.

After the fracas, Girl Scouts Executive Director Dorothy Stratton wrote to Page to thank him for his counsel during the period of the controversy. In her letter she said that at the height of the storm, "Mr. Dickey" (probably Charles O. Dickey of the House of Morgan) had asked her where she was going for advice. "When I told him we had gone to you," she wrote, "he said, 'you couldn't be in better hands.'"[133]

Page provided public relations counsel to the Girl Scouts until 1958, when he resigned from the Advisory Council.[134]

He continued to serve as a director of the Metropolitan Museum of Art to his death in 1960. From 1947 to 1951, he served on the museum board's executive committee. Perhaps his most important work for the Metropolitan during the period 1947-1960 was to help oversee museum public relations. When the museum formed a Dept. of Public Relations and Promotion in 1947, Page became an advisor to the new staff. From at least 1951 to his death, he was a member of the museum's Visiting Committee to the Dept. of Public Relations.[135]

Page continued to serve as a trustee of the Carnegie Corp. until November 1958, when he asked not to be reelected. His efforts to fund the Center for the Study of Liberty in America during these final days on the board have already been noted. He was also active as chairman of the Finance Committee to his 1958 resignation.[136]

During the 24 years he was a trustee of the Carnegie Corp., charities in which he was personally involved received at least $5.9 million in Carnegie Corp. grants. The biggest beneficiaries were Teachers College of Columbia University ($3.1 million) and the Council on Foreign Relations ($1.8 million).[137]

Other Carnegie trustees were involved in many of the same charities as Page. Nicholas Murray Butler was chairman of the Carnegie board during much of Page's trusteeship, and may have had more to do with the grants to Teachers College than Page. A majority of trustees had to approve any grant another trustee requested. Still and all, the charities with which Page was personally involved benefited rather well from Carnegie Corp. largesse while he was a trustee.

Page remained active with the Long Island Biological Assn. until 1958, when he resigned as vice president, director and executive committee member. During the period 1946-1958, perhaps because of his involvement with the atom bomb at Hiroshima, he took particular interest in LIBA's work on the effects of atomic radiation on heredity. He sporadically helped to raise local funds for the operation, and was a generous contributor to the laboratory's work himself.

Among his personal contributions to LIBA was a $300 gift in 1956 to be used specifically for research into the effects of the hallucinogenic agent lysurgic acid (LSD). The contribution is interesting in light of Central Intelligence Agency experimentation with LSD on unwitting American citizens at the time.

Page's children became involved in the work of the laboratory as he withdrew. Son-in-law Anderson Hewitt helped produce fund-raising brochures for the organization. Daughter-in-law Jane (Mrs. Walter H. Page II) served for a time as a LIBA vice president, and in the late 1950s, son Walter H. Page II became president of LIBA, later the Cold Spring Harbor Laboratories.[138]

Other causes to which Page devoted his time during 1947-1960 include:

• *The American Heart Assn.* Served on the National Campaign Planning Committee for the 1949 fund drive, and on the National Sponsors Committee for the 1950 effort. Among the people working with him were Winthrop Aldrich, Henry Luce, Arthur Hays Sulzberger of the *New York Times*, E. Tappan Stannard (until his death in an airplane crash) and Frank Stanton of CBS.[139]

• *New York Public Library.* Chaired the Utilities Committee for the library's 100th anniversary campaign to raise $10 million in 1948.[140]

• *American Arbitration Assn.* Served on the agency's 25th Anniversary Committee in 1952 at the request of General Electric Chairman Charles E. "Electric Charlie" Wilson.[141]

• *British Apprentice Club.* Continued to take an active interest, helping to raise funds at least through the mid-1950s. His son-in-law Anderson Hewitt, and to a lesser extent son Walter II and wife Mollie, helped him. The Pages' invitation list for a typical fund-raising dinner at the New York Yacht Club in the 1950s included the Arthur Hays Sulzbergers, the Henry R. Luces, the Laurance Rockefellers, the Charles Dollards, the Irving Oldses, the David Sarnoffs, the Cass Canfields and the Allen Dulleses.[142]

• *American Society of the French Legion of Honor.* Served as a sponsor for a dinner at the Waldorf-Astoria in 1954 commemorating the 150th anniversary of the establishment of the Legion of Honor. The list of guests attending is studded with names from the *Social Register.*[143]

• *American Fund for Westminster Abbey.* This fund-raising committee was formed to raise £100,000 (about $280,000 at the time) toward a goal of £1 million to make necessary repairs on Westminster Abbey. Probably because of the plaque honoring his father at the Abbey, Page took a special interest in the fund-raising effort.[144]

• *YWCA Centennial.* Beginning in 1952, a national committee began laying plans to celebrate the 100th anniversary of the Young Women's Christian Assn. with a $5 million fund-raising effort. Page declined an invitation from Mrs. Henry A. (Mary) Ingraham to join a committee to raise contributions from corporations, saying he could do a better job of getting money for the cause if he wasn't involved in the campaign machinery. With Mrs. Laurance Rockefeller heading the drive, it was difficult for Page to totally refuse involvement. Among other things, he revised the fund-raising appeal materials the YWCA planned to use to solicit gifts. He recommended that Kennecott Copper give $1,000 to $2,000. He probably had direct involvement in $10,000 gifts from AT&T and the Chase National.[145]

• *J. Pierpont Morgan Library.* Served for a number of years as a trustee of this research facility for scholars established in 1923 by J.P. Morgan Jr. in memory of his father.

• *Theodore Roosevelt Centennial Commission.* Served on the National Committee of Sponsors for a year-long observance of the 100th anniversary of Theodore Roosevelt's birth. Purpose of the celebration was to renew American appreciation of Roosevelt.[146]

• *Sportsmanship Brotherhood.* A Page neighbor, John Perry Bowditch, founded the first chapter of the Brotherhood, which was devoted to encouraging good sportsmanship in athletics. After Bowditch died, Page served on a committee to select a recipient for the first John Perry Bowditch Memorial Award. He was a guest speaker at the 1958 luncheon at which the award was presented to Avery Brundage, president of the International Olympic Committee.[147]

• *American Red Cross.* Participated in 1954 on a committee headed by American Red Cross Chairman E. Roland Harriman that studied how well the five Red Cross chapters in metropolitan New York were serving, and how strongly the public supported their work. Others involved in the small study group included S. Sloan Colt, Walter S. Gifford and Lindsley Kimball of the Rockefeller Foundation.[148]

• *Commission on National Voluntary Health Agencies.* Served on a small committee that charted a course of investigation for the Commission on National Voluntary Health Agencies from 1959 to 1960. The small study group and the commission it guided were prestigious. Among those involved in addition to Page were Lindsley Kimball, public relations counsel Tommy Ross, National Fund for Medical Education President S. Sloan Colt, Secretary of Health, Education and Welfare Arthur S. Flemming, former Secretary of Health, Education and Welfare Marion B. Folsom, Standard Oil of New Jersey Chairman Eugene Holman, *Time* publisher James A. Linen and Pan American World Airways President Juan Trippe.[149]

Overseer of Harvard and other educational service

PAGE DEVOTED a good deal of his time in the consultancy years in service to Harvard, Bennington, Teachers College of Columbia University and New York's Cooper Union.

He continued to serve as vice chairman of the board of Teachers College to July 1959, when he resigned.[150]

In March 1949, Hollis Caswell replaced William Russell as dean of Teachers College, serving until Stephen M. Corey succeeded him in September 1955. Caswell recalls Page as "the wisest man I have ever known." He called often at Page's Cedar St. office to discuss difficult problems. "He invariably helped," Caswell remembers. "He had the rare ability to cut away the superficial from a problem and reduce it to the central issue involved. He then could relate the resulting issue to ethical considerations and the basic purposes you were seeking to achieve. He never lectured, he never gave ready made answers, — he always analyzed in direct manner using your knowledge and experience to build upon."[151]

There was also a rigidity in Page that permitted him, once

he was convinced he was right, to stand by a decision. When Teachers College decided to close its experimental Horace Mann-Lincoln School, and the New York Supreme Court upheld its right to do so, Page defended the decision staunchly despite opposition to the closing among many of his close friends. He was not afraid to stand in opposition to public opinion when convinced his cause was just.[152]

From 1948 to 1951, Page chaired the Bennington Associates, a group formed to raise money for the school at the request of the new president of Bennington, Frederick Burkhardt. Page helped obtain a Carnegie Corp. grant to introduce a new history course at the college that traced themes through American history. He became interested in the course as a vehicle for getting students to study the history of freedom in America from colonization through modern times. Later, in the mid-1950s, Page was active on the New York Committee for Bennington's 25th Anniversary fund, an effort to raise $300,000 for the school. It did far better than had been expected, bringing in a total of about $1 million.[153]

In 1956, at the invitation of Irving Olds, he served on the Centennial Committee for Cooper Union, a unique tuition-free trade school in New York. The committee sought to raise $7 million for various improvements.[154]

Page's most extensive work for higher education in his consultancy years was for Harvard.

In the late 1940s, he served as a vice president of the Harvard Club of New York, and then as president of the club, although at one point he considered letting the presidency go to someone else because a few members complained about his attendance record at meetings while a vice president.[155]

In 1951, he ran a fourth time for a six-year term as a Harvard overseer. This time he was successful, receiving almost three times as many votes as he had in 1938, his last previous run for one of the prestigious posts.[156]

Under new President Nathan Pusey, imported from tiny Lawrence College (later University) in Wisconsin, perhaps because he had had the courage in that state to speak out against Sen. Joseph McCarthy, Harvard launched a massive

"Program for Harvard College." The Program was an effort to build new buildings, revise curricula, and above all, raise $100 million (later revised downward to $82.5 million) for the school. From the launching of the program to his death, Page played a major role in the fund-raising effort, the biggest campaign any American college had launched to that time.[157]

For his many accomplishments in life, and particularly for his work in service to higher education, Page was awarded two honorary degrees. Columbia University conferred the first, an honorary doctor of laws degree, in July 1954. The citation noted that for 25 years Page had served as a trustee of that school. Williams College of Williamstown, Mass., gave him another in 1959, noting his work as an overseer of Harvard and his efforts to encourage the teaching of American history.[158]

Helping other public relations professionals

MANY PUBLIC RELATIONS professionals, some well established, others young men on their way up, corresponded with Page or visited him at his office. Some sought his counsel. Some sought his friendship. Some hoped he would use his influence to get them jobs at firms such as Kennecott Copper.

Among the public relations professionals with whom Page was closest during his consultancy years were John W. Hill, Tommy Ross, Harold Brayman of the DuPont organization, Verne Burnett, who left General Foods in 1948 to form his own Verne Burnett Associates, public relations patriarch Pendleton Dudley of Dudley-Anderson-Yutzy, William Baldwin of Baldwin and Mermey and an exceptionally perceptive counselor for whom Page had especially high regard, Earl Newsom.

There was also a steady flow of young men through Page's office. He had a great interest in the young, and was always willing to take time from a busy schedule to talk to someone starting out in the public relations field.

Although Page had many contacts with public relations professionals, he remained relatively aloof from formal groups such as the Public Relations Society of America (PRSA) and its predecessors. To his death, Page abhorred the idea that people could be trained for public relations jobs by formal schooling, and resisted attempts to make a profession of public relations. He felt that an engineer or accountant with years of Bell System experience, someone who understood the company, would make a better employee in the AT&T Information Dept. than someone who had been trained as a journalist or mass communicator and who knew nothing about the company.

Family man to the end

ALTHOUGH THE CONSULTANCY years were busy for Page, he found adequate time to relax and enjoy life with Mollie, his children and grandchildren. He and Mollie frequently traveled to the Carolinas to shoot game birds. He fished in America and Canada. He played golf—not very well, but often. Only rarely did he sail on Long Island Sound during his last years.

He read prolifically in his final years. Now and then in the fall, he attended football games for relaxation, Above all, he enjoyed relaxing socially with old friends.

He dearly loved his grandchildren, who often visited County Line. He referred to them affectionately as "the destroyers," but he and Mollie liked to have them stay. In an undated letter scrawled to son John on the back of a Continental Oil pamphlet, he described a typical undertaking with the grandchildren:

> Yesterday was fair day at County Line. The fair was to raise money for the Eastwood School Library. The big room was full of tables with books for sale and hobbies for show. Stamp and coin collections, specimens of the twigs of all native trees, soap sculpture... The terrace had plants flowers and soft drinks for sale...

Every ten year old within ten miles was running over the house like a pack of beagles, while mothers, fathers, aunts and friends paid high prices to the youthful vendors. The twins as soft drink barkeeps were immense, although they drank more than a barkeep should...[159]

Beginning in 1947, Page devoted considerable leisure time to tracking down the history of bourbon distilling in America. He had an affection for bourbon whiskey, and wanted to know more about how it came into being. Although Walter Hines Page II held back most of his father's "bourbon file" from the papers given to the Wisconsin State Historical Society, sufficient references to the bourbon research are present to indicate he did a thorough job of scholarship.

There is something of the publisher in these last years of Page's life, represented by his involvement with the Stimson biography and autobiography and Executive Book Club. There is certainly a lot of the public relations pioneer in his work as a consultant and corporate executive. And we see something of the patriot in his work to establish the Center for the Study of Liberty in America. For his most important work as a patriot, however, we must look elsewhere.

Much of Page's time in the consultancy years was devoted to helping America fight the Cold War against the Soviet Union. These efforts by Page, which include his work in propagandizing for passage of the Marshall Plan and in helping to organize Radio Free Europe, are covered in the next chapter.

ENDNOTES

[1] Letter to author from American Telephone & Telegraph Co. Asst. Vice President J.V. Ryan, Oct. 10, 1975.
[2] Letter from Page to Chase National Bank head Winthrop Aldrich, April

18, 1946, Box 13, Arthur W. Page Papers.

[3] Information on Page's consulting fee from Chase National Bank is from letter to author from Chase Manhattan Bank Vice President Michael E. Carlson, Sept. 26, 1975. According to Carlson, Page's $25,000-per-year retainer was cut to $15,000 per year on Jan. 1, 1956; to $9,000 per year on Aug. 1, 1956, and to $5,000 per year on July 1, 1957.

[4] Raleigh, *op. cit.* p. 1.

[5] Letter from Page to Winthrop W. Aldrich, April 18, 1946, *op. cit.*, and Chase National Bank lease for Page's office suite, Aug. 28, 1946, Box 14, Arthur W. Page Papers.

[6] For a discussion of "the Perfumed Stockade," "the Establishment," "Wall Street," and "Madison Avenue," see Theodore H. White, *The Making of the President 1964* (New York: New American Library, 1965), pp. 81-88.

[7] Letter from Page to L.F. McCollum, July 11, 1952, Box 73, Arthur W. Page Papers.

[8] Letter from Page to Winthrop W. Aldrich, April 18, 1946, *op. cit.*

[9] Telephone interview with John W. Hill, *op. cit.*

[10] Letter to author from former Columbia University Teachers College President Hollis L. Caswell, July 16, 1971.

[11] Letter to Page from Chicago lawyer Laird Bell, March 14, 1947; letter to Page from Bell, April 1, 1947; letter from Page to J. Philip Weyerhaeuser Jr., May 12, 1947; letter to Page from Bell, June 2, 1947; letter from Page to Weyerhaeuser, June 20, 1947; and letter from Page to Arthur W. McCain, Chase National Bank board vice chairman, Feb. 16, 1950; Boxes 15 and 71, Arthur W. Page Papers. See also letter from Page to Weyerhaeuser, July 7, 1948, Box 18, in which Page discusses the importance of good employee relations to corporate success.

[12] See especially letter from Page to Col. Sosthenes Behn, May 6, 1948; letter from Page to Douglas Stewart, May 16, 1947; and letter from Stewart to Page, June 19, 1947; Box 15, Arthur W. Page Papers.

[13] Letter from Page to L.F. McCollum, March 20, 1951, Box 72, Arthur W. Page Papers.

[14] Letter from Page to Harvard historian Arthur M. Schlesinger Sr., Jan. 22, 1947, and Schlesinger's reply, Jan. 30, 1947, Arthur W. Page Papers.

[15] Arthur W. Page, "Notes on Public Relations Conference," speech at annual Bell System Public Relations Conference, June 27, 1947, Box 15, Arthur W. Page Papers.

[16] See especially letter from Page to Edward Pulling, Oct. 15, 1945, *op. cit.*, and letter from Page to Robert McDougal, Oct. 16, 1947, Box 16, Arthur W. Page Papers.

[17] Arthur W. Page, "What We Think about Held Orders," speech delivered *ca.* February 1946 to audience of Bell System employees, and Griswold, *op. cit.*, p. 14.

[18] See especially letter from Page to AT&T Secretary C.O. Bickelhaupt, Oct. 16, 1947; prospectus entitled "Certain Material Related to Employees' Stock Plans of the Bell System," July 11, 1947; letters to Page from investment counselor Arthur C. Flatto, June 22, 1951, and April 14 and Oct. 21, 1952; and letters to Page from AT&T stockholder Martha K. Mack, Jan. 13 and Feb. 6, 1956; Boxes 69, 15, 72 and 73, Arthur W. Page Papers. *Fortune* magazine perceptively covered AT&T's postwar efforts to finance its record construction program in a 1950 article entitled "Item: 12 Million New Telephones."

[19] Jack Barbash, *Unions and Telephones: The Story of the Communi-*

cations Workers of America (New York: Harper & Brothers, 1952), pp. 2-52

[20] *Ibid.*, pp. 55-59.

[21] *Ibid.*, pp. 63-70. The 1947 victory was temporary, not permanent, for American Telephone. In the early 1970s, AT&T management finally agreed to national bargaining with telephone worker unions.

[22] Letter from Page to Keith S. McHugh, Sept. 12, 1947, Box 16, Arthur W. Page Papers.

[23] Todd, *op. cit.*, p. 56, and letter from Page to Federal Communications Commission Secretary T.J. Slowie, Feb. 24, 1948, Arthur W. Page Papers.

[24] Letters to Page from Southern Bell Telephone Vice President Fred J. Turner, March 5, 1948, Box 70, Arthur W. Page Papers. In the Mississippi case, a chancery court judge enjoined the Mississippi Public Service Commission from denying a rate increase to Southern Bell on the grounds that denial would be equivalent to confiscation of the company. The Georgia Supreme Court ruled similarly against that state's Public Service Commission's denial of a rate increase Southern Bell had requested in Georgia. The two cases set important precedents for rate increase requests Bell System companies had filed in other states.

[25] Letter to Page from Southern Bell Telephone Secretary Peyton W. Greene, Oct. 24, 1949, and letter to Page from AT&T Secretary C.O. Bickelhaupt, Nov. 18, 1949, Box 71, Arthur W. Page Papers. See also Page's notecards.

[26] Certified statement of AT&T Secretary C.O. Bickelhaupt, *ca.* April 1950, Arthur W. Page Papers.

[27] Resolution of the board of directors of the American Telephone & Telegraph Co., Dec. 20, 1950, Box 72, Arthur W. Page Papers.

[28] Interview by author with Wisconsin Telephone Co. Public Relations Vice President John Paige, July 16, 1970. According to Paige, Arthur Page expressed his views of how Leroy Wilson had saved the Bell System to him at one of the Bell System public relations conferences.

[29] Letter from AT&T Director Samuel A. Welldon to AT&T Director Myron Taylor, July 3, 1951, Box 72, Arthur W. Page Papers.

[30] Letter to Page from C.O. Bickelhaupt, July 2, 1951, and letter from Page to Walter S. Gifford, July 6, 1951, Box 72, Arthur W. Page Papers.

[31] Letter from Page to Walter S. Gifford, July 6, 1951, *op. cit.*

[32] Arthur W. Page, pamphlet, "An Experiment in Business Letter Writing," published by the Pacific Telephone & Telegraph Co., San Francisco, 1952, pp. 7-8. The pamphlet was widely distributed throughout the Bell System

[33] Arthur W. Page, "The Political Situation," speech at Bell System Public Relations Conference, Jan. 12, 1951.

[34] Clipping of newspaper story concerning Ryerson's resignation from Northern Trust, sent to Page by Cleo Craig, Jan. 13, 1953, Box 74, Arthur W. Page Papers.

[35] Telegram from Page to W. Cameron Forbes, Jan. 26, 1955; undated itinerary for trip by Page and wife Mollie to Nassau, Miami and other points from Jan. 29 through Feb. 2, 1955; excerpt from American Telephone & Telegraph Co., Minutes of meeting of Board of Directors of Feb. 16, 1955; letter from Page to Cleo F. Craig, April 21, 1955; and letter from Forbes to Craig, May 7, 1955; all in Box 76, Arthur W. Page Papers. See also "AT&T Plans 72-Yr. Limit for Its Board Members," *New York World Telegram and Sun*, April 16, 1956.

[36] Todd, *op. cit.*, p. 58; and letter to Page from James F. Bell, March 23,

1957, with attachments, and Page's reply, March 25, 1957, Box 78, Arthur W. Page Papers.

[37] American Telephone & Telegraph Co., "Report of the Annual Meeting of Share Owners," Box 80, Arthur W. Page Papers. (Pamphlet.)

[38] *Ibid.* At the same 1959 annual meeting where stockholders approved the three for one stock split, President Frederick Kappel fended off a question from the floor about why AT&T was paying Arthur Page, a director of the firm, a $25,000-per-year consulting fee.

[39] See Drew Pearson's "Washington Merry-Go-Round" column datelined April 14, 1958, cited here from *New York Daily Mirror,* April 15, 1958.

[40] Letter from Chase National Board Vice Chairman Arthur W. McCain to Page and others, Feb. 14, 1950, *op. cit.*

[41] Page served on a number of Chase National Bank committees other than the two mentioned here. Letters regarding his service on these other committees are scattered in Boxes 72-76 of the Page Papers.

[42] Letter to Page from Chase National Bank Vice President Gus W. Campbell, Sept. 3, 1952, transmitting copy of "A Report to the New York City Staff of the Chase National Bank and the Chase Safe Deposit Co. on the Employee Opinion Survey Made by the President's Committee," and letter to Page from Chase National Bank Board Chairman John J. McCloy, June 9, 1953, transmitting copy of "The Chase Employees' Benefits Program," *ca.* May 1953, the latter in Box 74, Arthur W. Page Papers.

[43] Letter to Page from Chase National Bank Secretary Kenneth S. Bell, March 16, 1955, with attached "Statement of the Economic Benefits of the Merger of the Chase National Bank of the City of New York into President and Directors of the Bank of the Manhattan Co.," March 14, 1955, Box 76, Arthur W. Page Papers.

[44] See especially letter to Page from Chase Manhattan Bank Secretary Kenneth S. Bell, April 1, 1955, and letter to Page from Chase Manhattan Bank Secretary, Jan. 27, 1960, Boxes 76 and 80, Arthur W. Page Papers.

[45] Based on a March 1953 article in *Barron's* magazine by C.A. Clark Jr. entitled "Kennecott Copper Low-Cost Production Keeps Earnings Level High," pp. 22 and 25; John H. Davis, *The Guggenheims: An American Epic* (New York: William Morrow & Co., 1978), pp. 100-106; and memorandum to Page from Kennecott executive named Illanes, Jan. 21, 1952, the latter in Box 73, Arthur W. Page Papers.

[46] Memorandum to Page from Kennecott Vice President C.T. Ulrich, Dec. 10, 1946, Box 69, Arthur W. Page Papers.

[47] Letter to Page from Kennecott President C.R. Cox, April 29, 1953; letter from Page to Carroll Shanks of Prudential Insurance, Feb. 24, 1954; and letter to Page from Carl K. Lenz of Kennecott Copper, March 18, 1954; Boxes 74-75, Arthur W. Page Papers.

[48] For background on the election of González and the rise of the communist movement in Chile, particularly in the copper, nitrate and coal industries, see S. Cole Blasier, "Chile: A Communist Battleground," *Political Science Quarterly,* Vol. 65 (September 1950), pp. 353-75.

[49] Untitled diary of events experienced by Page, Stannard and Whelpley in Chile from Nov. 20 through Dec. 10, 1946, dated Jan. 2, 1947, Box 69, Arthur W. Page Papers. See also analysis of the effects of 1946 arbitration in Chile prepared for Kennecott by lawyer Henry S. Drinker, attached to letter to Page from Kennecott Secretary Arthur W. Cherouny, June 10, 1947, Box 69, Arthur W. Page Papers.

[50] Untitled manuscript dealing with Kennecott problems in Chile, Jan. 17, 1947, Box 69, Arthur W. Page Papers.

[51] See, for example, letters from Page to John J. McCloy, Jan. 5, 1948, and to Asst. Secretary of State Spruille Braden, May 28, 1947, Boxes 70 and 69 respectively, Arthur W. Page Papers.

[52] See especially letter to Page from Kennecott Copper President E. Tappan Stannard, Oct. 28, 1946, Box 69, Arthur W. Page Papers, and "American Holdings Abroad Now Vital, Clayton Declares," *New York Times*, Oct. 26, 1946.

[53] Untitled memorandum probably written by Page, Jan. 17, 1947, *op. cit.*, and letter from Page to Braden Copper executive F.E. Turton, Jan. 16, 1947, Box 69, Arthur W. Page Papers.

[54] See especially Blasier, *op. cit.*, and letter to Page from Braden Copper executive S.M. Arriola, May 10, 1949, Box 70, Arthur W. Page Papers.

[55] Letter to Page from Kennecott President C.R. Cox, with attachments, April 29, 1953, *op. cit.*; memorandum from Kennecott President E. Tappan Stannard to board of directors, Jan. 13, 1948; letter to Page from Kennecott Vice President and Treasurer C.T. Ulrich, March 19, 1949; memorandum from Stannard to board of directors, March 31, 1948; letter from New Jersey Zinc President Henry Hardenbergh to his board of directors, April 8, 1948; Boxes 70 and 74, Arthur W. Page Papers. Most of the letters mentioned have multiple attachments also used as sources.

[56] Letter to Page from Kennecott President E. Tappan Stannard, June 22, 1948, and letter from Page to Braden Copper executive S.M. Arriola, Oct. 26, 1949, Boxes 70-71, Arthur W. Page Papers.

[57] Letter from Page to Kennecott Director E.S. Guggenheim, Oct. 20, 1949, and Kennecott Copper Co., Minutes of Special Meeting of the Board of Directors, Dec. 20, 1949, Box 71, Arthur W. Page Papers. See also "Resigns Steel Post to Head Kennecott," *New York Times*, Dec. 22, 1949.

[58] See especially letters from Page to Kennecott President E. Tappan Stannard, May 23 and July 18, 1949; letter to Page from Stannard, May 3, 1949; letters from Page to Kennecott President Charles R. Cox, Feb. 21, 1950, and Feb. 26, 1951; letters to Page from Kennecott Asst. to the President Arthur S. Cherouny, March 20 and July 12, 1951 (with attachments); letters from Page to Cherouny, March 6 and 22, April 4, and July 16, 1951 (the March 22 letter is in memorandum format); memorandum, "A Public Relations Program for Kennecott Copper Corporation," prepared by Richard Strobridge of Cunningham and Walsh, 1949; Cunningham and Walsh proposal for a Kennecott product promotion campaign, *ca.* April 19, 1957; itinerary for visit of Page and C.R. Cox to Washington, March 29-30 (and possibly 31), 1950; letter to Page from Hewitt, Ogilvy, Benson and Mather executive Larry Nixon, March 29, 1951; memorandum probably prepared by Page outlining duties for proposed Braden Copper public relations staff in Chile, March, 1951; and letter from Page to Kennecott Asst. to the President John D. East, Feb. 8, 1952; Boxes 70-73 and 78, Arthur W. Page Papers.

[59] Letter from Page to Central Intelligence Agency Directorate of Plans Chief Allen W. Dulles, Aug. 18, 1952, Box 73, Arthur W. Page Papers, and Leonard Mosley, *Dulles: A Biography of Eleanor, Allen, and John Foster Dulles and Their Family Network* (New York: The Dial Press/James Wade, 1978), pp. 268-76.

[60] Letter to Page from Mrs. Learned (Frances A.) Hand, May 1, 1951, Box 72, Arthur W. Page Papers.

[61] Letter from Page to Mrs. Learned Hand, May 3, 1951, Box 72, Arthur W. Page Papers.

[62] Letter from Page to C.R. Cox, Aug. 22, 1951, Box 72, Arthur W. Page Papers.

[63] Letter from Page to C.R. Cox, Sept. 18, 1952, Box 74, Arthur W. Page Papers.

[64] Letter to Page from Kennecott executive Arthur S. Cherouny, Oct. 6, 1953, transmitting Minutes of First Meeting of Kennecott Contributions Committee, Box 74, Arthur W. Page Papers.

[65] See especially letter to Page from Kennecott Secretary Robert C. Sullivan, Oct. 1, 1953, Box 75, Arthur W. Page Papers. A copy of the A.P. Smith v. Ruth F. Barlow et al. case is in the Page Papers.

[66] Letter to Page from C.R. Cox, Dec. 10, 1956; memorandum by Page responding to Mormon Church contribution request, Dec. 18, 1956; letter from Cox to Page, Robert G. Stone, and Albert A. Thiele, Feb. 4, 1957; and letter to Page from Arthur S. Cherouny, April 1, 1957, with attachments; Boxes 77-78, Arthur W. Page Papers.

[67] See especially Minutes of Meeting of Kennecott Contributions Committee, March 7, 1957, attached to letter from Page to Arthur S. Cherouny, March 12, 1957; note to Page from Cherouny, July 2, 1959; and letter from Page to C.R. Cox, July 7, 1959; Boxes 78, 80 and 81, Arthur W. Page Papers.

[68] Letter from Page to Kennecott director Alfred P. Sloan Jr., May 9, 1957, and Sloan's reply, May 13, 1957, Box 78, Arthur W. Page Papers.

[69] See especially letter from C.R. Cox to all Kennecott directors, June 25, 1957, tucked with other documents regarding mandatory retirement for Kennecott directors in booklet entitled "Survey of Corporate Boards and Directors 1955"; letter from Page to Kennecott directors, Sept. 9, 1957; copy of resolution passed by Kennecott board and received by Page Oct. 11, 1957; and letter from H.O. Havemeyer to C.R. Cox, Nov. 5, 1957; Boxes 77-78, Arthur W. Page Papers.

[70] Letter from Page to C.R. Cox, May 11, 1959, Box 80, Arthur W. Page Papers. Page's resignation was effective May 15, 1959.

[71] Telephone conversation between author and Walter H. Page II, July 11, 1975. Walter H. Page II married into the Morgan family.

[72] In 1947, Continental Oil ranked 14th among America's major oil companies in terms of gross operating income (Standard of New Jersey, later Exxon, ranked first, with gross income of more than $2.3 billion, compared to Continental's $229 million), and 11th in terms of net income. See report binder, "Oil Companies Financial and Operating Comparisons for A.W. Page," attached to letter to Page from L.F. McCollum, May 14, 1948, Box 70, Arthur W. Page Papers.

[73] McCollum signed a ten-year contract to serve as Continental's chief executive on Nov. 19, 1947. The terms of the contract included a $125,000-per-year salary, an option on 50,000 shares of Continental stock and other benefits.

[74] Up to 1954, the Conoco Salary Committee reviewed pay increases for executives making $15,000 per year or more; from 1954 forward it reviewed salaries of $20,000 or more. See especially letter to Page from Conoco Secretary R. Warner Jr., July 6, 1950; Minutes of Meeting of Continental Oil Board of Directors, April 21, 1954, attached to letter to Page from Conoco Secretary P.J. Dominic, May 13, 1954; and letter to Page from Dominic, May 16, 1957, Boxes 72, 75 and 78, Arthur W. Page Papers. Background on the Conoco board fight over increasing the stock dividend in 1948 can be found in letter from Page to L.F. McCollum, Nov. 12, 1948; letter from James J. Cosgrove to Page, Feb. 14, 1949; and letter to Page from McCollum, June 21, 1949; Boxes 70-71.

[75] Letter from Page to L.F. McCollum, March 20, 1951, op. cit.

[76] Arthur W. Page, untitled speech to Continental Oil board of directors

at Fort Clark, Texas, April 9, 1951, Box 72, Arthur W. Page Papers. It appears that Page gave the same speech to a gathering of Continental Oil employees a day earlier. It ranks in magnitude with Page's "Industrial Statesmanship" speech.

[77] Letter to Page from L.F. McCollum, Feb. 3, 1950; letter from Page to McCollum, Feb. 9, 1950; letter to Page from Continental Oil Asst. to the President A.W. Tarkington, *ca.* February 1950; and internal Continental Oil Memorandum entitled "Proposed Program 75th Anniversary Celebration Continental Oil Co. as of July 21, 1950"; Boxes 71-72, Arthur W. Page Papers.

[78] Letter from Page to public relations executive Verne Burnett, Aug. 29, 1950, Box 72, Arthur W. Page Papers.

[79] *Ibid.*, and letter from Page to L.F. McCollum, Aug. 29, 1950, Box 72, Arthur W. Page Papers.

[80] Letter from Page to Verne Burnett, Aug. 29, 1950, *op. cit.*

[81] Letters from Page to Verne Burnett, July 31 and Aug. 8, 1950, and letter to Page from Burnett, Aug. 7, 1951, Box 72, Arthur W. Page Papers.

[82] Letter from Page to Verne Burnett, July 31, 1950, *op. cit.* The final anniversary celebration produced tangible benefits for Conoco.

[83] See especially letter from Page to L.F. McCollum, April 23, 1951; letter from Page to members of the Conoco board of directors Incentives Committee, June 26, 1951; letter from Page to McCollum, Nov. 2, 1951; and letter from Page to Standard Oil of California (Chevron) executive H.L. Severance, June 24, 1952; Boxes 72-73, Arthur W. Page Papers.

[84] See especially letter from Page to L.F. McCollum, Sept. 24, 1951; letter from Page to Westinghouse Electric executive E.V. Huggins, Oct. 16, 1951; and letter to Page from Lloyd F. Thanhouser, Oct. 11, 1951; Box 72, Arthur W. Page Papers.

[85] See especially memorandum from L.F. McCollum to all Conoco directors, April 10, 1952, with attachments; letter to Page from James J. Cosgrove, April 6, 1953; and letter from Page to McCollum, Aug. 28, 1953; Boxes 73-74, Arthur W. Page Papers.

[86] Letter to Page from Conoco Secretary P.J. Dominic, May 10, 1956, with attached memorandum by Lloyd F. Thanhouser, Box 77, Arthur W. Page Papers.

[87] Page discusses mandatory retirement age for Conoco directors in letter to L.F. McCollum, Dec. 31, 1956, Box 77, Arthur W. Page Papers. The letter he wrote to McCollum in January 1957, resigning from the Conoco board, is not in the Page Papers but Page refers to it in letter to McCollum, Jan. 15, 1958, Box 79.

[88] Letter from Page to L.F. McCollum, Jan. 15, 1958, *op. cit.*; letter from Page to P.J. Dominic, Nov. 20, 1958; letter from Page to Eugene J. McNeely, Dec. 18, 1958; and letter from Page to McCollum, Dec. 31, 1958; last three items in Box 80, Arthur W. Page Papers.

[89] Letter to Page from P.C. Lauinger, Nov. 20, 1958, Box 80, Arthur W. Page Papers.

[90] Letter to author from Prudential Insurance Co. News Service Manager James A. Longo, July 18, 1975.

[91] Telephone conversation with Westinghouse Electric Manager of Stockholder Relations Erias Hyman, July 17, 1975.

[92] Page was alerted to the Federal Trade Commission report by an item headlined "1,000 Biggest Firms Closely Interlocked" in AT&T's *Daily Digest.* The item was summarized from the March 12, 1951, issue of *Daily Compass.* See also Federal Trade Commission news release, March 7, 1951, at-

tached to letter from FTC official John T. Crittenden to Page's secretary, Marguerite Phelps, March 14, 1951, Box 72, Arthur W. Page Papers.

[93] See especially letter from Lloyd F. Thanhouser to L.F. McCollum, attached to letter to Page from McCollum's secretary, Olga H. Swanson, Aug. 21, 1951, Box 72, Arthur W. Page Papers. The Thanhouser letter excerpts the specific references made to Arthur Page in the FTC report.

[94] Victor H. Kramer, "Interlocking Directorships and the Clayton Act after 35 Years," *Yale Law Journal*, June 1951.

[95] See especially letter from Page to L.F. McCollum, July 19, 1951, Box 72, Arthur W. Page Papers.

[96] See especially letter from Lloyd F. Thanhouser to L.F. McCollum attached to letter to Page from Olga H. Swanson, Aug. 21, 1951, *op. cit.*, and letter to Page from McCollum, July 26, 1951, Box 72, Arthur W. Page Papers.

[97] Letter from Page to L.F. McCollum, July 19, 1951, *op. cit.*

[98] Arthur W. Page, untitled position paper on Senate Bill 1659 sponsored by Sen. Hubert H. Humphrey, sent by Page July 26, 1951, to E.V. Huggins of Westinghouse Electric, James Cosgrove of Continental Oil, Cleo Craig of AT&T and George Whitney of J.P. Morgan and Co., Box 72, Arthur W. Page Papers.

[99] Letter to author from Sen. Hubert H. Humphrey, Aug. 4, 1975.

[100] Letter to Page from James Van Toor, Oct. 16, 1945, Box 12, Arthur W. Page Papers.

[101] Kai Bird, *The Color of Truth* (New York: Simon & Schuster, 1998), pp. 88-90, and sheaf of memoranda in Page Papers, top manuscript dated May 1, 1946; memorandum written by Page outlining collaboration agreement between Henry L. Stimson and McGeorge Bundy, May 9, 1946; and letter from Page to Hawthorne Daniel, May 21, 1946; Box 13, Arthur W. Page Papers.

[102] Letter from Page to Henry L. Stimson, June 12, 1946; letters from Page to Harvey Bundy, July 9 and 12, 1946; letter from Page to Stimson, Feb. 13, 1947; letter from McGeorge Bundy to Page, April 14, 1947; letter to Page from *Collier's* magazine Editor W. Davenport, April 16, 1947; letter to Page from Harper and Brothers Board Chairman Cass Canfield, July 17, 1946; letter from Page to *New York Times* Managing Editor Edwin L. James, July 19, 1947, and James's reply, July 20, 1947; letter to Page from *Ladies' Home Journal* Editor Hugh McNair Kahler, Sept. 12, 1947; letter from Page to Stimson, Nov. 6, 1947; letter to Page from Canfield, Nov. 11, 1947, and Page's reply, Nov. 12, 1947; and letter from Page to *Life* magazine Editor Daniel Longwell, Nov. 25, 1947; Boxes 13-16, Arthur W. Page Papers.

[103] Bronson Batchelor invited Page to join the editorial advisory board on Oct. 29, 1946. Page didn't exactly accept—he wrote to Batchelor on Oct. 31 to say he'd be happy to discuss the matter when he returned from Chile if Batchelor hadn't filled the board by that time. Batchelor took the Page letter as an acceptance, and in late November, while Page was still in Chile, sent a letter to Page's New York office welcoming Page to the board. See letters from Bronson Batchelor to Page, Oct. 29 and Nov. 27, 1946, and Feb. 19 and July 31, 1947, and letter from Page to Batchelor, Oct. 31, 1946, Boxes 14-16 Arthur W. Page Papers.

[104] Letter from Page to Bronson Batchelor, July 23, 1947, Box 15, Arthur W. Page Papers.

[105] Letters from Page to Bronson Batchelor, Nov. 3, 1947, and Jan. 28, 1948, Box 16, Arthur W. Page Papers.

[106] Bird, *Color of Truth, op. cit.*, pp. 147-48, and letter from Page to

Hermann Hagedorn, Dec. 3, 1945, Box 13, Arthur W. Page Papers.

[107] Letter from Page to Elting Morison, Oct. 1, 1959, Box 60, Arthur W. Page Papers.

[108] Morison, *Turmoil and Tradition, op. cit.*

[109] Charles Warren Center for Studies in American History of Harvard University, *Annual Report* (1969-1970), p. 14. The report lists all works published by the Center for the Study of Liberty in America up to its absorption into the Charles Warren Center.

[110] *Ibid.*, p. 30.

[111] Carnegie Corp. records of interviews between John Gardner and Page, June 27, 1957, and between Gardner and Harvard Librarian Paul Buck, Sept. 12 and Dec. 12, 1957, copies in possession of author; and letter to author from Florence Anderson, Aug. 5, 1975, *op. cit.*

[112] See letters from Page to public relations executive Earl Newsom, Aug. 21, 1958, and Standard Oil of New Jersey Chairman Eugene Holman, Aug. 22, 1958, Box 57, Arthur W. Page Papers.

[113] Letter to Page from Woodrow Wilson Foundation President August Heckscher, June 23, 1960, and Page's reply, June 27, 1960, Box 81, Arthur W. Page Papers.

[114] Arthur W. Page and Fairman Dick, "A Plea for the Return of the Railroads to a Healthy Economy," booklet bound in plastic cover, Box 64, Arthur W. Page Papers.

[115] Raleigh, *op. cit.*, pp. 200-03.

[116] Letter from Page to Fairman Dick, Aug. 4, 1954, Box 36, Arthur W. Page Papers, and Raleigh, *op. cit.*, pp. 204-05.

[117] Report of the Working Group, Cabinet Committee on Transport Policy and Organization, November 1954, Box 37, Arthur W. Page Papers.

[118] Cabinet Paper 6, Eisenhower Administration, entitled "Report of the Cabinet Committee on Transportation Policy and Organization," Dec. 8, 1954, Box 39, Arthur W. Page Papers. See also Raleigh, *op. cit.*, pp. 212-14.

[119] Raleigh., *op. cit.*, pp. 209, 215-20, 223-27.

[120] Letter to author from E. Hornsby Wasson, July 1, 1971.

[121] For a full discussion of the provisions of the Smathers bill of 1958, see Raleigh, *op. cit.*, pp. 229-32.

[122] *Ibid.*, pp. 237-39.

[123] *Ibid.*, pp. 241-44.

[124] *Ibid.*, pp. 244-48.

[125] *Ibid.*, pp. 249-59.

[126] Arthur W. Page, "Report of the Project Director to the Metropolitan Rapid Transit Commission," May 1957, Box 52, Arthur W. Page Papers.

[127] *Ibid.*, and Raleigh, *op. cit.*, p. 259.

[128] Raleigh, *op. cit.*, pp. 260-64.

[129] *Ibid.*, pp. 264-66.

[130] Raleigh, *op. cit.*, pp. 268-70.

[131] Letters from Page to Mrs. Paul Rittenhouse, Jan. 15 and 30, 1947, Box 14, Arthur W. Page Papers. Page recommended several public relations consulting agencies.

[132] Letter to Page from Girl Scouts of America National Advisory Council Chairwoman Mrs. Frederick H. Brooke, May 5, 1947 and Page's reply, May 20, 1947, Box 69, Arthur W. Page Papers.

[133] Discussion of incident between Girl Scouts and American Legion is based on letter to Page from Miss Dorothy C. Stratton, Aug. 27, 1954, with attachments, Box 75, Arthur W. Page Papers. The attachments to Miss

Stratton's letter include: daily log of major developments in the incident prepared by Girl Scout headquarters covering the period Aug. 6-15, 1954; letter from Girl Scouts President Mrs. Roy F. Layton to Girl Scout council presidents, executive directors, national board and national committee members, Aug. 9, 1954; "Facts about the Girl Scout Handbook," Aug. 16, 1954; Girl Scout News Notes, Aug. 18, 1954; "Revisions in the Fifth Impression of the 1953 Edition of the Girl Scout Handbook"; Girl Scout news release, Aug. 9, 1954; "Daily Log of Major Developments in Handbook Controversy, Aug. 15-21"; and "Girl Scouts and Their Proficiency Badges," mimeographed letter dated Aug. 23, 1954.

[134] Letter from Page to Girl Scouts National Advisory Committee Chairwoman Mrs. Roy F. Layton, March 12, 1958, Box 79, Arthur W. Page Papers.

[135] Letter to author from Frances G. Oakley, July 29, 1975, *op. cit.* See also letters to Page from Metropolitan Museum official Dudley T. Easby Jr., June 2, 1947, and from Metropolitan Museum Board President Roland Redmond, July 25, 1947, Box 15, Arthur W. Page Papers.

[136] Letter to author from Florence Anderson, Aug. 5, 1975, *op. cit.*

[137] Charities with which Page was directly connected and the amounts of grants they received from the Carnegie Corp. between 1931 and 1958 include: Council on Foreign Relations, $1,815,624.10; Charity Organization Society and successor Community Service Society, $144,185; Farmers Federation Educational and Development Fund, $235,000; Teachers College of Columbia University, $3,097,600; Long Island Biological Assn., $81,667; Center for the Study of Liberty in America, $400,000; Metropolitan Museum of Art, $147,935; and Anna T. Jeanes Foundation, $13,500. According to Carnegie Corp. records, no grants were made during Page's trusteeship to Radio Free Europe or to the Foreign Service Educational Foundation. Grant amounts above are from letter to author from Florence Anderson, Aug. 5, 1975, *op. cit.*

[138] See especially letter from Page to Dr. Milislav Demerec, Nov. 30, 1949, and letter from Page to Long Island Biological Assn. President Amyas Ames, March 3, 1958, Box 79, Arthur W. Page Papers.

[139] Letter to Page from Andrew W. Robertson, Sept. 1, 1948, and Page's reply, Sept. 7, 1948; letter to Page from American Heart Assn. Asst. Director David S. Robertson, Oct. 1, 1948; letter to Page from Andrew W. Robertson, Sept. 27, 1949, and Page's reply, Oct. 3, 1949; and letter to Page from American Heart Assn. Chairman Harold E. Stassen, Nov. 11, 1949; Boxes 70-71, Arthur W. Page Papers.

[140] Letter from Page to Thomas Dunworth Jr. of New York Public Library Anniversary Committee, Dec. 10, 1948, Box 70, Arthur W. Page Papers.

[141] Letter to Page from Charles E. Wilson, Dec. 7, 1951, and Page's reply, Dec. 14, 1951, Box 72, Arthur W. Page Papers.

[142] A letter to Page from M.J.N. Eland of the Booth American Shipping Corp., May 9, 1955, Box 76, Arthur W Page Papers, indicates that Page was actively involved in British Apprentice Club financing at least as late as 1955. The invitation list mentioned is from a dinner probably held in the early 1950s; the undated list is in the Page Papers.

[143] Letter to Page from American Society of the French Legion of Honor President George A. Sloan, June 23, 1954, and letter from Page to Society Secretary M.A. Downing, Nov. 5, 1954, Box 75, Arthur W. Page Papers.

[144] Letter to Page from American Fund for Westminster Abbey Co-Chairmen William V. Griffin, Morris L. Ernst, and Langdon P. Marvin, Feb. 23, 1951; letter from Page to Griffin, Feb. 25, 1954; and letter to Page from

Ernst, March 3, 1954; Box 75, Arthur W. Page Papers.

[145] Letter to Page from YWCA Centennial Corp. Gifts Committee Co-chairwoman Mrs. Henry A. Ingraham, Dec. 10, 1952; letter from Page to Chemical Bank and Trust Chairman Baxter N. Jackson, Feb. 24, 1953; letter to Page from YWCA Centennial General Chairwoman Mrs. Laurance Rockefeller, Jan. 26, 1954; letter from Page to Kennecott Copper President Charles R. Cox, July 1, 1954; and letter to Page from Mrs. Ingraham, Sept. 30, 1954; Boxes 74-75, Arthur W. Page Papers.

[146] Letter to Page from Theodore Roosevelt Centennial Commission Director Hermann Hagedorn, Oct. 3, 1957, and Page's reply, Oct. 24, 1957, Box 78, Arthur W. Page Papers.

[147] Letter to Page from Sportsmanship Brotherhood Executive Director Daniel Chase, March 19, 1957; letter to Page from Chase, May 9, 1957; letter to Page and others from Chase, Dec. 1, 1957; undated Sportsmanship Brotherhood news release on awards luncheon planned for Jan. 23, 1958; and text of speech by Arthur W. Page at Sportsmanship Brotherhood luncheon, Jan. 23, 1958; Boxes 78-79, Arthur W. Page Papers.

[148] Letter to Page from S. Sloan Colt of 16 Wall Street (Bankers Trust Co.), Sept. 20, 1957; letter to Page from Rockefeller Foundation Executive Vice President Lindsley F. Kimball, Oct. 28, 1957; letter to Page from E. Roland Harriman, May 8, 1958; Boxes 78-79, Arthur W. Page Papers.

[149] Letter to Page from Lindsley F. Kimball, Oct. 30, 1959; Page's reply, Nov. 4, 1959; letter to Page from Rockefeller Foundation consultant Dr. Robert H. Hamlin, Dec. 10, 1959; and letters to Page from Kimball, March 11 and May 4, 1960; Box 81, Arthur W. Page Papers.

[150] Telephone conversation between author and Judy Suratt, *op. cit.*

[151] Letter to author from Dr. Hollis Caswell, July 16, 1971, *op. cit.*

[152] *Ibid.*, and decision of New York State Supreme Court Justice Botein in Teachers College, Plaintiff, *v.* Nathaniel L. Goldstein, Attorney-General of the State of New York, and General Education Board, Defendants, March 20, 1947.

[153] Letter to Page from Walter W. Stewart of the Institute for Advanced Study at Princeton, April 20, 1948; letter to Page from Bennington College Public Relations Director John Friend Noble, May 27, 1948; letter to Page from Frederick Burkhardt, May 20, 1948, Page's reply, May 24, 1948, and Burkhardt's reply, May 28, 1948; mimeographed newsletter from Burkhardt to all Bennington Associates, Nov 2, 1949; letter from Page to Burkhardt, March 23, 1950; mimeographed newsletter from Burkhardt to all Bennington Associates, June 22, 1950; letter to Page from Mrs. Richard S. Emmet, January 1955; letter to Page from Mrs. Marjory B. Hyde, Nov. 4, 1955; letter to Page from Mrs. George S. Franklin, March 13, 1956; and letter to Page from Oscar M. Ruebenhausen of Debevoise, Plimpton and McLean, Nov. 16, 1956; Boxes 70-71 and 76-77, Arthur W. Page Papers.

[154] Letter to Page from Irving S. Olds, July 25, 1956, and Page's reply, Aug. 28, 1956, Box 77, Arthur W. Page Papers.

[155] Letter from Page to Harvard Club President George Whitney, Nov. 19, 1947, and Raleigh, *op. cit.*, p. 49.

[156] Letter to author from Robert Shenton, *op. cit.* Page received 8,313 votes and ran third in the field in 1951, compared to 2,927 votes and a seventh place in 1938.

[157] Materials on Page's fund-raising for Harvard in the late 1950s are scattered in the Page Papers. See also Raleigh, *op. cit.*, pp. 4 and 60.

[158] Citation for honorary degree, Columbia University, July 1, 1954, Box

75, Arthur W. Page Papers, and Raleigh, *op. cit.*, p. 57.

[159] Undated letter to John H. Page written in hand of Arthur Page on back of a Continental Oil pamphlet dated May 1, 1952, Box 73, Arthur W. Page Papers.

CHAPTER NINE

Cold Warrior, 1946-1960

THE ANTECEDENTS of the Cold War can be traced to World War II. In the rapid Russian thrust through Eastern Europe to Germany, in Stalin's desire to set up a buffer in Central Europe, in the agreements unreached at Yalta and Potsdam, in the ambition of American internationalists to see their nation assume world leadership and in Russia's last-minute entry into the war in Asia, the stage for the Cold War was set.[1]

By the time of the ambiguous agreements of Yalta, the Soviets had already occupied Poland and installed a communist government. Stalin promised to hold free elections after the war. By V-E Day, Roosevelt and Churchill were already complaining he was not keeping his word. Then Roosevelt died, and Harry Truman had to face his failure at Potsdam to get firm agreements from Stalin on the future of Germany, Poland and the rest of Central Europe.

Walter LaFeber dates the start of the Cold War to early 1946. Josef Stalin, he contends, uttered the communist world's "declaration of war" in an election speech on Feb. 9. Winston Churchill, in his "Iron Curtain" speech in Missouri on March 5, fired the return volley for the West.[2]

Some argue the credit should go to President Truman, who on March 12, 1947, announced the Truman Doctrine to a joint session of Congress. He asked for $400 million in aid to head off communist threats in Greece and Turkey, and promised to help other nations facing communist insurrections.

Paul Nitze deserves some credit for drafting NSC-68, the blueprint for the Cold War. "Doing in the enemy is the right thing to do," Nitze held. "The communists (are) barbarians."

Well before the end of World War II, Arthur Page recognized that the postwar peace would be characterized by friction between the West and Soviet Union. He had lobbied among his influential friends, particularly in the State Dept., for a public relations effort to win support of American citizens and the people of uncommitted nations in the coming ideological struggle. The future, he felt, depended on the elite shaping the opinion of the masses.

In the fall of 1947, he was given a chance to build the sort of information machinery he thought the State Dept. needed, but he declined.

George C. Marshall, serving as secretary of state at the time, had been America's top soldier in World War II. In that capacity, he developed a respect for Page, a frequent visitor to the Pentagon. In October 1947, Marshall and his able deputy, Robert Lovett (Henry Stimson was fond of calling Lovett and John McCloy his "imps of Satan"), invited Page to become assistant secretary of state for public relations. Page considered the offer, but in a letter to Lovett explained that acceptance would force him to sever all the connections he had made to establish his consulting office. It would be difficult to renew the arrangements a few years later, after he had finished the State Dept. job.[3] So for the second time (the first had been in 1929), he turned down an assistant secretaryship in the State Dept.

Although Page refused the State post, he played important roles in the Cold War on the Stimson Committee for the Marshall Plan, as one of the founders of Radio Free Europe and as a consultant to the National Security Council.

The Stimson Committee for the Marshall Plan

MORE THAN A YEAR and a half before Page began taking part in the work of the Stimson Committee for the Marshall Plan, he was involved in behind-the-scenes maneuvering with Winthrop Aldrich, Charles J. Symington and others to privately finance postwar recovery in Europe.

In January 1946, he took part in a round of meetings with Aldrich, Secretary of Commerce Henry A. Wallace, Symington (a consultant to Wallace and uncle of Stuart Symington), Arthur Paul of the Commerce Dept.'s Office of International Trade and William McChesney Martin of the Export-Import Bank. At the meetings, the possibility of American banks forming a private capital pool to make economy-rebuilding loans to foreign nations was discussed. Page, who believed America should use its economic power to build a *pax Americana*, felt that both government and private capital would be needed. Fresh from his brush with communist unions in Chile, he advocated, as did Aldrich, denial of government loans to nations that did not welcome American trade and investment.[4]

In June 1946, President Truman named Aldrich to head a Committee for Foreign Trade, nicknamed the Committee of Twelve because it had a dozen prominent members. The committee, which reported to the National Advisory Council, explored ways in which private lenders could assume some of the responsibility for making foreign loans from the American government. Neither Page nor Symington were members of the Committee of Twelve, but both played roles in helping Aldrich map the issues and made recommendations to him.[5]

Marshall Plan planning began when President Truman recognized after the disastrous 1946-47 winter in Europe that the United States needed to do something to jump-start the war-blasted economy or watch Europe go communist. George Kennan wrote "Certain Aspects of the European Recovery Problem," delivered to Secretary Marshall on May 25. Undersecretary of State Dean Acheson formulated details of the program, while Republican Sen. Arthur Vandenberg played a key role in getting legislation passed. Among the dozen or so others who claimed a hand in the plan, Charles "Chip" Bohlen and William L. Clayton stand out. As for what to call it, Truman insisted it be named after George Marshall, who had succeeded Jimmy Byrnes as his secretary of state. It was Marshall who, upon returning from a trip to Russia, persuaded Truman that something had to be done to rescue Europe. Although the Marshall Plan (known formally as the European Recovery Program) was to be a direct policy enactment of the broader Truman Doctrine to aid beleaguered democracies, Harry Truman was sage enough to know that if his name was attached to it, it stood little chance of passing Congress.

Speaking at commencement at Harvard on June 5, Marshall outlined his eponymous plan, appealing for the United States to come to the economic aid of war-distressed Europe. His speech, foreshadowed a month earlier by one on a similar theme by Undersecretary Acheson, marks the start of the campaign for Marshall Plan passage.

By July 1947, Page had decided to his satisfaction that it was necessary for America to lend money to Western Europe, although he found the state socialism of many of the European nations distasteful. He had also decided it was necessary to reverse what he called "the half-Jewish policy of suppressing German industrialism."[6]

Henry Stimson entered the fray with an article entitled "The Challenge to Americans" in the October 1947 issue of *Foreign Affairs*. In the article, Stimson outlined the need for America to help put Europe back on its financial feet.

At the time the Stimson article appeared, Page was working with Robert P. Patterson (Stimson's successor as secretary of war from 1945 to early 1947, when he was succeeded by Kenneth Royall) to form a citizens committee to support the Marshall Plan in Congress and in the general electorate. The need for a blue-ribbon committee to mold public and Congressional opinion was suggested to Patterson by Alger Hiss of the Carnegie Endowment for International Peace (Whitaker Chambers of *Time* magazine would shortly accuse Hiss of being a member of the American Communist Party who passed state secrets to the Soviets) and Clark Eichelberger of the American Assn. for the United Nations.[7]

Who better to head such a blue-ribbon committee than

Stimson, the great legalist, moralist, internationalist and believer in the sanctity of international agreements?

The Marshall Plan became a major weapon in America's Cold War arsenal as well as a humanitarian gesture. Although the Soviet Union and communist states of Central Europe were initially invited to participate, the Soviet Union quickly backed away. That was fortunate, for had Stalin decided to participate, Congress would almost certainly have scuttled ERP. The Marshall Plan goal following Soviet withdrawal became economic buttressing of Western European states so their citizens would not find communism more attractive than state socialism or western-style capitalism.

From the summer of 1947 through the winter, the Stimson Committee for the Marshall Plan to Aid European Recovery was a major part of the administration's efforts to sell the Marshall Plan to Congress.

Henry Stimson agreed to serve as chairman of the committee, but his role was more titular than active. Robert Patterson, chairman of the executive committee of the group, was far more active in the persuasion effort. Members of Patterson's executive committee included Winthrop Aldrich, Dean Acheson, Frank Altschul, Allen Dulles, Clark Eichelberger, Alger Hiss (who was convicted of perjury in December 1948) and Arthur Page. Some 300 prominent Americans selected to confer status on the committee—industrialists, bankers, Hollywood personalities and government leaders—served as the committee's National Council.[8]

Between November 1947 and March 1948, the Stimson Committee spent $150,000 on a national persuasion and lobbying effort.

Early in the effort, the committee used its New York and Washington offices to inform the general public of Marshall Plan benefits. Efforts were launched to get a million signatures on petitions supporting the Plan. Some 1.25 million pieces of literature—pamphlets, speech reprints, newspaper and magazine article reproductions—were distributed to opinion leaders and the general citizenry. A speakers bureau was formed. Newspaper ads were placed in New York and Washington, the great centers of American power. Network radio broadcasts featuring prominent Americans speaking out for the Marshall Plan were arranged. Newspaper and radio news releases and radio public service announcements were sent to the media. Mat releases were sent to country newspapers not reached by the great wire services.

From January through March 1948, when Marshall Plan legislation was being considered in Washington, efforts were intensified. Marshall himself made a cross-country speaking tour to rally support from business and civic groups. A weekly newsletter was distributed to news editors and other opinion leaders. Selected transcripts of testimony favorable to the Marshall Plan before the Senate Foreign Relations and House Foreign Affairs Committees were distributed. Stimson Committee representatives provided information to legislators and representatives of the big interest groups in Washington such as the labor lobby. Chip Bohlen, George Kennan and other State Dept. representatives lobbied Congress. During March, when momentum for passage was growing, the Stimson Committee generated headlines by staging a meeting of its National Council in Washington. The national publicity encouraged voters to call, cable or write their representatives in Washington to urge passage.[9]

While a great persuasion campaign was executed, passage of legislation was probably helped more in the spring of 1948 by the democratic government of Czechoslovakia falling to one beholden to Moscow.

Marshall Plan legislation was passed and signed into law in early April 1948. Congress appropriated the first $5.3 billion of what was to be a $22 billion commitment over four years. Only $14 billion would actually be appropriated. With passage, "dollar diplomacy" became an even more integral part of American foreign policy. The massive flow of Marshall Plan dollars, resented as the Plan might have been in some Western European quarters, did much to stimulate the economic recovery of France, Great Britain, West Germany and the other participating nations.

Although Page had worked for passage of the Marshall

Plan, he rather quickly became disillusioned with it. In May 1949, Congress was considering a cut in the second-year appropriation of $568 million below recommended levels. John Ferguson, who had served as executive director of the Stimson Committee until the machinery was dismantled in March-April 1948, cabled Page and others asking them to do what they could to get Congress to reconsider. Page refused to help. He wrote Ferguson to say that he understood Western Europe in return for American dollars and tools had promised to lower or reduce tariffs and to establish convertible currencies to encourage American trade. He told Ferguson he didn't think the Europeans had met their part of the bargain. Reduced Marshall Plan expenditures in the second year might encourage them to do so, he noted.[10]

Some historians have viewed the Marshall Plan as a great humanitarian effort by the United States. Others have seen it as a self-serving effort that unnecessarily raised animosity in recipient nations such as France. One strain of criticism of the Marshall Plan, that it worked to the financial benefit of the New York banks, deserves mention in relation to Arthur Page.

A number of New York bank directors were active in the higher echelons of the Stimson Committee which helped create the climate for Marshall Plan passage. Among them were Page and Winthrop Aldrich of Chase National, Sosthenes Behn and Gerald Swope of National City Bank, Thomas J. Watson and Charles E. Dunlap of Morgan Guaranty Trust and Philip Reed and Ward Melville of Bankers Trust.

According to *Chicago Tribune* coverage, opportunities to earn commissions for extending risk-free Marshall Plan loans through letters of credit went almost exclusively to the banks whose directors had participated in promoting Marshall Plan passage by serving on the Stimson Committee. By the middle of 1953, the Chase National had collected commissions on more than $1 billion in such transactions, according to the *Tribune*. Altogether, the New York banks by mid-1953 had handled commissions on some $5 billion of the $6 billion or so in Marshall Plan business handled by private banks in

America. The *Tribune,* which had launched an investigation of the role of the New York banks in handling Marshall Plan money, and run some exposé articles, complained that from mid-1953 forward its investigation was stymied by Harold Stassen. Upon becoming foreign aid administrator, Stassen ordered a stop to publication of figures on private bank involvement in the Marshall Plan program.[11] Since total Marshall Plan expenditures were in the neighborhood of $12.5 billion, and private American banks had been involved in about $6 billion in letters of credit business already by mid-1953, it would appear that the role of the commercial lending institutions was considerable.

Also worth noting, although unknown to all but a few, was that the fledgling Central Intelligence Agency was siphoning large sums from the $200 million in local currency counterpart funds contributed by the 17 participating agencies. The CIA used the money to finance anticommunist activities in France and Italy and to fund sympathetic individuals and groups. Access to the counterpart funds was given specifically to Frank Wisner of the CIA, about whom we shall hear more in the upcoming discussion of Radio Free Europe.

Building a strong postwar military establishment

PAGE KNEW THAT for a *pax Americana* to work, the nation needed to back up dollar diplomacy with military might. Much of his work in the postwar 1940s was devoted to encouraging a strong military establishment in the face of considerable public pressure for demobilization.

In addition to campaigning for universal military traning, he was involved in high-level government discussions on the subject of merging the Army and Navy into a common Defense Dept.

As early as 1945, Page had been involved in discussions led by Secretary of War Stimson and Harvey Bundy on merging Army ground and air forces and Navy units under a single secretary and uniformed staff.[12] In 1947, that was accomplished by legislation creating the Dept. of Defense and Joint Chiefs of Staff.

During the period of transition to a unified Defense Dept., Page served as a consultant to Secretaries of War Patterson and Royall. When James Forrestal was named America's first secretary of defense in late 1947, Royall became secretary of the army and Page remained a consultant to him. He advised Patterson and Royall on matters such as the Army budget, public relations, lobbying for universal military training, Army morale and military government in Germany, Austria, Japan and Korea.[13]

Page favored UMT because he did not believe sufficient recruits could be attracted to a volunteer Army for America to effectively serve as a world policeman. His position shifted somewhat as the winds in Washington blew one way and another, but remained stable at the core.[14]

In addition to serving as an adviser to Patterson and Royall, Page also handled several specific assignments for the defense establishment in the postwar forties.

In February 1947, at the joint request of Secretary of the Navy Forrestal and Secretary of War Patterson, he agreed to serve on a special committee to investigate hazardous duty pay for aviators.

Since 1913, military aviators had been paid a supplement because of the dangers involved in their duties. The committee to which Page was named was to investigate if such extra pay should continue. Although named the Flight Pay Board, the committee was also to look into hazard pay for sailors in the Navy's submarine service. The group was headed by John Lord O'Brian, one of the most skillful lawyers to practice before the Supreme Court, a Harvard overseer and welcome White House visitor from the days of Woodrow Wilson forward. Albert Jaques of Prudential Insurance was its secretary, and Roane Waring of the Memphis Transit System was the fourth member.[15]

The group issued its final report to Secretary of Defense Forrestal in December 1947. Forrestal referred the report to the Advisory Commission on Armed Services Pay. The commission's recommendation that hazard pay for flyers and submarine crews be discontinued was ignored.[16]

Page advised Patterson and Forrestal on disposition of the joint Army and Navy Committee on Welfare and Recreation he had headed during the war. In early 1947 he recommended that the committee be dismantled. Forrestal disagreed. The committee was reconstituted in late 1947 with Lindsley Kimball as chairman. Page agreed to serve as a member of the reorganized group at Forrestal's request.[17]

He was a frequent speaker at classes of the Army Information School, which he had helped to establish. When Hanson Baldwin of the *New York Times* criticized the first session of the new National War College for devoting too little attention to public opinion, Page became a regular speaker at classes. Secretary of Defense Forrestal was so impressed with the content of Page's first speech to the National War College after other Navy officers brought it to his attention that he ordered transcripts distributed to all Navy commands.[18]

Page devoted considerable attention to providing public relations advice to the Army Chiefs of Information from Lt. Gen. J. Lawton Collins through Lt. Gen. Floyd L. Parks. From the 1954 appointment of Maj. Gen. Gilman C. Mudgett forward, however, his guidance declined.

Page campaigned in the postwar years for the Army and Navy to do a more effective job of making their points of view known to Congress and the general public. He advised Lt. Gen. Collins to prepare more polished presentations when asking money from Congress.[19] He urged the Navy to be more frank when speaking with the press, and above all, to be more vocal in presenting its views to the public.[20] He helped Maj. Gen. Parks prepare a cogent presentation on why public relations was necessary to the Army—a presentation made with desired effect to Gen. Dwight Eisenhower.[21]

In 1948, when questions arose over whether Army public relations problems should be handled by the Army's public relations officers or by the public relations staff of the secretary of defense, Page advised Army Chief of Staff Gen. Omar

Bradley that decentralization was essential. "The Secretary's office can't handle all the questions about all three Services put to it by the press and public," Page argued. "It must decentralize and let each handle its own." He recommended that the secretary of defense's public relations staff be responsible for developing national policy, but that applications of that policy be handled at the local level, just as Bell System local managers applied policies in their home towns that had been developed by AT&T's headquarters public relations staff in New York.[22]

He became annoyed when the Army dismissed the N.W. Ayer and Son advertising agency which had been handling its postwar recruiting advertising. He opposed firing an agency once retained, believing the threat of losing an account encouraged it to become dishonest, catering to a client's whims instead of providing what the client needed. AT&T, which had first retained N.W. Ayer in 1908, was still using the agency when Page died in 1960, the longest continuous agency-client relationship in American advertising history. When Secretary of the Army Royall asked Page in 1948 to sit on a committee reviewing the efforts of the new Army advertising agency, Gardner of St. Louis, Page refused, saying he did so because he disagreed with the Army's having changed agencies.[23]

In September 1948, Page testified before Ferdinand Eberstadt's Committee on National Security Organization (part of the machinery of the postwar Hoover Commission formed to reorganize the federal government, an office with which Page had been involved) on public relations in the military establishment. In his testimony, he outlined changes that he thought would both integrate the public relations activities of the Army, Navy and Air Force within the Defense Dept. and still leave the three branches sufficient autonomy to deal with their individual problems.[24]

Page several times during World War II had advocated that the Army establish civilian advisory committees to assist top-ranking officers. Such committees were formed, and from 1947 through at least 1957, Page served on the First

Army's Greater New York Army Advisory Committee headed by Julius Ochs Adler of the *New York Times*. He was assigned to the committee's press, radio and information media group, which included William Paley of CBS, Mark Woods of ABC, Roy Howard of the Scripps-Howard newspaper chain, William Randolph Hearst Jr. and Kenneth Dyke of NBC. The committee, with a total membership of around 70, advised the First Army commander, who in Page's day was Gen. Courtney H. Hodges, and thereafter, Lt. Gen. Willis D. Crittenberger.[25]

Birth of the National Committee for a Free Europe

PAGE'S OVERRIDING interest in his later consulting years was Radio Free Europe.

There was more than a casual link between the leadership structure of the Stimson Committee for the Marshall Plan and the hierarchy of the National Committee for a Free Europe (NCFE), parent organization of Radio Free Europe. Of the 35 individuals who initially served in the leadership councils of NCFE, 16, including Page, had been actively involved in the top levels of the Stimson Committee.[26]

Was the Stimson Committee the talent pool for NCFE leadership? Perhaps, but comparing membership of the Council on Foreign Relations in 1948-1949 with leadership of the Stimson Committee and early NCFE indicates the Council on Foreign Relations was the likely talent pool for both.[27]

Further, the concept of American propaganda radios predates the Stimson Committee. The State Dept. first sought to establish Radio Liberty to beam propaganda in Russian to the Soviet Union in August 1946. Gen. Lucius D. Clay, in charge of military government in American-occupied West Germany, objected to locating the Radio Liberty transmitters in Munich. His relations with the Soviets were still cordial, and he felt the propaganda operation would be counter to the spirit of the quadripartite occupation agreement between the United States, France, Germany and Russia.

Radio Free Europe (RFE) grew from talks held by George

Kennan with a few influential Americans early in the Cold War. Kennan, a diplomat, scholar and preeminent Soviet expert, in a July 1947 article in *Foreign Affairs* had called for the use of counterforce to contain the Soviet Union, arguing that it was in America's interest to block further Russian expansion. In the talks, he sought suggestions on how the State Dept. could best aid refugees from Eastern European communist regimes without risking a break in diplomatic relations with the Soviet bloc. Among those with whom he conferred were Joseph Grew, American ambassador to Japan at the time of the Pearl Harbor attack, and Gen. Clay. Dean Acheson, who helped formulate the Truman Containment Doctrine and the Marshall Plan and who became secretary of state in 1949, asked Grew to form an organization to deal with the refugee problem. Grew called on an old State Dept. colleague, DeWitt Poole. The two met at Grew's home, and agreed that the proposed organization should hold together an elite cadre of exiled Eastern European leaders ready to move into any power vacuum resulting from a counterrevolution in the satellite states.[28]

NCFE was incorporated as a nonprofit agency in New York on May 11, 1949. The organizers held their first meeting a week later.[29]

At the organizational meeting, Grew was named chairman of the board of directors, Poole was elected president and Allen Dulles was named chairman of the executive committee. Dulles, a Wall Street lawyer by trade, friend and neighbor of Page, had been a key operative in America's World War II Office of Strategic Services (OSS) intelligence arm. His experience in the cloak-and-dagger business in Switzerland during the war led him into involvement with the new Central Intelligence Agency (CIA) created by the National Security Act of 1947.

The day after the organizational meeting, at which Arthur Page was elected a director of the new organization, he wrote to Grew to say he would be willing to serve, but that he thought it wiser for Grew to find someone with a more well known name to be a director. Grew said he wanted Page, and he thus became a member of "the Forty-Niners," the group that did the initial shaping of the Free Europe organization.[30] Page, who had been a propaganda officer in World War I, was back in the psychological warfare business.

On the day he expressed his reservations to Grew about being on the NCFE board, Page wrote a fund-raising ad for the new organization and sent it to son-in-law Anderson Hewitt. Hewitt had left the J. Walter Thompson advertising agency to form his own firm, Hewitt, Ogilvy, Benson and Mather.[31] Page knew enough of the philosophy of NCFE the day after the charter meeting to write the ad copy, an indication he was in on earlier planning.

While NCFE grew out of the Kennan talks mentioned, it was very much a reaction to Cold War events. In February 1948, an election coup toppled the Benes régime in Czechoslovakia, replacing it with a communist government. Simultaneously, the Soviets stepped up sabotage at German ports through which the Allies were shipping supplies. Communist-led strikes crippled Italy and France.[32] These events led to reevaluation of America's intelligence operations.

In June 1948, George Kennan wrote national security memo NSC 10/2 which created an Office of Policy Coordination (at first called the Office of Special Projects) within the CIA. OPC was made responsible for covert operations, particularly those aimed at countering communist inroads in Europe. The OPC director was supposed to keep the State Dept. informed of what it was doing. However, that didn't happen. Headed by Frank Wisner, an ardent foe of communism who had been recommended for the job by Allen Dulles, OPC was soon operating independently of direction from either the secretary of state or Director of Central Intelligence Adm. Roscoe Hillenkoetter.[33]

Also in June 1948, the Soviet Union cut off land and water supply routes to West Berlin in an attempt to get the Western Powers to withdraw. The blockade was the first real test of the Truman Doctrine. Although the Berlin Airlift was conceived and started by Gen. Lucius Clay, who had been the logistics and supply genius of World War II, it was President Harry Truman who endorsed it. Rather than go to war to break the land blockade, Truman chose to approve the air route of supply. By the time the Airlift ended in May 1948, more than 1,600,000 tons of supplies had been delivered to beleaguered Berlin by American and British planes.

As part of a 1948 reevaluation of American intelligence services, President Truman appointed Allen Dulles, William H. Jackson and Mathias Correa to examine CIA operations. The outcome was National Security Council Report No. 50, written almost entirely by Jackson and Dulles. Their report was really meant for New York Gov. Thomas Dewey, whom the establishment confidently expected to be elected president. It went essentially unnoticed by Truman, who upset Dewey and was narrowly reelected in 1948.[34]

While the civilian directors of NCFE provided overt guidance for development of Radio Free Europe and related operations, covert funding and the real direction came from Frank Wisner and his subordinates at OPC. In 1949, the year NCFE was incorporated, OPC already had more than 300 agents at work and a budget of $4.7 million, with a stream of off-the-record capital ready to flow to it from Marshall Plan counterpart funds. The money for Radio Free Europe came from Wisner, and RFE was for all practical purposes Wisner's baby.

The true nature of NCFE/RFE funding remained secret until 1971, when Sen. Clifford Case introduced legislation that began overt government funding of RFE. Even after 1971, RFE contended its earlier funding came solely from contributions of individuals, businesses and foundations until 1975, when CIA Director William Colby, testifying in Washington, admitted that RFE had long been a CIA-funded front company.[35]

Although Radio Free Europe became the best known of its operations, the activities of NCFE were considerably more extensive than propaganda broadcasting. NCFE began operation with three committees that evolved into divisions.

The Committee on Intellectual Activity sought employment, often in academic and research posts, for Eastern Eu-

ropean exiles with leadership potential. In 1951, in cooperation with the French university at Strasbourg, the committee, which by then had become a division of NCFE, founded
the Free Europe University in Exile (*College de l'Europe Libre*)
which offered fellowships to young exile scholars from Eastern Europe. The college was soon dubbed a "school for spies"
by Soviet counterpropagandists.[36]

The mission of the Committee on Radio and Press, which
split into NCFE's Radio Free Europe Division and the Free
Europe Press, was to carry the voices and viewpoints of exiles back into their home countries by radio and print media. Early on, Yugoslavia was dropped as a target country
and the nations NCFE sought to influence became Poland,
Czechoslovakia, Hungary, Albania, Romania and Bulgaria.[37]

A new sense of urgency entered the Cold War in September 1949, when the United States learned the Soviets had
successfully tested an atomic bomb. In January 1950, America
began work on a hydrogen bomb, which it had by 1952. The
U.S.S.R. had a light version of the hydrogen weapon by 1953,
and a "super" version like America's by 1955.

The Committee on American Contacts was formed to make
refugee speakers available throughout America. An exile labor leader, for example, might be put on a circuit speaking
to American union groups.[38]

The fourth NCFE Committee on National Councils was created in early 1950 under direct supervision of Allen Dulles.
It was to organize exiles into national groups and then coordinate operation of the groups. The councils, which operated in America and abroad, remained under Dulles's control after his entry into the CIA. While they operated to some
extent in America, their main goal was to conduct espionage
and sabotage in Eastern Europe and Russia. Frank Wisner's
OPC recruited members from homeless expatriates wander-
ing around Germany. They were trained at a former Nazi
camp near Weisbaden. Many were KGB agents, but the CIA
would not learn that until much later.[39]

Allen Dulles rejoined the intelligence community in 1950
at the invitation of Gen. W. Bedell Smith, who succeeded Adm.

Hillenkoetter as head of the CIA. Caught completely by surprise by the North Korean invasion of South Korea in June 1950, President Truman had asked Hillenkoetter to resign. "Beetle" Smith, the new DCI, was a no-nonsense commander who had served as chief of staff for Dwight Eisenhower in World War II, and after the war been ambassador to Moscow, where he honed his dislike of communists to a sharp edge.

Smith, who had read the Dulles-Jackson-Correa NSA Report No. 50, asked Dulles to complete a six-week consulting task. In December, that task completed, he invited Dulles to join the CIA in a new post supervising secret intelligence collection and Frank Wisner's OPC (clandestine operations). Dulles accepted, resigned from the presidency of the Council on Foreign Relations and chose the title deputy director of plans for his new job. A few months later, Deputy Director of Central Intelligence William Jackson left the CIA, and Beetle Smith on Aug. 23, 1951, named Dulles to replace him.

Although Page was interested in all aspects of NCFE work, he was most active in raising funds for the organization. The first feeble efforts of NCFE to raise money, so that the impression might be given that NCFE activities were funded by private contributions, were the newspaper ads prepared by Hewitt, Ogilvy, Benson and Mather. These ads featured coupons to be clipped out and sent back to NCFE with cash contributions. The early advertising also featured testimonials from members of the National Committee for a Free Europe and other prominent American anticommunists.

Page persuaded Gen. Dwight Eisenhower, then president of Columbia University, to allow the use of his name, photo and endorsement in the early ads.[40] He had met Eisenhower in London during his War Dept. assignment for the Normandy invasion. Before Eisenhower left uniform to head Columbia, Page hosted a dinner in his honor to introduce him to 25 or so prominent industrialists and financiers.[41] As vice chairman of the Teachers College board, Page occasionally saw him in that capacity. Eisenhower, not particularly happy as president of Columbia, cheered up when President Truman called him back to uniform in December 1950 as supreme allied commander in Europe. The Pages and Eisenhowers now and again met socially until then.

Page helps found the Crusade for Freedom

IN LATE 1949, with Arthur Page leading the way, NCFE began laying plans for an elaborate fund-raising campaign that became the Crusade for Freedom. Page received a plan in January 1950 from the John Price Jones firm for the first campaign to raise $1 million.[42] Appended to the plan was a memorandum from Hewitt, Ogilvy, Benson and Mather outlining proposed advertising support.[43]

At the time Page got the John Price Jones recommendation, Abbott Washburn, on leave from his post as public services manager for General Mills in Minneapolis, was studying the needs of NCFE for a fund-raising and public relations staff. Washburn, who went on to a distinguished career with the Crusade for Freedom, as deputy director of the U.S. Information Agency, as a partner in the Washburn-Stringer public relations firm, as an executive in Clay Whitehead's Office of Telecommunications Policy and then as an FCC commissioner, submitted his recommendations in late January 1950.

Washburn recommended that as a first step NCFE form a Public Relations Policy Committee with Arthur Page as chairman, himself as vice chairman, and Nate Crabtree, who had been a public relations aide on the staff of Adm. Chester Nimitz in World War II (and who went on to become public relations vice president of General Mills before his death in 1965), as an assistant.

Washburn also recommended that NCFE hire a full-time public relations director, a full-time public relations agency and a full-time aide for Gen. Lucius Clay (Ret.), who had agreed to serve as chairman of the first Crusade for Freedom fund-raising effort. Clay, by then the creator and hero of the Berlin Airlift, was no longer an opponent of propaganda radio. At the crest of his popularity and on his way to becoming a business leader, he had by 1950 also recreated himself into an ardent anticommunist.[44]

In early March 1950, the Public Relations Policy Committee which Washburn had recommended was formed. It became the coordinating agency for the Crusade for Freedom. Its more well-known members, in addition to Page and Washburn, included Adm. H.B. "Min" Miller, who had been the principal public relations adviser to Adm. Chester Nimitz in 1944-1945 and director of public relations for the Navy from 1945 to 1946, Claude Robinson, founder of the Opinion Research Corp., Handley Wright, public relations vice president of the Assn. of American Railroads (and, in 1951, president of the Public Relations Society of America), and Frank Altschul, a well-known businessman who had married into New York's prominent Lehman family.[45]

Maj. Gen. Clarence L. Adcock (Ret.), who had been Clay's deputy in Germany, was hired as his assistant. NCFE ultimately retained three public relations agencies rather than the one Washburn had recommended—Baldwin and Mermey as the main agency, Roger Brown, Inc., to handle broadcasting arrangements and Flanley and Woodward for relations with women's groups.

In April 1950, Page was elected to the NCFE executive committee. In May, the executive committee assigned him overall responsibility for the Crusade for Freedom.[46] By the end of May, planning was well under way for the fall fund-raising campaign. Initial plans called for visits of "air cavalcades" of aircraft that had participated in the Berlin Airlift to major American cities, and for a visit to Europe by Crusade dignitaries. The European tour was to include a visit to Berlin, where the Crusade officers planned to hang a ten-ton "freedom bell" in memory of the Berlin Airlift, and to Munich, main site of proposed Radio Free Europe operations.[47]

The plans for the air cavalcade had to be cancelled when, on June 24, Dean Acheson informed President Truman, vacationing in Independence, Mo., that North Korea was invading the South. The next day, Acheson told Truman that large numbers of North Korean troops supported by Soviet-built tanks had moved across the 38th parallel into South Korea. Truman said, "By God, I am going to hit them hard." He went to the United Nations for a cease-fire resolution, and, the Soviet Union boycotting the U.N. at the time, got instead a resolution calling for U.N. member nations to intervene. The planes that were to have been used in the air cavalcade were now needed, along with warships and soldiers, in Korea.[48] Ninety per cent of the forces that would fight in Korea would end up being American.

Overall, the Korean conflict was an asset for the Crusade, making its work easier. Just as the communist coup in Czechoslovakia in February 1948 aided the Stimson Committee for the Marshall Plan by creating a climate for passage of Marshall Plan legislation, the outbreak of the Korean conflict created a climate in which Americans supported aggressive education (read "propaganda" or "psychological warfare") programs targeted at the Soviet Union and its captive satellites.

Despite the Korean conflict, Radio Free Europe went on the air on schedule on July 4, 1950. The first transmission was a short, symbolic one. Within weeks, RFE was broadcasting on a regular basis from a small 7.5- kilowatt mobile transmitter borrowed from the Army located near Frankfurt, Germany.[49] As the months passed, huge medium-wave transmitters went on the air from Munich, and shortwave transmitters at sites in Portugal began using curtain antennas to bounce signals off the ionosphere to target nations.

NCFE officials enhanced their domestic communication capabilities in July 1950 when the Advertising Council, a public service group formed in World War II to provide advertising at production cost to defense-related agencies, approved the Crusade for Freedom as a Council project. Hewitt, Ogilvy, Benson and Mather was named the volunteer agency to handle the account, and within a week of Council approval, it forwarded the first layouts for Crusade advertising under Advertising Council auspices.[50] The Advertising Council support of Radio Free Europe so begun did not end until well after Sen. Clifford Case in 1971 acknowledged publicly what only a few Americans but most of Soviet Intelligence had long known, that the main source of RFE funding was not donations from the public but the CIA.

The Crusade for Freedom was a division of NCFE until October 1950, when it was incorporated as a separate non-profit corporation. Its mission as a separate foundation was to act as the fund-raising arm and official publicity voice of NCFE. Lucius Clay was named chairman of the new foundation, Clarence Adcock its executive vice chairman and Arthur Page chairman of its executive committee. Directors, in addition to the three officers just named, were Allen Dulles, DeWitt Poole and Frank Altschul.[51]

The Crusade was given prestige and credibility by 80 or so prominent Americans who lent their names to the cause by serving on the National Crusade for Freedom Council. The roster included Sen. William Benton, Sen. J. William Fulbright, ex-OSS head William J. Donovan, William L. Green of the American Federation of Labor, Sen. Hubert Humphrey, theologian and Cold War philosopher Reinhold Niebuhr, David Sarnoff of RCA, Henry Luce of Time, Inc., and DeWitt Wallace of the *Reader's Digest*.[52]

Gen. Dwight Eisenhower, head of NATO, launched the fund-raising effort on Sept. 4, 1950, with a stirring and widely reported speech delivered over America's four major radio networks.[53] Films on the Crusade and its Freedom Bell were distributed to all television stations in America and widely shown in commercial movie theaters.[54] Hewitt, Ogilvy, Benson and Mather released proofs of 12 different newspaper ads to 10,000 newspapers and magazines, inviting the media to send for mats of whatever they wanted. The agency distributed 3,000 billboard posters and 25,000 car cards.[55]

Well before Crusade publicity peaked, Baldwin and Mermey, the main public relations agency, had to terminate newspaper clipping because it was buried in stories pouring in. The agency estimated that by Oct. 1, 1950, when it ended clipping, it had received clips of 20,000 stories, cartoons and editorials relating to the Crusade.[56]

Magazine publicity was equally potent. *Time* gave one of its covers to Crusade Chairman Lucius Clay, and a number of stories in the newsmagazine dealt with the effort. Baldwin and Mermey supplied materials for articles to *Coronet, Fortune, Look, Life, Newsweek, True, Freedom and Union, Scholastic, This Week,* the *New Yorker,* the *Saturday Review, Editor & Publisher, Public Relations Journal* and *The Reporter.*[57]

The Crusade and its local affiliates put out millions of flyers, leaflets, brochures, handbills and like items. Some 6.5 million copies of the main Crusade flyer, "Join the Crusade," were distributed.[58] Hewitt, Ogilvy, Benson and Mather received 11,930 orders for advertising mats, a result described by an Advertising Council executive as "by all odds the most successful campaign of its length (six weeks) ever conducted by the Council."[59] A good deal of publicity was generated when the Crusade's Freedom Bell, cast in England, was sent to more than 20 cities before being shipped to Germany.[60]

Formal conclusion of the first Crusade came on United Nations Day, Oct. 24, 1950, with dedication of the Freedom Bell in the bell tower of the Schöneberg Rathaus, West Berlin's city hall. By then, U.N. intervention in Korea was well under way, President Truman having committed American Army, Navy and Air units in June. The crowd that gathered in the Berlin platz for the bell ceremony was estimated at 250,000 by the *New York Times,* and at 400,000 by NCFE. Speakers included Dr. Ernst Reuter, mayor of Berlin, John J. McCloy, U.S. high commissioner in Germany, Lucius Clay (now representing NCFE rather than the American occupation government) and Gen. Maxwell Taylor, commandant of U.S. forces in Germany. The bell dedication ceremonies were broadcast over Radio Free Europe. Immediately after, reminiscent of the BBC-Overseas, Radio Free Europe made three peals of the Freedom Bell its distinctive station-break trademark.[61]

The Crusade received contributions of $1.3 million. On the surface, that would be a success.

What the Crusade did not report was cost. Figures on collections, much less costs, were never released to the public after 1950, although the amounts, derived from internal NCFE documents, are reported here. John Price Jones had estimated a campaign to raise $1 million would cost $100,000. The

1950 Crusade cost from $900,000 to $917,000 netting only $400,000.[62]

The $400,000 was totally inadequate to meet the financial needs of Radio Free Europe. In June 1950, Allen Dulles and two other auditors reviewed the first year of NCFE operation. According to their final report, NCFE's annual payroll was $500,000. Office space, travel, entertainment and other costs came to another $125,000. NCFE in addition had in its possession (or on order) radio equipment representing a capital outlay of $800,000 and was committed to a program of radio equipment acquisition of about $2.3 million.[63]

Although the Crusade for Freedom made much ado about being the funding arm of Radio Free Europe, its real mission was to act as a cover for the main source of NCFE funding. This funding source is referred to in the Page Papers, including in the Dulles audit just mentioned, as "the Foundation." "The Foundation" was of course the CIA or a CIA conduit.

Rather than an efficient fund-raising effort, the early Crusade was a massive persuasion (propaganda if you wish) effort, a major goal of which was to convince Americans of the need for the nation to fight Soviet influence in Eastern Europe. The 1951 Crusade ended up spending more on propaganda and fund-raising than it collected. Here was the massive effort to educate the public to internationalism that Page had called for in the mid-1940s.

All money raised by the Crusade went to the Free Europe organization, with "the Foundation" paying all costs incurred by the Crusade. Since "the Foundation" was the CIA, and the CIA was covering all costs of Crusade propaganda in America, then the CIA was funding a psychological campaign targeted at the American people which contravened legislation prohibiting it from conducting domestic operations.

In fairness, the Crusade propaganda was inane material, saying little that Americans didn't already pretty much believe about the Soviet Union and its satellites. It was hardly the sort of insidious, hateful propaganda put out by Goebbels' Reichsministry of Propaganda.

Still, a nagging doubt persists about the legality and ethicality of the CIA funding propaganda fronts used domestically against American citizens.

More important to the life of Arthur Page, the Crusade put a man whose integrity was normally above question, and who throughout his life had called for institutions to be honest, in the position of telling Americans that their donations were needed to keep Radio Free Europe on the air. That was a lie. The Free Europe organization was being secretly subsidized by tax dollars of citizens being asked to contribute.

In Page's defense, he made an effort to get government officials, including President Eisenhower, to be more honest about the true nature of Radio Free Europe funding.

Why did the Free Europe organization even bother with fund-raising? One answer is that government propaganda operations like the Voice of America and U.S. Information Agency, while fairly free in what they can say, must still conform to basic rules of international protocol. To violate these would be to invite diplomatic problems and protests. An operation funded and run by private citizens, on the other hand, has more freedom. When Soviet bloc nations complained to the State Dept. about Radio Free Europe, State could reply that the RFE operation was run by private citizens over which it had no control. The Crusade gave Radio Free Europe the cover of being an agency funded by contributions of private citizens who disliked Soviet tyranny.

A second reason for the Crusade cover operation, for which there is evidence in the Page Papers, is that the CIA and other government officials hoped that the Crusade eventually would raise enough money so that it could be said honestly that the Crusade was the sole funding arm of NCFE.

The 1951 and 1952 Crusades

HAROLD STASSEN, with the behind-the-scenes help of Abbott Washburn, Adm. Min Miller, Page and others, headed the 1951 Crusade for Freedom. It was an uneventful, low-keyed, disorganized effort.

In the summer of 1951, the Crusade experimented with its first "Winds of Freedom" balloon operation. Balloons carrying propaganda were released in Germany and allowed to carry their leaflets to the Soviet satellites. In ensuing years, the program became more refined as the Free Europe Press, the NCFE division responsible for the program, learned more about wind currents in Europe and refined timing devices for release of leaflets over wide areas.

As the balloon program grew, protests from the Soviet satellites mounted. The balloons were called a safety threat—it was claimed that a Free Europe Press balloon had downed a Czech airliner. The balloon operation was terminated at State Dept. request immediately after the abortive Hungarian revolt of 1956.[64]

At the CIA, Frank Wisner liked to boast of the capabilities of his "mighty Wurlitzer," able to spin out propaganda around the world. This Wurlitzer included not only Radio Free Europe, but Radio Liberty, which went on the air in 1953 with messages targeted directly at the Soviet Union, and Radio Free Asia discussed below. Despite Wisner's boasting, programming on these early psychological warfare weapons was primitive propaganda at best.

In late 1950, Royall Tyler of NCFE complained from Paris that refugees who came from behind the Iron Curtain said that without exception Radio Free Europe scripts were flavored more to the taste of Americans than Eastern Europeans. Further, he complained, the exiles on the air spoke with a tone of superiority that grated on their countrymen left behind. In terms of overall popularity behind the Iron Curtain, he claimed, RFE ranked last behind the BBC Overseas, the Voice of America, Radio Paris and Radio Madrid.[65]

To DeWitt Poole, Tyler said the sentiment of satellite nation refugees was that "RFE broadcasts rub... most listeners the wrong way or, still worse, simply bore them."[66]

The Crusade in 1951 appealed not only for donations to Radio Free Europe, but to a proposed similar effort to begin broadcasting to the People's Republic of China and other points in Asia.

In the early 1950s, Page became a member of the Committee for a Free Asia, a separate foundation set up along the same lines as the National Committee for a Free Europe.

The Free Asia Committee began broadcasting to selected points in Asia, including the People's Republic of China, in 1952. It also conducted print propaganda operations. The mission of penetrating the Bamboo Curtain by broadcast and print proved too complicated, however, and further, the operation irritated a number of Asian nations. Broadcasting by the Free Asia Committee terminated in 1953. In 1954, the Committee for a Free Asia changed its name to the Asia Foundation, and thereafter, the group devoted most of its efforts to working with Asian student groups and other ventures totally different in concept from what NCFE was doing. During the Committee for a Free Asia phase, Arthur Page functioned chiefly as a troubleshooter for Allen Dulles of the CIA.[67]

Min Miller served as chairman of the 1952 Crusade for Freedom effort. The campaign, shorter and more low-key even than the 1951 effort, was one of the least successful Crusades. Of course, it really didn't need to be successful. The main source of its funding, Frank Wisner's OPC, by this time had a staff of 3,000 and a budget of $84 million.

Abbott Washburn left the Crusade staff in early 1952 to work on the Eisenhower presidential campaign. He was replaced by a hard-nosed fund-raiser, Fred Smith, president of Fred Smith and Co. Soon after being retained, Smith began to complain about the incompetence of the Ivy Leaguers in paid positions on the staffs of the Crusade and NCFE. Shortly before Smith was relieved, he wrote a bitter letter to Min Miller in which he said he would be more enthusiastic about his work if "this crowd could be replaced with some hardheaded, intelligent individuals who had the sense to recognize that we are up against a tough lot of extremely able propagandists who can't be fought off by a lot of soft-headed, pseudo intellectuals who don't know the difference between a fleeing criminal and a political refugee..."[68]

The Ivy Leaguers did in fact embrace some criminals—fleeing Nazis and other despised individuals—putting on the air people it thought to be respected in their home countries who in reality were detested as opportunists, war criminals or worse.

Richard B. Walsh replaced Smith, but plans for the fall Crusade effort were in disarray. The Advertising Council quickly detected the chaotic state of affairs, and in late 1952 threatened to drop the Crusade project if weaknesses such as lack of organization at the local level were not rectified.[69]

Two events saved the Crusade. One was the election of Dwight Eisenhower, who upon assuming office in 1953 put the strong support of the White House behind it. The second was the takeover of the Crusade in the spring of 1953 by the American Heritage Foundation.

Consultant to the National Security Council

IN THE SUMMER and fall of 1953, Page served at President Eisenhower's request as a consultant to the National Security Council. He took part in discussions to develop strategy for defense of the continental United States as a member of the first consultant group on national security policy of the Eisenhower administration.[70]

The mission of the group was to analyze and debate the conclusions reached in "Operation Solarium," a set of voluminous studies by experts on continental defense. From the deliberations of the consultant group came the first full security policy statement of the Eisenhower administration.[71]

Eisenhower's respect for Page is obvious in letters in the Page Papers, in that Eisenhower asked him to serve as a consultant to the National Security Council and in the support he gave to Page's recommendations on national transportation policy covered in the last chapter.

Edward Raleigh, who interviewed Eisenhower shortly before his death, reported that Ike spoke most favorably of Page.[72] His respect for Page may in part explain why his willingness to lend the prestige of the White House to the Crusade for Freedom and National Committee for a Free Europe.

The American Heritage Foundation
revitalizes the Crusade

RADIO FREE EUROPE operations expanded dramatically during the period 1953 to the Hungarian revolt in early 1956.

President Eisenhower, who took office in January 1953, named Foster Dulles to head his State Dept. and Foster's brother Allen to head the Central Intelligence Agency. The dapper Allen Dulles was now in a position to implement Foster's rhetoric about freeing the "slave states" of Eastern Europe, but he would avoid any actions that would actually do that. Something of a snob, and not a very good administrator, he proved adept at vetting the social pedigrees of agents destined for top CIA slots to be sure they had the right family and Ivy League connections.

Page became increasingly important to NCFE operations during this period. Efforts to obtain larger corporate contributions for the Crusade resulted in the fund-raising effort becoming a pet project of some of the most respected industrial leaders in America.

In early 1953, the American Heritage Foundation, notable for having sponsored a 1947 tour through America of a Freedom Train loaded with historical documents and artifacts, and for a "get out the vote" campaign in 1952, took over administration of the Crusade for Freedom.

Arthur Page had been involved in negotiations which began in 1950 to merge the Crusade and the American Heritage group. He was interested in getting the Heritage Foundation's $250,000 treasury for the Crusade. The two main powers in the Heritage Foundation, Winthrop Aldrich and Thomas D'Arcy Brophy, rejected the early overtures aimed at merger.[70] The Heritage Foundation officers agreed, however, when asked by high government officials to take over the Crusade and run its 1954 fund-raising effort with an eye to eventual merger.

Page welcomed the Heritage alliance. He knew that early Crusades, while attracting much attention to Radio Free Europe, were failures at fund-raising. The 1950 Crusade raised only $1.3 million at a cost of $900,000, a $400,000 net. The 1951 Crusade, which ended in early 1952, raised only $1.9 million at a cost of $2 million, a net loss of $100,000. The third Crusade, covering a 16-month period from March 1952 to June 1953, raised $932,000 at a cost of $918,000.[73]

With the American Heritage Foundation agreement to put the Crusade on a more businesslike footing, the Advertising Council agreed to continue its support of the project.[72]

Henry Ford II of the American Heritage Foundation agreed to serve as the next Crusade chairman, and Winthrop Aldrich as treasurer. A Heritage-Crusade Operations Committee consisting of Page, Earl Newsom (public relations counsel to Ford and others), Leo Burnett (of the new advertising agency replacing Hewitt, Ogilvy, Benson and Mather), Harold Brightman, Allan Brown (of Union Carbide), C.M. Vandeburg, Thomas D'Arcy Brophy, Louis Novins, Theodore Repplier (of the Advertising Council) and Robert Robb was formed to supervise the overall effort. The John Price Jones organization was again retained to coordinate the drive.[76]

At about the time the Heritage group took over the Crusade project, Radio Free Europe was fresh from a new triumph. When Josef Stalin died in early 1953, RFE had brought first news of the event to the satellite states, scooping the communist news organs. To overcome jamming of its broadcasts, RFE had gang-transmitted, beaming the full power of all its transmitters first to one target nation, then another.[77] The RFE transmitters when ganged could broadcast at about one million watts in the shortwave spectrum. The strongest commercial radio stations in America broadcast at 50,000 watts in the medium-wave range.

Although Page was proud of RFE's coverage of Stalin's death, he was also irked by what he thought was a Crusade news release describing a meeting of exiles at Free Europe headquarters immediately after Stalin's death. According to the story, which a Crusade official said was written by an independent newsman and not the Crusade staff, the exiles had discussed whether or not the time had come for Radio Free Europe to make an open appeal for revolt in the satellite states. The news release contended the exiles finally decided revolt in the unstable situation was unwise and might lead to slaughter of innocents. Page curtly told the Crusade staff to stop issuing news releases and prepare for the American Heritage takeover.[78]

In June 1953, Page was named chairman of the NCFE executive committee, replacing John C. Hughes who had accepted an embassy post.[79]

Under Heritage sponsorship, American industrial leaders were integrated into the Crusade. In September 1953, President Eisenhower held the first of a number of dinners for business leaders at the White House to encourage their participation. Eisenhower held similar annual dinners thereafter, except in 1955, when Vice President Richard M. Nixon hosted the affair while Ike recovered from a heart attack.

The 1953 dinner included invitations to Henry Ford II of the Ford Motor Co., Cleo Craig of AT&T, Morse Dial of Union Carbide, Frank Abrams of Standard Oil of New Jersey (Exxon), Benjamin Fairless of U.S. Steel, John McCaffrey of International Harvester, Barney Balaban of Paramount Pictures, Edwin J. "Eddie" Thomas of Goodyear, John McCloy of the Chase National, Harlow Curtice of General Motors and other industrialists.[80]

Page handled much of the coordination work for the first and the successive Crusade dinners at the White House, usually working through Eisenhower aide Maj. Gen. Wilton B. "Jerry" Persons, whom Page had come to know when Persons was part of the Pentagon public relations machinery during World War II.

With the prestige of the White House behind the Crusade, corporate contributions climbed dramatically. Among the corporate gifts to the first Heritage-sponsored Crusade were $250,000 from Ford Motor, $250,000 from Standard of New Jersey, $150,000 from U.S. Steel, $100,000 from Goodyear, $100,000 from Union Carbide, $75,000 from AT&T and $50,000 from International Harvester.[81]

Page worked particularly to get large contributions from the corporations of which he was a director, and in most cases, got them. AT&T and Westinghouse became particularly generous givers.

Although the first Heritage-sponsored Crusade, which concluded in the spring of 1954, was the best-organized effort to that date, it still fell considerably short of the $5 million goal that had been set. The effort raised $3.1 million at a cost of $877,000.[82]

By early 1954, Radio Free Europe had 26 transmitters on the air broadcasting from West Germany and Portugal. The staff had learned from early mistakes. Programming was more sophisticated, and listenership was building.

RFE had stopped broadcasting to Albania by this time for two reasons. It wanted better broadcasting sites in Turkey to reach the country, and there were too few receivers in that tiny and poor nation (an estimated 15,000) to justify broadcasting from inadequate sites.[83]

In Munich, RFE maintained a gigantic card file on information from behind the Iron Curtain. Information came from monitoring broadcasts from behind the Iron Curtain and from constant surveillance of more than 300 satellite state publications.[84] The intelligence served two purposes. Information gathered from the satellite states allowed the station to keep news broadcasts up-to-date and thoroughly researched. Further, the extensive information, when evaluated and condensed into daily reports, became an important component of overall American intelligence.

Besides gathering news from behind the Iron Curtain, Radio Free Europe by early 1954 maintained 16 separate news bureaus manned by some 100 American and refugee journalists. This newsgathering and intelligence-collection operation was one of the most extensive in the world.[85]

Part of the mission of Radio Free Europe, obviously, was espionage—the secret (or sometimes not so secret) gathering of information about foes, and occasionally, about friends. The other part of RFE's mission was covert action—seeking to influence or change the way a country is governed.

As the first Heritage-Crusade effort drew to a close in the spring of 1954, the National Committee for a Free Europe changed its name to the Free Europe Committee to more closely identify the parent organization with its best-known family member, Radio Free Europe.[86] Much later, the Free Europe Committee changed its name again, to Radio Free Europe, Inc.

By this time, the Free Europe University in Exile was in operation in France, as was a Mid-European Studies Center in New York. The Free Europe Press was publishing a dozen or so magazines for exile groups around the world, and supervising the "Winds of Freedom" balloon operation, which had grown to impressive proportions. During 1954 and 1955 alone, the Free Europe Press sent an estimated 377 million leaflets into the satellite nations by balloon.[87]

In the summer of 1954, Arthur and Mollie Page traveled to Europe to inspect Radio Free Europe facilities. They also stopped in London, where Ambassador Winthrop Aldrich entertained them.[88]

Soon after his return from Europe, Page wrote to Secretary of State John Foster Dulles to say the American ambassador to Portugal (Lisbon was the site of Radio Free Europe's Raret shortwave transmitters) was incompetent. Dulles replied that the situation would soon be improved. A few months later, a new ambassador was appointed.[89] Page also suggested upon his return that a request by Portuguese strongman Salazar (whom Page had met in Portugal) to use the Raret transmitters to talk to the Portuguese colonies be exploited by RFE as a starting point to bargain for an American or Radio Free Europe transmitter site in the Azores.[90]

The CIA was impressed with the improved performance of the Crusade under American Heritage guidance. Thomas Braden of the agency asked Page, who had been named a trustee of the American Heritage Foundation, to use his influence to get the Heritage board to agree to oversee the Crusade for a second year.[91] The Heritage group agreed.

The 1954-1955 Crusade, the second under American Heritage sponsorship, again fell short of goal. The drive raised $3.0 million at a cost of $922,000, a slightly worse record than that of a year earlier.[92]

The approximately $2.1 million cleared by the 1955 Crusade came nowhere close to covering the budget of the Free Europe Committee (FEC). Mark Ethridge of the *Louisville Courier-Journal*, a member of the NCFE and successor FEC organizations (and of the Council on Foreign Relations), traveled to Munich in late 1954-early 1955 to see Radio Free Europe operations. In a confidential report on his return, he indicated Radio Free Europe had a fiscal 1954-1955 provisional budget of $6.4 million. That figure appears to be only for radio operations in Europe, and not to include other FEC operations costing at least as much again. Evan Thomas says in his book *The Very Best Men* that RFE and Radio Liberation/Liberty were spending $30-$35 million a year at about this time.[93]

While the 1954-1955 Crusade was coming to a conclusion in the spring of 1955, Page and other Heritage-Crusade leaders began making plans for the Crusade to become independent again. Page hoped to push the Crusade in progressive steps to an annual gross of $10 million, so that it could honestly be said that the Crusade was the main source of funding for Radio Free Europe. A turnover committee composed of Page, Earl Newsom, Sam Pryor of Pan American World Airways and Paul Weisl of Simpson, Thacher and Bartlett worked out details for the split.[94]

In mid-1955, with plans for a merger of the American Heritage Foundation and Crusade for Freedom abandoned, the Crusade again became an autonomous organization.[95]

The mood of the FEC staff in New York was anything but peaceful at the time the Crusade again became independent. In March 1955, Robert Lang, an ex-OSS officer who had long been the head of NCFE/FEC's Radio Free Europe division, resigned over a quarrel with the Free Europe Press, laying the problem squarely on Page's shoulders.

Lang was angry over the way the Free Europe Press had handled publicity in its balloon leaflets about Jose (Joseph) Swiatlo, a high-ranking defector from the Polish secret police. Swiatlo, while working for the secret police in Poland as a CIA mole, had at CIA instruction in 1949 fomented a purge by releasing false information claiming Noel Field, known to many ranking communists, was a CIA double agent. The CIA boastfully claimed internally (since the trick was top secret) that the ruse had resulted in 100,000 to 150,000 communists being jailed or executed.

Radio Free Europe, in one of its finer moments, had put Swiatlo on the air, and his broadcasts were probably responsible for an ensuing liberalization of the secret police establishment in Poland. Then the Free Europe Press maladroitly, and against the recommendations of the FEC's Polish Exile Council, began balloon distribution of a leaflet calling Swiatlo "a man who has known every shame" and worse. Swiatlo refused to cooperate with RFE further, and threatened to sue the Free Europe Committee. Lang felt the Free Europe Press action had compromised Radio Free Europe's credibility. He pointed out that RFE's credibility was already dangerously low before the Free Europe Press blunder, with Radio Warsaw broadcasting "frighteningly accurate" information linking RFE's Voice of Free Poland to the CIA.[96]

Regarding the Radio Warsaw charges, Soviet and satellite intelligence agencies likely knew early on that Frank Wisner's "Mighty Wurlitzer" was a CIA operation. In 1949, while RFE was being created, H.A.R. "Kim" Philby came to Washington to be the liaison between British and American intelligence services. He was in the close confidence of Allen Dulles, who would almost certainly have confided in him the true story of RFE and its missions. One of the Cambridge Four, Philby was a trained Soviet agent.

Page and his FEC executive committee decided to accept Lang's resignation, and named William J. Convery Egan, an ex-State Department officer, to replace him. Lang was assigned to conduct negotiations in Turkey for acquisition of a site for RFE to use for a transmitter and monitoring station covering the Balkan area.[97]

Lang's resignation was only one sign of growing internal friction at FEC headquarters in New York. Whitney Shepardson, serving as FEC president, asked to resign by March 1, 1956. Adolf A. Berle Jr., a cold warrior who, like Page, was part of the "Forty-Niner" group, said he was not surprised at Shepardson's action given the internal rivalries at FEC. "Half the shop is intriguing against the other half," Berle observed.[98]

As a major player in both FEC and the Crusade, Page had to worry about both fronts. Earl Newsom came to his rescue with public relations help for the Crusade, including a plan for intensively penetrating American schools with Crusade and Radio Free Europe messages. That left Page more free from Crusade planning to work with the CIA in finding an acceptable replacement for Shepardson.[99]

Gen. Willis Crittenberger (ret.), whom Page had known as an adviser to the First Army which Crittenberger had commanded before retirement, was hired to replace Shepardson as FEC president.[100] In another important personnel change made at about the same time, John M. Patterson, a State Dept. officer, was hired as executive vice president of the Crusade for Freedom. He served briefly as an understudy to Crusade President William A. Greene before replacing him.[101]

The 1955-1956 Crusade, headed by Standard Oil of New Jersey Chairman Eugene Holman, had as its ambitious goal the raising of $10 million to support the Free Europe Committee. The drive actually took in $2.9 million at a cost of $1.0 million, netting about $1.9 million.[102]

In 1956, Page tried to get President Eisenhower or another responsible government official to admit that the Radio Free Europe organization received some government funding. He called his effort "Project Candor." He became particularly concerned about the truthfulness of Crusade claims that citizen donations were the sole source of FEC funding when *Washington Post* Executive Editor J. Russell Wiggins wrote to Crusade Chairman Eugene Holman to say it troubled him that "all of us are selling this activity as a private endeavor. I think we are being somewhat less than candid about the source of its funds. There is, in my opinion, no reason why private persons should not assist the government in such an endeavor... However it is done there should be no deceit about the matter, and I am a little afraid there has been some deceit...."[103]

A few months after Wiggins wrote to Holman, Page drafted a letter for President Eisenhower which, if signed, Holman could use to answer embarrassing questions raised by people like Wiggins. In the letter, Eisenhower was to say he hoped the American people would eventually provide all the financial support Radio Free Europe needed, but in the meantime, he would pay from the president's discretionary funds to the Crusade for Freedom what money it needed to support the Free Europe organization. The letter Page drafted also quotes the president as saying he agreed with Holman that perhaps the time had come to tell the public the truth about the funding of Radio Free Europe.[104]

The State Dept. objected to disclosure of information about the government funding.[105] Eisenhower sent Holman a noncommittal letter making no mention of government funding instead of the letter Page had drafted.[106] Page made at least one more ineffective attempt to disclose clandestine funding, and then apparently gave up.[107]

While people like Wiggins were tactfully beginning to question the credibility of the Free Europe organization, a much more serious threat to Radio Free Europe's reputation in America and the Eastern European satellite states arose in the fall of 1956. From its inception, the Free Europe organization had been looking to the day when a counterrevolution might erupt in one or more of the satellite nations. On Oct. 23, 1956, such a revolt began in Hungary.

Radio Free Europe and the Hungarian uprising of 1956

JOHN FOSTER DULLES, secretary of state during most of the Eisenhower administration, had been critical during the 1952 presidential campaign of the Truman administration's containment policy. Containment would commit the United States to indefinite peaceful coexistence with communism, he contended. His view was that the proper course of action for America was to dynamically roll back the threat of communism. "We will abandon the policy of containment," he said, "and will actively develop hope and resistance spirit within the captive peoples."[108]

Some 100 million or so people lived in 1956 in the Eastern European shatter zone satellites of the Soviet Union that Radio Free Europe sought to influence. If these millions believed that Dulles's pledge would involve military aid in the event of a revolt, they might have looked to the short-lived uprising in East Berlin in 1953. America expressed sympathy, but did not actively intervene or otherwise help. The CIA station chief in Berlin appealed for arms, but was ordered to provide moral support only. Berlin was an object lesson showing that Dwight Eisenhower and Foster Dulles didn't intend to go to war over campaign rhetoric.

Events leading to the Hungarian revolt of 1956 began in 1955 when Nikita Khrushchev criticized repressive policies of Josef Stalin in a public speech. Poland took heart in the ensuing period of destalinization, and in the late summer of 1956, Premier Wladyslaw Gomulka emerged the victor in a dramatic showdown in which Khrushchev at first threatened to crush Poland with military force, but finally backed down.

Radio Free Europe by the time of the showdown in Poland was able to gang-transmit at a consolidated power of more than 1.2 million watts from 29 transmitters. Its newscasters gleefully reported events in Poland to the people of that country and to the other satellite nations.[109] In mid-October, Frank Wisner discussed with a CIA colleague what America might do if a full-blown revolt broke out in Europe. He didn't expect America to intervene, but thought that large quantities of weapons would be supplied.

On the eve of the Hungarian uprising, where dynamism would get its most severe test, Wisner had 5,000 refugee warriors—some well trained, some not—at camps around Germany. On loan from the U.S. Army were officers to lead them if they were needed.

On Oct. 23, with knowledge of the victory won in Poland, 300,000 Hungarian students joined by workers moved into the streets of Budapest demanding that Stalinist Ernö Gerö be replaced by Imre Nagy. Secret police with machine guns unsuccessfully tried to quell the uprising. The Soviets temporarily backed off. Nagy was allowed to replace Gerö.

On Oct. 24, Frank Wisner arrived in London for the beginning of a tour of CIA stations in Europe. On Oct. 28, the Soviets began to withdraw their armor from Hungary.[110] Radio Free Europe reported the new victories in Hungary with even greater relish. As Leonard Mosley put it in his biography of John Foster, Allen and Eleanor Dulles, "From his (Radio Free Europe) station in Munich, Wisner poured out propaganda to swell the stormy waters. And as the revolt increased in intensity and the anti-Soviet rebels took over in Budapest, he stepped up the signals, saying: 'Hold on. Your friends in the West are coming.'"[111]

What RFE actually did, at least at first, was intercept calls to arms being broadcast by transmitters the Hungarians had seized, and rebroadcast those calls at much greater signal strength back into Hungary. Freedom Fighters hearing the messages believed they were coming from the West, and that the West would intervene to help.

A tragic chain of events that doomed the Hungarian uprising then began to unfold.

On Oct. 29, Israel, angered by guerrilla attacks by Egyptian leader Gamal Nasser and encouraged by Great Britain and France, launched a lightning strike into the Sinai, almost destroying Nasser's army. A day later, Great Britain and France demanded that Nasser withdraw from the Suez Canal which he had seized. When Nasser refused, British and French planes began bombing Egyptian targets. Ground forces of the two Western European powers prepared to invade the Suez. Wisner was furious with the British, French and Israelis for launching a campaign just when it looked like the long-awaited revolution in Central Europe was beginning.

Some military advisors urged Secretary of State John Foster Dulles to provide American support for the Anglo-French invasion of the Suez, but he was in no mood to do so, nor, for that matter, to support the Hungarian Freedom Fighters. He seemed mainly concerned, as were other prominent members of the administration, with the mistaken belief that intervention might cost Dwight Eisenhower reelection in the looming American contest on Nov. 6, then only days away. At the CIA, Director of Central Intelligence Allen Dulles was in close touch with his brother Foster at State.

On Nov. 3, at the height of the crisis, John Foster Dulles underwent surgery for the cancer that would eventually cause his death. That made little difference for Hungary. The important decision not to intervene in the revolt there had already been made. As for the Suez, British and French military forces had by this time landed and occupied the Canal Zone. They would soon be dislodged, not by Soviet threats, and not by the forces of Egypt and the Arab bloc, but by U.S. threats and dollar diplomacy.

During this critical period, the new Nagy government said it was withdrawing from the Warsaw Pact, the Soviet Union's equivalent of the North Atlantic Treaty Organization. That was too much for Russia. On Nov. 4, 200,000 Soviet troops and 2,500 tanks and armored vehicles moved into Hungary, concentrating on Budapest. The military force brutally crushed the revolt. An estimated 30,000—50,000 if you believe some estimates—died in the ensuing slaughter. Revolt leaders and their families not shot by the Russians were loaded on boxcars and transported to Soviet gulags. Nagy was arrested and probably executed in 1957.

Wisner was a mental wreck by the time he arrived in Frankfurt on Nov. 5. On Nov. 6, Eisenhower was re-elected in a landslide. By Nov. 7, Wisner had moved on to Vienna, where he could meet face to face with the refugees pouring into Austria from Hungary. The last of the pitiful pleas for help were then clattering into the Associated Press teletypes in Vienna from freedom fighters who had occupied the AP offices in Budapest. On Nov. 8, the last of the Hungarian resistance was crushed.

At the U.S. Embassy in Vienna, Wisner listened with Ambassador Llewellyn Thompson to the radio broadcasts of the United Nations debate on Hungary. The U.N., distracted like America by the Suez crisis and the possibility of a world war, decided to do next to nothing. It passed a resolution condemning Soviet brutality. The Soviets protested. The resolution was powerless to stop the executions and deportations.

Wisner frantically cabled Washington during the revolt asking for American aid. He is said to have asked for an airlift to provide the freedom fighters with arms and trained reinforcements, especially antitank weapons and people who knew how to use them. He is said to have asked permission to at least commit the emigre cadres that had been trained to fight in just such a situation.

Probably with sincere regret, Allen Dulles tried to explain that active American help for Hungary would not be forthcoming. "How can anything be done about the Russians," the DCI asked, "when our own allies are guilty of exactly similar acts of aggression?"[112]

In the weeks and months and years after the failure of America to assist in the Hungarian revolt, Wisner suffered from increasingly severe bouts of depression, took to drinking heavily and began talking to his revolver. He retired from the CIA in 1962. Some said he was a victim of paranoia, of manic-depressive psychosis, of logorrhea (excessive and often incoherent talkativeness). Others contended Hungary had broken his spirit. Either way, he killed himself with a shotgun blast in 1965.

The West was horrified by news reports that leaked from Hungary. Newspapers were full of front-page photos of young Hungarian freedom fighters throwing gasoline-bottle bombs at Russian tanks, graphic evidence of the brave but futile resistance. Hungarian freedom fighters had broadcast frantic pleas directly to Radio Free Europe from transmitters they had captured—pleas for military help, weapons, food and medical supplies the fighters claimed Radio Free Europe had promised.

The abortive revolt in Hungary was the end of Foster Dulles's policy of rolling back communism through "dynamism," the turning point for a return to containment as U.S. policy toward the Soviet Union and the People's Republic.

Immediately after the Soviets crushed the revolt, reports critical of the role Radio Free Europe played in the tragic events in Hungary began to circulate in American and West German news media.

On Nov. 11, the Ridder newspaper group published a critical story filed by Walter Ridder from Vienna, where most of some 200,000 or so Hungarian refugees who had fled their homeland ended up. Ridder and his wife spent the evening of Nov. 11 in a restaurant in Vienna with Wisner, who ranted about how the American government let Hungary down, about how he had been personally betrayed and disgraced and about how much money had been spent on Radio Free Europe to foment the revolt America failed to support. In the story Ridder filed, he said America's failure to come to the aid of Hungary had led to a great loss of American prestige in Europe. "For some years now," he alleged, "the Voice of America and to a much larger extent Radio Free Europe, an independent U.S. broadcasting outfit, have been urging the people of Satellite nations to revolt, promising them all-out U.S. help in their efforts to throw off the shackles of Russian tyranny."

The Soviets blamed RFE for inciting the revolt. Wisner himself warned Allen Dulles in a cable on Nov. 12 that many refugees in Vienna were criticizing RFE broadcasts into Hungary. A CIA officer said later of Allen Dulles's behavior, "When he heard we'd been doing some pretty nasty things, and stirring up captive peoples to expect things that weren't going to happen, he justified it morally... as being for the sake of the country."[113]

Did Radio Free Europe incite the Hungarians to revolt, as some critics charged? The answer in several whitewash investigations was, "No, but don't let it happen again!"

Immediately after the uprising, Radio Free Europe was asked to provide tapes of all its transmissions during the revolt to the West German government, which translated and analyzed what RFE provided. Based on analysis of the tapes it had been given, the German government told the Council of Europe that although a few injudicious statements had been broadcast, the tapes did not contain comments which could be regarded as direct incitement to riot.

In a second whitewash, the Council of Europe issued a report absolving Radio Free Europe of blame. The German government asked, however, that Radio Free Europe in future broadcasts confine itself to objective reporting of news and eliminate commentary which could be interpreted to imply promises of Western aid in the event of new revolts in the satellite states.[114]

Charges of Radio Free Europe culpability in the Hungarian revolt appeared in many American publications, including *Time, Life* and the *Saturday Evening Post*, posing a considerable public relations problem. John Patterson, with the advice of Arthur Page, engineered much of the Radio Free Europe denial of involvement.[115]

While the Free Europe organization was not successful in liberating Hungary in 1956, it won a propaganda victory. During the period of turmoil, it used its exile councils—especially the Hungarian National Council and Assembly of Captive European Nations—to advantage in molding world opinion in favor of the freedom fighters.[116]

Page heads the Crusade for Freedom

WILLIAM A. GREENE resigned as the paid president of the Crusade for Freedom in November 1956. Page agreed to replace him, but not as a full-time paid president. John Patterson, the executive vice president of the Crusade, retained his title but became the full-time chief executive.[117]

At the time Page moved into the presidency, the Crusade effort for 1956-1957 was just beginning. Eugene Holman had agreed to serve as Crusade chairman for a second time.[118] President Eisenhower again held a dinner for America's industrial titans at the White House, with Page handling behind-the-scenes details and making recommendations on invitees.[119]

The 1956-1957 Crusade fared only slightly better than the year earlier effort headed by Holman. It raised $3.0 million at a cost of $922,000.[120]

Earl Newsom, whose public relations firm worked for Standard Oil of New Jersey (Exxon), had recruited Holman to head the 1955-1956 and 1956-1957 Crusade efforts.

Page recruited Westinghouse Electric President Gwilym A. "Bill" Price to head the 1957-1958 effort. Page was a director of Westinghouse. He and Price were trustees of the Carnegie Corp. Westinghouse was a major supplier of broadcasting equipment to Radio Free Europe. In a letter to Holman, Page said he would agree to stay on for another year as president of the Crusade if Holman would agree to serve as chairman of the Crusade's executive committee. Holman accepted.[121]

Protecting Radio Free Europe from Fulton Lewis Jr.

FULTON LEWIS JR., a news commentator with a column syndicated by King Features and a nightly radio news show on the Mutual Broadcasting System, in late 1957 unleashed the most vitriolic attack against Radio Free Europe to occur in Page's 11 years with the organization.

Exactly what motivated Lewis to make the attacks is unknown. It was extremely unusual at the time for a journalist to criticize CIA operations. Such behavior could easily result in accusations of disloyalty, lack of patriotism or even treason.

Perhaps Lewis was upset at being left out of the cozy journalistic circles that patronized the CIA. At the time, Joseph Alsop and his brother Stewart were the favorite sources when the agency wanted to leak information from the "pickle factory" (as operatives were fond of calling the CIA) through the press to the public. *Washington Post* Managing Editor Alfred "Fred" Friendly was another trusted friend in the media. James Reston, the Washington Bureau chief of the *New York Times*, spent hours talking to Frank Wisner and, "over the back fence," to his next-door neighbor Paul Nitze. Fulton Lewis Jr. was not a member of this insider group.

Lewis fired his first shot in a column dated Oct. 2, 1957.

He began by charging that the Central Intelligence Agency secretly funded Radio Free Europe. He didn't object to the secret funding, but criticized the clandestine spending of taxpayer money on what he termed a "pinko" broadcasting operation. He alleged that leftists who had supported Tito-style communism in Czechoslovakia, forced to flee from their homeland in 1948, had formed the Council for Free Czechoslovakia and then been "shoehorned" by the State Dept. into the Radio Free Europe organization. The group since, he charged, had been broadcasting for a Tito-style dictatorship in Czechoslovakia instead of demanding establishment of a Western-style democracy in their native land.[122]

Thereafter, Lewis fired salvo after salvo on the air and in print until he finally tired of the attack in 1958.

Lewis's reporting was at first naive and inaccurate. In his first column, he appears not to know of the Council of Free Czechoslovakia's financial ties to the Free Europe Committee, and makes other mistakes. As his campaign progressed, however, and dissidents within the Free Europe organization began to leak information to him, the attacks came ever closer to truth.

In mid-November 1957, Lewis attacked the annual Crusade junkets to Europe for prestigious volunteers, and charged regarding secret CIA funding that "Every intelligence organization behind and outside of the Iron Curtain knows the truth, but Mr. (CIA Director Allen) Dulles won't tell the American taxpayers."[123]

Lewis went on to charge that the "overall management in New York is in the hands of a troop of rich men's sons, drawing fancy salaries for playing an adolescent game of amateur foreign intrigue."[124] Behind Lewis's sensationalistic invective lies more than a degree of truth. As was the case at the CIA, the Free Europe Committee's management had a large proportion of Ivy League-educated scions of wealthy families (especially from Yale) handling day-to-day operations. Heading the Free Europe Press operation in New York, for example, was 31-year-old Samuel S. Walker Jr., a Yale graduate, grandson to one of the New York bank fortunes. His assistant in New York was another graduate of Old Eli, John Kirk, son of Columbia University President Grayson Kirk. Walker's chief assistant in Europe, responsible for the balloon operations suspended in late 1956, was Howard S. Weaver, in 1957 about to be recalled to New York because of alleged involvement in a black market cigarette scandal in West Germany. Weaver had been a friend of Walker's at Yale.

Lest "Old Eli" take all the blame, it should be noted that fully one-fourth of the top CIA officers in this period were from Harvard, and Princeton was far from underrepresented.

In December, using information leaked to him from inside the Free Europe organization, Lewis indicated Radio Free Europe's budget was $20 million annually, not counting capital (equipment) expenditures. He began to document examples of profligacy in the organization. More than 130 employees were still on the Free Europe Press's balloon operation payroll 13 months after the project had been terminated, he charged.[125] Posh apartments had been built in Munich to house RFE staffers. RFE claimed that rents from the apartments made them self-supporting, but Lewis said he'd learned that staffers were paying no rent. When the German government complained about staffers being given use of Army post exchanges and commissaries, RFE ordered a stop to the practice but provided an extra allowance of up to $1,000 per year in compensation.[126]

Much of RFE's problem with refugee groups stemmed from resentment among the exiles over lucrative jobs given by RFE to the chosen few.

The Crusade for Freedom's immediate reaction to the Lewis attacks was to refute specific charges when possible in internal memoranda, seeking to discredit the whole by discrediting small parts, but to avoid answering the Lewis charges in the news media. Free Europe officers, after Joseph Grew discussed the attacks with Allen Dulles, decided the wisest course was to avoid a national confrontation with Lewis which might give wider publicity to his allegations.[127]

Page, chairman of the Free Europe executive committee and president of the Crusade for Freedom, finally broke the

Free Europe silence. He wrote to Lewis on Jan. 6, 1958, to provide him with detailed information on six individuals Lewis had charged once worked for Radio Free Europe and then defected to their home countries. Lax RFE security had permitted them to leave in possession of valuable information, Lewis charged.[128]

The next day, Page wrote to Grew to say the Crusade board, the Advertising Council and others had reached the unanimous conclusion that the Crusade had to say something publicly to refute Lewis. He said he had gotten Allen Dulles to reluctantly agree, and sent Grew a draft letter to Lewis on which he (Page) was working.[129]

A few weeks later, in response to Lewis's repeated charges that Willis Crittenberger and Gwilym Price refused to meet with him or talk to him by phone, Page wrote to Lewis and said he would meet with him at Lewis's convenience.[130] A meeting between Lewis, Page, and other Crusade officials was not finally arranged, however, until late February 1958.

By the time of the meeting, the Lewis attacks were beginning to tell. Stockholders of corporations that made large contributions to the Crusade began writing for information about Lewis's allegations. A Crusade treasurer in Indiana had to resign when a female devotee of Lewis who had a substantial interest in the bank for which he worked demanded that he sever his connection with the Crusade.[131]

Before meeting with Crusade officials, Lewis broke one of the most damaging and perhaps best documented of his attacks, a report on the case of Fletcher Bartholomew, a General Mills meteorologist who had been loaned to the Free Europe Press to work on the balloon leaflet project before it was discontinued. In July 1957, Bartholomew was scheduled to return home. Before leaving Munich, he wrote a memorandum detailing what he saw as weaknesses in Radio Free Europe operations in Germany. Among other things, he gave reasons why he suspected considerable homosexuality on the Free Europe staff. Homosexuality in an intelligence operation was believed dangerous because it could open an agent to blackmail by hostile powers.

Bartholomew gave one copy of his memorandum to American Consul Edward Page Jr. in Munich, sent one copy to Whitney Shepardson at the Free Europe Committee in New York and sent a third to a friend who was to deliver it personally to Allen Dulles at CIA headquarters. On the day Bartholomew was to return to the United States with his family, he was committed to an Army hospital in Munich by a social worker purporting to be a psychiatrist. Without the knowledge or consent of his wife, Bartholomew was moved to an Army hospital in Frankfurt, Germany, and then, heavily drugged, flown to the United States. Samuel Walker, the young head of the Free Europe Press, apparently sought to keep the actions secret from Whitney Shepardson and other responsible Free Europe officials.

A secretary, concerned about violation of Bartholomew's rights, blew the whistle. Shepardson intervened, and Bartholomew was released after considerable anguish to himself and his family. He agreed to let Lewis make the case public. Lewis made the most of the story. The U.S. Army in Germany had clearly operated in violation of regulations in the intrigue involving State Dept. and Free Europe officers.[132]

After airing the Bartholomew case, Lewis turned to publicizing information about the corporations making the largest donations to the Crusade for Freedom, and to demanding in print and on the air that Congress investigate Radio Free Europe and the Crusade. Willis Crittenberger made a hurried trip to Washington to confer with Eisenhower aide Jerry Persons. Page suggested that Persons get from the CIA the Haskins and Sells audits of the Free Europe organization in case an investigation developed.[133]

By Feb. 21, 1958, Page had approved letters to the Mutual Broadcasting System and King Features Syndicate detailing Radio Free Europe's point-by-point refutation of some charges Lewis had made. Copies of the letters were made available for all MBS affiliates that carried the Lewis news broadcasts and to all newspapers carrying Lewis's column.[134] Page opted to pinpoint the Free Europe counterattack in the specific media which had given voice to Lewis's charges.

Page had planned to meet with Lewis immediately after the counterattack letters were sent to the news media. But on Feb. 20, Page's secretary wired Lewis to say he had become critically ill in South Carolina and would not be able to meet with Lewis as planned. A private plane had been hired to fly him back to New York for hospitalization.[135]

A meeting involving Lewis, Willis Crittenberger, Earl Newsom, John C. Hughes and a few others was held on Feb. 22.[136] Lewis made a few isolated attacks on the Free Europe organization after that, but for all practical purposes, his opposition ended. William Buckley of the *National Review* stepped into the fray in its waning days, offering to conduct an independent investigation of the Free Europe organization, but nothing came of his offer.[137]

Decline of the Crusade for Freedom

CRUSADE FOR FREEDOM collections gradually declined from the start of the Fulton Lewis Jr. attacks to Page's death.

The 1957-1958 Crusade effort headed by Gwilym Price of Westinghouse Electric raised $2.6 million at a cost of $931,000, considerably off from the year-earlier campaign headed by Eugene Holman.[138] The publicized goal of the effort had again been $10 million. By publicizing the annual Crusade goal, and saying nothing about how much money was actually collected or what the costs had been, the Crusade was able to give the impression it was taking in far more than it actually was. The $10 million figure was accepted as the approximate amount of annual collections by many a gullible person, and by the *National Review.*[139]

With some coaxing from Page, Gwilym Price agreed to head the 1958-1959 Crusade effort. The second Crusade chaired by Price raised $2.5 million at a cost of $918,000.[140]

In June 1958, knowing Willis Crittenberger wished to resign as paid president of the Free Europe Committee, Page sounded out members of the FEC executive committee which he headed about the possibility of hiring New Jersey lawyer and politician Archibald Alexander as a replacement. The executive committee and eventually the FEC board approved, and Alexander succeeded Crittenberger in February 1959.[141]

On July 1, Page resigned as president of the Crusade. He had been serving for two years in the post, and wished to devote more of his time to the affairs of the Free Europe Committee. John Patterson, executive vice president of the Crusade, became president.[142]

Following his resignation as Crusade president, Page devoted considerable time to organization of the Western European Advisory Committee for Radio Free Europe. This group was created in response to a pointed suggestion by Dr. Frans J. Goedhart, who had written the Council of Europe report absolving Radio Free Europe of blame in fomenting the Hungarian revolt of 1956. Goedhart had visited Free Europe headquarters in New York after writing the report, and felt he had been brushed off. His response was to warn Free Europe officials they would be wise to involve Western Europeans in their operations in the future.[143]

Despite his age, Page accompanied Willis Crittenberger on a trip to Europe in November 1958 to recruit members for the proposed council from England, France, Belgium, Germany, Italy, Sweden, the Netherlands, Denmark, Norway and Portugal.[144] Names of individuals to be recruited were supplied by "our friends and those consulted across the street." "Our friends" is a scarcely veiled reference to the Central Intelligence Agency.[145] The terms "our friends" and "our friends in the South" are used frequently in Radio Free Europe documents as code words for the CIA.

Page and Crittenberger were eminently successful. Prominent statesmen from all the Western European nations agreed to join the proposed Western European Advisory Committee for RFE. Perhaps the two "biggest fish" landed were Professor Hugh Seton-Watson, an outstanding British expert on Eastern Europe, and Robert Schuman of France, chairman of the European Economic Assembly and regarded as the father of the European Coal and Steel Community. (Although Jean Monnet was the primary architect of the European Coal and Steel Community, it was named after Schuman who announced it.) Frans Goedhart of the Netherlands was also invited and accepted.[146]

The first meeting of the Western European Advisory Committee was held in Paris on May 20-21, 1959.[147]

Although Page had hoped to stay out of Crusade for Freedom planning, he grew concerned when General Motors President Harlow Curtice, whom the CIA wanted to chair the 1959-1960 Crusade, declined. Earl Newsom came to Page's rescue, obtaining the services of Campbell's Soup President William B. Murphy. Page wrote in gratitude: "What a man is Newsom! He stands upon the burning deck when all the rest have fled; he thinks up three candidates where no one else had any, and delivers the first of the three."[148]

While Murphy was serving as chairman of the Crusade, board members voted to change the name of the organization from Crusade for Freedom, Inc., to the Radio Free Europe Fund. The change became effective on July 1, 1960.[149] At about that time, the Crusade effort was running about $300,000 behind the prior year's campaign as a trend toward deemphasis on fund-raising continued.[150]

Page remained chairman of the Free Europe executive committee and interested in the affairs of the Radio Free Europe Fund to his death a few months later in 1960.

Death in September

IN MARCH 1960, Page entered the hospital for two operations for diverticulitis (a disease of the intestines and bladder) from which he had been suffering.[151]

In early May, he was back at work in his office.

He returned to the hospital again in August, and died on Sept. 5, 1960, shortly before his 77th birthday.

He was survived by his wife Mollie, all four of his children and numerous grandchildren.

A few weeks before he died, the Chase Manhattan Bank's Trust Dept. had estimated assets in the name of Arthur Page at $123,000 and assets in the name of Mollie Page at $684,000. Page's estate was willed solely to his wife. Following her death and the tax collector's bite, the remainder of the estate went to the four Page children.[152]

In addition to having been a successful magazine editor and book publisher, Page had loomed as a giant in the developing public relations field from 1927 to his death in 1960. The *New York Times,* picking up a line it had used in a story about Page in 1957, said in his obituary that he had concerned himself with the future.[153] That he had done.

Of great importance, he gave public relations practice a model for others to imitate. He had shown and taught that the job of public relations in a modern institution was to forecast where public opinion was going, and to adjust the institution so that it would be in harmony with public opinion in the present and future.

Above all, he perhaps more than any other pioneer in the public relations field had stressed the importance of action in the public interest over publicity as the keystone of good public relations.

Of the several obituaries published, the one that perhaps best summarized Page's career appeared in the October 1960 issue of AT&T's *195 Broadway Magazine.* One paragraph is an appropriate epitaph:

> Upon joining the Bell System, Mr. Page set out to build a strong public relations organization. In visits to associated companies throughout the country, he defined the public relations role in telephone operations and clearly emphasized that good service was the foundation of good public relations.

ENDNOTES

[1] See, for example, the timetable of Dean and David Heller, *The Cold War* (Derby, Conn.: Monarch Books, 1962).

[2] Walter LaFeber, *America, Russia and the Cold War 1945-1971* (New York: John Wiley and Sons, 1972), p. 30.

[3] Letter from Page to Under Secretary of State Robert A. Lovett, Oct. 21, 1947, Box 16, Arthur W. Page Papers. A small pencilled note on the letter indicates the job Page was turning down.

[4] Letter from Symington-Gould Corp. President C.J. Symington to Secretary of Commerce Henry A. Wallace, Jan. 2, 1946; letter from Symington to Chase National Bank head Winthrop W. Aldrich, Jan. 2, 1946; letter from Symington to Page, Jan. 2, 1946; letter from Page to Aldrich, Jan. 2, 1946; letter from Page to Aldrich, Jan. 10, 1946, with attached memorandum probably by Page, same date; and letter from Symington to Export-Import Bank head William McC. Martin Jan. 10, 1946, Box 13, Arthur W. Page Papers. See also letter from Kennecott Copper President E. Tappan Stannard to Page and others, Oct. 28, 1946, Box 69, Arthur W. Page Papers.

[5] Letter from C.J. Symington to Winthrop W. Aldrich, July 16, 1946, with attachments; letter from Page to retired Chase National executive Shepard Morgan, July 26, 1946; letter from Morgan to Page, Oct. 3, 1946, with attachments; letter to Page from Aldrich, Oct. 7, 1946; and letters from Symington to Page, Oct. 17 and 29, 1946, with attachments; Boxes 13-14, Arthur W. Page Papers.

[6] Letter from Page to Ivison Macadam in London, July 18, 1947, Box 15, Arthur W. Page Papers.

[7] Memorandum from Page to Winthrop W. Aldrich, Oct. 2, 1947; letter from Page to onetime Secretary of War Robert P. Patterson of Patterson, Belknap and Webb, Oct. 14, 1947, with attachment; and letter from Page to Patterson, Oct. 15, 1947; Box 69, Arthur W. Page Papers.

[8] Lists of the officers, executive committee and National Council members of the Committee for the Marshall Plan to Aid European Recovery appear in two pamphlets published by the group, "The Marshall Plan Is Up to You" and "A Statement of Purpose," copies of which are in Box 69, Arthur W. Page Papers. Alger Hiss was a protégé of John Foster Dulles. When George Franklin Jr. in 1946 wrote a Council on Foreign Relations paper suggesting U.S. cooperation with Russia in the postwar world, it was Frank Altschul, then secretary of the COFR board of directors, who led the charge against foreign aid to the Soviet Union.

[9] Letter from John H. Ferguson to Robert P. Patterson, attached to letter from Ferguson to Page, April 9, 1948. The Stimson Committee for the Marshall Plan spent $152,000 on its persuasive campaign through March 1948. By the time of the final audit in late 1948, the committee had spent $168,000 on its efforts.

[10] Cable to Page from former Stimson Committee Executive Director John H. Ferguson, May 25, 1949, and Page's reply, May 26, 1949, Box 70, Arthur W. Page Papers.

[11] "Foreign Policy and Bankers' Profits," editorial, *Chicago Sunday Tribune*, Feb. 6, 1955.

[12] Letter from Page to Harvey H. Bundy, July 9, 1945, Box 12, Arthur W. Page Papers.

[13] Letter from Page to John Martyn of the Office of the Secretary of War, Jan. 28, 1947; letter to Page from War Department Administrative Asst. George E. Brewer, March 17, 1947; letter to Page from Secretary of War Robert P. Patterson, March 20, 1947; letter from Page to Secretary of War Kenneth Royall, Aug. 27, 1947; and draft of classified report on military government about which Page and Royall conferred, Sept. 22-23, 1947; Boxes

14-16, Arthur W. Page Papers.

[14] See especially letter from Page to Gordon Wasson, Jan. 15, 1947; letter from Page to Harry A. Batten of N.W. Ayer and Son, Feb. 3, 1947; letter from Page to Randolph Burgess, Feb. 10, 1947 ; and letter from Page to Gen. George C. Marshall, Feb. 28, 1947; Box 14, Arthur W. Page Papers.

[15] Letters to Page from James Forrestal and Robert P. Patterson, Feb. 27, 1947; letter from Forrestal to John Lord O'Brian, April 16, 1947; and letter from Page to O'Brian, May 16, 1947; Boxes 14-15, Arthur W. Page Papers.

[16] See especially letter from Page to John Lord O'Brian, Sept. 12, 1947; letter from O'Brian to Page and other members of the Flight Pay Board, Dec. 11, 1947; and letter to Page from James Forrestal, Dec. 27, 1947; Box 16, Arthur W. Page Papers.

[17] Letter from Page to Secretary of War Robert P. Patterson, Jan. 3, 1947; letter to Page from Patterson, Jan. 24, 1947; letter from Page to Patterson, Feb. 14, 1947; letter to Page from Maj. Gen. W.S. Paul, May 23, 1947; letter from Page to Paul, June 2, 1947; letter to Page from Secretary of Defense James Forrestal, Dec. 8, 1947; letter from Page to Forrestal, Dec. 18, 1947; and letter from Forrestal to Page, Dec. 8, 1947; Boxes 14-16, Arthur W. Page Papers.

[18] See especially letter to Page from Rear Adm. Felix Johnson, June 24, 1947, and copy of speech Page made at National War College on May 27, 1949, Boxes 15 and 22, Arthur W. Page Papers.

[19] Letter from Page to Lt. Gen. J. Lawton Collins, Jan. 31, 1947, Box 14, Arthur W. Page Papers.

[20] Letter from Page to Capt. A.E. Buckley, Feb. 24, 1947, Box 14, Arthur W. Page Papers.

[21] Speech prepared for Maj. Gen. Floyd L. Parks headed "Purpose of Presentation," Box 14, Arthur W. Page Papers.

[22] Letter from Page to Gen. Omar Bradley, June 11, 1948, with attachment, Box 18, Arthur W. Page Papers.

[23] Letter from Page to Secretary of the Army Kenneth Royall, Aug. 2, 1948, Box 18, Arthur W. Page Papers, and Raleigh, *op. cit.,* pp. 183-85.

[24] Raleigh, *op. cit.,* p. 179.

[25] See especially letter to Page from Gen. Courtney H. Hodges, March 6, 1947; letter to Page from Hodges, March 31, 1947; letter to Page from *New York Times* General Manager Julius Ochs Adler, April 25, 1947; Box 69, Arthur W. Page Papers.

[26] The individuals active at the top levels of the Stimson Committee for the Marshall Plan who became active in the early operations of the National Committee for a Free Europe were Joseph C. Grew, DeWitt C. Poole, Frank Altschul, Allen Dulles, James B. Carey, Herbert Lehman, Arthur Page, Laird Bell, Francis Biddle, William J. Donovan, James A. Farley, William Green, Charles R. Hook, Robert P. Patterson, Charles P. Taft, Matthew Woll and Darryl Zanuck. Conspicuously absent from NCFE is the name of Alger Hiss. In 1948, Hiss was accused by *Time* Senior Editor Whitaker Chambers of being a communist. Hiss sued Chambers for libel, but was ultimately convicted of perjury.

[27] Among the 1949 members of the Council on Foreign Relations who were particularly active in formation of the National Committee for a Free Europe were resident members Frank Altschul, Adolf A. Berle Jr., William J. Donovan, Lt. Gen. Hugh A. Drum, Allen W. Dulles, Herbert H. Lehman, Arthur W. Page, Robert P. Patterson and DeWitt C. Poole, and nonresident members Laird Bell, Joseph C. Grew, George F. Kennan and Spencer Phenix. See Coun-

cil on Foreign Relations, *Annual Report of the Executive Director* (1948-1949), pp. 61-70. Many Council members not active in NCFE formation became active in paid or volunteer capacities in the first decade of NCFE operation. As for COFR being the common pool for both the Stimson Committee for the Marshall Plan and NCFE, it's worth noting the Ivy League cast of the COFR. Of the 55 officers and trustees running the New York COFR operation in 1946, 35 were Ivy League graduates, with the heaviest representations from Harvard (12), Columbia (9) and Yale (7). According to the Peter Grose history of COFR, the favorite clubs of the leadership were the Century and Knickerbocker in New York and Cosmos and Metropolitan in Washington.

[28] Lucius Clay's opposition to Radio Liberty is from Jean E. Smith, *Lucius D. Clay: An American Life* (New York, Henry Holt, 1990), p. 285. Discussion of Kennan talks leading to Radio Free Europe is from Allan A. Michie, *Voices through the Iron Curtain: The Radio Free Europe Story* (New York: Dodd, Mead and Co., 1963), especially p. 11, and Robert T. Holt, *Radio Free Europe* (Minneapolis: University of Minnesota Press, 1958), especially pp. 9-10. See also Herb Altschull, "Radio Free Europe Hits behind the Iron Curtain," *Waterbury (Conn.) American*, Oct. 2, 1957. Kennan's July 1947 article in *Foreign Affairs* was bylined "Mr. X." Walter Lippmann, boycotted from publishing in *Foreign Affairs* by its editor, devoted 13 of his newspaper columns to discussing the article.

[29] National Committee for a Free Europe, "Memorandum on Organization and Operations," July 25, 1949, Box 71, Arthur W. Page Papers.

[30] Letter from Page to Joseph C. Grew, May 18, 1949, and Grew's reply, May 24, 1949, Box 70, Arthur W. Page Papers.

[31] Copy for newspaper advertisement headed "The National Committee for a Free Europe," May 18, 1949, marked "To A.F. Hewitt," Box 70, Arthur W. Page Papers.

[32] Mosley, *op. cit.*, pp. 240-41.

[33] *Ibid.*, pp. 243-44.

[34] *Ibid.*, p. 246.

[35] See especially following Associated Press stories: "Radio Free Europe Fund Probe Asked," *Milwaukee Journal*, Jan. 24, 1971, sec. 1, p. 12, and "Phone Eavesdrops Disclosed by CIA," *Wisconsin State Journal*, Aug. 7, 1975, p. 72,

[36] National Committee for a Free Europe, "Memorandum on Organization and Operations," *op. cit.*, and NCFE, "The Free Europe University in Exile: An Interim Report as of August 6, 1951," the latter in Box 72, Arthur W. Page Papers. The Free Europe University in Exile was dismantled in 1958, two years after the abortive Hungarian uprising of 1956.

[37] National Committee for a Free Europe, "Annual Meeting, April 3, 1950, President's Report," Box 71, Arthur W. Page Papers.

[38] National Committee for a Free Europe, "Memorandum on Organization and Operations," *op. cit.*

[39] Peter Grose, *Gentleman Spy: The Life of Allen Dulles* (Boston and New York: Houghton Mifflin, 1994), pp. 305-25; National Committee for a Free Europe, "Annual Meeting, April 3, 1950, President's Report," *op. cit.*; and Mosley, *op. cit.*, p. 289

[40] Letters from Page to DeWitt C. Poole, July 11 and Aug. 15, 1949; letter from Dwight D. Eisenhower to Page, Aug. 15, 1949; and letter from Poole to Page, Aug. 11, 1949; Boxes 22 and 71, Arthur W. Page Papers.

[41] See especially letter from Page to Winthrop W. Aldrich, March 25,

1946; letter from Page to Maj. Gen. A.D. Surles, March 28, 1949; and letter to Page from Gen. Dwight D. Eisenhower, April 5, 1946, Box 13, Arthur W. Page Papers.

[42] Letter to Page from John Price Jones Co. Vice President Erwin D. Tuthill, Jan. 13, 1950, Box 71, Arthur W. Page Papers.

[43] John Price Jones Co., "Analysis and Plan of Fund-Raising for the National Committee for Free Europe," December 1949, with appended "Battle Plan" of fund-raising campaign advertising support prepared by Hewitt, Ogilvy, Benson and Mather, Box 71, Arthur W. Page Papers.

[44] Memorandum from Abbott Washburn to DeWitt C. Poole, Jan. 26, 1949, Box 71, Arthur W. Page Papers. Biographical background on Crabtree is from "Nate L. Crabtree Is Dead at 58," *New York Times*, Feb. 1, 1965, p. 23. See also Jean Edward Smith's *Lucius D. Clay: An American Life, op. cit.*

[45] Letter from Page to Lucius D. Clay, March 10, 1950, Box 71, Arthur W. Page Papers.

[46] Letter to Page from National Committee for a Free Europe executive Theodore C. Augustine, April 3, 1950, and letter to Page from John R. Burton, May 8, 1950, Box 71, Arthur W. Page Papers.

[47] C.L. Adcock, memorandum entitled "Crusade for Freedom Progress Report No. 2," May 18, 1950, and letter to Page from James M. Lambie Jr., May 31, 1950, Box 71, Arthur W. Page Papers.

[48] Agenda, Crusade for Freedom Committee Meeting, July 7, 1950, Box 72, Arthur W. Page Papers.

[49] Michie, *op. cit.*, pp. 2-4. Michie was a Radio Free Europe executive for a number of years and his book should be approached as less than objective.

[50] See especially memorandum to Page from C.L. Adcock, Aug. 17, 1950, Box 72, Arthur W. Page Papers.

[51] See especially memorandum from C.L. Adcock to Page, May 31, 1950, and pamphlet published by Crusade for Freedom, "7 Fateful Years, Crusade for Freedom, Inc., 1950-1957," published *ca.* January 1958, Boxes 71 and 79, Arthur W. Page Papers.

[52] Memorandum from C.L. Adcock to Page, Aug. 17, 1950, *op. cit.*

[53] Text of Eisenhower's speech appears in *New York Times*, Sept. 7, 1950, p. 35.

[54] Memorandum to Page from C.L. Adcock, Aug. 17, 1950, *op. cit.*, and "Crusade for Freedom: The Story of a Smash Campaign," internal Baldwin and Mermey public relations agency memorandum, Nov. 15, 1950, Box 2, William H. Baldwin Papers, State Historical Society of Wisconsin, Madison, hereafter referred to as the William H. Baldwin Papers.

[55] Memorandum to Page from C.L. Adcock, Aug. 17, 1950, *op. cit.*

[56] Memorandum from Baldwin and Mermey public relations agency to Lucius Clay, Nov. 8, 1950, Box 2, William H. Baldwin Papers.

[57] *Ibid.*, and memorandum from M. Law Jr. and M.D. Kirkwood of Hewitt, Ogilvy, Benson and Mather to A.F. Hewitt, "Subject: Digest of HOBM Services to NCFE, July-October 1950," dated Nov. 10, 1950, Box 72, Arthur W. Page Papers.

[58] Memorandum from Baldwin and Mermey to Lucius Clay, Nov. 8, 1950, *op. cit.*

[59] Memorandum from M. Law Jr. and M.D. Kirkwood to A.F. Hewitt, *op. cit.*,

[60] For a more detailed description of the first Crusade for Freedom Campaign, see Noel L. Griese, "Radio Free Europe's First Crusade for Freedom

Fund Drive: Post-Mortem of a Cold War Campaign," paper presented at annual convention of Assn. for Education in Journalism, August 1972, Carbondale, Ill.

[61] National Committee for a Free Europe, *Annual Report* (1950), p. 13; Drew Middleton, "Berlin Dedicates the Freedom Bell," *New York Times*, Oct. 25, 1950, p. 19.

[62] The $1 1/3 million figure for 1950 collections is in the National Committee for a Free Europe's 1950 *Annual Report, op. cit.*, p. 13. The $900,000 cost figure is from letter to Page from Crusade for Freedom President John M. Patterson, May 11, 1960, Box 81, Arthur W. Page Papers, and the $917,000 figure is in letter from Thomas D'A. Brophy to Henry Ford II, July 26, 1954, Box 75, Arthur W. Page Papers.

[63] Allen W. Dulles, John C. Hughes and W.M. Jackson, "Audit Report on National Committee for a Free Europe," June 29, 1950, Box 71, Arthur W. Page Papers.

[64] Holt, *op. cit.*, contains a discussion of the Free Europe Press balloon propaganda operation, and recounts the protests of the Soviet bloc that the balloons posed a danger to aviation.

[65] Letter from Royall Tyler to DeWitt C. Poole, Oct. 23, 1950, Box 72, Arthur W. Page Papers.

[66] Letter from Royall Tyler to DeWitt C. Poole, Dec. 6, 1950, Box 72, Arthur W. Page Papers.

[67] See especially letter to Page from Committee for a Free Asia President Alan Valentine, May 5, 1952; letter to Page from Ray T. Maddocks of Committee for a Free Asia, July 9, 1952; letter from Page to Allen W. Dulles at Central Intelligence Agency, Nov. 21, 1952; letter to Page from Brayton Wilbur, July 15, 1953; and letter to Page from Brayton Wilbur, Aug. 6, 1954; Boxes 73-75, Arthur W. Page Papers.

[68] Memorandum from Fred Smith to Adm. H.B. Miller (Ret.), May 15, 1952, Box 73, Arthur W. Page Papers.

[69] The Advertising Council, "Report on Crusade for Freedom Campaign 1952," Feb. 25, 1953, Box 73, Arthur W. Page Papers.

[70] Letter from Page to Richard L. Hill of the National Security Council Special Staff, the White House, July 27, 1953, Box 32, Arthur W. Page Papers.

[71] Letter to Edward C. Raleigh from Robert Cutler, Aug. 20, 1964, in Raleigh, *op. cit.*, pp. 54-55. Cutler in 1953 was a Special Assistant to the President for National Security Affairs.

[72] Raleigh, *op. cit.*, p. 53 ff.

[73] Letter to Page from John R. Burton Jr., March 31, 1950; letter from Page to Burton, April 7, 1950; letter from Abbott Washburn to Lucius D. Clay, April 26, 1950; letter from Washburn to Page, May 2, 1950; and letter from C.L. Adcock to Crusade for Freedom officials, June 16, 1950; Box 71, Arthur W. Page Papers.

[74] Letter to Page from John M. Patterson, May 11, 1960, *op. cit.*

[75] Letter from Anderson F. Hewitt to H.B. Miller, Jan. 28, 1953, with attachments, Box 74, Arthur W. Page Papers.

[76] Letter to Page from Greater New York Crusade for Freedom Chairman James Farley, Feb. 13, 1953; John Price Jones Co., "A Preliminary Plan for the Crusade for Freedom Sponsored by the American Heritage Foundation," July 1953; and letter to Page from Heritage-Crusade Project Executive Director C.M. Vandeburg, Aug. 19, 1953; Box 74, Arthur W. Page Papers.

[77] Radio Free Europe memorandum prepared for Hickenlooper Com-

mittee attached to letter to Page from Whitney H. Shepardson, April 24, 1953, Box 75, Arthur W. Page Papers. See also Lang, *op. cit.*

[78] News release, not on official Crusade stationery, March 22, 1953; letter from Page to Crusade executive Richard B. Walsh, March 25, 1952; and letter to Page from Walsh, March 31, 1953; Box 74, Arthur W. Page Papers.

[79] Letter to Page from Adolf A. Berle Jr., June 8, 1953, and Page's reply, June 9, 1953, Box 74, Arthur W. Page Papers.

[80] Guest list for Crusade for Freedom dinner at the White House, Sept. 23, 1953, Box 74, Arthur W. Page Papers.

[81] List of 38 companies which gave $10,000 or more to 1953-1954 Crusade for Freedom, attached to letter from Page to ten Crusade for Freedom and National Committee for a Free Europe officers, April 19, 1954, Box 75, Arthur W. Page Papers.

[82] Letter to Page from John M. Patterson, May 11, 1960, *op. cit.*

[83] Crusade for Freedom pamphlet, "Your Crusade for Freedom," *ca.* December 1953; NCFE pamphlet, "National Committee for a Free Europe: Weapon in the Struggle for Freedom," *ca.* January 1954; and Stephen King-Hall, *National News-Letter*, March 11, 1954; Box 75, Arthur W. Page Papers.

[84] Stephen King-Hall, *National News-Letter*, March 11, 1954, *op. cit.*, and Leland Stowe, "They Hit the Communists Where It Hurts," *Reader's Digest*, February 1954, pp. 48-52.

[85] King-Hall, *National News-Letter, op. cit.*

[86] Letter to Page from National Committee for a Free Europe President Whitney Shepardson, March 9, 1954, Box 75, Arthur W. Page Papers. Shepardson had replaced DeWitt C. Poole as president of Free Europe.

[87] Figures on balloon leaflets vary from source to source. The 377 million figure cited for 1954-1955 is from amended version of a presentation Arthur Page made before the Advertising Council on Jan. 19, 1956, Box 77, Arthur W. Page Papers.

[88] Materials relating to the trip of the Pages to Europe from May 7 through June 21, 1951, are in Box 75, Arthur W. Page Papers.

[89] Letter from Page to John Foster Dulles, June 21, 1954, and Dulles's reply, June 24, 1954, Box 35, Arthur W. Page Papers.

[90] Letter from Page to Whitney Shepardson, June 29, 1954, Box 75, Arthur W. Page Papers.

[91] Letter to Page from Thomas W. Braden, April 27, 1954, Box 75, Arthur W. Page Papers.

[92] Letter to Page from John M. Patterson, May 11, 1960, *op. cit.*

[93] Memorandum from William J. Convery Egan to Whitney Shepardson, Subject: "Mark Athridge (sic) Survey of RFE Information Field Apparatus," undated, with attached 22-page report, untitled, headed "CONFIDENTIAL," Box 76, Arthur W. Page Papers. Content of report indicates it was written *ca.* March 1955. See also Evan Thomas, *The Very Best Men* (New York: Simon & Schuster/Touchstone, 1995), p. 61.

[94] Letter from Page to Allen W. Dulles at the Central Intelligence Agency, Feb. 9, 1955, Box 76, Arthur W. Page Papers.

[95] Crusade-Heritage Operations Group, Minutes of Meeting of April 13, 1955, and letter from Page to Crusade for Freedom Chairman William A. Greene, April 14, 1955, both items in Box 76, Arthur W. Page Papers.

[96] Letter to Page from Robert E. Lang, March 8, 1955, Box 76, Arthur W. Page Papers.

[97] Announcement of the executive committee of the Free Europe Committee, Inc., March 15, 1955, Box 76, Arthur W. Page Papers.

[98] Letter from Page to Joseph C. Grew, Dec. 19, 1955, and letter to Page from Adolf A. Berle Jr., Dec. 20, 1955, Box 77, Arthur W. Page Papers.

[99] See especially letter from Page to Central Intelligence Agency executive Cord Meyer, Jan. 12, 1956, and letters to Page from Earl Newsom, Feb. 6, 1956, and March 12, 1956, Box 77, Arthur W. Page Papers.

[100] Letter from Page to Willis D. Crittenberger, July 31, 1956, Box 77, Arthur W. Page Papers.

[101] Crusade for Freedom, Minutes of Meeting of Executive Committee of May 31, 1956, Box 77, Arthur W. Page Papers.

[102] Letter to Page from John M. Patterson, May 11, 1960, *op. cit.*

[103] Letter to Eugene Holman from J.R. Wiggins, Jan. 4, 1956, Box 77, Arthur W. Page Papers.

[104] Draft letter for President Dwight D. Eisenhower to send to Eugene Holman, attached to letter from Page to Earl Newsom, March 21, 1956, Box 77, Arthur W. Page Papers.

[105] Letter from Page to Adolf A. Berle Jr., May 23, 1956, Box 77, Arthur W. Page Papers.

[106] Letter from President Dwight D. Eisenhower to Eugene Holman, May 23, 1956, Box 77, Arthur W. Page Papers.

[107] Untitled speech probably made by Arthur W. Page, Dec. 17, 1957, Box 78, Arthur W. Page Papers.

[108] Blum *et al.*, p. 792.

[109] See Holt, op. cit.

[110] LaFeber, *op. cit.*, pp. 192-93.

[111] Leonard Mosley, *Dulles: A Biography of Eleanor, Allen, and John Foster Dulles and Their Family Network* (New York: Dial Press/James Wade, 1978), p. 419.

[112] *Ibid.*, pp. 419-420.

[113] Walter T. Ridder, "Hungarians Are Bitter: American Prestige Is Damaged by Failure to Back Patriots," *New Haven (Conn.) Register*, Nov. 11, 1956, and Mosley, op. cit., p. 289

[114] The CIA officer who spoke of Allen Dulles's reaction was Howard Roman, quoted here from Mosely, *op. cit.*, p. 289.

[115] See especially the following reports of the Council of Europe: M. Altmaier, "Radio Free Europe and Its Associates," Dec. 8, 1956; Countess Finckenstein, "Radio Free Europe Broadcasting Station and the Hungarian Uprising," December 1956; and M. Goedhart, "Radio Free Europe Report," April 27, 1957. Copies of all three can be found in Boxes 78-79, Arthur W. Page Papers. The authors for the most part had only hearsay evidence on which to base judgments.

[116] Many documents relating to Radio Free Europe's response to attacks appear in Boxes 77-79, Arthur W. Page Papers. See especially letters from John M. Patterson to Page, Nov. 14 and 16, 1956, Box 77, and letter to Page from Bernard Yarrow of the Free Europe Committee, July 9, 1957, Box 78. See especially undated bulletin, "Steps of the ACEN in Regard to Situation of Poland and Hungary," attached to letter to Page from Bernard Yarrow, Nov. 1, 1956, and "A Draft Report of the Hungarian National Council October 23-December 31, 1956," attached to letter from Yarrow to Page, Feb. 19, 1957, Boxes 77-78, Arthur W. Page Papers.

[117] Crusade for Freedom news release, Nov. 5, 1956, Box 77, Arthur W. Page Papers. The story appeared in the *New York Times* of Nov. 12, 1956.

[118] *Ibid.*

[119] Much of Page's time was devoted to telling Crusade for Freedom staffers whom to approach at the White House dinners for what favors and donations. He could be blunt in his instructions. When John Patterson asked him who could best approach James Farley to ask a favor, Page let the value he placed on his personal friendships show when he replied: "...(A)nybody can know Jim Farley. He doesn't know me from Adam's Off Ox but used to write to me almost affectionately by my first name." See letter from Page to John M. Patterson, Feb. 6, 1957, Box 78, Arthur W. Page Papers.

[120] Letter to Page from John M. Patterson, May 11, 1960, *op. cit.*

[121] Crusade for Freedom Campaign Newsletter, July 1957, and letter from Page to Eugene Holman, April 3, 1957, Box 78, Arthur W. Page Papers.

[122] Fulton Lewis Jr., "'Radio Free Europe Loaded with Pinkos!", King Features Syndicate column appearing in *New York Mirror*, October 4, 1957.

[123] Fulton Lewis Jr. column, *New York Daily Mirror*, Nov. 14, 1957.

[124] Fulton Lewis Jr., "Spend, Spend—And No Accounting," *New York Mirror*, Nov. 18, 1957.

[125] Transcript of radio broadcast made by Fulton Lewis Jr., Dec. 20, 1957, Box 78, Arthur W. Page Papers. Transcript may be erroneously dated.

[126] Transcript of radio broadcast made by Fulton Lewis Jr., Dec. 20, 1957, different text than that in fn. immediately above, Box 78, Arthur W. Page Papers. Transcript may be erroneously dated.

[127] Letter to Page from Joseph C. Grew, Dec. 27, 1958, with attached letter from Grew to Willis A. Crittenberger, Box 78, Arthur W. Page Papers.

[128] Letter from Page to Fulton Lewis Jr., Jan. 6, 1958, with attachments, Box 79, Arthur W. Page Papers.

[129] Letter from Page to Joseph C. Grew, Jan. 7, 1958, Box 79, Arthur W. Page Papers.

[130] Letter from Page to Fulton Lewis Jr., Jan. 24, 1958, Box 79, Arthur W. Page Papers.

[131] Letter to Page from John M. Patterson, Jan. 27, 1958, with attachment, Box 79, Arthur W. Page Papers.

[132] Transcripts of MBS radio broadcasts by Fulton Lewis Jr. on Jan. 28, 29 and 30, 1958, Box 79, Arthur W. Page Papers.

[133] Transcript of Fulton Lewis Jr. MBS radio broadcast of Feb. 4, 1958, and letter from Page to Deputy Asst. to the President Gen. Wilton B. Persons, Feb. 5, 1958, Box 79, Arthur W. Page Papers.

[134] Letter from Willis Crittenberger to Page, transmitting to Page draft letters addressed to Mutual Broadcasting System and King Features Syndicate, Feb. 18, 1958, Box 79, Arthur W. Page Papers. Printed versions of the letters are dated Feb. 21, 1958.

[135] Telegram from Ethel Betts to Fulton Lewis Jr., Feb. 20, 1958, Box 79, Arthur W. Page Papers.

[136] Transcript of radio broadcast by Fulton Lewis Jr., Feb. 26, 1958, Box 79, Arthur W. Page Papers.

[137] See "'Mr. Lewis and Radio Free Europe," editorial, *National Review*, March 29, 1958, pp. 297-300.

[138] Letter to Page from John M. Patterson, May 11, 1960, *op. cit.*

[139] "Mr. Lewis and Radio Free Europe," *National Review, op. cit.*

[140] Letter to Page from John M. Patterson, May 11, 1960, *op. cit.*

[141] Letter from Page to Adolf A. Berle Jr., John C. Hughes, Joseph C. Grew, Charles M. Spofford, Whitney Shepardson, H. Gregory Thomas and C.D. Jackson, June 5, 1958, and Page's agenda for annual meeting of Free

Europe Committee, Inc., Sept. 10, 1958, Boxes 79-80, Arthur W. Page Papers.

[142] Based essentially on Crusade for Freedom, Minutes of Meeting of Board of Directors, June 12, 1958, Box 79, Arthur W. Page Papers.

[143] Letter from F.J. Goedhart to Willis D. Crittenberger, Oct. 28, 1957, Box 78, Arthur W. Page Papers.

[144] Untitled brown binder in Box 80, Arthur W. Page Papers, containing itinerary for trip by Page and Willis D. Crittenberger to Europe Nov. 15-28, 1958.

[145] Memorandum from Richard J. Condon and Lewis Galantiere to Page and Willis D. Crittenberger, Sept. 26, 1958, in brown folder mentioned in fn. 139, p. 509.

[146] *Ibid.*, and letter from Page to Joseph C. Grew, Dec. 19, 1958, Box 80, Arthur W. Page Papers.

[147] "West European Advisory Committee Inaugural Committee Session, Paris, May 20-21, 1959," Box 81, Arthur W. Page Papers.

[148] Letter from Page to Earl Newsom, Oct. 29, 1959, Box 81, Arthur W. Page Papers.

[149] Letter to Page from W.B. Murphy, June 22, 1960, Box 81, Arthur W. Page Papers.

[150] Letter to Page from John M. Patterson, May 11, 1960, *op. cit.*

[151] Raleigh, *op. cit.*, p. 63.

[152] Letter to author from Arthur W. Page Jr., Aug. 19, 1975, and letter to Arthur Page Sr. from Chase Manhattan Bank Vice President Ernest R. Keifer, Aug. 16, 1960, in possession of author.

[153] "Arthur Page, 76, Consultant, Dies," *New York Times*, Sept. 7, 1960.

Selected Bibliography

Books

Binkin, Martin, and Eitelberg, Mark J., with Schexnider, Alvin J., and Smith, Marvin M. *Blacks and the Military*. Washington, D.C.: The Brookings Institution, 1982.

Bird, Kai.
    The Chairman: John J. McCloy, The Making of the American Establishment. New York: Simon & Schuster, 1992.
    The Color of Truth McGeorge Bundy and William Bundy: Brothers in Arms. New York: Simon & Schuster, 1998.

Blankenhorn, Heber. *Adventures in Propaganda*. Boston: Houghton Mifflin, 1919.

Blum, John M.; Catton, Bruce; Morgan, Edmund S.; Schlesinger, Arthur Jr.; Stampp, Kenneth M.; and Woodward, C. Vann. *The National Experience*. New York: Harcourt, Brace and World, 1968.

The Book of the Children of Allison Francis Page and Catherine Raboteau Page. Private printing, 1921.

Cohen, Daniel. *The Manhattan Project*. Brookfield, Conn.: The Millbrook Press, 1999.

Conrad, Will C.; Wilson, Kathleen; and Wilson, Dale. *The Milwaukee Journal: The First Eighty Years*.

Converse, Jean M. *Survey Research in the United States: Roots and Emergence, 1890-1960*. Berkeley: University of California Press, 1987.

The Country Life Press. Garden City, N.Y.: Doubleday, Page and Co., 1919.

Danielian, N.R. *A. T. & T.: The Story of Industrial Conquest*. New York: Vanguard Press, 1939.

Daniels, Josephus.
    Editor in Politics. Chapel Hill, N.C.: University of North Carolina Press, 1941.
    Tar Heel Editor. Chapel Hill, N.C.: University of North Carolina Press, 1939.

Davis, John H. *The Guggenheims: An American Epic*. New York: William Morrow & Co., 1978

Doran, George H. *Chronicles of Barabbas 1884-1934*. New York: Harcourt Brace, 1935.

Eliot, Charles W. *Harvard Memories*. Cambridge, Mass.: Harvard University Press, 1923.

Emery, Edwin. *The Press and America*. Englewood Cliffs, N.J.: Prentice-Hall, 1962.

Ewen, Stuart. *PR! A Social History of Spin*. New York: Basic Books/ HarperCollins, 1996.

Gaston, Paul M. *The New South Creed: A Study in Southern Myth-making*. New York: Vintage Books, 1973.

Gifford, Walter S. *Addresses, Papers and Interviews by Walter S. Gifford*. Private printing.

Gilbert, Martin. *The First World War: A Complete History*. New York: Henry Holt, 1994.

Golden, L.L.L. *Only by Public Consent*. New York: Hawthorne Books, 1968.

Gregory, Ross. *Walter Hines Page, Ambassador to the Court of St. James's*. Lexington, Ky.: University Press of Kentucky, 1970.

Grose, Peter.

Continuing the Inquiry: The Council on Foreign Relations from 1921 to 1996. New York: Council on Foreign Relations, 1996.

Gentleman Spy: The Life of Allen Dulles. New York and Boston: Houghton Mifflin, 1994.

Gruening, Ernest. *The Public Pays... And Still Pays.* New York: Vanguard Press, 1964.

Handlin, Oscar. *America, A History.* New York: Holt, Rinehart and Winston, 1968.

Heller, Dean, and Heller, David. *The Cold War.* Derby, Conn.: Monarch Books, 1962.

Hendrick, Burton J.
 The Life and Letters of Walter H. Page. 3 vols. Garden City, N.Y.: Doubleday, Page and Co., 1923.
 The Training of an American. Boston and New York: Houghton Mifflin, 1928.

Hiebert, Ray Eldon. *Courtier to the Crowd.* Ames, Iowa: Iowa State University Press, 1966.

Holt, Robert T. *Radio Free Europe.* Minneapolis: University of Minnesota Press, 1958.

Hyman, Sidney. *The Lives of William Benton.* Chicago: University of Chicago Press, 1969.

Josephy, Alvin M. Jr., ed. *The American Heritage History of World War I.* New York: American Heritage Publishing/Simon & Schuster, 1964.

Kirchberger, Joe H. *The First World War: An Eyewitness History.* New York: Facts on File, 1992.

LaFeber, Walter. *America, Russia and the Cold War 1945-1971.* New York: John Wiley and Sons, 1972.

Lankford, Nelson D. *The Last American Aristocrat: The Biography of Ambassador David K. Bruce.* Boston and New York: Little, Brown & Co., 1996.

Leavell, J. Perry Jr. *Harry S. Truman.* New York: Chelsea House, 1988.

Lifton, Robert J., and Mitchell, Greg. *Hiroshima in America.* New York: Avon Books, 1995.

Leuchtenburg, William E., ed. *Woodrow Wilson: The New Freedom.* Englewood Cliffs, N.J.: Prentice-Hall, 1961.

Lundberg, Ferdinand. *The Rich and the Super-Rich.* New York: Bantam Books, 1968.

Lyon, Peter. *Success Story: The Life and Times of S.S. McClure.* New York: Charles Scribner's Sons, 1963.

Marchand, Roland. *Creating the Corporate Soul: The Rise of Public Relations and Corporate Imagery in American Big Business.* Berkeley: University of California Press, 1998.

McCullough, David. *Truman.* New York: Simon & Schuster/Touchstone, 1992.

Michie, Allan A. *Voices through the Iron Curtain: The Radio Free Europe Story.* New York: Dodd, Mead and Co., 1953.

Morgan, Ted. *FDR: A Biography.* New York: Simon & Schuster, 1985.

Morison, Elting E. *Turmoil and Tradition.* Boston: Houghton Mifflin, 1960.

Morison, Samuel Eliot. *The Oxford History of the American People.* New York: Oxford University Press, 1965.

Mosley, Leonard. *Dulles: A Biography of Eleanor, Allen, and John Foster Dulles and Their Family Network.* New York: The Dial Press/James Wade, 1978.

Mott, Frank Luther. *A History of American Magazines.* Cambridge, Mass.: Harvard University Press, 1957. Vol. 4.

Nalty, Bernard C., and MacGregor, Bernard C., eds. *Blacks in the Military: Essential Documents.* Wilmington, Delaware: Scholarly Resources, 1981.

Page, Arthur W.
 The Bell Telephone System. New York: Harper and Brothers, 1941.
 Our 110 Days' Fighting. Garden City, N.Y.: Doubleday, Page, 1920.

Page, Arthur W.; Arnold, H.D.; Otterson, John E.; Fletcher, Harvey; Bown,

Ralph; Jewett, Frank B.; and Ives, Herbert E. *Modern Communication.* Boston and New York: Houghton Mifflin, 1932.

Page, Walter H. *The School That Built a Town.* New York: Harper and Brothers, 1952.

Peterson, Theodore. *Magazines in the Twentieth Century.* Urbana., Ill.: University of Illinois Press, 1956.

Pound, Arthur. *The Telephone Idea.* New York: Greenberg, 1926.

Raucher, Alan. *Public Relations and Business, 1900-1929.* Baltimore: Johns Hopkins Press, 1968.

Robertson, David. *Sly and Able: A Political Biography of James F. Byrnes.* New York: W.W. Norton, 1994.

Regier, Cornelius C. *The Era of the Muckrakers.* Chapel Hill, N.C.: University of North Carolina Press, 1932.

Smith, Jean Edward. *Lucius D. Clay: An American Life.* New York: Henry Holt, 1990.

Swados, Harvey. *Years of Conscience.* Cleveland and New York: World Publishing Co.-Meridian Books, 1962.

Sweeney, Maj. Gen. Charles W., with James A. and Marion K. Antonucci. *War's End: An Eyewitness Account of America's Last Atomic Mission.* New York: Avon Books, 1997.

Thomas, Evan. *The Very Best Men.* New York: Simon & Schuster/Touchstone, 1995.

Tuchman, Barbara W. *The Zimmermann Telegram.* New York: Macmillan, 1958, 1966.

Vail, Theodore N. *Views on Public Questions.* New York: private printing, 1917.

Winter, J.M. *The Experience of World War I.* New York: Oxford University Press, 1989.

Wynn, Neil A. *The Afro-American and the Second World War*, Rev. Ed. New York & London: Holmes & Meier, 1993.

Magazine Articles and Editorials

"Admiral Sims and Mr. Daniels," *World's Work*, March 1920, pp. 425-28.

"An American Navy at Last," *World's Work*, October 1916, pp. 608-09.

Archbold, John D. "The Standard Oil Co.: Some Facts and Figures," *Saturday Evening Post*, Dec. 7, 1907, pp. 3-5, 32.

"Arthur W. Page, Our New Director," *The Chase* (published by the Chase National Bank), March 1934.

"The Autobiography of a Magazine," World's Work Advertiser, *World's Work*, Vol. 1.

Baker, Franklin T. "The Model Preparatory School," *World's Work*, September 1903, pp. 3886 and 3889.

Baker, Ray Stannard. "Railroads on Trial," *McClure's*, March 1906, pp. 535-44.

Blankenhorn, Heber. "The War of Morale: How America 'Shelled' the German Lines with Paper," *Harper's*, September 1919, pp. 514-15.

Blasier, S. Cole. "Chile: A Communist Battleground," *Political Science Quarterly* 65 (September 1950): 353-75.

"California's Japanese Problem Solved," *World's Work*, February 1924, pp. 355-57.

Chapman, Henry G. "The Progress of Honesty," *World's Work*, March 1901, pp. 509-14.

Clark, C.A., Jr. "Kennecott Copper Low-Cost Production Keeps Earnings Level High," *Barron's*, March 1953, pp. 23 ff.

Crowther, Samuel.
"On the Trail of the Reds," *World's Work*, February 1920, pp. 341-45.
"Radical Propaganda—How It Works," *World's Work*, April 1920, pp.

618-24.

Cuniff, M.G. "The Post-Office and the People," *World's Work*, December 1903, pp. 4074-85.

"Destroyers to the Rescue," *World's Work*, October 1917, pp. 589-91.

Dosch-Fleurot, Arno. "Louvain the Lost," *World's Work*, October 1914, pp. A-H.

Doubleday, Frank N. "Some Impressions of John D. Rockefeller," *World's Work*, September 1908, pp. 10703-15.

Duffus, Robert L. "Salesmen of Hate: The Ku Klux Klan," *World's Work*, May-September, 1923, pp. 31-38, 174-83, 275-84, 363-72 and 527-36.

"The Editor," *World's Work*, July 1915, pp. 269 ff.

"England Is 'The Mother Country' in New York Public Schools," *World's Work*, Vol. 44, September 1922, pp. 458-60.

"The Federal Budget System," *World's Work*, May 1915, pp. 13-14.

"For Diplomacy," *Business Week*, April 14, 1945, p. 34.

Fosdick, Raymond B. "The Leisure Time of a Democratic Army," *Survey Graphic*, June 1942, pp. 280-85.

"Froth and Truth about Trusts," *World's Work*, November 1900, p. 18.

Gibson, Hugh S. "A Journal from Our Legation in Belgium," *World's Work*, August-December, 1917.

Gifford., Walter S. "The Changing Character of Big Business," *World's Work*, June 1926, pp. 166-68.

"The Gist of Sims' Criticisms," *World's Work*, May 1920, pp. 122-23.

"Governor Cox's Pro-Germanism," *World's Work*, September 1920, p. 427

Golden, L.L.L. "Public Relations: Lessons of History," *Saturday Review*, July 8, 1967, p. 62.

"The Great Standard Oil Fine," *World's Work*, September 1908, pp. 10633-34.

Griswold, George H. Jr. "How AT&T Public Relations Policies Developed," *Public Relations Quart*erly 12 (Fall 1967): 7-16.

Hale, William Bayard. "Woodrow Wilson: Possible President," *World's Work*, May 1911, pp. 14399-53.

Hanson, Ole.
  "Fighting the Reds in Their Home Town," *World's Work*, January 1920, pp. 302-07.
  "On the Trail of the Reds," *World's Work*, December 1919, pp. 123-26.
  "Smashing the Soviets in Seattle," *World's Work*, March 1920, pp. 484-87.

Hendrick, Burton J.
  "America and England: The London Letters of Walter H. Page," *World's Work*, August 1921, pp. 246-60.
  "The American 'Home Secretary,'" *World's Work*, August 1913, pp. 396-405.
  "The Case of Josephus Daniels," *World's Work*, July 1916, pp. 281-96.
  "New Page Letters," *World's Work*, June 1925, pp. 139-47.
  "Washington in the Summer of 1916," *World's Work*, June 1922, pp. 150-68.
  "The Zimmermann Telegram to Mexico, and How It Was Intercepted," *World's Work*, November 1925, pp. 23-36.

Holman, Charles. "How Siberia Got Rid of Bolshevism," *World's Work*, June 1919, pp. 135-47.

Houston, David F. "Eight Years with Wilson 1913-1921," *World's Work*, February-September 1926.

"Information, Not Argument," *World's Work*, August 1917, pp. 359-60.

Ingalls, Albert. "Ultra-Violet Transmitting Glass—Has It Made Good?", *Scientific American*, April 1929, pp. 338-43.

Jaques, W.K. "A Picture of Meat Inspection," *World's Work*, May 1906, pp. 7491-505.

"The Jews and the Colleges," *World's Work*, August 1922, pp. 351-52.

"Keep Up the Bars against Immigration," *World's Work*, June 1922, pp. 127-28.

Keys, C.M. "The Large Corporations," *World's Work*, August-September 1908, pp. 10571-90 and 10683-702.

Lawrence, Col. Thomas E. "Arabian Nights and Days," *World's Work*, July-October 1921, pp. 277-88, 381-86, 516-20 and 617-21.

Lewis, David L. "The Outstanding PR Professionals," *Public Relations Journal*, October 1970, pp. 78-80, 84.

Mabon, Prescott, C. "The Art of Arthur Page," *Public Relations Journal*, March 1971, pp. 5-9.

"A Magazine of International Affairs," *World's Work*, May 1922, pp. 13-14.

McAdoo, William Gibbs. "The Soul of a Corporation," *World's Work*, March 1912, pp. 579-92.

"Mr. Bryan's Retirement and Its Significance," *World's Work*, July 1915, p. 270 ff.

"Mr. Lewis and Radio Free Europe," *National Review*, March 29, 1958, pp. 297-300.

"Mr. McAdoo, Mr. Palmer, and Others," *World's Work*, May 1920, pp. 10-11.

"The Mystics Descent upon Washington," *World's Work*, March 1922, p. 457,

"A New Series of Letters from Walter Hines Page to President Wilson," *World's Work*, May 1925, pp. 25-26.

"A Notable Victory for Academic Freedom," *World's Work*, January 1904, pp. 4284-87.

"Opinion Survey Research Results," *Public Relations Journal*, February 1974, p. 35.

Page, Arthur W.

"The *Advocate* at the Inauguration," *Harvard Advocate* 78, p. 113.

"Are the Colleges Doing Their Job?", *World's Work*, September 1910, pp. 13431-39.

"Campaigning," *Harvard Advocate* 78, p. 15.

"Communications by Wire and Wireless," *World's Work*, January 1907, pp. 8408-22.

"The Cotton Growers," *World's Work*, January 1906, pp. 7049-59.

"The End of Blackwell's Tiger," *Harvard Advocate* 74, pp. 77-79.

"Ephraim's Fall," *Harvard Advocate* 74, pp. 37-38.

"A Fight for Conservation," *World's Work*, November-December 1910, pp. 13607-11 and 13748-60.

"The Fight for a Land Conscience," *World's Work*, November 1907, pp. 9588-93.

"A Half Hour's Freedom," *Harvard Advocate* 73, pp. 88-89.

"Henry L. Stimson—A Character Sketch," *Current History*, April 1929, p. 7.

"Houston of Agriculture," *World's Work*, December 1931, pp. 149-59.

"How the Wrights Discovered Flight," *World's Work*, August 1910, pp. 13303-18.

"Little Pictures of O. Henry," *Bookman*, June-August 1913, pp. 381-87, 498-508, 607-16 and October 1913, pp. 169-77.

"The Meaning of What Happened at Chicago," *World's Work*, August 1920, pp. 361-77.

"On the River Dan," *Harvard Advocate* 77, p. 28.

"The Real Conquest of the West," *World's Work*, December 1907, p. 9691 ff.

"The Rediscovery of Our Greatest Wealth," *World's Work*, May 1908, pp. 10223-28.

"Running a River through a Mountain," *World's Work*, September 1907, pp. 9322-30.

"Secretary of War Lindley M. Garrison," *World's Work*, July 1913, pp. 292-301.

"Some Profitable Statistics," *Harvard Advocate* 78, pp. 15-16.

"The Statesmanship of Forestry," *World's Work*, January 1908, pp. 9734-57.

"The Strength Test," *Harvard Advocate* 78, p. 86.

"The Truth about Our 110 Days' Fighting," *World's Work*, April-June 1919, p. 62 ff. and pp. 69-85 and 159-83.

"An Unfinished Story," *Harvard Advocate* 73, p. 69.

"A War Time Game," *Harvard Advocate* 75, pp. 108-09.

"Why the Allies Expect To Win," *World's Work*, February 1917, pp. 356-62.

Page, Arthur W., and McHugh, Keith S. "What Should a Business Do about Public Relations," *Advertising and Selling*, October 1946, pp. 41-42 ff.

Page, Ralph W. "From a Law Office to a Cotton Farm," *World's Work*, November 1911, pp. 114-17.

Page, Walter H.

"On a Tenth Birthday," *World's Work*, January 1911, pp. 13903-17.

"Study of an Old Southern Borough," *Atlantic Monthly*, May 1881, pp. 648-58.

"What the *World's Work* Is Trying To Do," *World's Work*, January 1913, pp. 265-68.

"Pan-Germanism in the United States," *World's Work*, June 1915, pp. 135L-135P.

Pratt, Sereno S.

"Our Financial Oligarchy," *World's Work*, October 1905, pp. 6704-14.

"The President—Why He Should and Should Not Be Reelected," *World's Work*, August 1916, pp. 367-69.

"Presidential Weather and Timber," *World's Work*, November 1910, p. 13574.

"Public Confidence and the Censor," *World's Work*, July 1917, pp. 243-44.

"The 'Publicity Men' of Corporations," *World's Work*, July 1906, p. 7703.

Rockefeller, John D. "Some Reminiscences of Men and Events," *World's Work*, October 1908-April 1909, pp. 10755-68, 10878-94, 10992-11004, 11101-10, 11218-28, 11341-55 and 11470-78.

Rhoad, Julie A. "Special Delivery," *American Legion* magazine, April 2001, pp. 34-35.

Schrag, Peter. "America Needs an Establishment," *Harper's*, December 1975, pp. 51-58.

Shaw, Adele Marie. "The True Character of New York Public Schools," *World's Work*, December 1903, pp. 4204-21.

Sims, William S., and Hendrick, Burton J. "The Victory at Sea," *World's Work*, September 1919-July 1920.

Sinclair, Upton. "The Socialist Party," *World's Work*, April 1906, pp. 7431-32

"A Spanish Edition of the *World's Work*," *World's Work*, February 1915, p. 374 .

Spargo, John.

"Bolshevism, A Caricature of Marx's Theories," *World's Work*, November 1919, pp. 28-36.

"The Psychology of the Parlor Bolsheviki," *World's Work*, December 1919, pp. 127-31.

"Why the I.W.W. Flourishes," *World's Work*, January 1920, pp. 243-47.

Speranza, Gino.

"The Immigration Peril," *World's Work*, November 1923-May 1924.

"Playing Horse with American History," *World's Work*, April 1923, pp. 602-10.

Stockbridge, Frank Parker. "With Governor Wilson in the West," *World's Work*, August 1911, pp. 14713-16.

Strother, French.

"Crime and Eugenics," Part 1, *World's Work*, December 1924, pp. 168-74.

"The New Leadership of Business," *World's Work*, June 1926.

Sullivan, Mark.

"Carter Glass—Sound Democrat," *World's Work*, May 1920, pp. 7882.

"Congress and the Alien Restriction Law," *World's Work*, February 1924, pp. 436-42.

"The Democratic Dark Horse Pasture," *World's Work*, July 1923, pp. 285-92.

"Who Will Lead the Democrats," *World's Work*, June 1924, pp. 146-53.

"This Is To Be No Pink Tea Campaign," *World's Work*, November 1920, p. 10.

"Those Who Voted against the Republic," *World's Work*, May 1918, pp. 13-14.

"The Trusts and Wages," *World's Work*, November 1900, pp. 18-19.

"Ultra-Violet Windows," *Science*, Vol. 70, pp. x-xiii.

"Who Owns Our Corporations," *World's Work*, May 1926, pp. 11-13.

Wiggam, Albert E. "The Rising Tide of Degeneracy," *World's Work*, November 1926, pp. 25-33.

Wilson, Robert F. "Sims, of the Successful Indiscretions," *World's Work*, July 1917, pp. 333-40.

"Wood and the 'Leading' Republican Candidates," *World's Work*, August 1920, pp. 12-13.

Wood, Kenneth P. "Understanding Fifty Million Customers," *Public Relations Quarterly* 12 (Fall 1967): 17-24.

Woodlock, Thomas F. "The Uplift in Business," *World's Work*, July 1904, pp. 4955-58.

Collected Documents

Cambridge, Mass. Harvard University. Walter Hines Page Papers.
Madison, Wis. State Historical Society of Wisconsin.
    Arthur W. Page Papers.
    John M. Shaw Papers.
    William H. Baldwin Papers.

Newspapers

Chicago Tribune, Feb. 6, 1955.

Daily Mirror (New York), Oct. 4, 1957, Nov. 14, 1957, Nov. 18, 1957, April 15, 1958.
Herald-Tribune (New York), Feb. 15, 1930, Feb. 9, 1945.
Milwaukee Journal, Jan. 24, 1971.
New Haven Register (Connecticut), Nov. 11, 1956.
New York Times, Dec. 19, 1899, Nov. 18, 1904, April 1, 1913, March 13, 1915, July 3, 1915, Aug. 5, 1915, June 4, 1916, July 22, 1916, Aug. 12-14, 1916, Aug. 16, 1916, Sept. 19, 1916, Oct. 13, 1918, Nov. 1, 1918. Nov. 9, 1918, Dec. 23, 1918, July 4, 1923, May 5, 1924, May 26, 1924, May 29, 1924, June 2, 1924, June 20, 1924, June 23, 1924, June 26, 1924, June 28, 1924, June 30, 1924, July 10, 1924, Oct. 28, 1924, Dec. 6, 1925, Nov. 24, 1926, Jan. 24, 1927, March 27, 1927, July 28, 1927, June 24, 1928, July 1, 1928, Nov. 18, 1928, Nov. 15, 1929, Feb. 15, 1930, March 22, 1930, Sept. 8, 1932, Dec. 22, 1932, Jan. 12, 1933, April 6, 1933, May 17, 1933, June 7, 1933, Oct. 18, 1933, Oct. 28, 1933, Jan. 10, 1934, Feb. 8, 1945, Aug. 7, 1945, Oct. 26, 1946, April 6, 1948, Oct. 25, 1950, Sept. 7, 1950, Nov. 12, 1956, Sept. 7, 1960, Feb. 1, 1965.
News Leader (Richmond, Va.), March 26, 1919.
Wall Street Journal, Dec. 14, 2000.
Waterbury American (Connecticut), Oct. 2, 1957.
Wisconsin State Journal (Madison), July 26, 1970, Aug. 7, 1975.

Unpublished Materials

Ellsworth, James D. "The Twisting Trail," 1936 memoirs, Mass Communications History Center, State Historical Society of Wisconsin, Madison. (Typewritten.)

Hamel, George F. "John W. Hill, Public Relations Pioneer." Master's thesis, University of Wisconsin-Madison, 1966.

Long, Norton W. "The Public Relations Policies of the Bell System: A Case Study in the Politics of Modern Industry." Ph.D. dissertation, Harvard University, 1937.

Moranda, George E. "Arthur Wilson Page: His Formative Years." Term paper, University of Wisconsin-Madison, 1963.

Raleigh, Edward C. "In the Public Interest: The Government Service of Arthur Wilson Page." Master's thesis, University of Wisconsin-Madison, 1965.

Oral Reminiscences

Hendrick, Burton J. *Oral History Project: The Reminiscences of Burton J. Hendrick.* New York, Oral History Research Office-Columbia University, 1972.

Page, Arthur W. *The Reminiscences of Arthur W. Page.* New York, Oral History Research Office-Columbia University, 1972.

Speeches

Griese, Noel L. "For One Brief Shining Moment." Speech at Southern Bell Telephone Employee Information Seminar, Atlanta, April 2, 1974. (Mimeographed.)

Page, Arthur W.

"Address." Speech at 1930 Bell System General Commercial Conference, May 1930. (Multilithed.)

"Coordination of Sales and Advertising Activities." Speech at Bell System General Sales Conference, January-February 1929. (Multilithed.)

"Fundamentals of Public Relations Program for Business." Speech at Seventh International Management Congress, Washington D.C., Sept. 20, 1938. (Printed pamphlet.)

"Industrial Statesmanship." Speech at public relations conference of the Chesapeake and Ohio Railway Co., White Sulphur Springs, Va., Oct. 27, 1939. (Multilithed.)

"Looking Forward in Public Relations." Speech at annual meeting of Association of Life Insurance Presidents, Dec. 2, 1943. (Multilithed.)

"Notes on Informal Talk by Arthur W. Page to Members of the Information Department on His Return from London." Speech, New York, July 19, 1944. (Multilithed.)

"Our Public Relations Today and the Outlook for the Future." Speech at New York Telephone Co. public relations course, December 1933. (Multilithed.)

"Philosophy of the Business." Speech at Bell System General Plant Conference, October 1928. (Multilithed.)

"The Problem of Forecasting Public Opinion in the United States." Speech at Bell System General Publicity Conference, April 1929. (Multilithed.)

"Public Relations." Speech at Bell System General Operating Conference, Briarcliff, N.Y., April 28, 1927. (Multilithed.)

"Public Relations.'" Speech at Bell System General Operating Conference, May 1928. (Multilithed.)

"Public Relations." Speech at Bell System General Operating Conference, May 1930. (Multilithed.)

"Public Relations." Speech at Bell System General Operating Conference, May 1931. (Multilithed.)

"Public Relations and Sales." Speech at Bell System General Commercial Conference, June 1928. (Multilithed.)

"Public Relations Today and the Outlook for the Future." Speech at New York Telephone Co. public relations course, Dec. 13, 1937. (Multilithed.)

"Social Aspects of Communication Development." Lecture at the Lowell Institute, Boston, Jan. 26, 1932. (Pamphlet reprinted from *Bell Telephone Quarterly*, April 1932.)

"Some Remarks on Public Relations." Speech to members of the Institute of Life Insurance, New York, Dec. 2, 1942. (Pamphlet printed by the Institute of Life Insurance.)

"Talk on Public Relations." Speech at New York Telephone Co. public relations course, March 28, 1932. (Multilithed.)

"The Telephone—A Coming Industry." Speech to employees of the Bank of the Manhattan Co., New York, November 1934. (Multilithed.)

Untitled speech at Bell System General Commercial Conference, June 1927. (Multilithed.)

Untitled speech at Bell System Publicity Conference, April 28, 1927. (Multilithed.)

Untitled speech at Bell System Traffic Conference, Nov. 11, 1927. (Multilithed.)

Untitled speech at Bell System General Operating Conference, May 1930. (Multilithed.)

"What Publicity and Advertising Can Do To Help Operation." Speech at Bell System General Operating Conference, May 1927. (Multilithed.)

Annual Reports

American Telephone & Telegraph Co. *Annual Report*, 1921-1922, 1924-1926, 1928-1930, 1932-1942.

Cold Spring Harbor Laboratory. *Annual Report*, 1974.

Council on Foreign Relations. *Annual Report of the Executive Director*, 1948-1949.

Farmers Federation of Asheville, N.C., Educational and Development Fund. *Annual Report*, 1931, 1934.

National Committee for a Free Europe. *Annual Report*, 1950.

Negro Rural School Fund-Anna T. Jeanes Foundation. *Annual Report*, 1932, 1934.

Panama Railroad Co. *Annual Report*, 1945.

Pamphlets

American Telephone & Telegraph Co. "Directors and Officers of the American Telephone & Telegraph Co. from Incorporation," Aug. 9, 1951.

American Telephone & Telegraph Co. "The Early Corporate Development of the Telephone," 1964.

Mabon, Prescott C. "A Personal Perspective on Bell System Public Relations," American Telephone & Telegraph Co., 1972.

Todd, Kenneth P., Jr. "A Capsule History of the Bell System," American. Telephone & Telegraph Co., 1972

Miscellaneous Materials

Catalogue of the Officers and Members of the O.K. in Harvard College. Cambridge, Mass.: Harvard University, 1885.

Final Report of the Telephone Rate and Research Department. Washington,

D.C.: Federal Communications Commission, June 15, 1938. (Plano-graphed.)

The First Catalogue of the Hasty Pudding-Institute of 1770. Cambridge, Mass.: Harvard University Press, 1936.

Harvard Class Album. Cambridge, Mass.: Harvard University, 1904, 1905.

Harvard University Register. Cambridge, Mass.: Harvard University Press, 1903-1904 and 1904-1905.

Olla Podrida. Lawrenceville, N.J.: Lawrenceville School, 1900-1901.

Lawrenceville School Register, 1901. Lawrenceville, N.J.: Lawrenceville School, 1901.

The Signet: A Centennial Catalogue, 1870-1970. Cambridge, Mass.: The Signet Society.

U.S. War Department. *The Lockhart Report,* by Jack S. Lockhart. Washington., D.C.: July 1946.

Who's Who in New York, 1924.

Index